ONE WEEK LOAN

Also by Chris Ryder

The RUC: A Force Under Fire

The Ulster Defence Regiment: An Instrument of Peace?

Inside the Maze: The Untold Story of the Northern Ireland Prison Service

(with Vincent Kearney)
Drumcree: The Orange Order's Last Stand

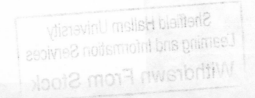

THE FATEFUL SPLIT

Catholics and the Royal Ulster Constabulary

Chris Ryder

Methuen

This paperback edition published by Methuen in 2004

10 9 8 7 6 5 4 3 2 1

First published in hardback in 2004
by Methuen Publishing Ltd
215 Vauxhall Bridge Road
London SW1V 1EJ

A CIP catalogue record for this book is available
from the British Library.

Methuen Publishing Limited Reg. No. 3543167

ISBN 0 413 77223 3

Typeset by SX Composing DTP, Rayleigh, Essex
Printed and bound in Great Britain by
Bookmarque Ltd, Croydon, Surrey

Contents

Acknowledgements

Illustrations
The author and publisher wish to thank the copyright holders for permission to reproduce the photographs in this book.

1. Sir James Craig, Prime Minister of Northern Ireland, 1921–40. © PRONI.
2. Sir Richard Dawson Bates, Minister of Home Affairs, 1921–43. © PRONI.
3. Sir Charles Wickham, Inspector-General, Royal Ulster Constabulary, 1922–45. © RUC GC Historical Society.
5. Royal Ulster Constabulary crest. © RUC GC Historical Society.
6. Special Constabulary at Newtownbutler, Co. Fermanagh, 1922. © Belfast Telegraph.
7. RUC officers operating a checkpoint on the border during the IRA's 1956–62 terrorist campaign. © PRONI.
8. Sir Richard Pim, Inspector-General, Royal Ulster Constabulary, 1945–61. © RUC GC Historical Society.
9. Captain Terence O'Neill, Prime Minister of Northern Ireland, 1963–9. © PRONI.
10. An RUC Shorland armoured patrol vehicle. © PRONI.
11. Major James Chichester-Clark, Prime Minister of Northern Ireland, 1969–71, and members of his Cabinet. © PRONI.
12. Police and army on joint patrol in Belfast in 1978. © Defence Press Office, Northern Ireland.
13. Anthony Peacocke, Inspector-General, Royal Ulster Constabulary, 1969. © RUC GC Historical Society.
14. William Craig, Minister of Home Affairs, 1963–4 and 1966-8. © PRONI.

Text

The author and publisher wish to thank the copyright holders for permission to reproduce text in this book.

Extracts from *All in a Life*, Dr Garrett Fitzgerald, reproduced with the permission of Gill & Macmillan Ltd.

Extracts from *Brookeborough* by Brian Barton reproduced with the permission of the Institute of Irish Studies, Queens University Belfast.

Extracts from *My Fight for Irish Freedom* by Dan Breen reproduced with the permission of Anvil Books Limited.

Extracts from *Police Casualties in Ireland 1919-22* ƒ Richard Abbott 2000 reproduced with the permission of Mercier Press.

For
Gerry Fitt,
and in memory of
Paddy Devlin,
who taught me that pragmatism
and accommodation are the essential
factors in promoting tolerance and reconciliation.

Author's Note

There's always much more that an author wants to include in his work than there is room for, even when writing at book length, a luxury for a journalist more used to the limitations of a newspaper page. That frustration, and the impulse to revise and expand, becomes all the more intense when significant new source material subsequently becomes available.

So it was with the history of the Royal Ulster Constabulary. Ever since I completed *The RUC: A Force under Fire*, first published by Methuen in 1989, many people offered additional insights and information to fill out the gaps in that work and, steadily over succeeding years, as once-secret official files have been declassified and opened for public inspection, an ever-more informative analysis of the life and turbulent times of the organisation has become possible.

Its transition from the Royal Ulster Constabulary to the Police Service of Northern Ireland in November 2001, as a crucial part of the slow-moving peace process, therefore seemed to be an appropriate point to revisit the subject and explore, with the benefit of this new material, one of the most intriguing strands of RUC history: the origins and evolution of the fatal estrangement between the RUC and the Catholic minority in Northern Ireland. (For convenience I have used the term 'Catholic' to include the nationalist and Republican standpoints, just as the Unionist and Loyalist groups are embraced by their common depiction as 'Protestant'.) This was the central issue that contributed to the failure to establish mutually acceptable policing arrangements, that critically exacerbated the social and political insolvency of the Northern Ireland state, and that generated a living legacy of hatred, controversy and difference which, albeit dwindling, still largely persists in many quarters.

I have to note that the National Archives (which incorporates the former Public Record Office) at Kew in west London takes a notably more permissive view of opening records under the thirty-year rule when compared with the Public Record Office in Belfast where, it is to be regretted, many papers relating to key events remain closed despite the fact that corresponding files are often available at Kew.

Nevertheless I am heavily indebted to the Deputy Keeper of the Records at the Public Record Office of Northern Ireland in Belfast and to the staff of the National Archives in London for permission to quote material from declassified official files which is included in this book. Other Crown copyright material is reproduced with the permission of the Controller of Her Majesty's Stationery Office and the Queen's Printer for Scotland. Because of the extent of my research I have not listed the official files consulted or quoted but I will endeavour to further assist any reader who contacts me via the publisher with a specific enquiry. I have also drawn on statements and evidence to the Bloody Sunday Inquiry which, in setting out the background and context of that ill-fated landmark, also informs the course of events described here.

There are too many people who have helped me compile an extensive body of research about the RUC over the last thirty or so years to name them all here. In any case, many would not welcome my doing so, but I wholeheartedly thank them all for their recollections, frankness and generosity with their time. Assistant Chief Constable Sam Kinkaid and former Assistant Chief Constable Alan McQuillan of the RUC/PSNI have both been extremely helpful to me in writing this book. As Chairman of the RUC GC Historical Society, Alan, together with the Curator of the Police Museum, Hugh Forrester, and his assistant, Harry Gibson, has also been of considerable assistance in making their archives available. I am also very grateful to Roy Black for sharing his records of the honours and awards earned by members of the RUC during its eighty-year history. I also wish to record my appreciation of the insights provided by former chief constables Sir John Hermon and Sir Ronnie Flanagan, and Sir Robert Porter, who was Minister of Home Affairs during the critical summer of 1969. Dr Garrett FitzGerald, the former Prime Minister of the Republic of Ireland, kindly talked me through his perceptions of policing in Northern Ireland and I thank him. Similarly, I appreciate the time of Fr. Sean McManus and others I met in Washington to discuss the same topic. Dr Georgina Sinclair, from the University of Reading, generously shared her research about the life and times of Sir Arthur Young. Chief Superintendent Stephen Grange and many of his colleagues in the South Belfast District Command Unit, past and present, also assisted me in describing the new beginning to policing designed to remedy the mistakes of history. Inspector Debbie Crawford at the Police Press Office in Belfast deserves particular thanks for her outstanding help in covering the final days of the RUC. I appreciate their help, as much as that of all my other sources, but stress that the conclusions I draw about policy-making and events are, of course, mine alone.

My good friend, David Cook, with whom I shared the travails of membership of the Police Authority for Northern Ireland from July 1994 until March 1996, generously helped me to track down some important legal cases during my research. Walter Macauley, whose encyclopedic knowledge of 'the troubles' rivals that of even the most sophisticated electronic databases, has once again been of invaluable assistance in pinning down elusive elements of my story. As ever, Yvonne Murphy, custodian of the political collection at the Linen Hall Library in Belfast, facilitated my research and I also wish to record my gratitude to Vincent Kearney for reading an early draft of the manuscript and making a number of very constructive suggestions to improve it. Jim McDonald also deserves a mention for his help in pointing me to useful sources and supplying constabulary anecdotes.

It is also necessary to record my thanks to a number of people and organisations for permission to reproduce copyright text and pictures. Hugh Orde, Chief Constable, allowed me to reproduce the PSNI crest, and the RUC GC Historical Society gave permission to reproduce the RUC crest. The Army Records Society and Trustees of the Imperial War Museum approved my request to republish extracts from the military correspondence of Field Marshall Sir Henry Wilson. Major Tim David at the Defence Press Office Northern Ireland facilitated my obtaining permission to reproduce the picture of a policeman and soldier on joint patrol in 1978. A full list of copyright acknowledgements appears on pp. vii-viii, although in some cases the copyright holder could not be traced.

In conclusion, I must thank my agents, Anthony Goff and Georgia Glover at David Higham Associates, for their customary sound advice and support. Thanks also go to Max Eilenberg at Methuen, for commissioning the book, Eleanor Rees, who edited the text with her incomparable skill, speed and insight, and the staff at Methuen, who produced it. Above all, I wish to acknowledge how my wife, Genny, supportively accepted my enduring preoccupation with 'the book' and ensured that there was always a bottle of cold white wine at the end of the writing day.

Chris Ryder
Belfast
August 2003

Introduction

'I want to shake the hand of an RUC man,' said a Saturday-night reveller, lurching out the door of a night-spot on Belfast's 'golden mile'.

'Well, you're just a minute too late,' replied Inspector Keith Gilchrist, looking at his watch. 'We've just become the Police Service of Northern Ireland.'

This exchange, immediately after midnight on the 4 November 2001, was how one officer marked the moment when, just months short of its eightieth anniversary, the embattled Royal Ulster Constabulary was consigned to history.

The name change had been recommended two years earlier by the Independent Commission on Policing in Northern Ireland, chaired by Chris Patten, the former Governor of Hong Kong. The commission was established under the terms of the Belfast Agreement, signed on Good Friday 1998, when an unprecedented cross-community coalition of political representatives and former terrorists, in conjunction with the British and Irish governments, gave approval to a comprehensive package of measures designed to bring about reconciliation and lasting peace.

Among the divisive issues the Patten commission sought to resolve was that of policing: 'a central issue in any society', the Agreement said. The Commission wisely decided not to dwell on the past, so its report, published on 9 September 1999, outlined, in 175 specific recommendations, a detailed vision for what it hoped, after thirty years of incessant conflict, would be 'a new beginning' for the police in Northern Ireland.

For many in the Royal Ulster Constabulary it was a deeply emotive and hurtful report. Those who had endured the violence, hatred and danger of the previous thirty years felt their courage, and the sacrifice of the 302 officers murdered trying to keep the peace in deeply divided Northern Ireland, were not being fully acknowledged. Losing the RUC name, and the 'harp, shamrock and crown' insignia they had acquired from the Royal Irish Constabulary in the early 1920s, was especially wounding. Some felt that the RUC was being all too hastily written off in the interests of political expediency.

However, looking to the future, the vast majority of police officers, especially those setting out on their careers, enthusiastically welcomed the Patten recommendations and the name change, the most symbolic aspect of the new beginning for policing. They saw it as freeing them from the handcuffs of a controversial history and providing an opportunity brimming with potential to serve the entire community in a peaceful and more normal environment.

The report recommended that policing must become a collective community responsibility, a partnership for community safety: another way of saying that policing was too important to be left to the police alone. In effect, what was needed to reverse the historic failure of policing was both a fresh approach on the part of the police and an entirely changed attitude to them on the part of the two main communities. New concepts of consent, co-operation and participation in the policing process would have to be forged.

A fundamental police reform process on such a scale was indeed long overdue, for the fault-line that had cut a swathe through policing in Northern Ireland ever since the turbulent 1920s was deep and lasting. The force, in the frank words of Sir Ronnie Flanagan, who would be its last chief constable, was 'white, male and Protestant' in its outlook. Patten's radical report was therefore a necessary catalyst to challenge long-standing mindsets within the police and on both sides of the sectarian and political divide and to trigger an avalanche of cultural and organisational reform. For generations, Protestants had generally regarded the police as 'ours', while Catholics looked on them as 'theirs', and Catholic alienation from the police was deep-seated. As the SDLP leader Mark Durkan said in March 2003:

> Throughout our history there has been no issue more difficult or more divisive than policing. It lay at the very fault-line in our society, exposing the deep gulf dividing nationalist and unionist. For them, the police were the rightful defenders of their laws and their order. For nationalists attitudes ranged from occasional resentment to relentless hostility against the strong arm of a state with which we could not identify.

Historically, therefore, Catholics neither co-operated with the police nor participated in the job. Patten found that only about eight per cent of the force (906 out of a total of 11,392 full and part-time officers) came from the minority community, a disproportionate representation as

Catholics accounted for forty per cent of Northern Ireland's population. The Patten report elegantly defined the central flaw in Northern Ireland's policing structures:

> The identification of police and state is contrary to policing practice in the rest of the United Kingdom. It has left the police in an unenviable position. In one political language, they are the custodians of nationhood. In its rhetorical opposite, they are the symbols of oppression. Policing, therefore, goes right to the heart of the sense of security and identity of both communities and, because of the differences between them, this seriously hampers the effectiveness of the police service in Northern Ireland.

The roots of this unhappy state of affairs lay in the turbulent events of the early 1920s when Ireland was partitioned in an effort to resolve the conflicting aspirations of those in the south of the island, overwhelmingly Catholics, who wanted Home Rule, and the mainly Protestant community in the north, who threatened an armed 'Protestant backlash' to maintain the union with Britain.

Giving evidence to the 'Bloody Sunday' inquiry in December 2002, the distinguished British civil servant Sir Arthur Hockaday, who was closely involved in the management of Irish affairs during his career in Whitehall, recalled a briefing he had written for Lord Carrington, then Secretary of State for Defence, on 31 December 1971 which said: 'The question of the "Protestant backlash" is perennial: and many policy decisions, from non-implementation of Home Rule in 1914 through partition in 1921 to internment in 1971, have been taken primarily to satisfy Protestant opinion.' To this list Sir Arthur could well have added the raising of the Royal Ulster Constabulary, for, as the settlement to partition Ireland was being hammered out, the Northern Ireland Unionists, while prevented from raising a purely military force, were instead allowed to enlist a 'swollen constabulary', putting thousands of Protestants into uniform and under arms with the full approval and financial support of a British government all too anxious to be rid of its Irish problem.

The 3,000-strong Royal Ulster Constabulary, which replaced the disbanded all-Ireland Royal Irish Constabulary on 1 June 1922, thus became the first line of defence for the fledgling Northern Ireland government. Despite the 1921 Anglo-Irish Treaty, the Belfast administration remained exceedingly fearful about an internal Catholic uprising and the prospect of invasion and takeover from the Free State, led by those who opposed partition. It had a paranoid fear that, in such an eventuality, the British government would not send its own military forces to a rigorous defence of the new border. Abandoned by their southern compatriots, the Catholic minority in the north refused to take up the 1,000 posts reserved for them in the RUC, not least because there was a marked lack of any official encouragement for them to do so. This reinforced Catholic fears that the RUC was nothing more than the 'armed wing of Unionism' to be used as an instrument of repression and discrimination against them. It was to prove a lasting and damaging perception. While the majority of Catholics ultimately came to a practical recognition of the new state, although never any identification with it, there was only ever a grudging acceptance, never consent, for the police. A minority of extreme Irish Republicans, who maintained that they should continue to fight for a united Ireland with or without any widespread support in the north and south for the cause, from time to time resorted to violence. For the self-styled and outlawed Irish Republican Army, the RUC were hated as defenders of the 'illegitimate' state, and prime targets. During periodic disturbances in the 1930s, 1940s (during the Second World War) and again in the late 1950s, seventeen police officers were murdered.

The most serious trouble erupted in the late 1960s when a civil rights movement, supported by a large number of Catholics and liberal Protestants in Northern Ireland, was exploited by Irish Republicans to foment disorder. When the Unionist administration of the day, with characteristic short-sightedness, refused to concede reform and used the RUC to crack down on the protests, the scene was set for years of brutal inter-communal conflict which would exceed even the bloody standards of earlier Irish history. Reporting on the violence and civil disturbances in Northern Ireland in 1969, which marked the start of these modern troubles, the tribunal of inquiry chaired by the then Mr Justice Scarman concluded:

> Thus there developed the fateful split between the Catholic community and the police. Faced with the distrust of a substantial proportion of the whole population and short of numbers, the RUC had (as some senior officers appreciated) lost the capacity to control a major riot. Their difficulties naturally led them, when the emergency arose, to have recourse to methods such as baton charges, CS gas and gunfire, which were sure ultimately to stoke even higher the fires of resentment and hatred.

In reality those fires had long been smouldering dangerously and the origins of the fateful split to which he referred substantially predated Scarman's comments. They could, in fact, be traced back for nearly half a century and would, in the end, another three decades on, critically contribute to the ultimate failure of the genetically flawed policing structures in Northern Ireland and the final demise of the RUC.

Drawing on new material disclosed at the Public Record Offices in London and Belfast and further research in Britain, Ireland and the United States, this book examines how Catholic alienation brought about the downfall of a unique police force by exploring three defining periods in that force's history, culminating in the Patten reforms which brought to an end its seventy-nine-year record of both courage and controversy.

Part One of the book, 'The Swollen Constabulary', examines the course of events from 1919 onwards, when the Northern Ireland state was being created. It recounts the way the fledgling RUC was tasked to maintain law and order and defend the border, and shows how its ethos was suborned by the Unionist administration and moulded to its political goals and prejudices despite a far-seeing report in 1923. Major-General Sir Archibald Montgomery recommended the RUC should be recast as a conventional civil police force, but his report was totally rejected by James Craig, the prime minister, and Richard Dawson Bates, his extraordinarily bigoted minister of home affairs, who was the RUC's unfortunate mentor.

Part Two, 'Breakdown', reconstructs the reprehensible way the under-strength and ill-equipped RUC was manipulated by Unionist politicians in 1968 and 1969, deployed against Catholics and committed to an unwinnable community conflict on the streets. It demonstrates how the RUC continued to be dogged by political antagonism and dispute, despite the abolition of the notorious B Specials and the short-lived efforts to reform it after the debilitating events of August 1969 and the onset of the years of conflict. Much important new material is disclosed about the decisively formative period from 1968 to 1973, when the civil rights campaign helped ignite slumbering sectarian tensions, brought about what a senior RUC officer described as a state of incipient civil war, and caused the RUC to be overwhelmed to breaking point. It shows how the British Army, as under-prepared as the RUC for the task it was asked to carry out, became inexorably sucked into what would become the longest continuous campaign in its illustrious history and reconstructs, in authentic detail for the first time, the bitter infighting between the two organisations, the personal rivalries and duplicitous political wrangling between London and Belfast which characterised the early stages of the conflict.

Finally, Part Three, 'The Point of No Return', looks at the far-reaching implications for the RUC of the crisis at Drumcree in July 1996, when, in accordance with the historical perception of Catholics, Chief Constable Sir Hugh Annesley surrendered to the force of Protestant threats and numbers, reversed his original decision and allowed the Orange Order's disputed march from Drumcree along the Catholic Garvaghy Road in Portadown. In retrospect this can now be seen as the decisive turning point for the embattled force. With even moderate Catholic opinion outraged by the U-turn and the heavy-handed vigour with which the protesters were dispersed by the police, all hopes that the RUC could be reformed by evolution rather than revolution evaporated. This time, for once, the threat of a Protestant backlash did not prevail. Three years later, in the wake of the historic Belfast Agreement, the Patten commission was instituted to map out the comprehensive new beginning for policing that Northern Ireland so badly required.

In recognition of its unparalleled record of individual bravery and sacrifice under fire – terrorists murdered 302 police officers and another 13,000 were maimed or injured during the years of conflict – the RUC was awarded the George Cross in 2000. The force thus shared, with only the Second World War population of the Mediterranean island of Malta, the distinction of having its collective acts of courage so formally acknowledged. A year later, in November 2001, it became the Police Service of Northern Ireland as the major programme of change designed, at last, to heal the fateful split got under way.

However, transforming the policing landscape was not without its difficulties. The transition from conflict to peace was compromised by hardline elements on both sides, who maintained a commitment to violence. The future of policing became a key bargaining point in the wider political negotiations aimed at consolidating the peace process. Years of distrust on the part of Catholics caused them to push for tough oversight measures and safeguards. As the terrorist threat subsided, a rising tide of criminality and racketeering presented the police with new challenges. From the outset, a legacy of bitterness, a tide of recrimination and distrust and a vast reservoir of grievance, inherited from the RUC, threatened to engulf the emerging new police service. However, just as the main body of their RUC predecessors had found the courage and commitment to do their honest best to serve and protect the entire community in dreadful times and circumstances, so the first generation of PSNI officers set about their task. With greater numbers of Catholics in police ranks than ever before, thanks to an affirmative-action recruitment programme, they have made an encouraging and visionary start. Only time will tell if they can finally bridge Northern Ireland's deep divisions and abate its sectarian hatreds to the point where they enjoy the consent and support of the entire community and become universally regarded by Catholic, Protestant and Dissenter as 'our' police.

PART ONE

The Swollen Constabulary

Chapter One
'Black Protestants'

There's a grandiose memorial by the side of the road at Soloheadbeg, some three miles from Tipperary in south-west Ireland, but not to the two policemen who were viciously murdered there on 21 January 1919. Instead, in telling testimony to Irish attitudes to policing, it glorifies their callous killers. The events of that bleak winter morning were a turning point of great significance in the history of policing in Ireland and the country itself, for the violent course initiated that day led directly to the partitioning of Ireland and the demise of the Royal Irish Constabulary over three years later. In its place, the new Free State government formed the Garda Siochana (Civic Guards), while in the Six Counties the Unionist government raised the Royal Ulster Constabulary.

For each of the five days before the ambush, a group of Irish Volunteers had been lying in wait for a police party due to escort a consignment of explosives to a remote quarry in the lush countryside around Soloheadbeg. On the fifth morning, Constables James McDonnell and Patrick O'Connell were delegated to report to the Magazine in Tipperary barracks, where gelignite was stored centrally under military control, to escort the delivery of the three half-hundredweight cases of high explosive (168lbs) and detonators. McDonnell, aged fifty-seven and born in County Mayo, had been a policeman for thirty-six years. He was a widower bringing up five children. Thirty-six-year-old O'Connell, a Corkman, was single and had served for twelve years. Both were well known in the locality and, according to Richard Abbot's study of 'Police Casualties in Ireland 1919–1922', McDonnell's 'great joke' was to ask children to spell 'rhododendron' and then teach them the correct spelling. Shortly after 1.30 p.m. the two policemen, walking behind the horse and cart with their Lee-Enfield rifles slung over their shoulders, were suddenly confronted by armed and masked men and shot dead in cold blood while the accompanying driver and a county council official looked on. The gang then escaped with the gelignite and the officers' rifles and revolvers, in their haste omitting to take the detonators, which were in the driver's pocket. In his memoir, *My Fight for Irish Freedom*, Dan Breen, the leader of the murder gang, recalled: 'Our only regret was that the escort had consisted of only two "Peelers" instead of six. If there had to be dead "Peelers" at all, six would have created a better impression than a mere two.' The ruthless ambush, a freelance operation by the local unit of the Volunteers, was designed, again in Breen's own words, to 'start the ball rolling. We were to begin another phase in the long fight for the freedom of our country.'

They succeeded, for the attack is now regarded as marking the start of Ireland's 'war of independence'. Quite coincidentally, two hours later that afternoon at the Mansion House in Dublin, the first meeting of the self-proclaimed Dáil Éireann (Parliament of Ireland) took place. At a general election a month earlier in December 1918, Sinn Fein, the political front for the Volunteers (soon to become known as the Irish Republican Army), had won seventy-three of the 105 seats. Despite the humiliating collapse of its Easter Rising in 1916, when an Irish Republic, independent of Britain, had been declared, the party had hugely benefited from anti-British feeling stoked up by the execution of fifteen of the insurgents and a later move to conscript Irishmen into the British forces to take part in the ongoing First World War. Emboldened by their landslide victory in the 1918 general election, the Irish Republicans decided they would not take their seats at Westminster but would instead establish their own parliament in Dublin as a bridgehead from which to step up their fight for independence. Encouraged by the double murder at Soloheadbeg, the Republicans now turned on the RIC with a vengeance, for although its members were overwhelmingly Catholic and Irish, the force had come to be seen as the eyes and ears of British rule in Ireland. Breen, who soon had a price of £1,000 on his head, regarded them as 'a pack of deserters, spies and hirelings'. If the British grip on Ireland was ever to be undermined and broken, the Republicans calculated, the RIC would first have to be swept aside. This policy, conceived by the Republicans' most far-sighted strategist, Michael Collins, was given the official sanction of the new parliament at its second meeting in April when Eamon de Valera, president of both Sinn Fein and the Dáil, called for the RIC to be ostracised: 'Their history is a continuity of brutal treason against their own people. They must be shown and made feel how base are the functions they perform and how vile is the position they occupy.'

With the ambush at Soloheadbeg the smouldering resentment against the police quickly flared into open hostility and boycott right across the country. Officers were gunned down mercilessly whenever the opportunity arose; whether they were on or off duty made no difference. Irish Republican leaders were convinced that if they were ever to break British rule in Ireland, they had first to break the RIC. The ruthless way the killers operated is well illustrated by the official report of the murder of fifty-year-old District Inspector Michael Hunt, who died on 23 June 1919 while supervising crowds dispersing after Thurles races in County Tipperary. The first entry on RIC Form 38, Notice of Outrage, reads: 'Murder'. Under the section headed 'Statement', the facts of the incident are outlined in polished handwriting:

> I regret to have to report that at 5.30 p.m. this date, DI Michael Hunt of Thurles was shot when returning in uniform from Thurles Races. When entering the square from New Street the DI was fired at three times in quick succession. Sergeant Joseph Grove 59311 and Constable Patrick Murphy 52292, who were about 15 to 20 yards in front of the late DI, turned around at once and saw him lying on the ground face downwards. They rushed to him at once, raised him up and carried him to the footpath. There was a rush in all directions from the scene by the very large crowd then returning from the races and there is no doubt the murderer got away in the crowd. [. . .] On receiving the report I went with a party of police to the scene and having seen that nothing further could be done for the late DI, we looked up suspects and searched every suspicious person. We also searched every person in the public houses, closed them out and moved off the crowds, but failed to get any trace of the assassin. I shall continue to make enquiries. It is likely that the murder was directed by persons who were anxious to remove the late DI, who had prosecuted several Sinn Feiners, and was an important witness in pending cases of a similar nature. Probably the murderer came from a distance and took opportunity of the Race Day to commit the murder.

The report is poignantly signed: 'S. Patterson Head Constable 56146 for DI killed'.

Throughout Ireland the vulnerability of the police to attack was considerable. In Dublin, the Metropolitan Police officers were highly exposed as, unlike the RIC, they mainly lived at home, not in barracks, and had to travel to and from duty. In no time they were reduced to doing nothing more than point duty on the streets of Dublin in daylight hours. As attacks on individuals escalated and the pace of the conflict in the country accelerated, police parties, usually consisting of a sergeant and up to six constables armed with revolvers, rifles and a shotgun, abandoned patrolling and simply tried to defend their stations, usually located in terraces of houses in villages. To drive them out the IRA launched raiding parties (more widely described as 'flying columns') numbering up to 200, who carried firearms, hand grenades, high explosive (gelignite and gun cotton) and petrol. The British Army's official account of the 1919–1922 campaign in Ireland, first opened for public scrutiny at the Public Record Office in London in April 2001, vividly records the scale of the attacks on the heavily outnumbered and outgunned RIC in the first half of 1920:

The rebels usually crept into the village under cover of darkness, and, in surrounding the barracks, took advantage of every available scrap of cover, such as stables and neighbouring houses from which the occupants had been ejected. They opened their attack by placing high explosives at the gable, or some other dead wall, exploding it with a short time fuse, and blowing a large gap in the wall. At the same time a hole was made in the roof, and petrol or other inflammable liquid poured in and set on fire. Rifle and revolver fire was then directed on all windows and exits. These attacks usually lasted for some hours, but, in spite of the fact that the police were as a rule outnumbered by anything from 20 to 40 to one, they almost in every case defended their posts to the last. If the explosion of the bomb or mine placed against the dead wall was fully successful, as in the case of Carrigtwohill, the attack was soon over, as the rebels rushed in and overpowered the police before they had time to realise what was happening. In one case near Cork City, a policeman played a violin all through the attack, although the barrack was on fire, and eventually this display of bravery played so much on the nerves of the attackers that they withdrew in haste. At Kilmallock, where the barrack was set on fire at the commencement of the attack, the defence was conducted by eight men under Sergeant Tobias Sullivan; the police held their barracks against several hundred rebels for over seven and a half hours, notwithstanding that under their very eyes, two of their comrades were burnt alive in the flames. The remainder had to continue the fight from room to room as the building collapsed bit by bit, and as more petrol was poured on it from the roof of a neighbouring house not exposed to the fire of the police. Eventually, when the whole of the building had collapsed, and there was nothing left to defend, this gallant little band of policemen charged the rebels with fixed bayonets and compelled them to retire hastily, but not before all except one of the RIC had been wounded. In spite of the manner in which the attack was launched and the long fight which followed, the police inflicted far heavier casualties on the rebels than they incurred themselves. Sergeant Sullivan, to whom all credit is due for the magnificent fight put up against such heavy odds, was subsequently promoted Head Constable and later to District Inspector, but, enraged at their defeat in Kilmallock, the rebels followed him from place to place, and eventually many months later they shot him like a dog under the eyes of his child in the public streets of Listowel, Co. Kerry.

As the frequency of such attacks on police officers and barracks increased, the men and their families were progressively driven from homes and stations in isolated areas and largely confined to heavily fortified garrisons in the larger towns. Even there they were singled out and ostracised. Telephone and telegraph wires to the barracks were cut. Shops and pubs refused to serve them. People walked out of the churches if a policeman and his family came to Mass. Women who associated with the police were seized and had their hair cut off. One officer recalled going into a shop, helping himself to produce to feed his family and then leaving the money on the counter because nobody would serve him. By mid-1920, morale and police efficiency had virtually collapsed. The RIC vacated half its 1,600 barracks, most of which were then burned out by the Volunteers, leaving a vacuum in which an alternative, Sinn Fein-managed, parish-based system of police and courts involving clergymen and others progressively thrived.

The Army records that as a result of this campaign 'the morale of the RIC [and Dublin Metropolitan Police] was naturally lowered considerably; they lost their old keenness and many indeed ceased to take much further interest. Although in the main a loyal body of men their morale had diminished and only two courses were open to their detachments: to adopt a policy of laissez faire and live or actively to enforce law and order and be in hourly danger of murder.' The flow of intelligence about 'rebels' and their activities also dried up with the loss of vital local knowledge caused by the deaths of so many police officers and the transfer of others for their own safety. As early as January 1920, after the murder of Second Assistant Commissioner William Redmond in Harcourt Street, Dublin, it was reported that there were 'barely half a dozen men' in the DMP Detective Division, which he headed, 'who could even identify the leading rebels'. On 31 May an exasperated Sir Hamar Greenwood, Chief Secretary for Ireland, told the cabinet in London: 'Our forces are still glued to the ground and we cannot succeed until our mobility is greater than theirs.'

In a bid to contain what had rapidly become a wholesale insurrection, the British government poured in troops and imposed martial law in areas where the violence was most acute. With RIC resignations flowing in at 200 a week compared with twenty-five before the war, and many officers simply 'hanging on for their pensions' – 2,000 were due to depart within the coming twelve months – the cabinet in London was concerned that a corresponding shortage of local recruits would rapidly lead to the collapse of the embattled force. So, early in 1920, the government encouraged British ex-servicemen to join the demoralised Irish police. Because of the speed with which they were recruited and deployed there were not enough items of police uniform to go round, so the men were issued with a mixture of police black and military khaki clothing, which promptly earned them the nickname 'Black and Tans'. By the spring of 1920, the government's cabinet committee on the Irish situation had determined that to get the speed and mobility required to out-manoeuvre the Volunteers, an eight-battalion 'gendarmerie' of British-recruited 'Auxiliaries' was also needed to 'stiffen' the RIC. In his memoir, *Voices and the Sound of Drums*, Paddy Shea, the son of an RIC sergeant who later became a distinguished civil servant in the Northern Ireland administration, says that those who flocked to join the Black and Tans were:

> [. . .] decent men and scoundrels, adventurers and frightened youths, domesticated family men and fugitives from deserted wives; they were English and Scottish and Welsh, Jew and Gentile. They came in all sizes and for all sorts of reasons, the most unlikely of which was, probably, to do a policeman's job. Once they passed an elementary test in reading and writing they were in without, apparently, much inquiry about character or background or much thought about suitability for police duties. Irish policemen, by and large, were unsophisticated, untravelled countrymen who said their prayers and did their duty as they saw it. The newcomers, they found, had neither religion nor morals, they used foul language, they had the old soldiers' talent for dodging and scrounging, they spoke in strange accents, called the Irish 'natives', associated with low company, stole from one another, sneered at the customs of the country, drank to excess and put sugar on

their porridge. To the men of the RIC they were a revelation and a plague and a Godsend. They brought help but they frightened even those they had come to help.

This new elite force, of mainly war-hardened, ex-Army officers, organised into loosely disciplined, often heavy-drinking, 100-strong companies, quickly imposed a reign of terror in the counties where IRA activity was most prevalent, but such was the spread and ferocity of the hit-and-run, tit-for-tat fighting that by mid-1920 their commander, Major-General Sir Henry Tudor, was seeking even more reinforcements. However, General Nevil Macready, the Army commander in Ireland, and other senior officials at Dublin Castle had already come to the private conclusion that no amount of coercion could settle the Irish question, although that view carried no immediate weight with the British government.

Nevertheless, the crisis did cause a reappraisal of the situation and in July, while still trying to carve out some political approach, the British government decided not to seek an early accommodation with Sinn Fein but first to engage in a policy of all-out reprisal and repression. The champion of this strategy was Longford-born Field Marshal Sir Henry Wilson, a staunch Unionist and close confidant of David Lloyd-George, the Liberal prime minister, with whom he had earlier shared approval of the introduction of conscription in Ireland. (Wilson was also very close to James Craig, the Unionist leader and future prime minister of Northern Ireland, and in due course he would resign from the Army, become the military adviser to Craig's Northern Ireland government and in February 1922 win the North Down seat in the Belfast parliament. Two months later he was assassinated on the steps of his London home by two IRA gunmen who were later hanged.)

From the outset, Wilson had been scornful about the conduct of the campaign in Ireland. In June 1920, he wrote to Winston Churchill, then Secretary for Air and War: 'I have absolutely no faith in the present regime as a semi-military, semi-police operation.' By May 1921, in a letter to General Henry Rawlinson, he was even more critical:

It positively makes one cry, this total lack of power of governing. In Ireland we have had one of the worst week-ends since the beginning of the rebellion, and it is perfectly clear to me that unless the 'Frocks' [politicians] shout out at the top of their voices and get England on their side, and then really set to work to stamp out this vermin we shall

lose Ireland, and with the loss of Ireland we have lost the Empire. I
want permission from the 'Frocks' [. . .] to send over between 20 and
30 battalions, from here, some more cavalry, guns, aeroplanes,
wireless, tanks, armoured cars etc. to place the whole of Ireland under
Martial Law, and hand it all over to Macready [. . .] to go on as we are
now, which is neither trying to knock out the murderers nor handing the
country over to them as a present, is sheer madness.

These events, primarily in the south of Ireland, were being monitored
most closely in the northern part of the island. Up to this point, the
Unionists and Protestants there, who had since 1886 consistently opposed
British efforts to impose Home Rule, which they equated with 'Rome
rule' by the Catholic majority, had watched developments with mounting
insecurity. In 1912, with Britain once more set to introduce the measure,
400,000 of them signed a 'Solemn League and Covenant' to resist. A year
later they illegally formed the Ulster Volunteer Force to do so and in
April 1914 defiantly landed 25,000 rifles and 3,000,000 rounds of
ammunition to give them the means. With the outbreak of war in August
1914, the Home Rule proposals were shelved for the duration, but
Unionist anxiety surfaced again after the 1916 Rising, becoming
progressively more acute as subsequent events unfolded.

In February 1920, with the war of independence raging, the British
government introduced new legislation in a bid to assuage the conflicting
demands of the nationalists and Unionists. There would be a large
measure of Home Rule for twenty-six counties but the six northern
counties would be allowed to maintain the union and have their own
parliament in Belfast. Under this Better Government of Ireland
legislation, common issues between north and south would be decided
through a new Council of Ireland while some issues, such as foreign
affairs, posts and telegraphs and customs and excise, were reserved by
London. This solution was not at all acceptable in the southern part of the
island, where the vast majority wanted to sever the British link, and only
reluctantly welcomed by the Ulster Unionist Council, who voted two to
one to accept it. At elections in May 1921, however, the Unionists won
forty of the fifty-two seats in the new Northern Ireland parliament. Sinn
Fein boycotted the elections in the south and refused to put up candidates,
and, in the absence of any others, the proposed parliament there never got
off the ground.

But even before the new northern legislature had come into existence,
the increasingly grave security situation in the south led London to take

the highly significant step of authorising the Unionists to raise their own security force, in the first official recognition of partition. The process had actually started in July 1920 when the government in London was seriously alarmed by the gravity of the situation that had developed in Ireland. Winston Churchill, now colonial secretary, who, like Wilson, wanted to 'raise the temperature of the conflict to a real issue and shock', suggested amassing a force of 30,000 local men in Ulster, thus freeing seven Army battalions for use in the south. Craig opportunistically backed the idea. Like many Unionists, he doubted the durability of Britain's commitment to them and nourished a nagging fear that it might tire of fighting, impose a form of Home Rule and leave them at the mercy of the IRA. What they actually wanted was independent control of a large, locally recruited force of 'reliable' men whom they could depend on for the defence of the Six Counties. The same month Dublin-born Edward Carson, an eminent barrister and fervent Unionist parliamentarian, told a Twelfth of July rally they would take the matter into their own hands if Britain 'is unable to protect us from the machinations of Sinn Fein'.

In reality, the Unionists had already taken matters into their own hands and moves to amass such a force had already begun. As the violence escalated in early 1920, many of the old UVF leaders revived their local units and put out patrols at night to help protect their homes and property. Many were armed with weapons imported in 1914 and carefully concealed in the intervening years for just such an hour of peril. In Fermanagh, according to Brian Barton's biography, Basil Brooke (who would later become prime minister of Northern Ireland) formed a cadre of fourteen men, one pair to do duty each night of the week, from among his own estate workers and then extended the network from townland to townland, forming what he grandly called a 'Vigilance Force' in a bid to depoliticise it and attract both Protestants and Catholics to become involved. This objective signally failed, partly from the political hostility of even moderate nationalists but also because of fear. Breaking ranks could well have attracted the violent attention of the IRA. In any case, Unionists so distrusted all Catholics that there was little enthusiasm to have them in the ranks. At that time, similar vigilante patrols were taking to the roads and streets at night in many areas, often in consort with the RIC. On 27 August 1920, for instance, a circular was issued from the Urban District Council Office at Bangor, County Down, stating that 'in view of the disturbances in some districts in Belfast and the excited state of mind resulting from recent occurrences, the Chairman of the Council, and Sergeant McNeice, have requested that the members of the Civilian

Patrol should be ostentatiously present . . . to come to the assistance of the police if necessary'.

The police and military authorities tried to assert more formal control of such activity by suggesting the issue of armbands and whistles to the men on such duty. Brooke, for one, vigorously opposed this as inadequate on the good grounds that the men were taking a great risk and should be armed for their own protection at least. The Ulster Unionist Council had earlier asserted its own control at a meeting on 24 June when it endorsed a proposal to revive the Ulster Volunteer Force, but it was not acting unilaterally. Within days Sir Wilfrid Spender, an English-born ex-Army officer who had been attached to the Ulster Divisions during the First World War, was approached in his workplace at the Ministry of Pensions in London and asked to go to Belfast to raise the Ulster Volunteer Force once again. According to Spender's records, the invitation came from Sir Hamar Greenwood, who told him that the enterprise had the tacit approval of Lloyd George but that 'it would be politically unwise to announce this publicly'.

Spender accepted and travelled to Belfast where he made contact with former UVF stalwarts like Brooke, Captain Robert Perceval-Maxwell, Brigadier-General Ambrose Ricardo and Lord Masserene. 'Many of them were war-weary but most of them responded to the request for their support in getting the UVF on to a proper footing,' he records. Before long even more 'Loyalists', as they came to be known, were out on patrol, mainly at night, informally co-operating with the hard-pressed RIC and Army to prevent IRA outrages. However, this dubious arrangement came to a head after an incident in Londonderry. UVF volunteers had gone to protect the Post Office after hearing that an attack was planned but were angered when a party of troops turned up soon afterwards and demanded they hand over their rifles. Spender immediately left for London, where he saw Greenwood and demanded that the police and Army be told the truth of the situation. He insisted that they be ordered to work with the UVF and make more active use of the intelligence they were obtaining from their local knowledge.

There was some opposition to this from Generals Macready and Tudor but they were overruled by London. UVF patrolling and military co-operation resumed and the men continued to keep their weapons at home, despite military objections. Spender and the other 'county commandants' were not satisfied and, with the support of Wilson and Craig, began to push for the government to raise an official Ulster Special Constabulary from the re-formed UVF. The county commandants and Spender discussed the demand at a meeting in Belfast City Hall with an emissary from Sir John Anderson, a senior official at Dublin Castle. His support appears to have clinched the issue and, on 8 September 1920, the British cabinet agreed.

By this time the conflict in the south was raging ever more violently and the political and security authorities were even more deeply divided about how best to resolve it. By August 1920, the Army believed there was only one solution to the state of affairs and that was to place all the Crown forces in Ireland under military control and discipline. The imposition of martial law throughout Ireland, the soldiers believed, would have solved the problems arising from the quadruple control of troops, RIC, Auxiliaries and Royal Marine detachments, the latter guarding coastguard stations on the west coast. In December 1920, a few days after Christmas, the deaths of three police officers during an elaborate ambush in County Cork caused the Army to begin taking official reprisals. On New Year's Day 1921, seven people associated with Sinn Fein in the same area were ordered out of their homes, which were then demolished by the Army.

With the passing of the Restoration of Order in Ireland Act in August, giving the forces tougher powers, some police officers, motivated by frustration, began taking the law into their own hands after the killing of comrades, a trend that accelerated in viciousness as the Black and Tans and Auxiliaries also became more and more involved in taking reprisals. On 21 November Michael Collins's formidable intelligence network pulled off its biggest coup when eleven British intelligence men, known as the Cairo Gang, were singled out and killed at a number of addresses throughout Dublin. That afternoon the Black and Tans opened fire into the crowd at a football match in Croke Park, killing twelve people and wounding sixty before officers from the Auxiliaries ordered them to stop firing. Later at Dublin Castle two prisoners were shot dead by police – while trying to escape, the authorities said, but few believed them.

For its part, the main body of native members of the RIC were both frightened and appalled by the excesses of the British imports to the force, feelings which contributed further to the flight from the ranks. Many left and went quietly over to the Republican side, but there was one notable act of public rebellion in June 1920 when Constable Jeremiah Mee and six of his colleagues at Listowel, County Kerry, protested and then resigned. Sir Hamar Greenwood, the chief secretary, addressed RIC officers at Phoenix Park to stress the need for discipline. His comments reflected the terms of a circular issued to the entire force by the deputy inspector-general from Dublin Castle two days earlier on 28 September. Headed 'Alleged Acts of Reprisal by Police and Soldiers', it stated:

> Many reports have appeared in the press of alleged acts of reprisal by police and soldiers. These accounts are generally thoroughly mis-leading and often misrepresent acts of justifiable self-defence as reprisals; but there are cases in which unjustifiable action has undoubtedly been taken. These cases are being carefully investigated. Meanwhile it is necessary to repeat and emphasise that reprisals will ruin the discipline of the Force and cannot be countenanced by those in authority. The great provocation under which men suffer who see their comrades and friends foully murdered is fully recognised, but the police are urged to maintain, in spite of this provocation, that self-control that has characterised the Force in the past.

In October Greenwood had to answer growing concern in the House of Commons about a particular event in Ireland:

> I found that from 100 to 150 men went to Balbriggan determined to avenge the death of a popular comrade shot at and murdered in cold blood. I find that it is impossible out of that 150 to find the men who did the deed, who did the burning. I have had the most searching inquiry made. But I cannot in my heart of hearts condemn in the same way those policemen who lost their heads as I condemn the assassins who provoked this outrage.

The same day in the Lords, Lord Curzon said that what was happening in Ireland was not guerrilla warfare. 'It is the warfare of the red Indian, of the Apache.' The government comfortably beat off opposition demands for an official inquiry into what was happening in Ireland but failed to silence the growing criticism. On 1 October 1920, the London *Times* commented that 'the name of England is being sullied throughout the Empire and throughout the world by this savagery for which the Government can no longer escape, however much they may seek to disclaim responsibility'. Early in 1921 Brigadier-General Hubert Gough, leader of the 1914 Curragh mutiny in which soldiers refused to help coerce Ulster into accepting Home Rule, articulated the continued concern about the situation: 'Law and order have given place to a bloody and brutal anarchy, in which the armed agents of the Crown violate every law in aimless and vindictive and insolent savagery. England has departed further from her own standards even [from those] of any nation in the world, not excepting the Turk and Zulu, than has ever been known in history before.'

In their record of the campaign, military authorities in Ireland stated that the British press was doing everything it could to vilify and misrepresent the policy of the government and the actions of the Crown forces. People at home in Britain appeared rather bored with the Irish situation, the Army record says, because 'we had no counter-propaganda either at home or abroad'. With regard to the issue of reprisals, the Army's concluding view is as follows:

> Is it to be wondered at therefore that men, who were not under military discipline and who were driven half mad by seeing their comrades shot down in cold blood, sometimes took the law into their own hands and indulged in unlawful reprisals. It is to be remembered also that these acts of reprisal – they were not numerous – were nearly always directed against individuals who, it was morally certain, had either taken part in, or were in entire sympathy with, the outrage committed. There are people who, from false sentiment and a lack of ethical knowledge, are more shocked at the burning of a house than at the murder which instigated it.

Meanwhile, in the north, with serious sectarian violence taking place, recruiting began for the Special Constabulary, whose ranks, it was envisaged, would be filled by the self-appointed UVF. A couple of days before recruiting began on 1 November 1920, Spender issued a memorandum to the Belfast battalions of the UVF encouraging them to enlist:

> I confidently rely on the Members of the Ulster Volunteer Force to do all they can to make the Special Constabulary Forces a success. Moreover, by restoring order in their own district they are making it possible for the Government to do more in the other parts of Ireland where the rebel forces predominate, and where our comrades are now being subjected to measures of terrorism. The Government has definitely recognised that there are two distinct elements among the population: Those who are loyal to the British Crown and Empire, and those who are not. The Government is asking the help of all Loyalists in Ulster, and proposes to arm with Firearms all those called on for duty, to confer certain privileges, to recognise them, and to indemnify them for injuries incurred by the performance of their duties.

This was a highly significant development in that it entitled the Unionists for the first time to regularise their irregular forces and bring them under legitimate authority. The system of enrolment was designed to make it easy for UVF members to enlist. Arrangements were made for application forms to be filled in and submitted in bulk from local UVF headquarters to the Selection Committee consisting of specially appointed magistrates who would consult with UVF officers 'so as to ensure that its members who join this Force are reliable and can be trusted with firearms', wrote Spender. In line with the organisational structure Spender had proposed at the earlier City Hall meeting, there were to be three classes of Specials. The 'A' class were full-time, paid at the same rates as the RIC (£3 17s. 6d. per week) and recruited from the twenty-one to forty-five age group. There was no pension but a bounty of ten shillings a week was payable at the end of service. Except for being confined to the six county area, the 'A's were for all practical purposes part of the RIC. 'B' Specials were part-time, unpaid, served locally, wore caps and armbands and received an allowance for wear and tear of clothing. Each man was armed and expected to do a four or five-hour duty one night a week and an entire night (eight hours) once a fortnight. 'C' Specials were simply enlisted for call-out in an emergency when they would be legally armed by the British government.

Soon afterwards Lieutenant-Colonel Fred Crawford, who had played the pivotal role in the UVF's 1914 gunrunning, stepped in to encourage the thousands of Orange Order members, who vigorously supported the Unionist demand 'to be armed & organised by the Government to protect their homes & persons', to join up. But, writing to Colonel Bob Wallace, the Grand Master of the Belfast Grand Lodge, he went on to reveal the real nature of the game-plan:

> The next point to be considered is who will be responsible for the safety of life & property when the new Government of Ulster is established & the troops are withdrawn, which they shall be? It will be the RIC, regular forces & A, B & C of Special Constables. Surely if this is a fact, the more Orangemen we have in that force, the better it will be for Protestant interests & the success of the Orange body itself. This seems perfectly patent. We must remember the old adage 'He who is not with me is against me.' Orangemen must come out now or be very sorry later that they have been neutrals, when they see Nationalists filling the ranks of an armed force where they might have been.

Despite these ambitions, the British government put its own man at the head of the Special Constabulary. Lieutenant-Colonel Charles Wickham, a Yorkshireman who had recently completed a two-year posting as a member of the British Military Mission to Siberia and been appointed RIC Divisional Commissioner in Belfast, was also given command of the Specials. As men signed up in their hundreds, Wickham and his staff officers took prompt steps to legitimise the carrying of arms by the new force. Permits, signed by the county commandant and with an official police stamp on the holder's photograph to prevent forgery, were issued to each man. In line with the 1920 Firearms Act, it authorised him to hold a stated firearm and ammunition at his dwelling house and when proceeding to or from duty. The third category permitted some Specials 'to carry for [their] protection when off duty, one revolver' and a specified quantity of rounds for it.

With so many 'reliable' men now officially under arms, Unionists believed that, like the Republicans with the IRA, they now had the independent means to back their own political demands with force, come what may in the uncertain days ahead. However, the creation of the Specials in this way, identifying them exclusively with the cause of Unionism, was the real starting point for what the distinguished British judge Mr Justice Scarman, half a century later, described as the fateful split between nationalists/Catholics and the forces of law and order. With Britain having effectively armed the Protestants, the Catholics in Northern Ireland, outnumbered six to four, were bewildered at being abandoned by Britain and their southern co-religionists to the uncertainties of partition, and deeply fearful of how they would be treated. It was no wonder then that in October 1920, as the Specials were being formed, Joe Devlin, the Nationalist MP for West Belfast, complained: 'The Protestants are to be armed for we would not touch your Special Constabulary with a forty-foot pole. Their pogrom is to be made less difficult. Instead of paving stones and sticks, they are to be given rifles.'

Fr John Hassan, a Catholic priest at St Mary's in central Belfast who compiled 'Facts and Figures of the Belfast Pogroms 1920–1922' under the pseudonym 'GB Kenna', recorded the development:

> The British Government, in the face of all protest, proceeded to organise and arm those Orange hordes – pogromists, looters, incendiaries and untried murderers a goodly portion of them – under the name of a Special Police Force. It need only be said that, as a body, their misdeeds surpass the worst that was even anticipated. It would be unfair, in

making this statement, not to add that there are, no doubt, many respectable and well-meaning men are to be found amongst them.

This critical standpoint and the manner of the raising of the Specials was to have long-standing implications for attitudes to law and order in Northern Ireland because, from the outset of the proposed state, it unambiguously identified law enforcement with the Unionist majority and imposed the impression that it was the Unionists alone who had responsibility for the task. As we shall see, events immediately ahead would reinforce this perception, and the deep fault-line thus created, which was to run divisively through Northern Ireland society for eighty years, was all the more dangerous because the violence since Soloheadbeg, in line with Northern Ireland's turbulent history, had also been characterised by ugly sectarianism.

In July 1920, nineteen people died and over fifty were wounded in sectarian clashes in Londonderry soon after a surge in nationalist support at council elections led to a nationalist majority taking control of the local council. The same month, 'disloyal workers' were driven out of the Belfast shipyards, triggering three days of trouble which left seven Catholics and six Protestants dead. The following month there was more sectarian trouble in Belfast and Lisburn after the murder of District Inspector Oswald Swanzy. By the end of August that year, when a night-time curfew was imposed in Belfast (which would not be lifted until 1924), twenty-two civilians were dead, 400 Catholic families had been made homeless and £1,000,000-worth of damage had been caused in some 180 malicious fires.

The first RIC casualty in Northern Ireland had occurred in May 1920 when Detective Sergeant Denis Moroney was shot dead while taking part in a bayonet charge to disperse rival sectarian crowds in Londonderry. On 26 September the force took its first casualty in Belfast when Constable Thomas Con was shot dead at Broadway on the Falls Road while on patrol. The Specials had been on the streets for a barely a month when they sustained their first fatal casualty, on 13 January 1921. That day a five-strong police party was escorting a postman delivering pension money between Crossmaglen and Cullyhanna in County Armagh when they were ambushed by an IRA 'flying column' of some fifty men armed with rifles and shotguns. The postman and an RIC constable were wounded in the fire-fight. The police party, unable to find the postman, withdrew with the wounded officer to Crossmaglen from where a party of reinforcements in a Crossley tender was sent out to rescue him. As they reached the scene of the earlier ambush, they also came under fire and Special Constable Robert Compston was shot. He later died from his wounds, as did the postman.

There now followed a sustained wave of sectarian violence in the north with twelve deaths and some twenty-five woundings in the first three months of 1921. Among the casualties were three RIC officers, Constables Robert Crooks and John McIntosh, both from Scotland, and Walter Cooper, an Englishman. The officers, all recently recruited Black and Tans, were posted from Gormanston to Belfast on 10 March as drivers. At 8.30 the next evening they were walking in Victoria Square, close to the city's main barracks at Musgrave Street, when they were attacked by four or five gunmen. Two of them died instantly from gunshot wounds, the third, Cooper, two days later in hospital. A civilian was also killed. Commenting on the incident in a report to Spender, the cabinet secretary, on 26 March, Lieutenant-Colonel Wickham said:

> The chief reprisal threatened was stopped under orders from this office. Had it taken place there would have been an almighty outcry from one end of England to the other. As you know Belfast city is a difficult place to deal with: once reprisals begin it is difficult to know where they will end. I am trying to arrange an increased force in the city which will enable us to take more drastic actions: primarily as a preventative but should further murders take place, to carry the war to the enemies' country.

More police deaths took place on 23 April when two members of the Auxiliaries, based in Sligo, were shot at the corner of Donegall Place and Fountain Lane in central Belfast. Cadet Ernest Bolam, a Londoner who had only been in the force for three months, died instantly. His colleague, Cadet John Bales, from Norfolk, who had joined up less than a month earlier, died the next day. That night, during curfew hours, two Catholic brothers were murdered in their home at 64 Clonard Gardens, Belfast. These deaths were regarded as reprisals and blamed on the police.

Elections for the new parliament took place on 22 May with Catholics protesting that many had suffered intimidation and violence to deter them from voting. Nineteen people were admitted to hospital with injuries including gunshot wounds. The new parliament was speedily inaugurated a month later, on 22 June, at Belfast City Hall by King George V. At the end of the day, as the king bade farewell to Craig aboard the royal yacht at Donegall Quay, he said: 'I can't tell you how glad I am I came, but you know my entourage were very much against it.' According to Lady Craig's diary, her husband replied: 'Sir, you are surrounded by pessimists, we are all optimists over here.' However, the concern for the king's safety was justified two days later when the train conveying the 10th Hussars mounted escort, sent from the Curragh to Belfast for the ceremonial opening procession from the Quay to the City Hall, was derailed by an explosion at Adavoyle, near Newry. Three soldiers were killed, another four injured and fifty-one horses were either killed or had to be destroyed. After the outrage, groups of Specials rounded up able-bodied men in Newry and the vicinity to dig a grave for the animals. The death toll could have been greater. A strong RIC detachment had also been sent from Dublin to Belfast to help line the route along High Street and Donegall Place. That morning, as Hugh McIvor, one of the party, recalled, they missed the return train:

> We were staying at the Horse Showgrounds off the Albertbridge Road and they put in blankets and a couple of bales of straw for us to lie on. After we did that duty somebody had been playing tricks and one of the fellas couldn't find his blankets and another fella the laces of his boots. Anyhow we were late in getting going and we had to march to the Great Northern Station. There was a special train for us but just as we went in they closed the gate. It must leave on time and away it went. So we got the second one a few minutes afterwards. Now we were fortunate to get that because the military one with the horses in was wrecked. A bomb lifted the whole section off the rail and it tumbled over and over and over. Aye, we were lucky in that.

The government's military adviser, Sir Henry Wilson, however, was far from optimistic about the way events were developing and disparaging about what he called the 'the complexion of James Craig's Parliament' in a letter to his friend General Henry Rawlinson, then commander in chief in India: 'As none of the Papists will take the Oath of Allegiance so the whole House is composed of Protestants, and the whole Police also of "Black [extreme] Protestants".'

Meanwhile, with the sectarian clashes continuing in Belfast and the entire island in violent turmoil despite his claim to 'have murder by the throat', Lloyd George decided, just two days after the opening of the Belfast parliament, to sue for peace and secretly invited the Ulster Unionists and Sinn Fein to unconditional talks. The first step was to negotiate a ceasefire, which came into force at noon on 11 July 1921. In an instruction issued to the police about the manner in which they should observe the truce, Wickham said its terms were verbal only, for a written agreement would have amounted to official recognition of the IRA. Wilson was deeply unimpressed by this development. In another letter to Rawlinson, he remarked:

> I simply cannot write what I think about inviting de Valera over. In your own cockney language, 'there ain't no bloody words for it'! We started the truce, so-called, in Ireland yesterday at 12 midday. What is going to happen I have not the faintest idea. We have something like 70 battalions over there now, and a whole lot of Field Artillery, without their guns, but mounted on their horses, as mounted infantry, and all the mechanical transport, aeroplanes, cavalry etc. that we can lay our hands on, but whether we are going to be told to withdraw the whole lot, or whether we are going to be told to carry out law and order, I have not the faintest idea, and to tell you a very great secret, no more has anybody else, except possibly, Michael Collins.

The military build-up had been ordered to ensure that Britain was seen to be negotiating from a position of strength. It was also intended to provide the ability to impose martial law on the entire island and to crack down quickly if the talks foundered and the truce collapsed. In the meantime, after murdering thirty-two police officers (five in the six-county area) in the month leading up to the truce, the IRA downed their weapons in accordance with a series of mutually grudging protocols agreed with the crown forces to maintain the fragile peace. The police were instructed they had to go unarmed both on and off duty and, in the north, to the fury of the Unionists, all patrols by B Specials were halted. In Belfast, news of the truce provoked yet another round of violence and death with thirteen Catholics and four Protestants losing their lives in the twenty-four hours before it came into force, according to the records kept by Fr Hassan. Within days, citing 'a murderous attack by Sinn Fein gunmen on the police in Belfast', the Craig administration was calling on the British government to revive the Restoration of Order (Ireland) Act to enable the police to respond. Despite the truce, another five Catholics and six Protestants died over the next few weeks and in a particularly bad flare-up over two days at the end of August nine Protestants and ten Catholics were killed.

Shaken by the situation and frustrated that the truce tied their hands in responding, the cabinet, chaired by Lord Londonderry, the minister of finance, went into an almost continuous crisis session over the next two days. Despite the creation of the Specials, Bates, the newly appointed minister of home affairs, gave them a disturbing report:

> The feeling among the rank and file is that the Government are either unable, or unwilling, to afford law-abiding citizens protection. The outbreaks, which have recently taken place, have shown that in many cases the Loyalist sections of the community are themselves taking organised steps to defend themselves against future attacks by Sinn Fein. The people cannot understand why having elected a Parliament, and the Government having been set up, that Government is not functioning. Every day that passes makes the position of the Ulster Government more difficult and increases the difficulties that the Ulster Government will have when they get into the saddle.

There were conflicting claims about responsibility for the violence. Archdeacon Convery, one of the most senior Catholic clergy in the city, had told Alfred Cope, the assistant under-secretary from Dublin Castle, that the Catholic population were 'terror-stricken, fearing attack and blamed the police and military authorities for not giving them protection'. William Grant, the Unionist MP for North Belfast, reported to Cope that 'the Unionists are living in dread' and also blamed the authorities. At one point Grant was called in to address the cabinet and graphically described the state of terror when mills and shops on York Street had been forced to close down while the street had been in the hands of snipers, who were not local men but were gunmen and good shots, who had been imported into Belfast for the purpose. Only that morning in Corporation Street, Grant stated, twenty had been observed with rifles and waterproof sheets, and another twenty, probably armed with revolvers, accompanied them.

Cope reported that 'the origin of the trouble was a bomb being thrown into a Catholic house from the Protestant end of a street occupied by Catholics and Protestants', and concluded: 'It was not the same situation as in previous disturbances, as this was not political, but Catholics versus Protestants.' JF Gelston, the Belfast police commissioner, said that the trouble had started after a man was beaten and spread widely after retaliation was taken. (The cabinet papers unfortunately do not record the religion of this original victim.) Because of the conditions surrounding the truce, he complained, 'the hands of the police were therefore tied'.

During the cabinet discussions, Bates criticised the 'apparent indifference' of the police and military authorities. 'This is not an ordinary riot, but the IRA,' he said, a view shared by other ministers who also clamoured for 1,000 A Specials based at Newtownards to be marched into the city and through the streets to restore public confidence and for the armed B Specials to be mobilised in their own localities. Colonel-Commandant Carter-Campbell, the General Officer Commanding, warned them that would be a breach of the truce and said the Army could cope. In answer to the ministers who wanted the power of internment restored to the military authorities, Cope replied that as both sides were shooting, both sides would have to be interned: 'The arrest of Catholics only would undermine the confidence of that side in the Crown Forces.' Of course, that was not the approach that the partisan Bates wanted the Army to take, but he could do little more than let off steam in a memorandum to the cabinet a few days later saying he was still not content that the Army was capable of restoring order. What the home affairs minister and his Unionist colleagues really wanted was the power and the means to crack down hard on non-Unionists.

Meanwhile political exchanges had started as soon as the truce had come into force, with three exploratory meetings between Lloyd George and de Valera in London before the end of July. By the end of September the two sides had agreed a formula for British and Irish representatives to meet 'with a view to ascertaining how the association of nations known as the British Empire may best be reconciled with Irish national aspirations'. A full-scale Anglo-Irish conference was convened and the two sides came together at Downing Street on 11 October for face-to-face negotiations.

Towards the end of November, however, at a particularly crucial point in the extraordinarily difficult and emotional talks, when the two sides were exchanging drafts of a possible treaty, the Ulster Unionists almost derailed the entire process. According to the *Whitehall Diaries* of Thomas Jones, assistant secretary to the British cabinet at the time, the episode 'badly poisoned the atmosphere'. Its origins appear to lie at a lunch in late October when, at Sir Henry Wilson's prompting, Craig entertained General Sir Nevil Macready, commander in chief of British forces in Ireland, and Major-General Archibald Cameron, the military commander in Northern Ireland, at his palatial home in east Belfast, not far from Stormont.

Craig had little faith that the Downing Street talks would produce a settlement and was more concerned about the readiness of the British government to defend the north when the initiative failed and the uneasy truce collapsed. As Craig told Wilson after the lunch, he was 'distinctly uneasy' after hearing that the generals planned to scrap two classes of the Special Constabulary and disband the third, in order to merge them into a very large military force for general service in Ireland. Craig believed this would leave Ulster entirely at the mercy of Sinn Fein, disorganise the 'Loyalist' party and, through denying it any means of defence under its own control, render the position of his government entirely untenable. He was also doubtful that Ulstermen would sign up for the new force in sufficient numbers. Craig wrote to Wilson suggesting that to avoid the situation in the south 'where there appears to be anything but harmony between the Military and Constabulary Authorities' he should 'approve of it' that Wickham, the Chief Constabulary Officer, should also hold a military appointment under General Cameron. 'I feel sure that we can rely upon his acquiescence in any arrangement which will prevent friction between the Military and Constabulary Forces,' said Craig.

Craig's views caused the military commanders to think again and a few days later Cameron, whom the RIC leaders had since commended to the prime minister as 'a Scot with staunch Protestant views', returned to Craig's home for another meeting. In the light of Craig's doubts about raising sufficient manpower for the new military force, Wilson had meanwhile suggested reforming the Ulster Division (the UVF-based force that had been sent to fight in the First World War) or further expanding the Special Constabulary Forces already existing in Ulster. Craig favoured the second option and stressed that while he thought they would not join up for general service throughout Ireland 'there will be no difficulty in getting from the "A" Constabulary any number of volunteers required to serve just outside the Six Counties for the better protection of our province. Our experience has made it quite clear that they are anxious to do so in Counties Donegal, Cavan and Monaghan, and Colonel Wickham, I know, feels that.'

Again pursuing a situation where he could at least influence military policy if he couldn't control it, Craig also pressed Wilson for his help in ensuring that 'when the truce ends' Ulster should be made independent of the commander in chief in Dublin and should have a local commander, reporting direct to the War Office. With his expectation that it was only a matter of time before the truce collapsed, Craig was further anxious that Macready's promise to get 13,000 firearms quickly delivered to Carrickfergus should be carried out. 'I hope there may be no question about this as previous promises have not been fulfilled and there would be very serious trouble if we lose a number of casualties at the beginning simply because arms are not available to let the people defend themselves,' said Craig.

Both Craig and his cabinet were gripped by chronic insecurity, fearing either or both external invasion from the south and internal subversion by nationalists. With sectarian trouble still a daily occurrence, notably in Belfast, despite the truce, they were also convinced that the IRA had used the lull to regroup and re-arm for a coming push to annexe the north. As the 1920 Government of Ireland Act prohibited them – and the southerners – from raising a military force, ensuring the adequate defence of Northern Ireland therefore remained a major preoccupation. These concerns, which could never be discounted given the unfolding uncertainties of the situation, provided the backdrop for a formal, minuted discussion on 7 November when Wilson and Sir Laming Worthington Evans, Secretary of State for War, met Craig and Spender at the War Office in London.

To the prime minister's immense satisfaction, the decision was reached that in the event of the truce breaking down the government of Northern Ireland would be responsible for its own law and order and martial law would not be applied. In addition, the War Office would lend senior and junior officers to help with the constabulary; all troops would be pulled out of Northern Ireland three days after the truce had been broken off (except for two battalions guarding the Army base at Ballykinler, County Down); and the War Office and Admiralty would undertake coastal defence with the agreement of the Northern Ireland parliament. It was further agreed that, in these circumstances, the War Office should supply arms, military material and stores on requisition by the Ulster cabinet and that the expense of all special enlistments into the RIC, ammunition, arms and other material, over and above the normal police garrison of the Six Counties, would be borne by the Imperial Exchequer. Taking advantage of these new terms, Craig immediately upped his requisition for rifles from 12,000 to 26,200 rifles with 5,240,000 rounds of ammunition.

When news of these War Office talks was relayed back to Dawson Bates in Belfast, whose individual concern about the vulnerability of the Unionist regime far exceeded even that of his prime minister and ministerial colleagues, he decided to put some wheels in immediate motion. So it was that on 9 November, a circular, classified Secret and signed by Wickham, was issued to the county commandants of the Special Constabulary. It proposed considerably expanding the Class C Special Constabulary force by 'obtaining the services of the best elements' of burgeoning cadres of 'unauthorised loyalist defence forces', many of which had sprung up under the auspices of Fred Crawford. The circular continued:

> The force is intended as a military one only, to be called out in grave emergency, to act in a military capacity. They will not of necessity be utilised for local defence, but may be drafted to any theatres of operations within the six counties. It is not intended that this force should interfere with or replace Class 'B' Special Constabulary, who remain a local force for local protection.
>
> The 'C' scheme, therefore, applies mostly to towns and cities where there is a population surplus to 'B' requirements. The most suitable class for this force are ex-soldiers, who possess already the necessary military training and knowledge of arms. As the matter is URGENT, replies should be sent at the earliest possible date.

Apart from its primary objective to meet Craig's aim of providing a locally controlled means for the defence of Northern Ireland, the Bates–Wickham initiative had the secondary purpose of keeping the task under official control and neutering the rival activities of Crawford. Earlier in 1921, the Northern Ireland government had made an official deal with him for the UVF arms and equipment, which he held in trust, to be formally loaned for the use of the Specials. Since then he had become the figurehead for hardline elements, who judged Craig and Bates far too accommodating in their approach to the situation. Crawford, who saw himself as the real saviour of Ulster and yearned for a more prominent role in events, had therefore created a secretive 'Ulster Brotherhood' and formulated his own plans for mustering a 150,000-strong militia and an elite detective force, 'Crawford's Tigers', to be offered to Wickham as the intelligence-gathering and investigative cutting edge of a drive against Republicans.

Almost inevitably a copy of what quickly became known as 'the Wickham circular' reached Collins, whose penetration of the RIC and British intelligence apparatus in the south had played a considerable part in forcing a reluctant Lloyd George into negotiation. Just as Craig and Bates were alarmed at the prospect of the Free State moving against the north, Collins and his negotiating team were similarly anxious about the effect of the Unionists raising such a force. Apart from the threat it would pose to Catholics in the northern area, its potential activities along the proposed border could only complicate further Collins's increasingly problematic task in getting a settlement that would head off a violent clash between those in the south pragmatically prepared to settle for partition and those who vowed to fight on for an all-Ireland Free State. To maximise the negotiating advantage gained from acquiring the circular, Collins had it leaked to the *Irish Bulletin*. Its existence, never mind its disclosure, was an acute blow at a highly inopportune moment for a British government which was allegedly neutral in the peace talks.

The Wickham issue was thus adroitly exploited by the Irish negotiators to compound British embarrassment. Collins told Jones his delegation had got letters from Ireland saying they were being fooled by the British government and that preparations for a civil war were at full blast in Ulster with the connivance of the War Office. Such an issue could not have arisen at a less favourable moment, with the treaty talks precariously balanced between success and failure, and Jones, who clearly regarded the hardline Wilson as the ultimate architect of the proposed force, later told colleagues it was pity the hardline field marshal had not gone for a voyage around the world.

At 10.30 a.m. on 23 November, Lloyd George convened a meeting at 10 Downing Street to deal with the matter. Sir Hamar Greenwood, the chief secretary for Ireland, Macready and Major-General Tudor, the policy adviser to the RIC, all denied any foreknowledge of the circular although they admitted having held contingency discussions with Craig. Lloyd George accepted the consensus view that it was Bates who had pressured Wickham into issuing the circular. At the end of the hour-long meeting he instructed Worthington Evans to go and see Craig at his London hotel to stress that the proposed force was illegal and secure a repudiation of the circular. Late that evening, after Craig had agreed, Jones contacted the Irish delegation to formally advise them that the circular had been issued without the knowledge or approval of any British ministers, that the proposition it contained was illegal and that, while Craig and Wickham understandably wanted to bring illegal Loyalist forces under official control, the circular had been withdrawn and no further action was being taken to raise such a territorial force. Craig was also forced to send a telegram to Bates in Belfast in similar terms:

> My attention has been drawn to the terms of Colonel Wickham's circular of November 9, with regard to the recruiting Class 'C' of the Special Constabulary, which I approved in the event of the Truce being terminated, but for their formation into a regular military unit the Constabulary has never been transferred to the Government of Northern Ireland. The recruits may be taken as police, but not into a

military force for organisation. I am returning on Saturday morning, when I will explain the legal position. Meanwhile the circular must be withdrawn.

For their part, the Irish side accepted the explanation and assurances and their attention again turned to the more fundamental issues involved in defining a new Anglo-Irish relationship, but the episode had aggravated existing suspicion and distrust which would linger in their minds and colour future events.

After several more weeks of brinkmanship, heart-searching and tough bargaining, Lloyd George issued an ultimatum on 5 December that the war would be resumed if the draft Anglo-Irish treaty was not immediately concluded. After a final round of talks, it was finally signed at Downing Street in the early hours of 6 December 1921. It confirmed that the southern counties would form a new Irish Free State while the six northern counties, already partitioned off and given their own subordinate parliament, would remain under British rule. A Boundary Commission would be appointed to delineate and confirm the precise line of the future frontier. Wilson, the diehard Unionist and imperialist, was not impressed by the outcome or the politicians who had sired it. Writing to a colleague a week later in a derisory and disillusioned tone, he said:

The state of chaos in Downing Street and in Ireland increases every day, and there is no question at all that if the highest art and form of statesmanship is to reduce an absolutely peaceful, quiet, thriving country into a hell then Lloyd George is a master. Egypt will follow Ireland, and India Egypt, and then we shall be left with Silesia, Constantinople, Jewland and Mesopotamia. These will follow in succession and then we shall be left with England, that will follow in succession and then we shall be left with Ulster, and from there we shall have to start again and build an empire. Don't laugh, because bear in mind always that Portugal once had an empire, and even Venice.

Wilson's feelings were not entirely shared in Belfast, however. On 22 November, even before the Treaty had been signed at Downing Street, Craig's administration had assumed responsibility for the security of Northern Ireland, ironically at the very height of the circular affair and amid another upsurge of violence. The next day, according to Fr Hassan's records, four Protestants and ten Catholics died in violent incidents in the city. In the face of the continued unrest in Belfast the Northern Ireland cabinet met with General Carter-Campbell that day and again demanded that the Special Constabulary should be utilised to bolster Loyalist morale and to prevent a further upsurge in violence. Again the GOC was against the proposal, pointing out that use of the Specials would violate the truce. However, he did agree that more troops would be put on the streets.

With control of security now in their own hands, although they were still forbidden from raising a military force under the terms of the 1920 Government of Ireland Act, Craig and Bates now pushed ahead with a major expansion of the Specials, announcing plans to expand the A force to 4,200, increase the B Specials to a strength of 8,500 and put up to 22,000 C Specials under arms. At a cabinet meeting on 28 November Craig said that 'under no consideration was it possible to reduce the Constabulary below the limits required to ensure life and property within the province. No Government could last which did not perform this elementary duty.' He would rather 'incur bankruptcy than fail in this respect,' he added. Craig also said he was sure the British government would endorse this necessity and generously fund it. 'As soon as circumstances permit, I will gladly insist on drastic reductions of this force,' he concluded, taking account of what were growing doubts in Britain about the conduct of the force and the cabinet's sensitivities about paying for it.

Liberal British opinion was now thoroughly outraged by newspaper reports of the ongoing sectarian conflict in Belfast and the reputation of the Specials. In an editorial in March 1921, the *Manchester Guardian* had said:

> The Special Constabulary, drawn almost exclusively from the ranks of the Orange Lodges and the Unionist Volunteers, was nominally raised to protect life and property and to maintain order, not to become a force of terrorists exercising powers of death over their Catholic neighbours, for in the Ulster Unionist mind Catholic and Sinn Feiner are synonymous. Ulster's case against a single parliament for Ireland has always rested on its alleged fear of persecution. It will be a bad beginning for the Ulster parliament if its establishment coincides with the dragooning of the Catholic minority in the six counties by an armed Protestant force administering a sort of lynch law.

Early in 1922, despite the inevitability of civil war in the new Free State between those in the provisional government, led by Collins, who accepted the Treaty and partition, and de Valera and others who wanted to fight on for the whole island, there was serious anxiety about the deeply unstable situation in the north. Collins was concerned that British policy seemed to amount to giving Craig and the Unionists the money and an unfettered hand to build up an all-Protestant Special Constabulary to terrorise Catholics. He recognised that Unionist insecurity lay at the heart of the problem, so, spurred on by London, Collins met Craig on 21 January 1922 in a bid to establish co-operative north–south relations. The encounter resulted in the first Craig–Collins Pact. For his part Craig undertook to stop the attacks on Catholics and protect the thousands who had been expelled from their jobs, notably in the Belfast shipyards. Collins agreed to bring an end to the eighteen-month-old 'Belfast boycott' which had led to goods from the north being burned or destroyed. Most significantly, Collins had given Craig an assurance that he did not wish to coerce the north into union with the Free State. Both also resolved to create a mechanism, other than the envisaged Council of Ireland, to act as a clearing-house in resolving disputes and differences between the two parts of the island.

During his trip to London, Collins also met Greenwood at the Colonial Office to discuss the future of the RIC. For their own differing reasons, the new administrations in both Dublin and Belfast called for its immediate disbandment. Collins, who had personal reservations about the wisdom of complete disbandment rather than reform, went along with the widespread and deep-seated prejudice against the long-established force in the south, although he quickly singled out a number of officers and, especially, detectives to provide a framework of training and experience for the Garda Siochana (Civic Guards) organisation he was already planning to replace it.

But as far as Craig, Bates and the Unionists were concerned, the RIC was riddled with Catholics and Republican sympathisers and was not to be trusted. Above all they saw in the development an opportunity to get more 'reliable' men under arms to assist in the 'defence' of Ulster. 'Reliable' was code for Protestant. Within a week of the London meeting the phased disbandment was under way. At that stage there were nearly 13,000 regulars and 5,000 'temporary' police, the Black and Tans and the now notorious Auxiliaries. These non-Irish officers, the first to be stood down, were concentrated under formal military protection in Dublin, Gormanstown, Mullingar and the Curragh before being discharged and escorted to the mail boats for England. A former member of the force said it was like the Wild West most nights, with a lot of drinking and revelry as they waited to to go home. To ensure that the Auxilaries dispersed to their homes throughout the country rather than congregate for what the authorities feared would be an extended and rowdy drinking spree after being shipped out from Dublin to Liverpool each was given a payable order for his final salary and bounty which could only be cashed at the post office closest to his own address. In a short time many of them re-enlisted in the service of the Crown and departed to join the Palestine Police.

By the end of March the RIC had been withdrawn from nineteen counties altogether and concentrated into a number of disbandment centres in the other seven counties of the south. One of these locations was at Gormanston, just north of Dublin, where almost 1,000 vehicles and tons of equipment were gathered for handover to the new Irish government. The acquisition by the southern government of several hundred of the very latest Crossley, Ford and armoured Rolls Royce vehicles with substantial quantities of machine guns, rifles and ammunition caused near apoplexy among the Unionists, who were convinced they would soon be turned against themselves.

As the Irishmen were discharged they were generally escorted in groups to railway stations and ferry ports or to the border, protected from attack by often hostile or, at best, grudging IRA parties. Some were not so fortunate. Contemporary newspaper reports describe how IRA parties intercepted and screened the departing RIC men, searching for those on their 'blacklist'. Several were abducted and reportedly murdered.

On 4 April, after a farewell parade at the Phoenix Park depot, the RIC was formally disbanded in the Free State. During May the House of Commons in London debated the disbandment of the force and passed an act, mainly dealing with pensions. Many MPs paid tribute to the force. One member calculated that one in twenty of its members had been murdered and one in twelve wounded in the preceding two years. Sir Hamar Greenwood praised the men of the RIC as 'the pick of the Irish race'.

From the 1916 Easter Rising until the truce in July 1921, 456 members of the RIC had been killed as a direct result of the political violence: fourteen in 1916, one in 1918 and twelve in 1919. In 1920 171 died and another 230 lost their lives in 1921. In 1922, twenty-nine were murdered. Eleven members of the Dublin Metropolitan Police also died during these years of violence. In addition, over the same period another ninety-two RIC officers lost their lives, including thirty-three who were accidentally shot, twenty who were kidnapped and never returned and sixteen who committed suicide.

Soloheadbeg is not the only place where this grim death toll of overwhelmingly Irish-born police officers murdered by fellow Irishmen is ignored. Shamefully, there is not a single monument to the RIC dead in what is now the Irish Republic. Despite the changes in public and official attitudes in recent years, so that the sacrifice of all Irish men and women in war and conflict is supposed to be equally recognised, the RIC remains despised and forgotten. To the shame of the Irish state, which officially reveres their killers, the only official memorial for the men of the RIC is a nondescript plaque in the crypt of St Paul's Cathedral, London which reads: '1836–1922 – In memory of the Royal Irish Constabulary and of the officers and men who fell in the discharge of duty during the existence of the force and in the Great War 1914–1918.'

Chapter Two

'An Unfortunate Mentor'

There could have been no worse architect for the development of policing in Northern Ireland or more unfortunate mentor for the Royal Ulster Constabulary than Richard Dawson Bates. As minister for home affairs, he clung disastrously to office from the formation of the Northern Ireland government in 1921 until he was forced from power at the mid-point of the Second World War in 1943. Bates was an uncompromising bigot who regarded all Catholics as nationalists and, as such, enemies to be distrusted and neutralised in every conceivable way. For many years, he imposed his deeply partisan views and discriminatory values on the ministry and the police and the way they exercised their varied powers and responsibilities. More than any other Unionist figurehead, through his lack of principle, his prejudice and inadequacies he helped create the factory of grievances that the new Northern Ireland state so quickly became. The legacy of distrust, discrimination and maladministration that he played such a part in creating imposed a heavy cost on future generations of all those who lived in Northern Ireland. In particular, the partisan way he steered the RUC into being and the role he set for it handicapped the force from birth and ensured that the fateful split from the Catholic community remained in perpetuity. As a direct consequence, long after his own political demise and even after his death, the force, manacled by his shortsightedness and prejudice, was, like the RIC before it, inevitably destined for a place of notoriety in Irish history.

Bates, born at Strandtown in east Belfast, followed his father and uncle into the legal profession and the long-established family firm of E and RD Bates, whose offices were in Mayfair Buildings at Arthur Square in central Belfast. Close by, at 25–39 Arthur Street, was the head office of Dunville and Co. the whiskey distillers, the highly prosperous family firm of James Craig and the source of his considerable wealth. The two men became close after Bates was appointed part-time secretary to the Ulster Unionist Council (at a salary of £100 per annum) when it was formed in 1905, a political partnership that would endure for almost forty years. Bates also became politically intimate with Edward Carson and built up a network of contacts with local Unionist associations throughout Ireland, which enabled him to provide much of the organisational muscle for the ongoing campaign against Home Rule. He was heavily involved in the crucial events from 1912 onwards: arranging the massive demonstration against Home Rule at Balmoral showgrounds in Belfast on 9 April and organising Ulster Day and the signing of the Covenant the following September. In 1913 he helped found the Ulster Volunteer Force and from his office in its headquarters at the Old Town Hall in Victoria Street, Belfast, was actively involved in the conspiracy to smuggle arms into Northern Ireland in 1914.

In 1920, after his election to the first Belfast parliament, representing the Victoria Division of east Belfast, Bates immediately became Craig's home affairs minister, responsible for the highly sensitive issues of law and order, local government and electoral affairs as well as a ragbag of other functions including prisons, roads, road transport, bridges, ferries and the registration of clerks of the petty sessions. Lord Londonderry, the aristocratic education minister, pertinently observed in his journal that Bates's experience as what we would nowadays call a party political 'fixer' was 'no training for the duties of Home Secretary and his support and standing in the Six Counties [was] not high enough to give him that general support and confidence which are such factors in successfully controlling a government office'. Other colleagues had a similarly low opinion of him. GC Duggan, a civil servant, also described Bates as 'unimpressive in physique and bearing, the frequent despair of his civil service staff driven to waylay him, even in the street, in order to obtain urgent decisions'. Duggan also observed that he was 'a man who made a point of being unpunctual for appointments on the ground that he declined to be a slave of time' and recalled that Bates had 'such a prejudice against Catholics that he made it clear to his Permanent Secretary that he did not want his most juvenile clerk or typist, if a Papist, assigned for duty to his ministry'. Some years later, in 1934, Bates wrote to a senior colleague advising him not to use the telephone to his office as he had discovered the telephonist was a Catholic.

Bates believed simply that Protestant ascendancy and Unionist dominance were the best ways to preserve Ulster, and as a hardline party hack he acted accordingly. For the next twenty years he was given free rein by Craig, who used him as a means 'to stop Catholics always coming squealing to me' on law-and-order matters. (To finance his grandiose lifestyle at Magherabuoy House, near Portrush on the north Antrim coast with views across the North Atlantic, he both clung to public office and operated his law firm until in 1943, according to Spender, an openly incompetent Bates was in such poor health that 'he seems incapable of giving his responsible officials coherent directions on policy'.)

The process of creating a new police force for Northern Ireland began on 31 January 1922, immediately after the decision to disband the RIC, when the new parliament in Belfast formally approved Bates's request to appoint a Committee on Police Reorganisation. Its deliberations lasted barely a month before Bates pressed them for an interim report, which was submitted on 28 March. It was a short and superficial document. The main recommendation was that there should be a new 3,000-strong single force under a single command for the whole of Northern Ireland, to be called the Ulster Constabulary. Setting the new force firmly in the Unionist firmament from the outset, the committee also submitted that the king be asked to award the 'Royal' prefix 'in recognition of their loyalty in the most arduous and dangerous circumstances and [because] it would also give great satisfaction to the loyal population of the Northern area who have always been noted for their attachment to the Throne and Constitution'. Representatives of both the RIC and Special Constabulary made submissions to the committee, each contending that it was entitled to special treatment in recruiting for the new force, and some committee members favoured quotas for both the ex-RIC and A Specials. The committee finally agreed that 'in the appointment of officers of the force the Minister of Home Affairs should have a certain latitude' and 'the claims of any suitable officers of the Special Constabulary should be considered', but it cautioned against packing the new force with transferring Specials, pointing out that 'to become members of a permanent police force, special qualifications are necessary, which are not to be gained by service in a temporary police force'.

The committee's most controversial recommendation was that a one-third quota of the new force should be recruited first from among the existing Catholic members of the RIC, then, if any portion of the quota was still not filled, from the overall Catholic population. Several members of the committee recorded reservations. One said he did 'not consider it wise to raise the religious basis of the Force further than to say that reasonable representation should be given to all religious classes in the six counties, provided they take the Oath of Allegiance'. (This proposed provision effectively excluded many Catholics who were, of course, averse to swearing allegiance to the crown.) Another strongly objected to 'the formation of the new Police Force on sectarian lines. I quite admit that in policing counties, cities and districts consideration should be given to the proportion of Protestants and Catholics in such counties and districts. Further than this I am not prepared to go.' GC Duggan, then acting assistant secretary at the Ministry of Finance, also entered a similar reservation:

> I concur with the view regarding the undesirability of fixing the composition of the new Police Force on sectarian lines. The effect of the Committee's recommendation will in all probability result in a considerable number of eligible Catholic members of the RIC being shut out from the new force. Recruiting for the new force will hardly follow normal lines, so far as its religious composition is concerned, for some years to come, and, therefore, there are strong grounds for not applying any sectarian formula to the enlistment of every suitable member of the RIC.

Bates, who harboured deep suspicions about the inclusion of Catholic members of the RIC, surprisingly ignored these reservations and the committee's main proposals, including the one-third Catholic quota, were incorporated into the Constabulary Act (NI) 1922, passed by the Belfast parliament in May. It seems that the Catholic quota was swallowed, however uncomfortably, for good practical reasons. There were simply not enough trained and experienced Protestants to assimilate from the overwhelmingly Catholic RIC and, in order to make the new force quickly effective, Bates had little choice. In any case, with a third of the population Catholic and, in the eyes of the northern government, potentially subversive, it also recognised the need to have 'eyes and ears' to ensure law and order and the very existence of the new state could be maintained. Recruiting advertisements inviting applications for enrolment in the Ulster Police 'without distinction of creed' from former members of the RIC, members of the Special Constabulary and 'a limited number' of the Dublin Metropolitan Police had already appeared in newspapers on 30 March 1922. As the committee had requested, the new force was indeed awarded the Royal prefix on 29 April. 'A gratifying announcement,' said the *Belfast Telegraph*: 'This announcement will, we are sure, be received with intense pleasure by the people of Northern Ireland and it will tend to give them an added pride in the force which is now in course of formation.' It is worth noting that the 'Royal' prefix was not a distinction 'earned' by the new force. It was merely awarded as a sop to Unionist opinion. For nationalists it was a meaningless bauble, but one that was nevertheless quietly resented.

At this point the new Northern Ireland state was gripped by anarchy and uncertainty, factors aggravated by what British civil servant SG Tallents described as 'the historic cleavage of race, temperament and religion in the six counties'. The division between Protestants and Catholics in Belfast, he wrote, 'is almost absolute, greater, I should say, than the division between Pole and Jew in Warsaw'. Despite the Craig–Collins pact, in January, north–south relations had not warmed and the sectarian violence in the north had intensified, especially in Belfast. In the first five months of 1922 there were 283 deaths by violence and 427 people wounded, as well as incidents related to the new border. Among Catholics there was a passive refusal to recognise or deal with the northern government and their political leaders were refusing to take their seats in the Belfast parliament. Above all, there was continued distrust and fear among the Unionists that, despite the widening split between those for and against the Treaty and partition, the Free Staters in the south would inevitably combine and move against the north, or some of its territory, sooner or later. Tallents said, 'The Protestant community of the north feel that it is an outpost of civilisation set precariously on the frontiers of Bolshevism. It believes that the British government has betrayed it and at best that its cause is misunderstood in England.'

Craig was in fact deeply fearful that either the British government or the Boundary Commission, to which he was opposed, would seek to change the status or area of the Six Counties, with consequences which he outlined in a letter to London on 15 December, a week after the Treaty had been concluded:

> Far from feeling that I have exaggerated the situation, I believe that civil war is not necessarily the only end to which we have to look forward under the terms of the Treaty. So intense is local feeling at the moment, that my colleagues and I may be swept off our feet, and, contemporaneously with the functioning of the Treaty, the Loyalists may declare independence on their own behalf, seize the Customs and other Government Departments and set up an authority of their own. Many already believe that violence is the only language understood by Mr. Lloyd George and his Ministers.

In reply, Chamberlain chose to be conciliatory. 'I know that you yourself desire peace and I cannot believe that men whose loyalty is their pride are contemplating acts of War against the King,' he wrote.

However, when Craig repeated the threats in a speech to his own Parliament on 6 February – 'We cannot consent to any alteration, of our boundary except by mutual agreement . . . by that we stand, no matter what the consequences' – alarm bells began to ring loudly in London, where, for the first time, the cabinet showed apprehension about the political wisdom and financial cost of its current policy which amounted to even more openly arming the Protestants. The grim implications of this policy were spelled out in a secret cabinet memorandum on 18 March 1922.

> In the face of language like this, it is impossible to assume that the formidable forces now being organised under the guise of police are directed solely against the danger of invasion from the South. The British Government has armed and is paying for forces, which, it is told by the one who controls them [Craig], will in certain eventualities be turned against itself. It is difficult to avoid the conclusion that the Government of Northern Ireland has succeeded in assuming the military functions specifically reserved to the British Government, simply by calling their forces 'police'. Our equivalent force of police in Great Britain would make at least 800,000, or in Germany about 1,300,000 men. What would France say if Great Britain allowed Germany to maintain well over a million 'police' armed with rifles.

At this point, apart from their plan to raise the 3,000-strong RUC, Craig, Bates and the government had at their disposal 4,346 A Specials, 20,000 enrolled B Specials (seventy-five per cent of them armed) and an indeterminate number of C Specials, many legally armed with the old UVF's smuggled weapons. Another 1,000 A Specials were being recruited and, as we shall see, plans were being hatched for all manner of additional manpower and armaments. 'The whole of these Specials are Protestants, if only for the reason that Catholics are averse to taking the Oath of Allegiance,' said the British cabinet report. (The reality was more complex than that, as we shall also see.) Turning to what should be done, the memorandum continued:

> In view of the disturbed conditions of Northern Ireland, it would be reasonable to suppose that its Government would require a regular police force equipped with firearms and larger in proportion to the population than would be needed for a community of commensurate size and area in Great Britain. It would naturally be supported by

special constables, to be called out in case of emergency. But such constables would not be equipped with firearms. It is a clear principle that a situation with which regular police armed with rifles and supported by special constables armed with batons are unable to deal, is one which calls for the intervention of the military forces of the State; when a Government enrols, drills and arms with rifles large numbers of specials, the distinction between military and civil control has broken down.

The situation was a novel one, for it was the first time in the history of the British Commonwealth that a dominion (the Irish Free State) was separated from the United Kingdom by a land frontier only. The paper went on to say that if either of the two Irish governments 'lost its head' and advanced forces into the territory of the other, it was the clear duty of the 5,000 British troops in Ulster to take control of the border and stabilise the situation. This important analysis went further by raising, for the first time, the need 'for gradually confining the functions of the northern government to genuine police work' and using financial sanctions to reduce the forces and enforce such a policy. This paper effectively set the lines for the battle over the constabulary and security that Belfast and London would fight over the coming years.

At this time, the true nature of the sectarian monster the British government had allowed the Ulster Unionists to create was outlined in a perceptive and astonishingly frank paper circulated throughout the senior ranks of the Constabulary. The 'A' force, the unidentified author said, consisted of:

> [. . .] good material on the whole, but owing to rapid expansion and want of moral courage in excluding undesirables, you have a large leaven of a bad type [. . .] there is much trouble from drink and consequent indiscipline. As a police force they have no chance. The A's belong to one section of the population and, although they serve mostly away from their immediate homes they form a distinctly partisan force and it is impossible to expect from them that impartiality that is necessary in an efficient police force.

But turning to the 'B' Class, the officer paints a far more chilling picture. Again decrying the lack of 'leaders of the officer class' and good NCOs, he said: 'But the most serious drawback to this class is undoubtedly the fact that they are drawn from the Protestant section of the population and mainly from the more extreme side. Roman Catholics are eligible for Special Constabulary but the local commanders including some County Commandants refuse to enlist any that apply.' Pointing to the fact that 'at the present time . . . antagonisms, racial, religious, and political, are at fever heat everywhere . . . and with arms in their personal possession, under altogether inadequate control,' he adds:

> [. . .] deplorable results inevitably follow [. . .] and from that ensues equally inevitable reprisals and counter-reprisals. Now when a police-man or soldier in Southern Ireland was shot it was to some extent an impersonal business – reprisals might and did occur by outraged comrades and counter reprisals followed. But in the case of B Specials it is otherwise. A B patrol is bombed, several local men are killed or injured by local men of the other side and at once you have established a group of personal blood feuds which will last for generations to come.

The writer said it was useless to expect impartiality from such a force. He recorded that, in many areas, moderate-thinking Loyalists who declined to serve in the B Specials had been 'coerced by the more ardent spirits'.

> Criminal acts by B specials have been and are 'cloaked' and evidence is unobtainable. The local authorities are not blameless in the matter, they have not set their face against reprisals and many of them are afraid of their men. It is hard to imagine how these B men will ever be disarmed. The danger of this force cannot be exaggerated.

By illustration of the state of affairs existing in many localities, the report explained how a head constable, in command of sixty to eighty B men in a district, would go to the leading nationalist, whom he had probably known amicably since childhood, and tell him that he would control his own 'hotheads' as far as he could. At the same time he would produce a list, with the nationalist's own name at the top, and tell him that if any B man was touched the list would be 'attended to' with him first.

In another contemporary memorandum, Brigadier-General Ambrose Ricardo, a veteran of the First World War and a former district commandant, expressed his own equally frank views about the quality and behaviour of the Specials:

There can never be any possibility of establishing confidence and security so long as the B Force, the ordinary Protestant countryman and in many cases corner boy, is supplied with arms and clothing by his Government and 'authorized' to get 'on top' as it were, of his RC neighbour. The latter resents it all the time, and even the most respectable and constitutional Nationalist gets more bitter as the record of raids and abuses by the uncontrollable elements pile up and harmless and innocent people suffer.

He goes on to describe how B men known to the authorities to have committed murders remained free.

In the first case the men were arrested and subsequently released, in the second the authorities were afraid to attempt an arrest, and in both cases the reasons given are true, i.e. they 'can get no evidence', because the unfortunate people who witnessed the tragedies were subsequently warned that if they identified the B men they would 'go down' next. North of Ireland Protestants are not saints, they have always been taught to hate RC's and it is against all reason to expect that untrained, undisciplined and almost wholly without supervision, they can be armed, uniformed and entrusted with police duties – human nature cannot rise to that right away.

Events on the ground underlined these informed analyses and the continued inflammability of the situation, not only along the uncertain frontier but throughout the Six Counties and, as always, in the traditional sectarian flashpoints of Belfast. Cross-border tension reached crisis point early in 1922 after a series of events triggered off by the arrest of ten Monaghan footballers in County Tyrone. It was alleged that they were on their way to Londonderry to free prisoners who were under sentence of death there for killing a prison officer and Special Constable William Lyttle with chloroform during an escape attempt from the city prison. The IRA responded promptly on 10 February by crossing the border and kidnapping a reported seventy Unionist hostages from the Fermanagh–Tyrone border area. Some were held under heavy guard at the Ballybay barracks in County Monaghan while others were transferred to Dublin. The *Belfast Newsletter* described the kidnappings as an act of war and called on the British government to fulfil its obligation to protect the lives of its citizens in Northern Ireland.

A day later cross-border relations deteriorated even further after a clash at Clones railway station in the Free State. There were two ways to travel from Belfast to Enniskillen by rail, the quickest being through Clones. Before partition speed was the only criterion but in the tense days of early 1922 it could only be described as foolhardy for a party of eighteen armed Specials to choose the cross-border route. Clones was in fact the last of several stops in the south, and by the time their train reached the station a cadre of armed IRA men had formed up on the platforms and set up machine guns. Their leader, revolver in hand, approached the carriage where the Specials were travelling and when he called on them to surrender was promptly shot dead. After an intensive fire-fight lasting several minutes, a sergeant and three of the Specials lay dead. One escaped the gunfire and the RIC later smuggled him back across the border; the others were taken into custody by the IRA.

The government in Belfast was now at boiling point and in an angry telegram to London called on Churchill, the colonial secretary, to order British troops to take effective action. Churchill took the view that the blame for the heightened tension was attributable to those in Belfast insensitive enough to have despatched the Specials across the border and he accepted Dublin's account that the Specials had fired first. The British government had anyway no desire to confront the new Dublin administration, fearing lest it collapsed, allowing de Valera and his anti-Treaty hardliners to take over with even more serious consequences for north–south relations and possibly the complete fragmentation of uncertain British policy in Ireland. Nevertheless, over succeeding days Craig continued to press for action. He reported alleged information that the IRA was massing considerable forces in Monaghan for a cross-border attack and demanded that the army command in Dublin supply him with a fleet of nearly 250 military vehicles, 150 guns and wireless sets. Churchill was unimpressed by the barrage of telegrams from Belfast and suspected, quite rightly, that the Unionists were thinking of mounting their own expedition across the border to rescue their kidnapped kinsmen. Such an expedition, he warned Belfast, would be illegal. Churchill, acting in concert with Collins, tried to defuse the situation by urging the northern government to release the Monaghan footballers in exchange for the kidnapped Unionists, some of whom had already been freed. Craig protested that the law in Ulster must take its course, which earned him both private and public rebukes from Churchill. 'I do not for one moment compare prisoners who have been taken lawfully and are being proceeded against at law in the courts with persons who have been kidnapped – but I do ask men of goodwill not to take fine points in matters of such character,' he told the House of Commons.

Churchill also chided Craig over the continued outrages in Belfast, which he said were 'worse than anything which has occurred in the south'. In the three days after the Clones incident thirty people had been murdered in the city. His remarks about the serious disturbances in Belfast were soon further underlined by another atrocity, one which would earn enduring infamy. On the night of 24 March five armed men, who have never been conclusively identified, smashed their way into the home of Owen McMahon, a Catholic publican, at 8 Kinnaird Terrace, adjacent to the high, grey stone walls of Belfast prison on the Crumlin Road. His wife and a maid were tied up, then Owen, his six sons and Edward McKinney, a barman who lodged in the house, were taken into the sitting room, lined up against a wall and shot one by one. All died except for the youngest son, John, who survived the massacre by hiding behind the sofa.

The McMahon murders chilled the blood of the Catholic community, and when the young survivor spoke of the killers being men in uniform, it was widely accepted that they were in fact Specials acting in reprisal for an IRA attack in Victoria Street, Belfast, the previous day when two patrolling Specials, William Charmside and Thomas Cunningham, had been shot dead. The British government, more deeply alarmed than ever by the spiralling violence in Belfast and with ever more credible evidence that there was a 'murder gang' operating within the Specials, summoned both Craig and Collins to London. Collins was under severe pressure from the frightened Catholics in the north who refused to engage with the new northern regime and regarded him as their only saviour. Many were convinced that the Unionists planned to drive them out of the north into the new Free State, the process now called 'ethnic cleansing'.

The discussions resulted in the second Craig–Collins pact, agreed in London on 30 March 1922. Churchill's aim was to establish a working relationship between the governments in each part of the island, with a view to restoring at least some semblance of law and order. To succeed, it was necessary to overcome the nationalist minority's passive hostility to the new northern state by drawing them into both recognition of and participation in its processes. So, tackling the areas of greatest immediate distrust, there was a plan for an advisory committee to oversee increased Catholic recruitment to the police; outrages were to be investigated by a committee with members from both religions and IRA activity in the Six Counties was to cease. Following the failure to secure re-employment of the 10,000 displaced Catholic workers, as provided for in the failed

January pact, the British government also allocated £500,000 to fund relief work schemes and to provide for the 23,000 made homeless in the rioting. A senior official reporting back to London from Belfast had noted the high rate of unemployment – one in five – and remarked: 'One has only to see the groups of unemployed men and youths hanging round the street corners to realise what fuel they provide for disorder.'

These potentially far-reaching proposals, had they been fully enacted, would have had a profound and long-term effect not only on north–south relations but on those between Protestants and Catholics in Northern Ireland itself. The Unionists, and Bates in particular, however, drew no distinction between the factions in the south for and against the treaty; as far as they were concerned, both posed a threat to the very existence of Northern Ireland. De Valera's faction was the mailed fist. Collins was equally menacing but, in their view, he wore a velvet glove. In the event, Craig, who was personally more pragmatic, proved when confronted by hardliners like Bates and the hardmen on the streets to be both unwilling and unable to implement the agreement. This became clear within hours when Collins, under the terms of the pact, sought urgent information about yet another sectarian atrocity in Belfast. This time a party of Specials from Brown Square barracks had gone on a violent rampage in Arnon Street after an RIC constable had been shot dead nearby. Two men were killed in their houses, while in a third house a sledgehammer was used to murder the occupant. His seven-year-old son was shot in the head and died a day later. Craig ignored several requests from Collins for more information about the Arnon Street killings, implicitly defying the terms of the newly signed London pact, and refused to constitute a formal investigation of precisely the type envisaged to help bring about an end to the violence. His defiance was entirely consistent with his real attitude at the time and effectively ended the Pact, although some efforts did continue to implement its main provisions.

Despite London's anxieties about their belligerent posture over the border – 'what we have we hold', as Craig had come to express it – and dubious security policy, the Belfast government brazenly continued to press for even greater resources, under its own control, for the defence of Ulster and the suppression of internal strife. There remained an overwhelming belief and fear that it was only a matter of time before there would be a co-ordinated invasion from the Free State and an uprising to bring down the northern government. The frenzy was fed by 'intelligence' reports outlining drilling, forces massing and the like, which never came to pass. Obtaining sufficient money for defence was therefore a constant preoccupation. At a Belfast cabinet meeting on 13 March, Craig said it was 'necessary to see the present crisis through, no matter what the cost. There is no doubt that strong action on securing respect for law and order will prove cheaper in the end.' He was also pressing for what he called 'the concentration camps' in the north 'to be emptied of Free State prisoners so that he could round up rebels and detain them.

The principal architect of the strategy was Sir Henry Wilson, who had now retired from the Army and become an MP. Over a fortnight in March 1922, for a fee of ten guineas a day plus his travel expenses, Wilson had drawn up a blueprint and recommended that his protégé, Major-General Arthur Solly-Flood should be appointed as military adviser to the government. The recommendation was accepted and the general, Irish-born, with a distinguished military record in the Boer and First World Wars, promptly arrived in Belfast. There he quickly established himself and a military staff in offices adjacent to Wickham's at Atlantic Buildings at Waring Street, Belfast, which was shared with such colourful tenants as the agent for the Legion of Frontiersmen and the Ulster Anti-Prohibition Council. He was also supplied with living accommodation at Danesfort House, a grand Victorian residence in the Malone area which the general eventually shared with his CID 'intelligence gatherers'.

Solly-Flood wanted a force of 3,000 RUC men, 2,220 A, 25,000 B and 15,000 C Specials – effectively putting into uniform and arming one in four of the able-bodied Protestant male population. To equip the force he requested 23,000 rifles, 15,000 bayonets, 5,000 revolvers, 1,000 Verey pistols, 10,000 truncheons and a quantity of mortars and Vickers and Lewis machine guns. Other items included signalling equipment, portable searchlights, fourteen motor boats and 150 bicycles. Elements of the force were to be at 'one minute notice' for duty in turbulent areas and there were plans to hand out revolvers to factory owners for use by 'tried' men in an emergency. Solly-Flood himself would preside at the head of this force as Director of Public Security. Before long he had also formulated a 'wanted list' of IRA activists for internment.

With staff costs, accommodation and administrative expenses, uniform clothing and cooking and bedding all included, the bill the British government was being asked to pay totalled £5,306,080. A later official estimate submitted to London put the cost at £6,000,000, or £5 a year per head of the Northern Ireland population. Craig said it was a costly business: 'The British Government in the end will have to recoup us for getting Ulster back into the condition that it ought to have left us in to hand over.' Tallents, who had been sent to Belfast to assess the situation, warned Churchill, chairman of the cabinet's Irish Committee, in June 1922 that the British government could be embarrassed in justifying these large and future payments for schemes devised by Solly-Flood 'on the assumption that [it] will bear the cost, but without consultation with any expert military or police authorities of the British Government'. However, despite concerns about the conduct of the new government, London, sensitive to the accusation that the Six Counties was being left defenceless, authorised interim funding and ordered some of the arms and equipment to be shipped on 'loan' to Belfast, on condition it would be returned when the situation eased. The question of the money for longer-term expansion remained pending.

In the meantime, mainly on account of pressure from London and the need to placate their intended paymasters, Craig and Bates grudgingly engaged in what were largely empty rituals to get the peace-building committees working as envisaged in the pact. There was, in fact, more obstruction than enthusiasm, generosity or energy on the part of them and their officials. They accused the southern authorities of impeding the transfer of experienced civil servants to the north and refusing to hand over records. On 29 June, Spender listed the grievances in a letter to Tallents and ended: 'Undoubtedly our main cause of complaint is that the activities of the IRA in Northern Ireland have been maintained and that the number of outrages directly attributable to the IRA are very numerous.' The most senior civil servant at the Ministry of Home Affairs was similarly critical: 'By appointing extremists on these committees, the southern Government have displayed little anxiety to help the authorities here.'

These sentiments were well out of line with Clause 1 of the second Craig–Collins pact on 30 March 1922, which had optimistically stated: 'Peace is today declared', and Clause 2, which went on to say: 'From today the two governments undertake to co-operate in every way in their power with a view to the restoration of peaceful conditions in the unsettled areas.' Reflecting the importance of policing in calming the situation, the next clause outlined specific measures to tackle the problem. According to the deal, the police in Belfast were to be organised so that Special patrols in mixed districts and those carrying out house searches would be composed 'half of Catholics and half of Protestants'. It was agreed that an advisory committee, composed of Catholics, was to be set up to assist in the selection of Catholic recruits to make the overwhelmingly Protestant police more representative of the entire community. In a bid to curb the excesses of the time, it was agreed that all police on duty, except the usual secret service, would be in uniform and officially numbered and all arms and ammunition issued to police were to be deposited in barracks, in charge of the military, with an official record to be kept of everything issued and used when an officer was on duty.

In a pre-emptive strike to deflect any criticism from London, Craig sent a telegram to Collins on 3 April, the day before the RIC's disbandment parade, expressing 'anxiety to proceed at once in giving effect to the agreement' and remarking that the 'first essential is the appointment of your Catholic Police Committee'. He asked Collins to co-operate with the northern government and appoint representatives on the committee without delay. In a detailed letter next day dealing with other aspects of the agreement, Craig told Collins that he had already contacted Dr Joseph MacRory, the Bishop of Down and Connor (the diocese in which Belfast was situated) about the establishment of the committee, and that the police authorities had been notified of the steps required to give full effect to it. However, in the immediate aftermath of the Arnon Street killings, Collins took the view, in a telegram to Craig the same day, that setting up the committee to investigate outrages, provided for by Clause 5 of the agreement, was more urgent.

This proposition was discussed at length on the late afternoon of 5 April in Dublin when Collins, Arthur Griffith, President of the Dublin Parliament, and William T. Cosgrave, the minister for local government, met a deputation representing Catholics from Belfast headed by the bishop. He was accompanied by Father Bernard Laverty, the Administrator of St Patrick's in Donegall Street, a man of highly peaceful instincts who believed that 'the Specials were the source of all the troubles in Belfast' on the basis of information he was given by Catholic police officers and later provided in affidavit form for Collins. The other delegates were Fr John Hassan, who was closely monitoring events for his later published account of the Catholic ordeal in Belfast, Dr Russell McNabb, a pro-treaty Belfast Sinn Feiner who had attended the London Pact talks at Collins's request, Frank Crummey, the intelligence officer for the IRA's 3rd Northern Division, and one S McArdle, an engineer who had been expelled from his workplace during earlier sectarian clashes. During what was later minuted as 'considerable discussion' the deputation heard that the IRA and Sinn Fein supporters were very much against the Oath of Allegiance proposed for the new northern police force. At the end of the meeting it was decided that the Police Advisory

Committee should be set up at once and nominees, including those present, were agreed. It was also confirmed that there should be a joint inquiry into the murders and nominations to take part in that were also made. Fr Laverty expressed concern about the safety of his police informants and promised to convey the names to Collins so that they could be brought to Dublin for their own safety.

On 11 April, by letter to Craig, Collins stated that he hoped to be in a position to supply the names of his representatives on the Police Committee 'within the next day or two', but he failed to do so. This was surprising in the light of the Dublin meeting and indicated that background pressures were already at work. In letters of 12 and 25 April, Craig reminded Collins that he had not yet received the missing nominations. In response to the second letter, Collins telegraphed Craig nominating twelve persons to constitute the Police Committee and expressed regret that owing to an 'oversight' on his part the names had not been sent earlier. In the meantime, with Craig and Bates refusing to co-operate in throwing any light on the atrocity in Belfast, which was highly embarrassing for them, a major dispute had arisen about the remit and powers of the other joint Protestant–Catholic committee to 'hear and investigate complaints as to intimidation, outrages etc'. On 7 April, the Belfast cabinet had immediately taken the posture that what its official papers referred to as the 'Roman Catholic Committee' had no administrative power, no power to summon witnesses, nor to call for official reports – it was 'to act merely as an Advisory Committee to the Ministry of Home Affairs and to exercise powers of moral suasion over the inhabitants'. Bates wrote to them on 20 April: 'I feel certain that the Committee . . . will be able by its powers of suasion to do much to foster a true spirit of conciliation between all classes of the community.' Although he later granted working expenses of a paltry £100 a month ('all payments of course to be vouched for'), it was barely half the £2,500 a year they had requested and effectively hobbled them in setting about their task with any vigour. Such hostility was also a significant factor in preventing the Police Selection Committee from achieving anything of value. When Collins finally learned of Belfast's opposition to a formal investigation of the Arnon Street incident, he wrote, on 27 April, to Craig: 'Let me state here that I cannot take any part in assisting you in the formation of a Police Force for your area until I am clearly convinced that the lives of its members will be safe and that it will be able to do something to restore law and order in Belfast.'

Despite the antagonistic sentiments affecting both sides, Bates wrote to the bishop on 2 May (merely because his was the first name on the list, he said) to find out when and where it would be convenient to hold a meeting of the Police Selection Committee, so that he might arrange for a representative of the police to attend 'in order to confer with the Committee and to supply such information as may be required'. The bishop replied on 4 May, saying that on account of his many duties it would not be possible for him to lend much practical assistance to the committee, but that Father Laverty would make the necessary arrangements for a meeting. Bates corresponded with Laverty and received a speedy reply suggesting a meeting on 9 May and specifying St Mary's Hall, in the centre of the city, as the most suitable place.

There now developed disputes about whether the committee was a voluntary or a government one, who should summon the members, and the availability of the hall, which had shortly before been raided by Specials who seized arms and documents, closed down the IRA liaison office that had been operating there since the truce in July 1921 and commandeered the premises from their Catholic trustees for use as a base. A slight postponement of the meeting was then proposed, since General Solly-Flood was away from Belfast and could not attend. In the end they convened the first meeting in the ministry offices at Scottish Provident Buildings, adjacent to the City Hall in Belfast, on Tuesday 16 May. Apart from Solly-Flood, the government side was represented by Wickham, then designate inspector-general of the incoming Royal Ulster Constabulary, JF Gelston, Police Commissioner for Belfast, Colonel Goodwin and Samuel Watt, the permanent secretary at the Ministry of Home Affairs.

McArdle, one of the Catholic nominees, withdrew before the meeting and only seven of the original twelve attended: Fr Laverty, Fr Murray, the Administrator of St Mary's, Chapel Lane, another central Belfast church, Alderman Frank Harkin, an ex-soldier who supported Joe Devlin, Dr Russell McNabb, H McAleenan, a bookmaker, Charles Magee, an accountant, and Frank Crummey, with his IRA connections something of a *bête noire* for the other side. Some months earlier the police had wanted him transferred from his teaching post at Conway Street school, in a Unionist area. A short time later, in November 1921, the school was closed after an arson attack and he was currently unemployed. As his son was also implicated in IRA activities and had been apprehended in east Belfast with papers containing details about the movements of County Inspector Harrison, Solly-Flood and Wickham were deeply suspicious of him.

The three-hour meeting began with a statement by Solly-Flood explaining that they had a common object, namely the restoration of order in the city. He intended to mete out justice impartially and he welcomed the committee's appointment as evidence of a desire on the part of the Catholic population to assist. The immediate aim was to find suitable Catholics for enrolment in the Special Constabulary and he asked for names to be submitted in the usual manner. The Catholics asked for details of service but immediate deadlock resulted once Watt and Wickham pointed to the long-established rule which prohibited constables from serving in their native districts. The Catholics pointed out that since the committee was appointed for Belfast only it could not nominate Catholics from outside districts. Wickham suggested that the difficulty might be met by mobilising Catholic B Specials, when recruited, and using them in the Catholic areas, in conjunction with the regular constabulary. The meeting was then adjourned for both sides to consider their position.

What the committee was proposing was, of course, diametrically opposed to what Craig and Bates intended. They did not want any Catholics in the constabulary if they could help it and the prospect of forming Catholic sections for Catholic localities would have been equally unacceptable. Such a force once armed, they feared, would simply have gone over to the IRA. Faced with this situation, Solly-Flood sought to sidestep the issue. After some members of the committee had left and the room door was standing open, Solly-Flood informed those remaining that their functions were purely advisory and confined to the recommendation of suitable Catholic candidates for the constabulary. He indicated that the more names submitted, the better he would be pleased and emphasised the fact that the committee was not a government body and therefore could have no voice in the organisation of the Constabulary, whether Regular or Special.

What the minutes of this meeting do not reveal is the scope of the debate then taking place within Belfast's embattled Catholic community about the implications of partition, the treatment of Catholics under the new regime and their attitude to the police, a particular issue that would periodically flare up and never be fully resolved for the next eighty years. Sinn Fein elements opposed to the Treaty continued to attack the police, a tactic that provoked the violent reprisals which so terrified and imperilled the entire community. More pragmatic elements, including Bishop MacRory, favoured the Catholics taking up the quota of places already reserved for them in the RUC and joining the B Specials in strength, as was now being explored, even though both acts amounted to recognition of the northern government. However, there were voluble elements, not all anti-Treaty voices, who so despised the Specials for their unpunished crimes and unchecked conduct that they could not support such a move. As always there was the shadow of the gunman: it was abundantly clear that the extremists would regard any Catholics joining the Constabulary as traitors and thus, in a phrase that would echo down the years, legitimate targets.

With the RIC now limping towards disbandment throughout Ireland, continued hostility to them had been graphically underlined again in a parallel wave of IRA violence in Northern Ireland, inspired and approved by Collins, whose real aim was to rattle the Craig government. On the night of 2/3 May, in County Londonderry, a number of mills and other buildings owned by Loyalists were burned down, and in an attack on police at Bellaghy and Ballyronan a sergeant and three constables were killed. Within a short time, seven Catholics in the same area were murdered in retaliation. The intensity of the attacks built up throughout the month and even Wickham himself was warned to 'go carefully' after 'information' was received 'that your murder has been decided on'. At the end of May, a weekend of arson and violence culminated on the Monday morning with the first political assassination of the troubles when IRA gunmen murdered William J Twaddell, a member of the northern parliament, who was shot in the centre of Belfast on his way to open up his drapery shop at Lower North Street.

Hours after the assassination, the Unionists finally chose repression rather than conciliation with the northern minority and accommodation with the south. The main instrument of repression was the truly draconian Civil Authorities (Special Powers) Bill, fashioned within the Ministry of Home Affairs and passed by the Belfast parliament a month earlier. Under its provisions, the minister could arrest without warrant and intern without trial. Prisoners could be flogged or executed. Coroners' inquests could be dispensed with. Land and property could be commandeered for security purposes. Organisations, meetings, publications and gatherings could be prohibited by ministerial order. If any unforeseen crisis developed, the minister was empowered 'to take all such steps and issue all such orders as might be necessary to preserve the peace'.

After the crisis cabinet meeting, Bates issued the first order under the Act outlawing the IRA and four other Republican organisations and decreeing that membership of them, promotion of their aims or possession of documents relating to them would be an offence. That night detachments of Specials, backed up by the military, began a series of swoops throughout the Six Counties. By dawn they had made 300 arrests. 'We are officially informed that the numerous arrests effected early this morning are . . . the culmination of plans that have been in preparation for several weeks past to cope with the insidious machinations of the IRA,' reported the *Belfast Telegraph*. Within a short time the number in custody had topped 400 and many were detained without trial. In due course they were held on the prison ship *Argenta*, moored first in Belfast Lough, later off Larne Harbour.

It was against the background of these fraught events that the Police Selection Committee gathered for its second meeting on 31 May. This time Solly-Flood, Wickham, Gelston and Watt, who was in the chair, were joined by Catholic delegates: Laverty, McAleenan, Crummie and Daniel Dempsey, a Post Office worker with Sinn Fein sympathies who had not been at the first meeting. Four of the original attenders were absent. Solly-Flood got the proceedings off to a brusque and uncompromising start by stating that after consideration he could not 'in any shape or form' accept the proposal that one third of all the constabulary in Belfast should be Catholics, nor could he disclose the present numbers of the constabulary, a point consistently pressed by Crummey, who again, to the general's clear discomfort, prodded him repeatedly for information about police tactics and methods. On the other hand, albeit with impatience, Solly-Flood repeated his offer to have Catholic B Specials mobilised full-time to maintaining law and order in Catholic areas. ' I would take as many of these men as I possibly could,' he said. 'Now that is how the matter stands and that is the only basis of discussion that I can permit this afternoon. I have very little time to give to any more of the discussion that took place last time.' The sticking point about Specials serving in their own areas remained, with Watt, Solly-Flood and Wickham refusing to budge from what they said was long-established RIC practice. Referring with apparent horror to the prospect of men resident in Belfast doing police duty on the streets of the city, Watt asked: 'You think that that would be a proper thing?' 'It may not be proper, but very improper things are going on at the present time,' replied McAleenan.

In the unstructured discussion that followed the members of the committee were asked if they could use their influence to attract Catholics from beyond Belfast to enlist for service in the city. 'In view of the reputation which the Specials enjoy amongst the Catholics, I do not think that you would get them,' said Fr Laverty. He favoured sending out mixed patrols of ten Catholic and ten Protestant Specials. 'I think the Catholics would not fire on them because they would be afraid of shooting their own and it would be the same thing with the Protestants. It would be safer to have them mixed. Besides it would help to break down bigotry,' said the priest.

Despite the cordial tone of the discussions it was apparent neither side really wanted to move. The government was deeply opposed to what it clearly feared would be a 'fifth column' coming into the constabulary and causing unthinkable complications to its defence strategy. The Catholics were feeling the heat from their own community and were unwilling to move, not least because Watt, Solly-Flood and Wickham were so unyielding, using an old RIC practice as a fig-leaf for the uncompromising political position they had been required to adopt.

The meeting ended on a sinister note. During the discussion, Crummey complained that the previous Saturday he had been fired at six times from a stationary Lancia police tender. 'It is a miracle that I am present here today,' he said. Before it ended, Crummey again intervened to report that on a recent night during curfew, Dr McNabb, who had been at the first meeting but was absent that day, had fled his house after five men made an attempt to break in through the rear. Fr Laverty, who lived nearby, confirmed that he had heard knocking and got up from his bed. 'I saw a number of men. I could not tell what they looked like. I was afraid he was going to be murdered, right enough.' Two nights later, according to Crummey, a party of Specials 'attended his house again and we understand it was official this time. It is very hard to know when a man is coming to murder you and when he is coming to arrest you. That is the difficulty.' Watt said he knew 'nothing at all about the thing' and the committee then adjourned for a week.

About the same time as the meeting ended and some half a mile away, several shots rang out in the Millfield area of Belfast at the foot of the Falls Road. Two Special Constables who had been on patrol there fell to the ground wounded and were shot again by their attackers who escaped using the evening home-going crowds for cover. One of the constables, Andrew Roulston, died later from his injuries. In his record of the city's violence, Fr Hassan describes what happened next as 'probably the most hideous date in the two years of horrors in Belfast'. Large numbers of the Special Constabulary immediately rushed into the district and began firing machine guns and rifles indiscriminately from armoured vehicles and Lancia cage-cars. The first casualty was a horse pulling a van. As it fell dead, riddled with bullets, many people crouched behind it for cover as the bursts of firing continued. With the streets now deserted, much of the gunfire was aimed through the windows and doorways of nearby houses. After a lull, the firing intensified again later in the evening about eight or nine o'clock, and soon afterwards some Specials broke open the doors of McEntee's public house in King Street and looted the large stock of drink. Later still, some of the men, by now in a pretty drunken state, drew up in front of St Mary's Presbytery, also in King Street, where three priests, including Fr Murray from the Police Selection Committee, and their domestic servants lived. Volleys of shots were fired into the residence, smashing all the windows and puncturing holes in the inner walls and ceilings. The disorder had spread like an uncontrolled bush fire through several other parts of the city and, over the succeeding twenty-four hours, at least eight Catholics and two Protestants perished in the violence and well over eighty Catholic families were driven from their homes. In some cases streets were burned from end to end. In one burned house firemen found a man and woman who had been shot before the building was set alight.

At midnight on 31 May, in the midst of this turmoil, the RIC ceased to exist in the north. Its 3,000-strong rearguard remaining in Northern Ireland had tried to maintain a low profile. With generous compensation and pensions awaiting them, the men were loath to run avoidable risks. In the run-up to the changeover, the IRA however had stepped up action against the police and murdered twenty-three Specials and ten RIC men between the decision to disband in January and the end of May, when what remained of the force was finally stood down. The last RIC officer to die in service was twenty-three-year-old Constable Henry O'Brien, who was shot dead outside Cullingtree Road Barracks in Belfast on 29 May. Given this violent backdrop, it was not surprising that there was no pomp or ceremony when the Royal Ulster Constabulary came into being on 1 June 1922. 'You were one day an RIC man and the next day you were an RUC man. You carried on just the same as if nothing had happened,' said Constable William Britton, then serving in Killyleagh, County Down, one of the 986 RIC officers who transferred directly into the new force.

For those, like Britton, who were already stationed in Northern Ireland the transition was a seamless one, but for many others joining the RUC was a far more trying experience. Among many of the discharged RIC men who made their way north by train from Dublin to join the RUC was John Regan, who reached the rank of county inspector. When the train started he left his coat and hat with his baggage in the first class compartment and, wearing a cap and old waterproof coat, got into the third class as far away from it as possible in case the IRA checked the passengers leaving the Free State. Several ex-RIC men made the journey by sea from Dublin to Glasgow and back to Belfast to avoid having to cross the border, and at least one man walked along the railway line from Monaghan to Armagh to sign on. Other discharged RIC men, like Hugh McIvor, who had returned to the relative safety of their homes in the north after being discharged, also re-enlisted.

> I was standing in Cullybackey one day talking to another man and I saw two policemen riding through on bicycles. I recognised one of them and I shouted at him but he wouldn't turn round and I shouted again and then he came back. 'Oh!' he said, 'I thought they'd followed me and I was afraid to look round.' He'd transferred over from the RIC to the RUC you see. They advised me to rejoin, which I did, and I was posted to Annalong at once because I was already trained.

The violent events of the week in which the RUC was born dictated that the circumstances for making progress on Catholic participation in policing were thus even more unpromising when the third meeting of the Police Selection Committee was held on 7 June. The further diminished attendance, with only the two priests and one other Catholic delegate, David McCluskey, a publican, turning up to see Watt, Solly-Flood and Wickham, reflected the new low. This time it was an angry Fr Murray, rather than Solly-Flood, who set the uncompromising tone. At the outset of the meeting he stated that he intended to take no further part in the Committee's deliberations. Two of its members, Dempsey and Crummey, the man who was too inquisitive about the constabulary for Solly-Flood's liking, had been arrested. Two others were sought by police arrest parties but had evaded capture and were accordingly prevented from attending. He went on to describe what he said was the deliberate attempt to assassinate himself and his colleagues after the Millfield shooting. Specials, of whom 'some were in such a state that they should not have had rifles in their hands', fired into McEntee's public house for fifteen minutes and then turned their fire on the nearby Presbytery. Eyewitnesses told him the Specials had said, 'We'll give them a jerk,' before opening fire with about twenty-six shots actually hitting the residence. 'You would be far better without police than with the class you have,' remarked Fr Laverty.

The rest of the meeting consisted of recriminations. The Catholics recounted details of other outrages in recent days and complained about the unwillingness of the police and soldiers to protect them from the rioting mobs, often when in sight of the violence. Solly-Flood and the government side bemoaned the lack of witnesses afraid to give evidence and the continued unwillingness of the Catholics to put forward nominations for the B constabulary to serve in their own areas. The meeting ended in agreement – that nothing could be done – and the committee never met again.

The failure of the committee was to have lasting consequences for policing in Ulster and there would not be any official effort to involve Catholics in the process for almost another fifty years. It fizzled out because the Catholic representatives not only irrevocably distrusted the northern government but also succumbed to intimidation from their own extremists. The Belfast government had anyway no real desire to make the scheme work. They were unyielding during the negotiations and, in an official account afterwards, the ministry seriously misrepresented what had taken place. 'The object of the Roman Catholic Committee's representatives was apparent: to break down the whole machinery of the RUC as at present existing; to find out the strength at the disposal of the Northern Government; by their continued demand for the abolition of Specials and the institution of martial law to prove to the world that the Northern Government could not govern.' The account concluded: 'At present the tendency for Roman Catholics to leave the RUC is most pronounced and it is highly probable that in a short space of time there will not be one single Roman Catholic Constable throughout the force.' (This was a ludicrous misrepresentation for, as we shall see, and as the ministry well knew from its own figures, there were many Catholics among the officers who had transferred from the RIC to the RUC.)

If both sides had persevered with more vision, generosity and courage, a formula might well have emerged which, through this Catholic bridgehead in the constabulary, in time would have created minority confidence in them and further encouraged Catholics to participate in policing. Despite the machinations of Bates to exclude Catholics from the RUC, Fr Laverty, for one, had urged a group of fifty ex-RIC Catholics to stay in post. Over the years such plurality could well have taken the politics out of policing and, through accountability to both communities, when crises developed, might have prevented the consolidation of the rift with Catholics seeing the RUC as the armed wing of the Unionist Party: 'ours' in the eyes of the Protestants, 'theirs' to the Catholics.

As it was, in June 1922, with the Belfast government now well embarked on its crackdown – which included the introduction of flogging – and the divided IRA now preoccupied by the civil war in the south, Craig successfully pressured Churchill into sending British troops, backed up by artillery, into action to repel IRA units who had earlier occupied part of Fermanagh near Belleek and Pettigo. In London on 22 June two IRA gunmen, reputedly acting on Collins's orders, assassinated Sir Henry Wilson outside his home at 36 Eaton Place in Belgravia, while in Northern Ireland the sickening series of tit-for-tat massacres, some of them carried out by Specials, continued, and an incident at Cushendall, County Antrim, the next day brought to a head the rising concern in London about events in Northern Ireland and the behaviour of the Specials.

According to the initial police report, a combined military and police patrol was ambushed and three local men, identified as IRA members, were killed after a police vehicle came under fire. 'All arms and identities were removed from the killed and wounded by women.' However, the Nationalist MP Joseph Devlin challenged this account of events in a letter to Winston Churchill soon afterwards and asserted that 'wilful murder' had taken place. Devlin claimed that John Hill and John Gore (an ex-soldier and former internee) had taken cover in a shop in the village when shooting began. Gore surrendered and was shot dead. His brother Patrick was allegedly only saved from death by the intervention of an angry local Special. By Devlin's account, James McAllister was shot three miles from the reported ambush, after being stopped while riding his bicycle. While he was being assaulted by Specials, a soldier said, 'If you have any humanity, and you want to kill him, shoot him at once'. A Special then placed a revolver in McAllister's mouth, and fired. Devlin noted that the inquest had been held in nearby Ballycastle, not Cushendall, and remarked that 'no evidence was admitted except as to the cause of death'. The MP rounded on the government of Sir James Craig in his scathing conclusion: 'The state of terrorism which exists in the Cushendall district, consequent upon the murder, constitutes the gravest possible indictment of the system of tyranny, outrage, and intimidation which is in operation under and with the connivance of the Northern Government.'

Not least because British troops were involved, Churchill decided that the government must act to demonstrate its impartiality towards the two Irish states and could not ignore the incident. Craig replied on 20 July saying that while he had no objection to an inquiry, 'judicial or otherwise', Solly-Flood was quite satisfied that a cleverly arranged ambush had been prepared in Cushendall 'and that in defeating it the

Specials and Military had acted with propriety and discretion'. He felt it unfair that the British government should heed allegations of murderous acts by the Constabulary whilst ignoring the bravery and discipline generally shown by the force. Churchill ignored Craig and appointed FT Barrington-Ward, the Recorder of Hythe in Kent, to conduct an investigation. It was held in private, and in his report to the British government on 9 September 1922 Barrington-Ward rejected the evidence of Specials and British soldiers that they had fired and killed in self-defence:

> No one except the police and military even fired at all [. . .] I am unable to accept the evidence of the Special Constabulary from Ballymena. I am satisfied that they did not tell me all they knew about the circumstances in which three men died, and in view of the reports made by the military officers at the time and the evidence given by them before me, I do not believe that none of the police entered any of the houses.

Churchill, accepting Barrington-Ward's verdict on the killings, sent Craig a copy of the report on 12 October 1922, urging action against the Specials involved. The northern government appointed JR Moorhead, the Chief Crown Solicitor, to re-interview the witnesses, after which their own report rejected Barrington-Ward's conclusions and vindicated the actions of the Specials. Moorhead's comment on the course of his investigation is indicative of the atmosphere of the time: 'I find on the part of many of the civilian witnesses a sentiment distinctly hostile to the Special Constabulary, and I would think it probable that the Special Constabulary might entertain a similar sentiment in the opposite direction.'Certainly Richard Best, Attorney-General of Northern Ireland, left no doubt about his thoughts on the affair, rejecting Barrington-Ward's findings on the grounds that they are 'largely based on the conclusion that no one except the police and military even fired at all on the occasion in question, and his report throughout hinges on that conclusion'. He went on to say: 'To anyone with experience of Irish witnesses there is nothing extraordinary in the number of civilians from a place like Cushendall, dominated up to recently by the IRA, coming forward to testify falsely against the Crown forces . . . any statements made by the people of Cushendall should be received with the greatest caution.' The British government acceded to Craig's request not to publish Barrington-Ward's report lest it embitter local feeling, now that normal conditions had been restored. The Cushendall killings further compromised any possibility that Catholics would trust either the police or the justice system.

The IRA was now more preoccupied with events in the south, where the divisions between them over partition had evolved into civil war, causing many of the northern 'Shinners', as one police report described them, to flee over the border to join one side or the other. The death of Collins in an ambush in County Cork in August removed the major thorn in Craig's side over his conduct of affairs in the north. The anti-treaty leaders, now far too preoccupied with the ongoing conflict, put their inclinations for the reclamation of the Six Counties on hold. The uneasy peace on the border itself was illustrated in September after a Specials patrol from Londonderry challenged and apprehended six men, armed with rifles, who were standing by a Crossley tender which had strayed some 400 yards inside Northern Ireland territory. The men were returned after a judge ruled that their detention was punishment enough for the incursion and the vehicle was allowed to be collected from the barracks in Londonderry after negotiation, by coded telegrams through the Colonial Office in London, to ensure that it would be going back into the hands of the Provisional government and not the anti-treaty forces.

By now Solly-Flood was becoming increasingly frustrated that his advice and schemes seemed to be falling on deaf ears. In August, the Cabinet rejected his latest grandiose plans for a four-tiered, 30,000-strong constabulary with an intelligence-gathering responsibility and himself at the helm. As a result, in petulant letters to Craig and Bates, he disavowed all responsibility for command of the constabulary and delegated the maintenance of law and order to Wickham. He wanted to revert, he stated, to his original terms of appointment as military adviser to the prime minister. Craig was not unhappy about this and sent him a placatory 'unofficial' letter to his residence in Abergavenny, Monmouthshire, saying that 'as Wickham has to carry on it might be as well to let him feel the full weight early as late, and you, as our military adviser, can give him the advantage of your ripe experience and technical knowledge'. In a simultaneous letter to Lord Londonderry, Craig wrote that the General failed to understand the British government 'would repel any invasion from the south – if it ever should come to that' and that Ulster could not stand the taxation that would be necessary to pay for his 'quasi-military, Territorial Special Constabulary'. Solly-Flood, however, was not to be placated. On receipt of Craig's letter, he dashed off a handwritten reply saying that 'the rift within the lute is firstly Dawson

Bates's inability to keep in view the ultimate situation and secondly Wickham's complacency. I have found the latter throughout far too pleased with himself, his ideas and his methods.' In a scaremongering letter to Craig, dated 5 September 1922, after his return to Belfast from holiday, he gave further vent to his feelings:

> Unrest amongst the loyalists is again becoming pronounced. This is due to their having heard of the impending [constabulary] reductions in the immediate future. Should outrages occur during the coming winter, loyalists will assuredly take the law into their own hands because they are under the impression that the Government are not protecting them. Should this occur I am afraid those who have hitherto acted as leaders will be powerless and the situation will be beyond rectification by the Government. Sinn Feiners are returning in numbers from the South, including a considerable proportion of gunmen. It is immaterial from the point of view of the Northern Government whether these profess to be Free Staters or Irregulars, for the rank and file of the IRA change their coat to suit the occasion, while the leaders, on their own showing, have before now combined in a plan for united action against Ulster, and will do so again in the future. It is most irksome to be continually crying 'Wolf', but, as I have already informed you, I view the future with grave concern.

By this time there was a groundswell of opposition to Solly-Flood among even the most uncompromising Unionist leaders and the party rank and file, many of whom were also active in the constabulary. They were becoming increasingly irritated by his empire-building activities and found him a threat to their own authority. Over the summer, Spender and others had warned the prime minister of this feeling and Lord Derby, the British Secretary of State for War, had advised Craig that if he intended to keep Wickham, he should retain the general solely as a military adviser and pay off his staff, whose duties very largely duplicated those of Wickham's. In fact Craig had first moved to clip Solly-Flood's wings that July, when he ordered a halt to searches of Catholic monasteries, churches, chapels and convents because 'they would turn public opinion against the government'. In another bow to religious sensitivity, this time Protestant, following a complaint from a clergyman, Craig directed that musketry training by the constabulary should not take place on Sundays and, when inclement weather rendered this necessary, that the hours of divine service should be avoided.

Over the summer the general's growing unpopularity was compounded by an embarrassing 'blunder which has impaired the confidence of the Northern Government in the Intelligence Department under his control', in the words of a senior Home Affairs official. The episode originated with the appointment of AP Stapleton as a clerk in the Registry at the Military Advisers' Office in July 1922. On Saturday 19 August he left the office, having applied for leave for two days on the Monday and Tuesday. During his absence it was noted that fourteen sensitive files were missing. They contained details of security measures at Belfast and Larne prisons, defence plans for some security installations, notes about individuals requiring special military protection and a plan to put a wireless transmitter in the spire of St Malachy's Chapel in Belfast. Immediate enquiries established that the unmarried man had disappeared from his lodgings at Botanic Avenue and that his parents, who resided in the Springfield Road area, had no knowledge of his whereabouts. It soon transpired that one of Solly-Flood's staff, Colonel Dyson, the officer in charge of personnel, had shortly before been alerted to the fact that Stapleton was a Roman Catholic and, as such, in those paranoid circles, a potential threat to security. However, he decided to take no further action because since November 1920 the former lieutenant in the Royal Irish Rifles had worked as a civilian clerk for the Army at Victoria Barracks in Belfast, where he had 'given entire satisfaction' and was duly recommended for the move to Atlantic Buildings.

Solly-Flood's credibility was further damaged by another blunder in his department soon afterwards. On 29 September, acting on information that 'armed men would attend and guard' a concert and dance to be held at St Columba's School, in the Ballyhackamore district of Belfast, one of Solly-Flood's intelligence officers authorised a raid: 'Search all persons present and arrest any on whom anything seditious is found. Women searchers should accompany the party.' In the event, without consulting the local police, the Specials swooped on the wrong premises and nothing of an incriminating nature was found. Spender learned of the débâcle and asked, on behalf of the prime minister, for a report. District Inspector Spears, the police commander in east Belfast, said: 'The people frequenting this hall are Catholics of a harmless and respectable type and the local police could have told the raiding party that nothing irregular was likely to be found there.' A subsequent minute from the Ministry of Home Affairs to Spender laid the ultimate blame for the error on Solly-Flood, who had already aroused enmities within the ministry and was rapidly running out of goodwill with the police command and the government itself. 'The fact that the CID did not apparently know the name of the premises which they proposed to raid is a striking commentary on their methods,' it said.

Throughout the autumn, the general continued to inundate Craig and others with increasingly bombastic letters and demands. He said that Wickham might make a good RUC inspector-general in normal times but that 'he is not capable of organising in peace any more than he is capable of commanding in war, all the Constabulary forces which are necessary for preserving the integrity of Ulster'. He waded in to complain when he found the Army in Northern Ireland was obtaining supplies of biscuits from Dublin and oats from Buncrana at a time when goods from the north were being boycotted in the Free State. (The Army took no notice.) On another occasion he suggested that 'malefactors' might be more effectively apprehended by patrols equipped with running shorts and rubber-soled shoes. 'The secret of success in these patrols is silence and celerity,' he wrote. In another unsuccessful bid, he demanded that his men be put in control of the *Argenta* prison ship, a proposition passed to Craig from Spender with this caustic comment: 'I think that in view of the fact that one of his own staff proved to be a spy, it is a little rash of him to suggest that the CID is competent to take over the staffing of the ship.'

In October, with his advice now routinely being ignored or dismissed, Solly-Flood told the cabinet he could not accept their model for the immediate future of the constabularies because it still 'leaves important points such as homogeneity, allaying jealousies and dual control rampant as heretofore'. In a minute he suggested his position had now become 'invidious and redundant'. Macready, the Army's commander in chief, came to the support of Solly-Flood and his ideas and, in a memorandum to the Belfast cabinet, vouched his concern that Wickham was only just able to hold his own as inspector-general. At its meeting on 4 October, the cabinet decided to clarify its 'defence' policy and Solly-Flood's position. His latest 'scheme' was not being implemented 'owing to political considerations', and henceforth 'he is to advise the Prime Minister and the Cabinet – and them only – regarding the general defence of the Six Counties against outside aggression . . . in the event of an attack upon the Border or a 'rising' within the Six Counties, the Military Adviser will be asked to assume supreme command of such forces under the jurisdiction of the Government of Northern Ireland as are required for Military operations.'

The general was stripped of his responsibility to gather intelligence. His CID in future was to come under the authority of the minister of home affairs and his bid to control the constabulary was also rejected. The cabinet 'thought it was better that the whole of the Constabulary forces should be under one command – that of the Inspector-General'. Undeterred, Solly-Flood opened unilateral negotiations with the War Office with the object of handing the reserve C1 constabulary over as a territorial Army unit. Bates found out about his plotting and sent a coded telegram alerting Craig, who was in London, on 23 November: 'Military Adviser has approached officers of C1 but latter loyal to us.' Through his officers, Solly-Flood had actually tried to get the eight colonel commanders of the C1 to sign a document saying they were a military formation, which would have paved the way for the London government to take them over. The loss of such a potentially large force, whose mobilisation was a key element in the northern government's defence plan, was unthinkable, and Craig and Bates reacted furiously to the 'entirely unauthorised' initiative 'which is against Cabinet authority and calculated to cause unsettlement throughout the Constabulary Forces'.

Over the summer of 1922 the net effect of these events had been to restore a fragile sort of peace to the troubled north, but the violence became progressively more sporadic in the latter half of the year. After the violence of May and June, the Lord Mayor of Belfast, reflecting the widespread shock in the city at the continued destruction and death, called for a ten-day truce which then extended indefinitely. By September, the city commissioner reported there had been 'no organised outrages on a large scale with which the city was unfortunately familiar up to a few months ago. I am of the opinion that the winter is more hopeful than it seemed a couple of months ago.' It was the same picture elsewhere. H Connor, the Commissioner for Londonderry, reported to Belfast on 26 September that 'during the month the City and County has been more peaceful than at any time during the past two months'. From Lisburn, the County Inspector for Antrim reported that 'the county is in a very peaceable state and shows a marked contrast to the position at the beginning of the summer'. From Down his counterpart declared 'a gratifying improvement in the state of the County', and from Omagh, District Inspector John Gorman reported 'a marked improvement within the past three or four months' in Tyrone and expected 'there should be no serious outrage on a large scale'. The only cautious note came from EV Gerity, the County Inspector for Fermanagh:

Beyond doubt, the conditions in County Fermanagh are largely influenced by the course of events in the Free State, owing to the very extended border line. It is, therefore, unsafe to predict what might happen. I do not expect serious trouble here unless the Republicans in the Free State get the upper hand. Should the Free Staters get the upper hand (and maintain it) I would expect some arrangement by which peace would be assured.

By now Solly-Flood was under attack on other fronts as a result of the internecine warfare and the extravagant conditions and salaries enjoyed by the elite members of his empire. Back in June the minister of finance had protested 'most strongly' that the furnished Danesfort House, 'with its greenhouses and large pleasure grounds [rented] at very considerable cost', was being used as offices rather than living accommodation as intended, after the general sought to acquire another similar property as a residence. The Ministry of Finance also sent in an accounting officer to examine the books and concluded that the general had flouted the Northern Ireland authorities by agreeing to inflated salaries, above Army rates, for his staff, and that he should be personally surcharged for the excess. The unfortunate Colonel Dyson, who had earlier failed to vet the spy in his registry, was also threatened with surcharge for taking it on himself to authorise the travelling expenses of officers coming from London to join the department in Belfast.

There now followed a rundown of the staff and by mutual agreement, Solly-Flood himself agreed to give up his command at the end of the year. His parting shot was yet another extravagantly documented proposal for an Ulster Volunteer Constabulary providing 'Defence not Defiance; Economy combined with Efficiency; and Evolution not Revolution'. In an accompanying memorandum to Craig he warned that while 'a comparative peace now reigns' the prime minister should not be 'gulled into a false sense of security'. He also sent him a personal letter in which he quoted some verses from Rudyard Kipling's 'If' and said: 'It bears a curious analogy to my existence in Northern Ireland recently.' The general was given a great send-off from the quay, the *Belfast Telegraph* reported a few days before Christmas, but no one was sorry to see him go, especially Wickham, whose position as the inspector-general of a unified constabulary was now unchallenged.

With the Six Counties more tranquil than could ever have seemed possible at the beginning of the year, Craig sent a handwritten Christmas message from Stormont Castle, Belfast, to be duplicated and individually copied to every member of the Royal Ulster and Special Constabularies.

I wish to place on record my high appreciation of the splendid bearing and discipline of the Officers and Men of the different branches of Constabulary whom I have had the honour to inspect. It has been an unqualified pleasure to me to observe a material increase in efficiency and a continued fine attendance on Parade, which testify to the loyal spirit animating all Ranks. I fully realize that what I have witnessed is typical of the entire Force and I am confident that if ever I am privileged to inspect further Districts they will prove equally efficient. The Government of Northern Ireland thoroughly understands its indebtedness to the Constabulary Forces and I am glad to avail myself of this opportunity of placing it on record and, at the same time, of thanking you personally for your services and of tendering you all good wishes for the New Year.

James Craig

At the final cabinet meeting of that tragic and turbulent year, a few days before Christmas, despite the fragile peace and a large measure of unfinished business, he announced he was going off for a month on holiday.

Chapter Three
Advice Unheeded

Just before 8 a.m. on 8 January 1923, the motor car and driver until recently assigned to General Solly-Flood waited at the quayside in Belfast for the disembarkation of two important passengers who had travelled overnight on the ferry from Fleetwood, Lancashire. One was Major-General Sir Archibald Montgomery, the other his aide, Colonel H Knox. With the agreement of Craig, they had been sent from the War Office in London on a secret mission to examine the future organisation of the constabulary and set it within a framework of financial limits that would be acceptable to the British government. The arrangement, made at a meeting between Lord Derby, the British war minister, and Craig in December, was primarily to satisfy Stanley Baldwin, the Chancellor of the Exchequer, that the vast constabulary expenditure was 'value for the money'. Confirming the situation in a letter soon afterwards, Derby, who strongly supported 'the necessity for a large Constabulary Force in Ireland', said, 'I think that in order to satisfy him we shall have to let the officer we send over make suggestions with regard to the cost of your force as compared to, say, the cost of Territorials in England.'

It was already official policy in Belfast, although not on the extravagant lines proposed by Solly-Flood, that when things were quiet the RUC should provide a conventional policing service, on the well-established lines of the old RIC, with back-up from a Special Constabulary. When things became serious then, 'by a turn of the screw', in the words of the Army's commander in chief, the constabulary could be switched to a military role to defend the frontier and the state. There was still a mighty obsession within the northern government that it must retain this doomsday capacity under its own control, despite repeated British assurances that the Army would be deployed to repel any cross-border invasion.

The continued insecurity in Belfast was largely due to the unfinished deliberations of the Boundary Commission and the ongoing indecision about the exact line of the border between north and south. The favoured option was to use the traditional county boundaries of the northern six, Londonderry, Tyrone, Fermanagh, Armagh, Down and Antrim, to delineate the northern state, but the provisional government, under pressure from northern nationalists in many affected areas, especially south Armagh, was pushing to include as many of them as possible in the Free State, however untidy the resulting frontier. The lack of a clear outcome to the ongoing civil war compounded the uncertainty in Belfast, as did the fear that industrial unrest in Britain or events elsewhere in the Empire could compromise London's commitment to protecting Northern Ireland. As County Inspector Harrison had recently told Tallents, 'the Government wish to control absolutely a force for which Great Britain pays. They say that events in Great Britain might arise necessitating a call on Imperial troops. Nothing should be done to weaken the Northern Government while this possibility at her gates remains uncertain.'

There was another unspoken imperative in keeping so many men in uniform: unemployment. Craig and Bates were anxious to preserve a united Unionist façade during what they regarded as days of still great peril for their fledgling state. With so many of the potentially militant working-class men engaged in the constabulary and earning good money, there was little incentive for unrest amongst them. Furthermore, given the critical disenchantment among the Protestant working class with the government's grudging welfare policies, creating 'IRA scares' and fomenting sectarianism was frequently to prove a useful tactic for the Unionist Party in quelling criticism and maintaining unity. Fear of the IRA, exaggerated out of all proportion to the actual threat, would in fact be one of the key elements enabling the party to hold together an otherwise illogical coalition of the landed gentry and artisan classes and, defying all political convention, to remain unchallenged in power for half a century.

Montgomery and Knox reported expeditiously and at length on 12 February, noting that 'in our opinion' the inspector-general's task of maintaining, organising and training a force of some 40,000 is 'too great for any one man'. Drawing a distinction between the long term and the current emergency, they said the semi-military Special Constabulary should continue in existence while the present period of unrest continued but should ultimately be disbanded. Then, they recommended, the civil policing and state security functions should be split, in line with the practice in Britain, and in the long term there should be a permanent Royal Ulster Constabulary and a military Territorial Force, under the wing of the Army commander in Northern Ireland and the War Office, although its members would not be called on to serve outside Northern Ireland unless the Belfast government consented. The two senior soldiers, obviously aware of the undisciplined record of the Specials and fears about what the rogue elements in uniform might still do in the volatile uncertainty of the ongoing emergency, warned of the need for discipline in the territorial force:

> Such a force, in an elementary stage of organization, in possession of arms and ammunition, cannot but be a source of possible danger should the members become disaffected. It is true that in the special circumstances which obtain in Northern Ireland such disaffection is unlikely, but still it is a possibility which should be considered and in a force of 28,000 men it is hardly reasonable to suppose that there will not be some individuals who may at times act in a manner which is undesirable in Government forces.

Wickham, who already had, of course, the unenviable task of trying to control and discipline such militant elements, took the view that 'the only way to keep the Special Constabulary on correct lines is to have it attached as nearly as possible to the regular police'. He was also opposed to the creation of the Territorial Force for related reasons. Pointing out that the current C1 stand-by force was 'a highly political body formed originally for the absorption of a dangerous independent Orange force which was organising itself for action', he said that if it were turned into a territorial force it would be 'permanently stained with politics and its future thus prejudiced'. He also feared that such a force might become a source of embarrassment if, at any time, differences arose between the imperial and Northern Ireland governments. 'It would then be more than likely that the rank and file of the Force would refuse orders from their Imperial officers, and a difficult situation would thus be created.' Wickham favoured disbanding the C1 force when opportunity allowed and replacing it with the unlikely ideal of a new force open to both creeds.

Craig and Bates, however, still fixated by the need for independent control of as large a 'constabulary' force as possible, were opposed to any loss of power. Furthermore, unlike Wickham, they would not have suffered the slightest embarrassment in using it to confront the Free State, and even Britain, if such a conflict of interest ever arose. So, for differing reasons, Wickham, Craig and Bates all found the Montgomery plan utterly unacceptable and rejected it, although they knew doing so would not help them in the ongoing fight for money from the London government to fund what Whitehall now referred to as Northern Ireland's 'swollen Constabulary'. Earlier, Craig had persuaded the Treasury in London that 'there was no cheaper way of maintaining the peace in Ulster' and had secured £2,750,000, two years' funding for the Special Constabulary. The £650,000 cost of the RUC was paid for separately out of the total grant to the Belfast government to provide public services. He now needed to go begging again but, before doing so, he turned once more to Lord Derby.

In an effort further to impress on his ally the efficiency and effectiveness of the local forces, Craig invited him to make a five-day visit to Northern Ireland early in 1923. In the event Derby, accompanied by his private secretary and valet, made a three-day visit and was lavishly entertained by some of the aristocracy. Among the several events organised for him was a grandiose march-past of 1,300 officers of constabulary at Newtownards Camp and a drumhead religious service for an equally large assembly at the Ormeau Park in Belfast. Despite its straitened circumstances, the government spent £8,000 staging the events and mustering the officers from all parts of Northern Ireland. Among the extravagances was £900 for erecting a thirty-foot flagpole, a saluting stand and tiered seats for 800 people and providing 300 men's latrines at the Belfast park. With Derby's help and Craig's combination of moral blackmail and bluster about the dire consequences of what would happen if the British did not pay up, the money question was soon settled for that year, but the advent of Ramsay McDonald's Labour government in 1924 brought the indulgence to an end. They took the view that while the existence of such large police forces gave Northern Ireland a sense of security and obviated the effects of unemployment, the continuance of substantial assistance from the British Exchequer could only be temporary, not least because the British government and parliament had no control over the armed forces maintained by the expenditure.

With the flow through the money tap being reduced, Craig and Bates had to take some hard decisions about the financing and strength of the various forces during the remaining years of the 1920s. Despite mutinous behaviour by redundant A Specials in Belfast and Londonderry, the number of men under arms was progressively reduced and by 1930 a pattern was set which, save for the duration of the Second World War, would remain, unchanged for some forty years. Despite its great reliance on the constabulary whose 'courage and discipline' ministers regularly acknowledged in parliament and elsewhere, the government showed little generosity in providing for it. The ministry, in fact, imposed a bureaucratic web on the RUC which, for many decades ahead, would enmesh it in crippling procedures to account for everything from buttons to batons in minute detail and ensure that the force was run on a shoestring, however uncomfortable or inconvenient for the personnel. The pattern of parsimony was firmly set by the end of 1923 when, despite repeated requests, the ministry failed to supply gas burners to light the huts at the Newtownards Camp, causing the police officers based and training there to live in darkness at night. Despite his several written pleas that 'the surgery is not a place that can do without a stove', the commandant could not even get the ministry to repair the chimney pipe. In later years, as motor cars became more common, the ministry would instruct the suppliers to remove the heaters from vehicles destined for the police in case the constables patrolling in them became too comfortable.

With the Montgomery report left to gather dust in a filing cabinet in the Ministry of Home Affairs' new offices at Ocean Buildings, adjacent to Belfast City Hall and a short stroll from Bates's legal practice, the backbone of the northern government's defence remained the RUC. With the relative peace that was consolidated in 1922–23, priority was given to bringing it up to its 3,000 establishment and restoring routine policing, which had been virtually non-existent for some three years. It was a considerable task. As Tallents had reported back in June 1922: 'On the day of [RIC] disbandment, the Northern Government, faced with a state of affairs which would have tested the best police force in Europe, found itself with a regular force of about one-third of its proper establishment practically unsupported by any system of criminal intelligence.' By February 1923, some eight months after its creation, RUC strength had only reached 2,130 and the force relied on 1,582 'Barrack Reinforcements' drawn from the 3,560-strong A Special platoons to help carry out its work. Many of the men were tied down guarding barracks that had been hastily set up in commandeered buildings in troubled areas such as the Falls Road library in Belfast, but as the situation continued to settle down from 1923 onwards and the Specials were run down these outposts were steadily closed and the police reverted to the old RIC barracks network.

One of the main problems had been attracting sufficient Catholics to fill the one-third quota reserved for them. A month after its inauguration, there were 400 ex-RIC Catholics among the 1,100 officers enrolled in the RUC but by October 1922, according to a parliamentary answer, the Catholic strength had only increased to 434 compared to 896 Protestants.

With the collapse of the Catholic Police Committee and Bates's underlying lack of enthusiasm for having ex-RIC officers and Catholics in the organisation at all, the remainder of the 1,000 places reserved for Catholics were quickly re-allocated to Protestants to bring the RUC up to full strength. Addressing parliament in Belfast in May 1924, shortly before the second anniversary of the RUC's formation, RD Megaw, the barrister and MP for Antrim who was deputy to Bates, reported that the force was finally within 100 places of reaching its 3,000 establishment and that 1,362 former RIC were now serving alongside 1,378 transferred from the Special Constabulary. 'This had brought about the happiest results and as they had worked together, so had efficiency increased,' he said.

At this point the overall Catholic proportion of the force peaked at twenty-three per cent before steadily declining as the former RIC officers retired and were replaced by Protestants, many from the Special Constabulary, who were actually to comprise half the force strength well into the 1950s. By 1935 Catholics still made up some seventeen per cent of the entire force and were well represented in the supervisory ranks, but by 1966, according to a parliamentary answer, Catholic participation was not sustained and overall numbers had fallen to ten per cent, at which approximate level they would hover until the outbreak of the Troubles in 1968. At no time were Catholics ever enrolled in sufficient numbers to fill the one-third quota originally envisaged. Such was the sensitivity about Catholic numbers, however, that at the very outset Bates had a detailed table prepared showing the religious affiliation of the entire command structure, whether they had come in from the RIC or the Special Constabulary and whether they were of Irish, Ulster or English origin. Wickham and the seven officers in his inspector-general's department were all Protestants, as were the four senior depot staff. Two of the seven county inspectors and ten of the thirty-nine district inspectors were Catholics, a total of twelve among the fifty-eight most senior officers, well under the one in three Catholic proportion envisaged for the entire force. Of this higher echelon, twenty-two were Irish, twenty-nine from Ulster and seven were English. Twelve of them had come in after service with the Special Constabulary, the remainder from the RIC.

The religious composition of the new force and the allocation of these top jobs was watched very closely by the Unionist community, within which there was a considerable extreme and suspicious element, vociferously critical of the Unionist party leadership and the government. They despised and distrusted the old RIC and opposed any vestige of

Catholic influence in its replacement. This view was strongly shared by a Protestant ex-RIC officer, District Inspector John W Nixon, who had most recently been serving in north Belfast, where his tough approach had earned him popularity among these elements and considerable notoriety among Catholics. So, when Bates passed him over for promotion to one of the county inspector posts, Nixon and his associates were far from happy.

Thus began the Nixon affair, which, as we will see, would become a defining episode in the history of the RUC. It began on 11 July 1922, when Nixon articulated his grievance in a closely typed, two-page letter, which was widely circulated among those critical of Craig and Bates and their policies. In what amounted to an embittered sectarian rant, Nixon pointed out that four of the seven new county inspectors were from the Free State and only three from Ulster. He continued: 'I tried to do my best to defeat the conspiracy against Ulster, whether I was successful or not I cannot say, but I was vain enough to hope that I had gained the confidence of a good many loyal people in Belfast and Fermanagh [where he had previously served]. I also think that my District in Belfast was more orderly than other Districts, and it would have been better but for the following facts.' Nixon went on to state that on 4 January 1922, he saw Fr Sebastian, the Catholic Rector of Ardoyne, coming out of the commissioner's office in Belfast. 'The same evening an order was issued to me from the Commissioner that Special Constabulary were not to be employed in Ardoyne or Bone areas. This was emphasised several times subsequently, and in the end no police but the Leopold Street men were allowed to be used there.' In Nixon's book, many of the Leopold Street RIC were in sympathy with the IRA and from that day on, as he put it, 'the IRA got a bit out of hand, and committed various murders and other outrages'. Nixon went on to claim that this and similar orders 'rendered him powerless' to search for arms and prevent murders.

> It's a common saying here that loyalty to Britain does not pay, and I
> hope that the same will not be said about Ulster, but it is very hurtful
> to be rejected by those whom you considered your friends. Personally
> I attach little importance to the promotion itself except that I feel as if
> the Sinn Feiners and their friends were laughing at me for getting left
> after all my exertions against them. My name and record is I hope as
> well known to the loyal people of Ulster as that of any of the men
> appointed to the higher positions over me.

Nixon was born in County Cavan, and joined the RIC in June 1899 at the age of twenty-two. He became the youngest ever district inspector and one of the minority to rise through the ranks into the officer class. After the war of independence broke out in 1919 he earned three commendations for his 'exceptional zeal, perseverance and ability in the performance of duty' before he was appointed to take charge of Belfast's troubled C District, working from Brown Square. Prior to formation of the RUC Nixon filled out a form to serve in the new force, and on 11 May he was offered an appointment as district inspector, which he accepted four days later. A contemporary newspaper account says of him, 'keen disciplinarian though he may be, it is safe to say there is no more popular officer in the service'.

By the summer of 1922, however, it is also safe to say, there was no more notorious officer, for among Catholics Nixon was widely reputed to be the leader of the 'police murder gang' responsible for a series of reprisal killings, including such recent atrocities as the McMahon family murders and the killings in Arnon Street. In Dublin, thanks to RIC officers from Leopold Street, who gave information to Fr Laverty for onward transmission, Collins was well aware of this connection. Papers from the time, retained in the Irish National Archives, contain well-authenticated accounts of the gang's activities, heavily based on eye-witness testimony and affidavits from other RIC officers, who were outraged by the ruthlessness and illegality of what was going on. In one such report Nixon, a Methodist, is described as 'a religious fanatic who preaches in the police mission'. Apart from Nixon, senior officers involved are identified as County Inspector Harrison and Head Constable Giff, who regularly mutilated his victims with a bayonet, as well as numbers of constables and Specials. Collins was making repeated complaints to London about the situation in Belfast and, in particular, the conduct of the security forces, and it is inconceivable that he did not raise the issue of this 'murder gang' directly with Craig during their exchanges concerning the first and second pacts earlier in the year.

When Bates first heard about the Nixon letter he decided to ignore it, but having learned how widely it was circulated and after receiving many, in his words 'intimidatory', resolutions from a variety of Orange Lodges, his view changed. In a letter to Craig, who was on one of his ever more frequent and prolonged breaks at Cleeve Court, his Thames-side retreat in Berkshire, Bates said: 'I propose to allow Wickham to take whatever disciplinary action he may consider necessary.' Bates said this would mean demanding a withdrawal of the letter and, on refusal, the setting up of a court of inquiry to consider a disciplinary charge against Nixon. His resolve to tackle Nixon could not have been more explicit: 'The steps which we propose taking will probably mean the dismissal of Nixon from his position, and will be followed by an outcry among certain of the extreme Protestant element. You will observe that Nixon has behaved extremely badly in accepting the position in May of DI, and in the meantime utilising his position to ferment disaffection in the Police Force and among the supporters of the Government.'

However, by the time Craig replied two days later, saying he could not conceive of 'a more injudicious or improper letter' and taking the view that the case was a matter of discipline best left entirely in the hands of Wickham, Bates was having second thoughts. Through membership of the Orange Order, the Protestant working class was able to make its views very clear to the ruling classes 'in lodge' during regular meetings. Vulnerable to such pressure because of their reliance on the grassroots for votes, the politicians ignored sentiments expressed in this way at their peril. So, when Nixon's supporters adroitly exploited their access to let Bates know they intended to push the matter to extremes and bring about the removal of Wickham and his deputy, Gelston, if needs be, Bates speedily enlisted the MP Lloyd Campbell to see if there was a solution that would render the disciplinary action against Nixon unnecessary. It became apparent very quickly that Nixon and his faction were not to be easily placated and on 4 September, Bates's deputy, RD Megaw, minuted Craig to see if he wanted to appeal to 'the heads of these organisations . . . to use their influence in the cause of preserving the peace'. Craig was still uncompromising and sent a stiff note by return saying the matter should 'be proceeded with at once'.

> In my opinion there has been undue delay which has given the opportunity for unwarranted interference and agitation. In cases of the kind in future I hope that immediate action will be taken; outside bodies have no jurisdiction and no right to interfere. With regard to the suggestion that I should see the heads of certain organisations with a view to seeking their influence, I hold most strongly that such would be an injudicious step. It would create a most awkward precedent and the same organisations would claim the right to criticise the transfer or dismissal of any Police Constable in whom they were interested.

While this missive was in transit to Belfast, Megaw wrote again to Craig advising him that Campbell and Solly-Flood had received an overture to see if Nixon's resignation would be accepted if offered.

'Campbell seems to think that it would afford a way out of a bad business – that the government would take no responsibility for the advance and would not be committed in any way – I should like a hint.' Twenty-four hours later, Megaw again wrote to Craig, reporting that Wickham had insisted on taking personal charge of the case and pressing ahead with disciplinary charges, but adding: 'I think that he is quite keen to have Nixon's resignation and would accept it.'

For unclear reasons, Craig himself now changed his mind and intervened, ordering an effort to settle with Nixon and instructing Wickham to take no disciplinary action for a week. The intermediary this time was the MP, Captain Herbert Dixon (later Lord Glentoran), who represented Belfast East in both the London and Belfast parliaments. At the end of the week, when Craig found out that there had been no progress because Nixon was on holiday by the sea at Newcastle, County Down. Spender contacted Wickham, obtained his address and, in a letter on behalf of Craig, urged the MP to 'get in touch with him very quickly and not wait till the end of his leave, which would mean another month's agitation'. A flavour of the 'agitation' that was going on can be gleaned from a letter to Craig on 25 July from a Mr Albert Hogg, who resided at Cregagh in east Belfast:

> The one man who fought Sinn Fein tooth and nail for the last four or five years has been deliberately overlooked. Those who favoured the enemy through cowardice now get the plums. I understand that Roman Catholic priests have access to our government offices. I suppose that would account for this business.

More formal protest came by way of many hostile resolutions passed by arms of the Loyal Orders such as the Sinclair Seamen's LOL and the Adam and Eve Royal Black Preceptory. Typical of these was one from the members of Castleton LOL 867 on 27 July, a copy of which was quickly forwarded to Bates at the ministry:

> The members in Lodge assembled hereby move the following: 'That we passed a vote of Censure on the Minister of Home Affairs, Sir RD Bates, for his disloyalty to the Protestant electors of Northern Ireland and demand that he shall immediately dismiss the City Commissioner, Mr. JF Gelston, for his Roman Catholic tendencies and giving position of trust, and positions where confidential correspondence must pass through their hands, and for his maliciously turning down Mr. Nixon in

the recent police appointments, and we are determined to leave no stone unturned until Mr. Nixon receives an appointment worthy of the dignity of the high services he has rendered to Ulster and the Empire.'

Despite the avalanche of such sectarian sentiments reaching them, the most powerful pull on Craig and Bates seems to have been exerted by Sir Joseph Davison, the leader of the Orange Order, who was renowned for his outspoken anti-Catholicism. After presiding at what he described as a meeting of 'prominent and influential citizens' he requested a meeting with Craig to 'lay before you the grievances expressed by those present with regard to District Inspector Nixon'. Although the official files remaining from the time do not explicitly record what happened next, there were two important developments. All talk of dealing firmly with Nixon stopped and, remarkably, given the recorded attitude of Craig and Bates, all action against him ceased. The only clue contained in the files comes in a handwritten letter to Craig from Dixon sent from the Constitutional Club at Northumberland Avenue in London on 19 September. 'My dear Prime Minister,' he wrote:

> I send you Nixon's letter which I received yesterday. I think it is as satisfactory as could be expected after the interview and I hope it is the end of the trouble. I enclose you a copy of a letter I sent him in reply. I sent this because it might be thought that the Home Sec. or the IG [inspector-general] had shown weakness by not bringing him before a court as was threatened [and] that I had been sent by the Government to make him apologise and failed. This is a case certain to be made by interested persons. Nixon's friends are sure to see this letter and it breaks that case. The IG has no official knowledge of the case and anything that was done by me was only out of goodwill. Could you please return Nixon's letter and my reply, as later they may be of value.

Unfortunately, neither of the letters Dixon mentions survives in any official records. But Bates's version of the about-turn is given in a subsequent letter (23 October 1922) to Craig explaining his part in the mysterious turn of events.

> In my opinion he [Nixon] is entirely responsible for the agitation which has sprung up. I decided, on careful consideration, not to take action against Nixon as I did not wish to make a martyr of him in such a critical stage in our Police Force, and, because I had no <u>official</u>

knowledge of the breach or discipline in question. Originally, Mr Nixon was a capable DI within certain limits, but latterly he has mixed up in politics and, undoubtedly, has shown a strong party feeling which is unbecoming in a police officer. In his District he has also allowed the feeling to develop that there is only one law and that for the Protestants, and in consequence the Protestant hooligan is allowed to interpret in his own fashion the laws of the country.

In the midst of all this turmoil, in August 1922, Bates was asked to grant permission for RUC members to become members of the Orange Order. Hitherto police, and indeed military, regulations placed stringent curbs on political activity by police officers. RIC members were specifically prohibited from voting at parliamentary elections, their oath of office disbarred them from membership of political or secret societies and the Code prevented them from expressing or manifesting any sectarian or political opinions. The request came in a letter marked 'personal', addressed to fellow Orangeman Bates at his home as 'Dear Sir and Brother'. It was dated just three weeks after the RUC came into existence on 1 June 1922, and in it the Anchor Purple Star Electricians LOL 811 said that a number of ex-RIC men wanted to know 'authoritatively but if necessary privately' if they could resume the Orange membership they had kept in abeyance and attend Lodge meetings in plain clothes 'the same as they do to Masonic meetings. You will understand that men of this type loathe anything underhand, hence their request to me to try and find out.'

Bates put the letter into official channels for consideration and, despite the weight of RIC precedent, decided in August that 'Members of the RUC may be allowed to remain in or join the Orange Order but should not attend the meetings in uniform nor should such attendance in any way interfere with their duties.' Not surprisingly, within a few months, in January 1923, an Orange Lodge confined to members of the RUC was formed. It took the name 'Sir Robert Peel Memorial Temperance Lodge Loyal Orange Lodge 1334' and soon boasted a membership of about 300, a tenth of the entire RUC. The first Worshipful Master was none other than the troublesome District Inspector Nixon, and in another extra-ordinary development, given the ongoing tussle between them, Bates himself was the guest speaker at the first Annual General Meeting of the Lodge later in 1923. In the King's Birthday Honours on 30 June the same year, clearly as part of the political climb-down by Craig and Bates, who would have had to recommend it, Nixon was honoured with the MBE. His assuaged friends in the Shankill area of Belfast quickly formed a committee and appealed for subscriptions 'to give practical effect to the esteem and appreciation' in which he was held. Plans were made for a function and they wrote inviting Craig to attend. Spender replied in October declining the invitation pointing out that 'it is not in accordance with the customs of service in the Royal Ulster Constabulary for officers to receive any form of testimonial' and 'in these circumstances Mr Nixon will no doubt already have let you know that he will be unable to accept the very kind expression of appreciation which it was the intention of yourself and others to show him'. The snub drew a pointed letter to Craig from Robert Armstrong, the sub-district commandant at Shankill Barracks, a few days later on 9 November: 'Even if there was such a rule, one would have thought that having regard to the terrible time through which Mr. Nixon passed in defending the citizens of this district and the loyal citizens generally, we might be permitted to do him this little honour and thereby show that the loyal law-abiding people of the district do not forget, as the Government seems to have forgotten, services loyally rendered in a critical period.'

Spender responded promptly, confirming the general practice that officers should not accept testimonials. He added that Craig 'cannot quite understand the paragraph in which you state that the Government seems to have forgotten the services loyally rendered in a critical period by Mr Nixon, since Mr Nixon's name was included in the Honours List, which is the normal way for giving recognition of the appreciation of the Government for services rendered'. The highly ambiguous nature of these exchanges cannot have been lost on Spender, for there had already been another sinister twist to the Nixon case which had given the prime minister very good grounds to keep his distance. It came after a murder at Oldpark Road just after 10 p.m. on 4 September 1923. John Shevlin, aged thirty-four, and his brother, both Catholics, had just locked up the Admiral public house, which they had bought only five weeks earlier, and parted to go their separate ways home. Three gunmen quickly approached John and fired two shots. He staggered into the roadway and fell under a passing tram. The police report states that it took 'a good twenty minutes to extricate him before he was conveyed to the Mater hospital where life was pronounced extinct. The area is a Protestant one and the crime is believed to be political.'

The next day, Megaw deemed the occurrence important enough to personally brief Craig in a handwritten letter sent to his English retreat. The police, he reported, did not think the motive was robbery and were convinced 'the perpetrator is one of the Protestant gang'. He went on:

The misfortune in regard to our chance of capturing the murderers is that Nixon is the DI in charge and his probable complicity with certain civilians in the neighbourhood ties his hands. He made no raid on dangerous persons following the affair and stated that it was useless as it was an IRA exploit. I know the difficulties in connection with Nixon, but I greatly fear that his retention is a weak link in our police.

Craig, in another U-turn, quickly replied from Cleeve Court: 'I feel strongly that if N is to be removed or transferred it should be done at once, otherwise your Ministry will be subject to very severe attack at a later date, as all the circumstances will soon be forgotten. I feel sure that Bates and you will carefully consider this aspect of the case.'

A £1,000 reward, publicised through posters and newspaper advertisements, attracted no new information about the murder and an inquest on 13 September concluded that death 'was caused by shock and haemorrhage following gunshot wounds wilfully inflicted by some members or members of an unlawful assembly'. In reporting the verdict to his superiors, the police officer dealing with the case added to the mystery: 'Nothing has transpired except what I committed verbally to Mr Heggart and which is perhaps better unwritten.' There are no surviving details of this information. On 13 October, Bates himself called for a fuller report from the police. In transmitting the request, Watt, the most senior civil servant in his ministry, directed that the murder file should now be classified Secret. The reply, on behalf of the inspector-general on 29 October, also revealed nothing about the dubious background to the murder. 'Every item of information received has been thoroughly investigated and statements taken but up to the present without any beneficial results. I suggest it is perhaps as well that the actual course of inquiry should not be reported in a case of this kind but could, if required, give details verbally.' On 2 November, Bates made a handwritten note on the file that he had spoken to the policemen involved. No details of the discussion are recorded and there are no more entries or papers in the murder file, held at the Public Record Office in Belfast, to indicate any further developments. Indeed, nobody ever appears to have been charged with the murder.

Whatever the truth of Nixon's apparent role in this serious crime, he was soon involved in more trouble. At a meeting of the Peel Lodge on 3 January 1924 he made outspoken political remarks which were promptly reported back to his police superiors and the government. Nixon was clearly spoiling for a fight, and the authorities knew that the Dublin government had an embarrassing dossier on him and his past activities. This was not conclusive evidence but would have been convincing enough for Dublin to use to stimulate concern in London about what seemed to be incompatible links between the RUC and the militantly Protestant Orange Order.

With the government's connivance, Wickham moved to limit the potential damage by issuing a circular outlining revised regulations about the political activity of RUC members on 17 January 1924. In the two-page document, which was ordered to be posted in every barrack and station, Wickham pointed out that RUC members were allowed to vote at parliamentary elections and join certain approved secret societies, a right not enjoyed by the RIC:

> It will be realised that these privileges are not to be used in any way likely to impair the efficiency of the force generally, or of its individual members, or to weaken the confidence of the public in the impartiality of the force. It would, for instance, be improper for any member of the force to abuse their privileges by expressing or manifesting political or sectarian opinions, though it is, of course, in no way intended to interfere with the private political or religious beliefs of any member of the force. Members of the Royal Ulster Constabulary should not, therefore, take any part by speaking, or entering into discussions, at meetings where political or sectarian opinions are expressed, or by organizing or assisting in organizing meetings or gatherings at which political or sectarian speeches or discussions are likely to take place.

Nixon was unmoved by what was, in effect, an explicit personal warning that he must toe the line. At another Lodge meeting on 29 January 1924, attended by a member of the government and at least two MPs as well as three newspaper reporters, he made further explicitly political remarks, according to reports in the Belfast papers the next day. He warned that although the Six Counties were intact, the border was surrounded by the enemy, who had artillery, armoured cars and aeroplanes, and every engine of war supplied to them by the Imperial (British) government. The opinion down in the Free State was that they were going to get a big slice of Ulster but the response of every leader among Protestants and Orangemen who had expressed himself on that matter, so far as he knew, was 'not an inch'. (Nixon prided himself on being the originator of the phrase which became part of the Unionist political vocabulary.) Apart from its political content, Nixon's speech was highly untimely for Craig, who was in the middle of crucial discussions with London and Dublin in a bid finally to resolve the line of the border.

Nixon was promptly accused of breaching the terms of the earlier circular. A few days later, on 4 February, a file containing the newspaper reports and initiating disciplinary charges was sent to Nixon at his barracks. Two days later he was suspended from duty pending the outcome of a disciplinary hearing at which he was to be charged with various breaches of orders by making a political speech. 'I have never known an officer or man of the RIC to be suspended except when charged with a criminal offence or gross insubordination,' he complained. Forwarding a file about the affair to Craig on 7 February, Bates, who was now back in anti-Nixon mode, wrote: 'I have no doubt whatever that Nixon's action in making the speech he did was intentionally in defiance of the Inspector-General's instructions of 17 January 1924.'

Supporters of the suspended policeman arranged a 'monster demonstration' for the night before he was due to appear in front of the formal inquiry. It was extensively advertised by posters, some of which were provocatively fly-posted over an entire wall of Nixon's Brown Square Barracks. According to the *Belfast Newsletter*, a crowd of some 10,000, led by bands playing lively airs, marched from the Shankill Road through the city centre and back again. During speeches outside the City Hall, Nixon was lavishly praised. Next morning, 14 February, the Constabulary Court convened at the Musgrave Street barracks in central Belfast. Two county inspectors presided but the proceedings were adjourned without making any progress because of legal argument about the way the case had been laid against Nixon and whether or not Bates, whom Nixon had summoned as a relevant witness, should attend to give evidence. Two days later the court adjourned again, this time at the request of Nixon's solicitor. Meanwhile Nixon had been sent a letter by a sympathiser offering to produce a witness who would question the impartiality of one of the county inspectors. This man claimed to have overheard a conversation in the Victoria Hotel in Newry the previous December where another county inspector recounted his colleague's confided view that Nixon was 'a companion of the scum of the Shankill Road' and that while 'the authorities were afraid of him' he would 'get his deserts' when an opportunity arose.

When the inquiry assembled for the third time on 19 February, after Nixon denied the four charges, it became clear that the case against him was to be outlined by three newspaper reporters who had been present at the meeting. However, a barrister representing them announced that the journalists would not be giving evidence lest it should be submitted that they were informers, detectives or police note-takers. The hearing adjourned after the prosecuting district inspector asked for warrants to arrest the three reluctant witnesses. Next morning a crowded courtroom waited with keen anticipation for the arrested men to appear, but after a confused twenty minutes during which several of the principal participants milled about the room it became clear the court would not sit. Later in the day Wickham announced that he had dissolved the court because he had come to the conclusion that 'it had been rendered absolutely abortive owing to the intimidatory methods' used by Nixon's supporters. These included the usual batch of letters (like the one quoted above) and resolutions but also at least one threat of murder. On receipt of Wickham's report, Bates took legal advice and, on 24 February, issued instructions to the inspector-general to summon Nixon before him 'as a subordinate' without legal representation. Accordingly, Nixon was ordered, at one hour's notice, to attend at the inspector-general's office at 3 p.m. on 21 February.

When he arrived he found only Wickham, his deputy Gelston and a shorthand writer present. According to Nixon, Wickham said that he had been directed by the government to put a list of queries to him and that he should answer only yes or no. The first question asked if he had attended a meeting described as a 'social' at the Clifton Street Orange Hall on 29 January. The transcript records that Nixon replied: 'Not a social.' The remaining six questions, containing sections of Nixon's reported address, were put to him and he was asked each time if they were his words. Nixon replied to the first quotation by saying: 'I have already been charged in connection with this matter and it is unfair and unlawful even to a criminal to question me.' Nixon answered the remaining questions by saying: 'Same answer as number two.' Before leaving he protested about not being allowed consultation with his legal adviser. On 28 February, after the governor, the Duke of Abercorn, had rushed back from London to authorise the action, Nixon was told he had been 'removed' from the force on a full RIC pension of £433 a year. His supporters had already announced a 'Six County-wide' protest about the case and planning meetings had taken place in Clifton Street Orange Hall. While there was plenty of vociferous support for his cause, there was little money. Efforts by Head Constable Giff to collect a five-shilling subscription from each constabulary officer in C District were halted when District Inspector Roger Moore intervened and warned he would 'take disciplinary action at once if any collection of the sort was made in these Barracks'. The ban was circumvented by a five-shilling levy being imposed on members of the Peel and other Orange Lodges.

In the event a protest meeting took place at the Ulster Hall at 8 p.m. on 15 April 1924. The main auditorium was packed to capacity with an overflow crowd outside who all sang the hymn 'O God our help in ages past' to open the proceedings. When Nixon made a delayed entrance a short time later they sang 'For he's a jolly good fellow', and cheered him as he took his place on the platform. At the end of the two-hours-and-forty-minute meeting the crowd passed resolutions of protest at his dismissal. After the rally Craig was again inundated with resolutions from Unionist bodies and the Loyal Orders. All received the same reply: the prime minister was absent, ordered on a sea cruise by his medical adviser, and their letters would be drawn to his attention on his return. The matter was raised several times after that in the northern parliament.

Bates always insisted that the agitation got up on behalf of Nixon was 'the greatest bit of cant and humbug he had ever heard in all his life. The speech was made by Mr Nixon in open defiance of the order of the Inspector-General.' The government refused to reinstate him. Nixon then entered politics and became both a Belfast councillor and later an MP, where he remained a thorn in Bates's side, constantly accusing the Minister of 'victimising him to placate and gratify the enemies of Ulster' and frequently abusing parliamentary privilege to pursue his many vendettas and grievances without the fear of legal sanction in the libel courts. For the rest of his days, fearful that the IRA would catch up with him, he carried a revolver in the glove compartment of his car. He died from heart trouble in the Royal Victoria Hospital in Belfast on 11 May 1947, aged seventy.

Although Nixon fought two major libel actions in subsequent years, winning £1,000 from the *Derry Journal* and £1,250 from the London publisher Methuen for alleging that he was involved in reprisal killings, including the McMahon murders, his notorious reputation has never been either persuasively proven or vindicated. Many of the crucial records from the time are incomplete. There is no doubt, however, that his indictment was a grubby political episode carried out to forestall any embarrassment to the government, who first set out to sack him, backed down in the face of pressure, decorated him and then, in the end, only acted when Nixon's own publicly confrontational attitude left them no choice. The handling of the case was not, as it should have been, a symbol of police discipline, propriety and impartiality. Nixon was the subject of first a sordid cover-up and finally supreme political hypocrisy. The legacy of the case, and the unprincipled conduct of Craig and Bates, is that it identified the RUC even more firmly with the Unionist side of the divided community in Northern Ireland. More importantly it was a defining episode for the Unionist government in its ability to play dirty politics with the force for its own ends, a flaw that would have a lasting corrosive effect on policing structures and the RUC's reputation and credibility with Catholics, who long used the Nixon case to question the moral integrity of the force and its standards of impartiality.

However, on another important symbolic issue Bates failed to impose his wishes on Wickham and the police force. This parallel saga began in October 1922, soon after the RUC's formation, when Bates commissioned designs for new insignia including a badge incorporating the crown and Red Hand of Ulster. After some modifications to the badges and buttons, suggested by Wickham, new drawings were approved by the Governor, Craig and Bates and an order was placed with a firm in Birmingham in March 1923. A month later, when samples were sent to Belfast for approval, Wickham took the view that the badges were not satisfactory. Soon afterwards, RUC and Special Constabulary officers let it be known that they were opposed to the new designs and favoured continued use of the RIC's harp and crown insignia with the word 'Irish' being replaced by 'Ulster'. Bates agreed to consider a new design but specified that the Red Hand of Ulster must be included.

In June 1923, in a bid to marshal the strong opinions that were now being expressed within the force, Wickham wanted to establish a representative committee to deal with the issue. A minute to the ministry stated that the men who had to wear the badges should have their say but Bates and officials overruled. The issue was allowed to simmer until October, when the ministry asked Wickham for a report on opinion within the force. He replied saying that the earlier designs had been 'unanimously condemned' and that the officers strongly favoured the amended RIC version. Bates, obviously as averse to its badge as he was to the old RIC, was still insistent that the Red Hand should be included and he ordered more designs and sample badges to be obtained. When these were submitted to Wickham in April 1924, he scorned each one in considerable detail.

By October, Wickham had rejected a number of further designs: 'The RUC is a semi-military organisation which I think places itself on a somewhat different plane to other police forces and requires therefore a "Corps" badge around which corps tradition and sentiment can grow in the same way as battalions of the lines have their own badges and not the arms of the counties whose names they bear.' Meanwhile, the force took the matter into its own hands. Each time new items of uniform were received, the new insignia were removed and replaced with those of the RIC. In a bid to break the long impasse, in January 1925 the Ministry even considered offering a prize of £5 or £10 through a public competition for a suitable design. In the end, later that year, the government bowed to the wishes of the men and approved the use of the amended RIC badge, a singular victory for the force over its political masters which was never to be repeated.

While the Nixon affair and the row over badges were running their courses, the stabilising of the situation throughout the Six Counties which had begun in the latter half of 1922 continued. Fears of a 'recrudescence of political outrages' in County Tyrone proved to be ill-founded when, according to District Inspector John Gorman, a number of ambushes of B Specials turned out 'to be the work of a few half-hearted, isolated irresponsibles'. In another tangible sign of changing attitudes, County Inspector J McNally reported from Newry that a considerable number of Catholics had shown up at the Special Constabulary sports. 'Three months since not one of them would have attended,' he said. He also reported that in Banbridge a leading Sinn Feiner 'at variance with another' had now invoked the aid of the Crown courts against him. JC Dudgeon, the District Inspector of Antrim, caught the prevailing mood in a report to the inspector-general on 22 September 1922:

> There is little doubt that both sides are pretty sick of conditions that have prevailed. The Nationalist minority are scarcely more anxious than the Unionist majority for a settlement which will allow the life and trade of the country to develop as it should. All have had enough of fighting, and the Nationalists here realise that conditions in Ulster are at least 500 per cent better than in the South.

This point was echoed in another report from the border county of Fermanagh, where County Inspector Gerity reported 'a disposition on the part of the RC population to recognise the Northern parliament. This change of feeling is due largely to the uncertainty of life and insecurity of property in the Free State. Many have expressed themselves glad they were not living in the Free State.' For his part, JF Gelston, Belfast City Commissioner, suggested 'all branches of the Constabulary should be encouraged to cultivate a friendly disposition towards all classes in their areas and so encourage the people generally to rely on the police and to furnish them with information when a crime is committed'. He reported that armed 'hold-ups' and robberies in Belfast had 'decreased to a gratifying extent due in some measure to the augmented police force being available to deal with ordinary crime instead of being fully occupied in endeavouring to preserve the peace between rival factions'. Police figures underlined the dramatic improvement in the situation. The number of outrages recorded by the police dropped from 4,502 in 1922 to 1,330 in 1923. Across all the indices of crime and disorder there were corresponding reductions: indictable offences fell from 5,103 to 1,412; firearms offences were down from 352 to 150 and malicious injuries reduced from 1,545 to 188. In 1922 there had been 231 murders in Belfast. In 1923 there was one.

With a more pragmatic and optimistic mood developing, the government now had a perfect opportunity to think again about the sort of society that it should be creating within its partitioned territory. By 1924 it was quite clear that the pro-treaty forces had come out on top in the civil war and that the Free State, however resentfully, would be sufficiently preoccupied with binding its own wounds to think about invading the north. In any case, the British government had given its solemn undertaking to defend the frontier, which was finally settled along the existing six-county border in December 1925. At the same time nationalists, recognising that their best interests lay in making a practical accommodation, however uneasily, with the new state, began to recognise and co-operate with its emerging administrative organisations. But the government's ingrained religious bigotry had now been compounded by a siege mentality and they set about establishing the IRA as a perennial bogeyman to justify the continuing need for heavily armed constabulary forces to maintain their defences.

The consequences for law and order, the cement that holds any society together, were especially unfortunate. With the emergency effectively over, there was in fact a golden opportunity to make a fresh start, especially with the RUC. Montgomery and Knox, with impressive foresight, had recognised this and urged that it should become a civil force charged exclusively with the maintenance of order and the enforcement of the law. 'As far as possible it should be relieved of duties of a semi-military nature,' they had stated. From his well informed standpoint Brigadier-General Ricardo expressed a similar view:

> [. . .] it is impossible to see how this new force can ever hope to 'make good'. They get all the odium as they have to carry the responsibility,

and all complaints and claims come to them from the public, yet they
have no control whatever over the Special Constabulary, who create
much of the trouble. There is only one way the new Force can come
into its own, and that is by controlling the B Specials, allowing the A
Force to pass over to the semi-military side, and making certain that the
RUC police HQ people are permitted to run their own show, entirely
separated and away from the military side.

Ricardo added: 'Our own Northern Cabinet, I believe, will never
acknowledge defeat or rise to the actualities of the present situation,' and
he was right. The visionary advice to create a civil police was totally
ignored. By contrast, in the Irish Republic the first commissioner of the
unarmed Garda Siochana, Michael Staines, who led the 380 founding
members of the new force through the archway to take possession of the
police headquarters in Dublin Castle, spelled out their ethos: 'The Garda
Siochana will succeed not by force of arms or numbers but on their moral
authority as servants of the people.' Despite initial problems, this infant
organisation emerged intact from the turbulence of the civil war and
eventually succeeded in establishing its authority throughout the country.

If the northern government had shown similar vision and courage, and
relied on the same principles, the history of policing in Northern Ireland
would probably have been very different. With the fresh start envisaged
by Montgomery, Knox and Ricardo but unheeded by Craig and Bates, the
RUC would have been a more acceptable organisation and, in time,
Catholics might have been persuaded to come forward in sufficient and
greater numbers. Instead, by maintaining its armed, paramilitary ethos
and twin mandate to defend the state and keep the peace, the RUC was
fatally handicapped. Its identification with a highly partisan government
fuelled the lasting perception that it was indeed the 'armed wing of
Unionism', enforcing the dominance of the new state through the
repressive provisions of the 1922 Special Powers Act.

In 1923, in a move to minimise nationalist or Catholic (for Unionists
there was no distinction) influence and participation, elections by
proportional representation were abolished, the franchise was weighted
in favour of Protestants and local government electoral boundaries were
redrawn to ensure that the two-third Unionist community dominated the
one-third Catholic minority. Figures from the late 1930s all too clearly
demonstrate the resulting nationalist disadvantage. In the city of
Londonderry, for instance, 27,062 electors were allocated only eight
council seats while 18,097 Unionists were able to elect twelve

representatives. The imbalances were carefully preserved. Houses were seen as equating with votes, so were always built in Protestant areas and never allocated to Catholics. All of this was justified as being necessary to 'defend the state' otherwise Catholic votes would bring it down.

Sectarian attitudes were endorsed and encouraged from the highest level. Back in 1920, Craig had publicly approved the practice of violently driving Catholics from their jobs in the Belfast shipyards. On 12 July 1932, from an Orange platform, he had proudly uttered: 'Ours is a Protestant government and I am an Orangeman.' A year later, in 1933, Basil Brooke appealed to Loyalists 'wherever possible to employ good Protestant lads and lassies' and told them he had 'not a Roman Catholic about his own place'. The same Twelfth day, Major JH McCormick, a Belfast Unionist MP, said a Protestant who employed a Catholic was a traitor to his country and warned 'Rome would be in power in twenty years both inside Parliament and outside it'. Soon afterwards Brooke returned to the subject and said that ninety-nine per cent of Roman Catholics were disloyal, a view promptly endorsed by Craig, speaking in parliament on 20 March 1934: 'There is not one of my colleagues who does not entirely agree with him and I would not ask him to withdraw one word he said.' These exchanges were all the more contemptible in that they took place at the height of three years of renewed sectarian violence between 1932 and 1935.

As the remarks demonstrated, discrimination against Catholics was encouraged and institutionalised in every sphere. Catholics therefore never accounted for more than ten per cent of the civil service and only achieved something like six per cent of the higher grade jobs. In 1937, the Nationalist MP Cahir Healy calculated that in the city of Londonderry only nineteen per cent of the wages and salaries paid by the local Council and Regional School Committees were paid to nationalists, who numbered 61.3 per cent of the population. In Belfast, where one in four of the population was estimated to be Catholic, only four per cent of the payroll was received by the minority community.

The police were not immune from the pressures of this institutionalised sectarian culture. On 2 August 1929, for instance, the Reverend WE Hurst, on behalf of 'the large majority' in Moira, County Down 'who were of the Church of Ireland persuasion', wrote to Bates complaining that 'we have had 7 or 8 Roman Catholic Sergeants in succession and we feel we have been rather unfairly treated, so we kindly ask you to send us a Churchman this time'. The good clergyman thought the sergeant was to be transferred after detecting two of his constables breaching discipline by being in a public house. Bates replied that as the sergeant had been doing his job properly there was no question of him being transferred.

Despite the gulf between them and the police, Catholics too were not above applying pragmatic sectarian pressure. At the end of January 1931, when a Catholic head constable in Portadown was due to retire, Joseph Connellan, a Nationalist MP, sent a letter to Bates pointing out that there were only three Catholics among the twenty-nine police officers stationed in the town and enquiring if 'the usual practice' was to be followed in having one of the two most senior posts filled by a Catholic. Shortly afterwards, Joe Devlin MP followed up the issue with an identical plea. 'Please give this your usual good attention and have this request of mine agreed to,' he wrote to Bates. 'The Catholic residents of Portadown will be most grateful for this concession.' Bates replied to both in similar terms. 'If and when a suitable opportunity occurs, every effort will be made to meet the point you make,' he said.

These exchanges illustrate the insidious and mutual bigotry that so speedily flourished and thrived at the heart of Northern Ireland society and generated periodic convulsions of inter-communal, sectarian violence. In the early 1930s two RUC officers were shot dead by the IRA during a prolonged series of disturbances in Belfast and elsewhere, and during the Second World War four RUC officers and two Special Constables were killed when the IRA, calculating that 'England's difficulty is Ireland's opportunity', in the words of a slogan daubed on walls, tried to sabotage the war effort by stealing arms and gathering information about industrial and military targets, which was passed to the Nazis through contacts in Dublin. There was a lull for a time after the war but by the early 1950s, a spate of terrorist attacks and new raids to steal arms were clear signs of a resurgence of militant Republicanism which culminated, at the end of 1956, in a co-ordinated series of attacks on police, military and other targets along the border and throughout Northern Ireland. It was the most serious assault on the northern state since partition and by the time it fizzled out in 1962, 605 outrages had been recorded and six RUC officers killed. The campaign was, however, a signal failure as the IRA's violence failed to secure any public support for the cause of a united Ireland and was vigorously condemned on both sides of the border.

Dealing with the onslaught reinforced the Unionists' siege mentality, nourished anew their fear of the IRA and its objectives and reinforced anti-Catholic attitudes, as was all too evident from the contents of a private journal maintained by a senior Special Branch officer who served in Belfast from 1941 until he was forced to retire after a heart attack in

1952. An election campaign in 1950 produced a set of scathing insights into the conduct of Unionist politicians. 'Election duty,' he recorded on 20 February. 'Unionists as usual causing trouble wanting to go into opposition areas, abetted by the election agents of the candidates of whom Baillie [the Unionist party agent] is a particularly evil specimen who does all he can to whip up sectarian feeling. Labour giving no trouble at all and doing everything we ask. Even anti-partitionists and Sinn Fein, much as they hate us, are being reasonable. Tory behaviour generally almost enough to make one pro-Republic of Ireland.' Four days later after polling, there were further observations arising from the tradition of holding provocative victory marches.

> Except for [the Reverend Godfrey] MacManaway [a fiery Church of Ireland preacher who blended 'no surrender' politics with the Bible] all behaved reasonably by Northern Ireland standards. He assembled his usual crowd of scoundrels and paraded the constituency; fortunately it was a very wet night and the crowd melted considerably as it proceeded. Sidelights on the election: scoundrels on MacManaway's lorry, he with them, shouting 'F' the Pope, singing 'Dolly's Brae' and 'the Sash [my Father Wore]' on the edges of RC areas. MacManaway, himself, at Sandy Row referring to RC's as 'bloody Fenians' and being applauded by Basil Brooke, the PM, and [Edmond] Warnock, ex-Minister of Home Affairs, presently Attorney General and prospective Lord Chief Justice. Warnock twitting MacManaway with being afraid to go up the Falls Road at Broadway and telling him that he, Warnock, had done so. He made sure first that he had lots of police in the area. No bigger coward exists. Every time some political joker threatened him on the telephone he demanded a radio car at his home all night.

Royal visits were another perennial source of tension and imposed a large burden on the police. In July 1953, Queen Elizabeth spent three days in Northern Ireland as part of a post-coronation tour of the United Kingdom. During the visit, the queen was serenaded by Lambeg drummers outside Government House at Hillsborough and carried out a packed programme of engagements. But behind the scenes, the inevitable sectarian shadows over Belfast prompted more manipulation of the police by the Unionist government. Between May and August 1953, a period which spanned the coronation and Northern Ireland visit, a contemporary police report reveals that forty-six of the 136 police officers in B Division (the Falls Road area of Belfast), were 'exclusively employed in guarding

[Union] flags from interference' and 'rioting was averted only with the greatest difficulty on numerous occasions'.

With similar problems arising throughout Northern Ireland, Sir Richard Pim, then Inspector-General of the RUC, issued a circular to the force indicating how they should handle the problem. But the Stormont government took exception to Pim's instruction and in August 1953 he wrote asking for political direction. In November, Pim was summoned to a meeting chaired by the hardline Edmond Warnock, who was now attorney-general. Afterwards an official noted: 'The general feeling was that it should not and could not be admitted that the flying of the union jack could lead to a breach of the peace and that persons objecting to the union jack were not entitled to do so and were certainly not entitled by right to protection while doing so.'

Later the same day the RUC submitted a revised draft circular, leaving out the controversial paragraph which visualised the removal of the Union Jack in 'extreme circumstances' and pledging that the RUC would 'give all possible protection to the flying of the union jack'. Referring to the status of the Irish flag, they also promised 'to ensure that the police will not merely be content with the removal of a tricolour but will institute proceedings where necessary'. Over the next month, as the Ministry of Home Affairs began work on legislation to give legal force to the circular, Pim appears to have had second thoughts about the situation and on 30 December 1953 dispatched a five-page, closely typed memorandum to the ministry.

> Speaking not as Inspector-General but simply as a loyal Ulsterman, the idea of singling out the union flag for special mention in an Act of Parliament does not appeal to me. I feel it would be liable to create, particularly in the minds of those outside the province, the entirely erroneous impression that the union flag cannot be flown in Northern Ireland except under the protection of an Act of Parliament and that the police are at present powerless to deal with any interference with it. I think also that such an Act would provide all those opposed to the government of Northern Ireland with a powerful propaganda weapon.

Pim also expressed fears about 'tying [his] hands' and 'those of the members of the force' by laying down in law that the police must never, under any circumstances, remove the Union flag.

Inside the ministry, Pim's long letter was re-typed and alongside it a highly dismissive commentary, typed in red, was provided by a senior official for the then minister of home affairs, George B Hanna, a Queen's Counsel like Warnock before him. In a highly caustic conclusion, it said: 'It is politically impossible to defend any suggestion that a man may not fly the flag of the country on his own property whenever he wants to. If the other side are not disposed to exercise that amount of tolerance, the penal clauses of the Act will provide the means of teaching them to do so.' When the cabinet considered the legislation in January 1954, Hanna reported that the inspector-general was 'unduly apprehensive' and his reservations were swept aside. The legislation was passed a few months later and, although it did not specifically prohibit the display of the Irish tricolour, it banned any flag or emblem 'likely to cause public disorder'.

What happened a decade later was inevitable. Having ignored sober police advice, Northern Ireland's myopic political masters once again doomed the unfortunate RUC to be thrust into the firing line. After the collapse of its 1956–62 campaign, the Republican movement turned to social agitation on a large scale, seeking to draw attention to the multiple disadvantages their Unionist rulers imposed on the Catholics of Northern Ireland. Their protests and political activities soon brought them into open conflict with Unionists, notably, the Reverend Ian Paisley, the militant anti-Catholic preacher who was then emerging at the head of a more extreme and uncompromising strand of Unionism. During the 1964 general election, Paisley publicly demanded the police use the 1954 Flags and Emblems legislation to remove a tricolour from the window of the Republican election headquarters, at Divis Street, Belfast, otherwise he would lead a march to do so himself. Despite the fact that the flag was exhibited in the middle of an exclusively Catholic area and was unlikely to have provoked anyone who had not gone well out of his way to be offended, the Unionist government surrendered to Paisley and ordered the RUC into action, setting off several days of the worst street rioting in the city since the 1930s. Although the trouble was swiftly suppressed and Northern Ireland continued to enjoy a phase of unprecedented prosperity, the tranquillity would prove to be short-lived.

PART TWO

Breakdown

Chapter Four

A Community in Revolt

When Emily Beattie was allocated one of two newly constructed council houses in Caledon, County Tyrone, on 13 June 1968 she could never have imagined that the decision would mark the start of the most violent period in Northern Ireland's history. Towards the end of 1967, as the builders put the finishing touches to them, the Catholic Goodfellow family, with three small children, the youngest just nine weeks old, took unauthorised possession of one of the new houses at Kinnard Park. They were among 269 mainly Catholic people on the council's waiting list desperately looking for a home. With only twelve houses under construction, and given the anti-Catholic track record of the diehard Unionist councillors whose say-so allocated them, they saw their hopes of getting one legitimately as non-existent. The situation was a snapshot of all that was wrong with Unionist-controlled Northern Ireland society and politics.

Some eight months later, during the afternoon of 18 June, five days after Emily Beattie was granted her new residence, a cadre of bailiffs acting for the owners, Dungannon Rural District Council, evicted the Goodfellows from it. So the next afternoon, during an acrimonious debate, Austin Currie, the local Nationalist member of the Northern Ireland parliament, complained bitterly about a situation where a nineteen-year-old unmarried Protestant woman could be allocated a publicly financed house ahead of many obviously more needy families, some of whom had been waiting for years. Currie's anger was all the greater because he had learned that Miss Beattie's tenancy seemed to be the fruits of political pull. She worked as a secretary for a prosperous Armagh solicitor, Brian McRoberts, at the time the prospective Unionist parliamentary candidate for West Belfast and legal adviser to the council. Throwing his notes across the floor of the parliamentary chamber in exasperation, Currie stormed out. The following morning, 20 June, he entered Miss Beattie's proposed dwelling and commenced a sit-in. It did not last long. Within a few hours a party of Royal Ulster Constabulary officers, including Miss Beattie's brother, arrived and he was manhandled out. In many Catholic eyes, the force was now irrevocably identified as anti-civil rights.

Before these retrograde events at Caledon, the emergence of the liberal Unionist Captain Terence O'Neill as prime minister had stimulated a mood of optimism and change. The time was ripe for fundamental reform but Unionist extremists were determined to thwart any efforts to achieve equality between Catholics and Protestants or to improve relations with the south, and when O'Neill paid a courtesy call on some nuns, as part of his outreach programme to demonstrate that the Catholic community had a respected place in the life of Northern Ireland, they vowed to bring him down. Ever since 1925, when the partition settlement had been finalised, successive governments in London had gladly turned a blind eye to the conduct of affairs from Belfast. Nobody wanted to resurrect the convulsions of Ireland which, as Churchill had so graphically said in 1921, 'forced generation after generation to stop the whole traffic of the British empire in order to debate her domestic affairs'. By convention, therefore, they were never raised at Westminster, where, over the years, the twelve MPs from Northern Ireland were anyway Unionists with no inclination to do so.

However, in 1966 Gerry Fitt, a colourful nationalist leader with socialist leanings, who already sat at Stormont, broke the Unionist monopoly on the seats by becoming the West Belfast MP. Helped by sympathetic British Labour MPs, he led the cry for the government in London to force O'Neill to confront his critics more rigorously and deliver on the many reforms he bravely admitted were necessary. Significantly, Fitt did not look to Dublin for redress. 'I simply want the same rights for my constituents in Belfast as apply in Birmingham or Manchester,' he said. Fitt's objective was closely in tune with the mood of contemporary Catholic opinion in Northern Ireland. Among the younger elements, like Currie, whose memories of the tribulations of the partition period were not first-hand, there was a pragmatic willingness to accept the status of Northern Ireland provided they got fair play, a standpoint helped by the fact that they enjoyed an altogether higher standard of living than their compatriots in the south. Thanks to hefty British subsidy the people of Northern Ireland enjoyed parity with the rest of the United Kingdom in the levels of social and welfare payments, a high standard of education and the benefits of the free National Health Service. However, among Unionists, a siege mentality still thrived and there were fears as vivid as any ever held by Craig or Bates that, given half a chance, the Catholics would rise up with IRA support and frogmarch them into a united Ireland. So they perpetuated gerrymandering and discrimination to prevent Catholics getting any share of real political power.

Because Unionist leaders were not courageous, generous or far-sighted enough to recognise the mood change among Catholics in the early 1960s and initiate reform, they made a major error. By attempting to stifle, rather than meet, even at that overdue hour, the growing clamour for reform within Northern Ireland, even after the warning signalled by the events at Caledon, their bigotry and sectarianism condemned Northern Ireland to its subsequent tragedy and, indeed, would cause Britain to review the very nature of the union they so cherished. For the RUC, caught in the middle, the coming ordeal was completely unforeseen.

The changing nationalist mood in Northern Ireland in the 1960s was heavily influenced by events of momentous historical significance elsewhere: the Russian invasion of Czechoslovakia; the assassinations of Martin Luther King and Robert Kennedy; the student riots in Paris and the worldwide protests against the United States' involvement in the Vietnam war. But the greatest inspiration for people in Northern Ireland, strongly wedded as they were to the concepts of struggle and martyrdom, was undoubtedly provided by the civil rights campaign for black people in the United States. By early 1968 a similar civil rights movement was well under way in Northern Ireland, campaigning for peaceful reform within the existing partition set-up. It contained a broad church of Republicans, liberals, socialists, Catholics, Protestants, Unionists, nationalists and even a prominent communist. The IRA, which had embarked on a course of subversive political action through infiltrating groups campaigning on these very social and economic issues, was heavily represented by what is best described as an undercover element, some with communist tendencies. For the moment the traditional Republicans, whose violent tactics had been discredited by the failure of the recent border campaign, were forced to take a back seat. Boosted by events in Caledon, the civil rights movement next took to the streets and organised a protest march in nearby Dungannon which was prevented by the police from entering the town centre. The way the police handled the situation further hardened Catholic hostility to them after they faced the civil rights marchers and were content to have the counter-demonstrators at their backs. As at Caledon, it appeared as if the RUC was at one with the anti-nationalist faction, that it shared their cause. For the civil rights activists, it was a disappointing re-affirmation of old allegiances, that the RUC was not 'their' police and they could expect neither even-handedness nor impartial treatment from its officers.

The first major venture of the civil rights movement was a march in Londonderry on Saturday 5 October 1968, the venue pointedly chosen because the city manifested many of the most serious shortcomings they were campaigning to rectify in Northern Ireland society. Religious discrimination was blatantly evident; bad housing conditions were compounded by unfair allocation procedures; electoral boundaries were unequally drawn and the franchise was unfair, with businessmen, predominantly Unionists, having extra votes and many people, mainly Catholics, having none at all. With a Protestant minority ruling a Catholic majority, it was no wonder then that 'One man, one vote' was their most fundamental objective. The other major reforms they demanded were the disbanding of the all-Protestant B Specials and the repeal of the infamous Special Powers Act. In 1936 the National Council for Civil Liberties had said that with this act the Unionists had created 'a permanent machine of dictatorship under the shadow of the British constitution'. Its draconian potency was quickly demonstrated after the march was announced. The government promptly utilised the legislation to ban it, the decision being taken by Bill Craig, the current minister of home affairs, a man cast in the same bigoted political mould as his predecessor Bates.

A solicitor by profession, Craig had served a term as minister of home affairs in 1963 and 1964, when he had pushed through the first major reform of the RUC since its formation. Exploiting the greater mobility provided by cars and radio communications, seventy-eight smaller police stations were closed and operations were concentrated on 178 remaining, some with only limited opening hours. Police employment terms were modernised to give them a fixed forty-four hour working week with prescribed time off. The real object of the exercise was to save money and one of the yardsticks used to measure the efficiency of stations was the amount they spent on postage each week. Those with a low outlay were deemed not to be busy enough. After he had held other ministerial posts, Craig was reappointed by O'Neill to Home Affairs in 1966, but as the groundswell of criticism gathered force, he speedily shed his progressive reputation and sided with the hardliners. The same year, defying Special Branch advice, he tried to prove his tough credentials by proscribing 'Republican Clubs' who were primarily interested in social agitation.

Despite the Londonderry march ban, which at least some senior RUC officers shrewdly forewarned would have pyrrhic consequences, hundreds of civil rights marchers formed up on the afternoon of 5 October at the Waterside railway station and began to walk along Duke Street towards Craigavon Bridge. Ahead of them the police had positioned a couple of grey-painted tenders to block the narrow street and were grouped in front of it to halt the marchers. The first rank advanced slowly towards the cordon, ignoring police loudhailer warnings about the illegality of the demonstration. Fitt, who was at the head of the column, vividly recalls that as they came within a few yards of the police he noticed they had drawn their batons.

> Suddenly there was a big push from behind and we were propelled forward. A sergeant grabbed me and pulled my overcoat down over my shoulders to prevent me raising my arms. Two other policemen held me and I was batoned twice on the head. A stinging pins and needles feeling followed and I could feel the blood coursing down my neck on to my shirt. As I fell to my knees I was roughly grabbed and thrown into a police van. At the police station I was shown into a room with a filthy wash basin and told to clean up. But I was not interested in that. I wanted the outside world to see the blood, which had dried all over my face. The police were confused about what to do with me and eventually I was driven to Altnagelvin hospital where my wound was stitched but the police would not let the doctors put a bandage around my head in case it provoked the crowds who had gathered.

The official police report of the incident, claims that Fitt was not assaulted at all but suffered his head injury, according to the sergeant concerned, when a marcher's placard on a pole was swung towards the police. When Harold Wilson, then British prime minister, summoned O'Neill and his senior ministers, Craig and Brian Faulkner, to London on 4 November to discuss the disturbances, he criticised the handling of the situation in Derry and said that in the absence of an impartial inquiry, he would find it hard to defend the Northern Ireland government's continuing responsibility for its own law and order. If the Northern Ireland government was so confident that no undue violence had been used on this occasion, there was no reason why an impartial inquiry should not be ordered, Wilson said. He then referred to the graphic television pictures of the clash, and O'Neill limply tried to imply they misrepresented what had occurred because they had been shot by a cameraman from the Irish state television service, Radio Telefis Éireann. Craig, however, reacted vehemently to Wilson. Emphasising that the incident had given him 'no cause to regret his confidence in the RUC', he said the government must demonstrate its confidence in the police force. According to the official note of the meeting he said: 'No inquiry should be ordered unless there was justifiable cause for ordering such an inquiry and an inquiry ordered as a result of political pressure could only undermine the confidence of the police and shake the authority of the government in its task of maintaining law and order.' He added that if it had not been for 'the efficiency of the RUC, violence would have continued in Londonderry for many days'.

The marchers and their sympathisers were having none of that and their MPs mounted a sustained campaign alleging police brutality during a series of increasingly acrimonious exchanges in the Stormont parliament. Craig vigorously defended the police and denied issuing tactical instructions. On 22 October, Harry Diamond, who represented the Falls division of Belfast, said the minister's 'Pontius Pilate act will carry no conviction anywhere', and asked if it was 'the attitude of an officer and a gentleman that the [County] Inspector [William] Meharg, in charge of the operation, gave the instruction publicly: "Give it to the bastards"?' Although Craig defended Meharg as 'deserving the highest credit', the officer himself refused to leave it at that and, later the same evening, confronted Diamond at his Belfast house insisting that as a 'Christian gentleman' he never used language like that. Despite Craig's unyielding bluster, the Stormont administration was ultimately forced to concede a formal inquiry, led by the Scottish judge Lord Cameron, who later concluded that the police handling of the demonstration was 'ill co-ordinated and inept' and that they had used 'unnecessary and ill controlled force'. It said the batoning of Fitt had taken place 'at a time when no order to draw batons had been given and in circumstances in which the use of batons was wholly without justification or excuse'.

The clash at Duke Street amounted to the crossing of a watershed but no one yet recognised how dangerously the smouldering embers of Ireland's turbulent history had been fanned into flames. In the immediate aftermath, Wilson moved swiftly to defuse the escalating disorder by insisting that O'Neill accelerate the implementation of reforms. As far as the majority of Catholics were concerned, delivering them would provide the basis for long-term peaceful co-existence within the existing borders of Northern Ireland. There was no significant demand for Irish unity despite the strength with which many Catholics cherished the long-term aspiration. What was remarkable was that, for the first time, a significant number of Catholics and moderate Protestants were working together in the civil rights movement to create a better state of affairs. However, a subversive minority of modern Republicans and radical student hardliners committed to a united Ireland, refused to settle for any compromise short of that and, agitating under cover of the civil rights banner, provoked more and more serious riots and confrontations between themselves, hardline Unionists and the RUC. On the other side, extreme

Unionists opposed any reform, which they regarded as concessions to the Catholic minority, and in the upper echelons of the Unionist Party there was turmoil as the reformers fought, increasingly in vain, to maintain forward momentum. The Reverend Ian Paisley, an uncompromising and fiery figure, rapidly emerged as the main street leader and his bellicose activities played a significant part in raising tension.

Between October 1968 and the summer of 1969 the RUC fought vainly to control the rising tide of public disorder. From the outset they were under the unyielding political thumb of Bill Craig, whose decisions Lord Cameron would later describe as unwise and unfortunate. From them, the report said, flowed 'widespread resentment' among Catholics who were roused to participate in demonstrations 'as a token of indignation and protest'. Cameron was also disparaging about Craig's bans on marches which 'placed upon the police an impossible strain and burden . . . and only served to engender a wide measure of popular hostility towards the police'. Over succeeding weeks, civil rights marches were invariably met by a counter-demonstration of extreme Unionists, normally led by the increasingly confrontational Paisley, his threatening activities always skimming close to the letter of the law.

Thanks to the years of under-investment in training and equipment, the RUC was singularly unprepared for the task it now faced. With 3,030 officers, only thirty more than its initial strength in 1922, manpower was woefully inadequate. There had been no co-ordinated public order training and protective equipment such as shields and helmets was outdated and in short supply. The Army hurriedly produced some stocks for the hard-pressed force but all too frequently police parties could be seen fending off volleys of bricks and bottles with dustbin lids commandeered from nearby premises. The RUC and the people of Northern Ireland both paid a heavy price for the lack of investment in training, manpower and equipment and the historic failure to divorce the police from day-to-day political control. In dealing with the disorder both the RUC and the Ulster government were further forced to operate in the unprecedented glare of the international media spotlight for the first time, with the bones of fifty years of unchallenged Unionist hegemony being picked over ever more critically by amazed outsiders.

A month after the first Londonderry clash, Wilson publicly warned that if O'Neill was overthrown by extremists, with the implication that the reform programme would be halted, the British government would have to consider reappraising its entire relationship with Northern Ireland. He was no admirer of the Ulster Unionists and was determined to do something about the social and political situation that had been allowed to fester. Wilson had a parallel anxiety that the steadily escalating sectarian confrontation and street violence could drag Britain more directly into the maelstrom so, in mid-November 1968, he asked his home and defence secretaries to find out in what circumstances British troops could be called on to assist with suppressing civil disorder. The prime minister's alarm bells had been set ringing after Eddie McAteer, the Nationalist Party leader at Stormont, visited the Home Office in London on 14 November. During his discussions with the minister of state, Lord Stonham, he referred to the RUC's use of the Royal Navy's Sea Eagle base in Derry during the recent clashes in the city when fifty members of the Reserve Force had been accommodated there. McAteer expressed concern that a naval officer had been quoted in a local newspaper saying they 'would always be pleased to assist in any way with the maintenance of law and order in Northern Ireland'. Although military commanders had approved the facility, Wilson caused reverberations around Whitehall after officials sent him a note of the meeting. He wrote: 'We must know where we stand. I am not so much concerned about what Stormont might ask as what our reply would be.'

Wilson was deeply reluctant to be sucked into the worsening conflict in Northern Ireland, nor did he want to appear to be sending British soldiers to confront civil rights marchers and maintain the Unionist regime, whose shortcomings were now being internationally condemned. So, on 6 December 1968, the chief of the General Staff, Sir Geoffrey Baker, sent a signal classified Secret to Lieutenant General Sir Ian Harris, General Officer Commanding at the Army's Northern Ireland Headquarters in Lisburn: 'You will understand the great political sensitivity of this subject and hence the importance of referring to Ministry of Defence if humanly possible before repeat before acceding to any request for the use of troops in aid of the civil power.'

A few days later, a reporter from the *Guardian* rang the Home Office in London to say the newspaper had learned that the Governor of Northern Ireland, as the representative of the Queen, could order the troops out in aid of the civil power but that he had been instructed not to do so because the government did not want the risk of British soldiers confronting civil rights demonstrators. An official note records that 'to keep the temperature as low as possible we replied that the question was a pretty academic one'. Nevertheless, with the story on the front page of the paper on 12 December the topic was firmly imprinted on the political agenda. Given the government's signal reluctantance to commit troops, a course it calculated would be 'politically embarrassing', the strategy now became one of aiding the RUC as much as possible in order to stave off any possible call for military assistance. Thus requests for the use of military facilities were approved and arrangements were made to loan riot control equipment as well as a fleet of Land Rovers, although, in the end, the vehicles were not needed.

In the meantime, lawyers in several Whitehall departments had been trawling through their books to answer Wilson's query about the use of troops, and their combined efforts formed the substance of a paper signed by Baker on 9 December. The official view was, as set out in the Manual of Military Law, that under common law the military had a duty to come to the aid of the civil power if requested. The advice also pointed out that in extreme or urgent circumstances, there was nothing to prevent a local district inspector of the RUC requesting assistance from a local military unit, whose commander could be deemed to be in breach of Queen's Regulations if delay or refusal 'would be likely to bring about a worsening of the situation or prejudice the success of an intervention'. Ministers were also warned that the GOC and his subordinates could not be relieved of their legal obligation to assist without a change in the law: 'It would not, therefore, be possible to ensure that consultation was always carried out before troops were committed in Northern Ireland.'

Denis Healey, the defence secretary, was now acutely concerned about the political dimensions of the issue. With the London government responsible for controlling the armed forces and the Belfast government obliged to maintain law and order, he was worried the military could be plunged into the midst of a political conflict if Belfast requested troops without consultation or for a task of which London did not approve. Healey therefore pointed to the need for some 'machinery of government' to enable urgent consultation to take place and give clear instructions to the GOC in Northern Ireland if the civil authorities in Northern Ireland asked for military assistance. 'The Secretary of State does not like the idea of the military in Northern Ireland using rifle butts to quell a riot without reference to him,' said a minute from his private secretary. In contrast to the reluctant but growing conviction in Whitehall that it was only a matter of time before the troops were needed, the prospect of military involvement was judged to be a remote one in Belfast. At a meeting there, in December 1968 between Baker and Anthony Peacocke, Deputy Inspector-General of the RUC, who was shortly to step up to lead the force, the policeman said he could not foresee any likelihood of the Army being called upon until the police were quite unable to cope and 'the guns were out'. At that point the security crisis in Northern Ireland was steadily deteriorating. A four-day march from Belfast to London-derry by the People's Democracy was repeatedly ambushed and attacked by Protestant extremists and there was serious rioting when it reached its destination on 4 January 1969. A week later in Newry, police vehicles were set on fire and pushed into the canal when more trouble developed during a civil rights march. That day, for the first time, in compliance with what he said was no more than a 'prudent military measure', Lieutenant-General Harris put a company of troops (about 100 men) on four hours' notice to move.

Soon afterwards, O'Neill called an 'Ulster at the crossroads' general election, for 24 February, in a bid to outflank a stridently critical Craig, whom he had sacked in December, and other opponents of reform. The gamble failed and despite being almost fatally defeated, O'Neill pledged to fight on. Within a month, though, on 31 March, the Ulster Unionist Council seriously undermined what little authority he had left when it passed a vote of confidence in him by only seventy-seven votes: 338 to 263. In the early hours of that morning, before the meeting, there had been a highly sinister development when an explosion caused £500,000 worth of damage to a vital electricity transformer at Castlereagh in south-east Belfast. The Special Branch instantly blamed the IRA, a view conveyed verbally to O'Neill and Robert Porter, the newly appointed home affairs minister, when they visited the scene to inspect the extensive damage. 'Oh, I don't think so,' replied O'Neill. 'I think this is some of my own people trying to tell me to go.' The Belfast government immediately announced that 1,000 B Specials were to be mobilised to guard similar vital installations. Within a week another explosion took place, this time causing damage to a water main linking Lough Neagh to Belfast.

Meanwhile the police were being faced with virtually nightly public disorder as civil rights marchers and Protestant counter-demonstrators confronted each other in towns and villages all over Northern Ireland. The most sustained clashes were in Londonderry, where trouble had been constant since the first clashes the previous October. Saturday 19 April was a particularly violent day; when a police officer had to fire shots in the air to escape from the midst of a violent crowd. The local hospital treated eighty-six police and seventy-nine civilians injured in the clashes. Overnight, in two more explosions, the main water pipe linking the Silent Valley reservoir to Belfast was severed and the cross-border electricity interconnector at Kilmore, County Armagh, was knocked out. That

Sunday morning, after a meeting of the new Security Committee which had been formed to manage the emergency, it was decided that soldiers would be requested to help guard sixteen key utility installations or Vital Points (water, electricity and communications installations: VPs, in military parlance). A simultaneous signal from Army headquarters at Lisburn to the chief of the Defence Staff pointed out the lack of any independent intelligence information but, citing 'relations with the RUC of the finest', said that, in their view, the weekend sabotage had been carried out by 'skilled operators' led by a man who had recently broken away from the mainstream IRA. London promptly agreed to provide 120 troops.

With the faltering O'Neill government plagued by yet another internal dispute, this time over when 'One man, one vote' would be brought in, there was a another explosion near Dunadry on 24 April, interrupting the water supply to a large part of Belfast for the second time. Later that day the government announced two military helicopters would join the security operation to maintain surveillance on water and electricity mains. Twenty-four hours later, a further blast at Annalong, County Down, aggravated the water shortages and, for the first time troop reinforcements were requested. Despite the growing political and military concern in London, a battalion of 500 was flown to Northern Ireland and tasked to help guard forty-eight Vital Points in remote rural areas. The army force now totalled 850 soldiers equipped with firearms and CS gas, which they were ordered to use first rather than open fire on any attackers. The political storm now enveloping O'Neill became so strong he decided not to carry on and announced his resignation on 28 April. (He later claimed that the explosions 'quite literally blew me out of office', a judgement vindicated the following October after Thomas McDowell, a forty-five-year-old quarryman with links to the outlawed UVF and Paisley's Free Presbyterian Church, died in a premature explosion while attempting to blow up an electricity pylon near the border. RUC investigations then uncovered extreme Protestant culpability for the earlier attacks.)

The Thursday after O'Neill's departure, 1 May, Captain James Chichester-Clark was elected to succeed him. With an atmosphere of crisis still hanging over the government in Belfast, the new prime minister set out to get a rapid grip on the deteriorating situation and give the public some reassurance that events were indeed under control. On 7 May, Harold Black, the cabinet secretary, wrote from Belfast to the Home Office in London with a request that would entail a further significant military commitment: assisting the eighty-strong Harbour

Police in guarding the Belfast Harbour Estate where the oil refinery, strategic oil stocks, two electricity generating stations, the main sewage pumping facility, the dry dock and building dock were all listed as being at risk. Harris, who judged there was no particular threat to justify the request, had already turned it down locally and sent some officers to advise on better co-ordination of the Harbour Police and the civilian security firms, with guard dogs, who were routinely engaged there. His decision was endorsed by the Ministry of Defence who advised the Home Office on 9 May that such a move 'would mark a significant step in the further involvement of HMG' in Northern Ireland and, quite probably, result in a need to further increase the number of troops there.

The Belfast government did not know, and most pointedly was not told, that at the weekly meeting of the London cabinet on 7 May, far from committing more troops, the startling proposition of staging a complete military withdrawal from Northern Ireland was raised. A note of the discussion says: 'It was suggested that the use of troops in sporadic disturbances of a relatively minor character might well tend to lead progressively to their use in more serious disorders, ending in full military intervention, and that the best course might be to withdraw them from Northern Ireland now.' Healey and James Callaghan, the home secretary were asked to consider the possibility and consequences of such a policy. At the same meeting concerns were expressed at the poor quality of intelligence being obtained about events and personalities. These were the two issues of most interest to the chief of the General Staff, Geoffrey Baker, when he was immediately despatched on a three-day fact-finding mission. What he had to say in a withering report on his return was far from encouraging reading for either the ever more beleaguered administration in Belfast or the increasingly perplexed government in London.

The RUC was behind the times, poorly led and administered and with a sadly inefficient Special Branch, so badly organised and run that speculation and guesswork largely replaced intelligence, the general reported. 'Of all its weaknesses, the latter requires the most urgent action to rectify,' he commented, adding with clear incredulity that neither they, nor the Northern Ireland government, had the remotest idea as to who was behind the recent sabotage incidents. The general was also scathing about Peacocke, now inspector-general, who objected to what he called 'interference from ministers' and told them only what he deemed they should hear. Such was the state of the relationship between the force and government that at his one-hour meeting with Chichester-Clark, the general found him defensive of the RUC's sensitivity to 'outsiders' and sympathetic to the fear that taking up the offer of expert Home Office advice to help improve performance might damage morale.

Having stressed the urgent need for much better intelligence product, the General encouraged the parties to get together without delay. They did so before he departed Northern Ireland and so he was able to report that the home affairs minister, Robert Porter, had held a four-hour meeting with the Security Service and Military Intelligence officers recently attached to the Special Branch, and the prime minister himself had a working lunch with them all 'during which no punches were pulled in outlining the RUC's weaknesses'. The Security Service, in its own report to the Home Office, corroborated what General Baker had said and condemned Peacocke's own Internal Security Committee as 'a bad piece of machinery'. They believed it could be made much more effective if Harold Black, the cabinet secretary, presided. 'This would create two-way traffic between the Security Committee of the cabinet and the RUC and would prevent the cabinet being told only what the RUC wanted them to hear,' the report said. Whitehall was already moving secretly to help plug the intelligence gap. On 21 April, the cabinet's ministerial committee on Northern Ireland ordered the security services to acquire independent sources, unknown to the authorities in Belfast, to supplement information on 'matters where Northern Ireland sources might be ineffective or unreliable'. The task was passed to the Joint Intelligence Committee who set up an Ulster Working Group to come up with a solution.

Baker was also concerned about the deployment of troops and highly doubtful that it was even necessary. He suggested:

It would make better sense either to call-up more B Specials, recruit 'bluebottles' (on the lines of the War Department Constabulary) or even make greater use of private organisations such as Securicor. There is no doubt that the Northern Ireland Government must do more to stand on its own feet. It is too easy a solution for them to fall back on the use of soldiers.

He therefore suggested that during Chichester-Clark's imminent visit to London he should be tactfully pressed on the 'the general state of the RUC, and in particular the Special Branch and 'the need for the Northern Ireland Government to establish a greater degree of self-sufficiency, thus being able to release the Army'. In their preparation for the meeting with

Chichester-Clark, the Home Office, again prompted by the Security Service, also decided to raise worries about the capacity of the RUC who were 'for the tasks they now have to perform, woefully thin on the ground'. The Security Service said that out of a total force of 3,000 the most the RUC could bring to bear for a particular disturbance was 600: 'They could only deal with three simultaneous disturbances in different places; four would be beyond them.' In earlier correspondence, Harold Black had revealed just how overstretched the force had become in the six months since the sustained campaign of demonstrations, marches and rioting had commenced. The brunt of the disturbances was borne by the Reserve Force, 250 men organised into eight platoons, with two of them (sixty men) constantly held on standby in Belfast ready to be sent anywhere in Northern Ireland.

Alan Wright, who was a member of the Reserve Force at the time, recalls an occasion when he was told to report for duty one morning to go to Londonderry and did not get home again for ten days. 'We were put up in a building belonging to the B Specials which became a dormitory for thirty men with one cooker and two wash-hand basins and everybody was still expected to appear clean and tidy for duty.' Other officers shared similar workloads. One recalls going off on a Friday night to Lurgan and performing duty in each of the Six Counties before he got home again the following Friday. 'All I took with me was a flask and a lunchbox of sandwiches and we had an awful job getting food as there were absolutely no facilities to cater for us. We slept in our tenders.' With so many personnel away from their stations for extended and unpredictable periods, it was left to the walking wounded to keep routine policing going. One officer nursing a broken leg was propped up each morning in the front office of a suburban Belfast station and spent the day answering the phone and dealing with visitors.

Reflecting anxieties that were again not fully shared with Belfast, London was also exercised about the way the RUC would react if the situation reached crisis proportions. In contingency planning earlier in the year, the judgement was that in the event of direct rule the RUC would 'loyally' support it. However, in the event of an illegal or unacceptable government coming to power, the expectation was that the RUC might divide into factions: one supporting the new administration, another UK rule, with many officers simply resigning. The planners also posed the question of whether the RUC and B Specials might have to be disarmed in the event of Britain deciding to 'depose' an illiberal or reactionary government. Summing up the lengthy briefing prepared for Callaghan, an official wrote: 'One gathers that Major Chichester-Clark is sympathetic to expansion [of the RUC] which naturally will cost money. But it is a long business. Meanwhile, naturally, the military commitment should be reduced as quickly as is compatible with safety.' The conventional wisdom at that point was that the low-key military deployment would be over in six months at most. The fear was that the street disorder would worsen, the overstretched RUC would not be able to cope and even more troops would be requested.

Meanwhile, on the opposite side of Whitehall from the Home Office, as the cabinet had ordered, the potentially explosive Top Secret document considering a complete military withdrawal from Northern Ireland had been prepared by the Ministry of Defence. At that point the armed forces contingent in Northern Ireland was 5,420 Army, 400 Royal Navy and 1,600 Royal Air Force. Together with 4,650 dependents and 5,070 locally employed civilians they occupied forty-five locations and contributed several million pounds a year to the local economy. The main Royal Navy facilities were the Joint Anti-Submarine School at Londonderry, an aircraft servicing workshop at Sydenham and an Armament Depot at Antrim for repairing and modifying the Mark 8 torpedo, the primary weapon of the submarine fleet. The RAF in Northern Ireland operated long-range maritime reconnaissance from Ballykelly and potential maritime strike and air defence from Aldergrove, both in fulfilment of NATO commitments. Workshops at the civilian-manned maintenance unit at Aldergrove maintained the airworthiness of Buccaneers, Canberras, Phantoms, and Varsity aircraft. Operation of the joint civil–military Air Traffic Control and Air Defence Radar at Bishop's Court was another responsibility.

Before the emergency, the Army's only direct operational concern with Northern Ireland itself related to the existence of the land frontier with the Irish Republic and the long history of IRA infiltration and disturbance. The MoD study said: 'There are, therefore, no direct operational reasons why the withdrawal of all service facilities from Northern Ireland should not be feasible. If all service facilities were withdrawn, assuming that the necessary sea and air transport resources were made available, the withdrawal of personnel with their dependents, stores, fuel, ammunition and vehicles and equipment would take about three months.' The main military considerations were that hasty temporary arrangements would have to be made to provide the necessary accommodation in Great Britain and that it would cost tens of millions of pounds to replicate some of the most vital military facilities. The drawback was that while this was being done Britain would be likely to incur criticism from NATO for resulting gaps in the alliance defence shield such as the loss of the Northern Ireland Territorial Army commitment, which would have a considerable effect on the operational capability to reinforce the British Army of the Rhine in emergency. The only enduring consequence of the withdrawal would be the probable loss of the four per cent of the British armed forces being recruited in Northern Ireland and the likelihood that traditional Irish regiments such as the Irish Guards, could therefore not continue in being.

The issues were summarised in a short minute for the Chiefs of Staff Committee on 20 May. The total withdrawal of all service personnel would be feasible but it would be a cumbersome and embarrassing operation. The minute raised an additional factor – the moral one – of whether the withdrawal of forces at short notice could be justified without giving the Northern Ireland government notice and time to build up a suitable security force to replace them. 'In no other "dependent territory" have we withdrawn before ensuring that the local government had adequate security forces at its disposal,' it noted.

Whatever the military assessment, there were, of course, formidable political consequences to be taken into account in contemplating such a far-reaching decision. Denis Healey and James Callaghan objectively spelled them out in detail for fellow ministers. A pull-out would inevitably aggravate the combustible situation in Northern Ireland, affect public opinion both inside and outside the United Kingdom and undermine Britain's standing in the world. It would leave the British government vulnerable – in practical, moral, constitutional and legal terms – to criticism for disowning its responsibilities, particularly among the minority groups in Northern Ireland. They would be blamed for the local economic effects of a withdrawal and Unionists, who would see the pull-out as a betrayal, might feel they had to adopt more repressive measures against the minority to maintain security. At the same time, the ministers said, the more extreme factions in the civil rights movement and the IRA might well see the decision as an opportunity to foment even greater disorder. The Dublin government, they continued, would probably not encourage these extremists directly but, politically, would find it hard to discourage them and would almost certainly feel obliged to reassert its own claim to sovereignty over the whole of Ireland and exert pressure to that end in the United Nations and elsewhere. The ministers concluded:

A final consideration is whether, if the Northern Ireland Government found itself wholly unable to maintain order, or if it collapsed altogether, the troops would have to return. If lives were being lost and property destroyed on a large scale, or if democratic government in Northern Ireland had come to an end, both domestic and world opinion would be critical and would demand that HMG should intervene directly, on whatever scale might be necessary, in what would after all remain a part of the United Kingdom. If, as is probable, this inter-vention could not be achieved without the use of troops, their task would be very much more difficult if they had severed the contacts which provide them with local intelligence, had lost their existing bases, and were obliged to undertake what might almost amount to the invasion of a hostile country.

In such circumstances, there was 'a probability that a greater degree of intervention would be required than if we were able to take swift action to prevent a conflagration with forces available on the ground'. In the end, these were the clinching considerations and the government decided against the withdrawal of the armed forces from Northern Ireland. The fact that such a radical step had even been considered was not disclosed to the administration in Belfast. (By now more and more of the secret classified documents about Northern Ireland circulating in Whitehall were coded with the additional legend: UK Eyes Only.) But the fact that such an apparently unthinkable proposition, with such symbolic significance and potentially dangerous consequences, was studied in such depth marked a major turning point in British policy towards Northern Ireland. While Northern Ireland nominally remained part of the United Kingdom, the Union was no longer entirely secure or sacrosanct.

Neither was Belfast told that the Home Office had looked at the possibility of sending in British police officers as an alternative to soldiers. The concept of mutual aid was well established in mainland Britain, where neighbouring forces helped each other out in dealing with major incidents when additional manpower was required. The RUC had never been included in such arrangements, although Scotland Yard had from time to time been asked to supply one or two senior detectives to help crack the comparatively rare phenomenon of a murder. However, the idea remained in abeyance for the time being. The prospect of flying in police reinforcements was fraught with problems, for, unlike the Army, police officers would have to be consulted and agree to the move; they would also be unarmed and unfamiliar with the law and geography of

Northern Ireland, and there were, anyway, legal difficulties about their powers and status if called on to operate there.

When the subject of further military assistance was raised by Belfast thereafter, London adopted a posture of discouragement; if the troops had to go in, that would amount to failure to maintain law and order, one of the core tasks of the Northern Ireland government. At Stormont, where control over justice and the police had been for so long one of the most effective instruments of Unionist power, the warning did not sink in and its implications were not even considered.

Rising tension through May and June 1969, with the customary policing burden arising from Orange parades being aggravated by a continuing series of civil rights demonstrations, inevitably culminated in widespread rioting in mid-July over the Twelfth, the climax of the annual marching season. The trouble was all too reminiscent of the 1920s and 1930s with the same localities and streets once again becoming sectarian battlegrounds. Even the most innocuous incident had come to spark off serious disorder. On the evening of Friday 16 May, for instance, a drunk fell down the stairs at Belfast's Edenderry Inn public house on the Crumlin Road. As the man lay injured, a customer called an ambulance and the publican called the police. A crowd soon gathered to watch the ambulance and when a police party in riot gear arrived scuffles developed. After a man was arrested, stones were thrown at the police, initiating a mêlée lasting forty-eight hours during which the police came under sustained attack as they tried to separate rival crowds. Sporadic but vicious clashes continued in the area for nearly a fortnight.

In this locality, and elsewhere in Belfast, vigilante groups, many of them manipulated by people with known IRA connections, were springing up and seeking completely to exclude the police from Catholic areas. For some years previously routine patrolling had been scaled down and the police moved cautiously, always getting back-up, when called into what had become known as 'no-go' areas. Anti-RUC feeling within the entire Catholic community was now running so strongly that efforts to maintain a police presence in many parts had virtually ended. More than ever before, they were seen, rightly or wrongly, to be on the Protestant side and there was a growing barrage of criticism of their activities, finding expression at community level meetings and in parliament where politicians such as Gerry Fitt and Paddy Devlin were drawing attention to RUC inadequacy as part of a campaign for fundamental police reform.

Devlin had been particularly tenacious in following up one particular incident. Back in January, the civil rights march from Belfast to Londonderry had been halted or diverted on several occasions by counter-demonstrations, but on the last leg of its journey the seventy marchers were ambushed by a 200-strong crowd gathered at Burntollet Bridge, on the main road between the two cities. Despite a police escort of some eighty officers, the attackers, armed with nail-studded cudgels and other weapons, pelted the march with heavy stones and then tore into the marchers, injuring many of them. In his autobiography, *Straight Left*, Devlin recalled how People's Democracy activists acquired newspaper photographs of the incident and visited areas in south Derry and east Tyrone, identifying a considerable number of the attackers, a very high proportion of them B Specials. With this evidence, Devlin tabled 452 parliamentary questions each asking if a named person was a member of the RUC or the B Specials. 'In spite of the fact that hundreds of them were identified this way, only a handful were ever charged with offences,' he wrote. 'I reckoned that more than a quarter of the replies I received were deliberately misleading and that those preparing the replies for the minister deliberately conspired to obstruct me.' Cross-questioning exposed the fact that the Ministry had far from complete records of the membership of the force. In parliament Robert Porter told Devlin: 'I do not accept that there was anything improper or half-hearted in the carrying out of these investigations.' But there was, in fact, constant stonewalling by the minister and senior officers as a mountain of allegations of heavy-handedness or brutality on the part of the police built up.

By far the greatest *cause célèbre* of this period was the case of Samuel Devenney. On the 19 April 1969, he was standing at the front door of his home at 69 William Street, Londonderry, with his son and two family friends. They were watching the ebb and flow of prolonged rioting between groups of youths and the police following the earlier banning of yet another civil rights march in the city. Some time after 8.30 p.m., as the rioting intensified, they went into their house and tried to close the front door. As they did so, a number of youths being pursued by the police pushed past them into the house, some going upstairs, others into the back yard. According to a subsequent investigation of events by a Scotland Yard team, a party of RUC officers in hot pursuit forced open the Devenneys' front door but did not make any attempt to apprehend the youths. Instead they kicked and batoned forty-two-year-old Devenney in front of some of his nine children, ranging in age from three to twenty-one. He was left lying on the floor with blood pouring from a number of head wounds and with his dentures and spectacles broken. During the incident, RUC officers also batoned and kicked sixteen-year-old Catherine Devenney, who was lying on a sofa recovering from surgery, and left her unconscious. Her older sister Ann twice flung herself across her father to protect him and was kicked, pulled up by her hair and thrown across the room against the fireplace. Before they left the police also beat Harry Devenney, aged twenty-one, with a baton and struck two family friends, one of whom was left unconscious.

Samuel Devenney was taken straight to hospital and released after three days but after suffering a coronary thrombosis he was re-admitted within twenty-four hours and remained there until 19 May. He died on 17 July 1969. His family took the view that his death was caused by the effects of the police assault and the attendance at his funeral, estimated at 30,000, underlined the extent of public concern about the incident and police involvement in it. Although a general amnesty in respect of all criminal offences committed between 5 October 1968 and 6 May 1969 prevented any prosecution in the case, an RUC investigation was carried out and failed to identify the officers concerned because of what was later described as a 'conspiracy of silence' within the RUC. The Scotland Yard detectives also failed to expose the perpetrators but did identify four officers who allegedly knew what happened but 'were in fear of retribution from colleagues' if they told the truth.

In due course, after considering all the evidence, including the fact that Devenney had a heart condition prior to the assault, an inquest ruled that he had died from natural causes. The Scotland Yard team examined medical evidence from seven sources, including those who had treated the dead man and an independent consultant employed by his family. Their views on the relationship between his injuries and his death varied and they declined to reach any conclusion. The minister responsible, Porter, like his predecessor Craig, consistently denounced complaints about police conduct and cases like this as part of an organised 'smear campaign' against the police. This unyielding attitude – the RUC right or wrong – only compounded the degree of alienation with Catholics. Some effort to recognise and alleviate Catholic concerns would have paid enormous dividends. In reality, with police morale crumbling, acts of indiscipline were becoming more commonplace as they inexorably lost their grip on the situation on the ground.

In London, Northern Ireland's seemingly unstoppable slide to the brink of anarchy was being very carefully monitored and there was fresh consternation when news came through from Belfast that the intelligence liaison officers, who had been put into RUC headquarters had relocated to a 'nearby military installation', the Army's Kinnegar Ordnance Depot in Holywood, after what Sir Martin Furnivall-Jones, the head of MI5, described as 'a modest amount of friction'. At a meeting of the Joint Intelligence Committee in London on 31 July, he said 'there was always the danger of friction when a security liaison officer tried to drive the local authorities too fast'. Another source of contention, the spymaster reported, was Peacocke's concern that intelligence material he had concealed from his own ministers might find its way back to them after it had been reported to London by the Security Service officers. His request to be copied in on the reports they were submitting to London was firmly turned down.

A few days later, Belfast revealed to London the first significant sign that events were beginning to outstrip the capacity of the RUC to cope with them alone. Writing to Callaghan on 4 August, Chichester-Clark asked for the threshold at which the police could use CS gas to be lowered. The RUC had long held stocks of CN gas and respirators, but earlier in the year the Home Office had explicitly warned Belfast not to use it because of fears about its long-term effect on humans. In any case, the respirators to protect the RUC officers from its effects were obsolete. London refused to release supplies of CS gas during prolonged disturbances over the Twelfth period in Derry because agreed conditions were not in place. So, on 17 July, after a formal request from Belfast, the British government approved an arrangement to make Army supplies of CS gas and 300 respirators available to the RUC for use when approved by the home affairs minister and when there was no other option to break up disorderly crowds except opening fire on them or calling in troops.

Porter, whom British diplomats in Belfast regarded as 'a politician against his will with a strong literal [*sic*] conscience and no more than an ordinary breadth of vision', decided that as he would have to authorise use of the gas, he wanted to experience the effects to satisfy himself they were not 'unduly severe'. So one afternoon he was flown from Stormont to the windswept military ranges on the beach at Ballykinler, County Down, where, after working out the wind direction, a soldier set off a gas grenade and the minister stepped downwind into the path of the cloud of acrid, white smoke. 'My nose and eyes started streaming, my throat and chest was irritated and I experienced laboured breathing. It was very, very uncomfortable,' he recalled later. 'However, after about ten minutes or so, I began to feel OK again and decided the gas was a relatively humane way of coping with riot conditions. It could be said to be preferable to baton charges which leave the police open to allegations of brutality,' he concluded.

Now, before the existing protocol had even been exercised, Chichester-Clark was asking for an even lower threshold enabling the use of the gas to contain rioting and protect property. Foreshadowing 'the next potentially difficult period in Londonderry' on 12th August, he said, 'my colleagues and I hope that such will not be the case and that even, if there is trouble it can be contained by conventional methods', but he warned that if use of the gas was denied 'unpalatable alternatives would otherwise have to be considered'. London duly authorised the request and all eyes were focused on the forthcoming Apprentice Boys parade. In Northern Ireland military involvement was now regarded as inevitable, a view most reluctantly shared in Whitehall, still officially anxious to defer military involvement. So senior military officers had been taking all measures short of actually putting soldiers on the streets to prepare for eventual deployment. The preparations had included two half-day seminars with the police about how they would work together, but when the call finally came, in the late afternoon of Sunday 3 August, it was found that the necessary apparatus was not yet in anything like smooth working order.

The previous day serious trouble had erupted in the ironically named Unity Flats area on the fringe of Belfast city centre. It began at lunchtime when rival crowds clashed just before a Junior Orange parade was due to pass the Catholic-occupied block of flats. By early evening, when the parade returned, a crowd of some 3,000 had gathered and sporadic trouble intensified as the evening wore on, later spreading to the Shankill and Ardoyne. At ten o'clock the next morning, Sunday, having sent his exhausted and injured men home to recuperate, Harold Wolseley, the Police Commissioner for Belfast, contacted the commanding officer of the Second Battalion of the Queen's Regiment, based at Palace Barracks, Holywood, and warned that if the trouble continued he might need assistance. Lieutenant-Colonel J Fletcher accordingly put a company of his troops on two-hour standby from four o'clock that afternoon. As the police feared, more trouble did flare in mid-afternoon and as the largely Protestant crowds increased, they made ever more violent assaults on the police struggling to prevent the mob reaching the flats. As cars were set alight and the burning and looting of premises began, the RUC called in an armoured car, a water cannon, a barrier-breaking vehicle and Land Rovers to try to disperse the rioters but the 200-strong force of police, many of whom were still suffering from the strain of the previous day, fought an increasingly losing battle to retain control.

Shortly before 5 p.m., Wolseley spoke to Fletcher who had come to his office at Castlereagh, advised that all police reserves had been committed and asked for troops to help restore order. This crucial decision had the support of Sam Bradley, the city's deputy police commissioner. The request was immediately referred to Army headquarters at Lisburn where the chief of staff, Brigadier Tony Dyball, said the troops could not be committed until political approval had been given from London. In the meantime, Wolseley contacted Peacocke, who was attending an emergency cabinet meeting at Stormont, and told him he had requested military assistance. Peacocke was far from pleased that such a grave step had been taken. Although he always claimed that what he called the 'political angle' played no part in his opposition to the move, the Belfast cabinet was now highly concerned about the 'constitutional implications' and had discussed their very serious reservations about them that afternoon. So, although a company of troops (about sixty) was moved to the police station at Castlereagh as a precaution about 6 p.m., there was great relief that they did not need to be deployed after Peacocke called in additional police from outside Belfast who were helped by bad weather to bring the trouble under control. 'Rain stopped play,' said the military report, noting the soldiers returned to their barracks at 2 a.m. on 4 August.

After the weekend, there was a flurry of clarifying contact between Belfast and London. On the Monday, London warned again of constitutional consequences if troops had to be used, including the possible suspension of the parliament and government. The Labour administration was concerned not to be seen to be propping up Unionist failure with British soldiers and above all was unwilling to allow the Stormont authorities to give orders to the military. Ministers feared they would simply be used as a stick to beat Catholics. The stern tone of the warning was such that Harold Black was sent to London the next day under political orders to argue that it would only be necessary for London to take over responsibility for 'law and order' if the troops went in and that stripping Belfast of its other powers should not arise. During the day, London took the view that if the troops were simply needed for a swift firefighting operation and quickly returned to their barracks, constitutional consequences would not arise. The more likely scenario, they believed, was one of prolonged Army intervention and that raised 'insuperable difficulties' .

Black reported back to Chichester-Clark and Porter after his meeting but there was anger in Belfast when this proposition was spelled out in the *Financial Times* next morning, asserting that troops could only be used after the Stormont government had surrendered its political authority to Westminster. The article said:

The British Government's view is that it would be the height of folly to allow its troops (or police) to be under the political direction of another Government which, rightly or wrongly, is regarded as essentially Protestant in outlook and which would use the troops to deal with disorders which were religious in origin. Ministers believe that it would be equally unacceptable for troops to be used – no matter whose direction they came under – if they were there to maintain law and order for the existing Northern Ireland Government.

As soon as he read the paper, Chichester-Clark first rang Porter and then telephoned Callaghan at his home in Sussex, following up his call with an irate letter to Callaghan in which he expressed his 'irritation' on reading 'regular press references to the use of "British troops" [here] as if it were some sort of external territory. The British Army is our Army too. I and many Ulstermen have been proud to serve in it,' Chichester-Clark declared, adding, 'It never for a moment occurred to us that its role in relation to Northern Ireland differed in any way from that role in relation to Great Britain.' Complaining that they had been put 'in an almost impossible situation', he said:

> The grave decision as to whether the civil power can no longer cope with a situation ought surely to be made on law and order grounds and not on political ones. I do not think it is right that the decision should be taken with a sword of Damocles hanging over our heads.' [. . .] You should be in no doubt that any move to replace a representative Government, freely and democratically elected as recently as February of this year, would be wholly unacceptable to the great majority of Ulster people. I must make it clear to you that the people of Northern Ireland are as determined to have their own Government as the people of the South were from 1919 on; and you should seriously consider the history of how Dublin Castle tried to cope with Sinn Fein at that time. As matters now stand, newspaper speculation about your intentions – which does not entirely misrepresent your thinking as you made it known to me – could have the most unfortunate effect of encouraging further disorder on the part of those whose aim has always been to overthrow the Government of Northern Ireland. Anyone who seeks that end and who reads in the newspapers that use of the Army may involve suspension of that Government, is surely going to redouble his efforts to escalate matters to a point where the police can no longer control the situation.

Chichester-Clark and Porter flew to London forty-eight hours later and held a two-hour meeting with Callaghan and his senior advisers. Before their arrival Callaghan's private secretary circulated a note to Downing Street, the Foreign Office and the Ministry of Defence stating that he was 'going to rest on his position' and 'leave it to the Northern Ireland ministers to make the running'. Although there was indeed great anxiety about the likelihood of a peaceful outcome to the looming march in Derry, there was little sense at the meeting that the commitment of troops, with the threatened 'consequences', was actually imminent. Indeed there was a clearly hypothetical flavour to the exchanges. Chichester-Clark and Porter made it clear they now accepted that, at the very least, implicit in any use of troops would be some surrender of their responsibility for law and order. Porter conceded that 'that would mean someone sitting in my seat'. But that was not enough for Callaghan and Sir Philip Allen, his permanent secretary, who insisted that such a straight division of functions was difficult to envisage. The question of the RUC having to transfer its loyalty to the UK government could cause difficulties and might involve even more troop commitments, said Callaghan. They strongly favoured a complete transfer because law and order would inevitably affect the entire range of government policies. When Chichester-Clark suggested these could be retained in Belfast, with the Northern Ireland administration acting on an 'agency' basis for the British government, Callaghan agreed to look at the implications. Returning to the RUC, he repeatedly urged the Northern Ireland leaders to speed up the expansion of the RUC from 3,000 to 3,500 within twelve months and by similar increments thereafter. An offer to pay a special under-manning allowance to attract the additional recruits was also made, but they still forecast it would take three years to make the target. Chichester-Clark and Porter, clearly sensitive to RUC morale, warned Callaghan that his plan to send two British police advisers to Belfast should be very carefully handled in case the force thought the assistance was being imposed on them.

This meeting was remarkable for it amounted to the British government repudiating, for the first time, the partition settlement of almost half a century earlier. From the Belfast perspective, it was momentous in that the Northern Ireland administration was offering partially to surrender its prized responsibility for law and order, one of its core powers. Despite this incredible new political vista and its potentially volatile conse-quences, which were clearly spelled out to them at its meeting on 11 August, the Northern Ireland cabinet agreed that Porter should feel free to take the initiative to call for military assistance if necessary. This decision, it was said, was taken in the light of the earlier police difficulties on the streets, and not with any specific prospect that it would be invoked in the light of the march next day. Regardless of the implications, the much-criticised Northern Ireland government was not prepared to delay calling in troops for political reasons to stave off what they now understood would be the most fundamental redefinition of the Belfast–London relationship since partition. Hitherto, reform in the teeth of the Troubles was firmly within the existing framework. With soldiers on the streets, there would be an entirely new and uncharted situation and the British government was making it clear they wanted to take control. Nevertheless, his colleagues bravely authorised Porter, the appropriate minister, to do what he thought was necessary entirely on security grounds even if that meant their own position being compromised.

As the 15,000 members of the Apprentice Boys of Derry converged on the city for their annual march the next day, Tuesday 12 August, there was still a growing sense of crisis. Over preceding days there had been more sporadic trouble and, in the graphic words of the subsequent Scarman report, the point had been reached where 'the sectarian disease that was infecting society was too deep-seated to respond to a Prime Minister's appeal or to police action. The two communities, sometimes from choice, sometimes under compulsion, but always in conditions of wretchedness and misery, fell apart into their respective "ghettos", where at least they had a sensation of security.' After Porter decided to let the march go ahead rather than ban it, the police concentrated 700 officers in the city, one fifth of their entire strength, but hopes that it would take place without trouble proved to be in vain. At 2.30 p.m., as the long, colourful procession passed through Waterloo Place, where thirty police and a crowd barrier were sited, a handful of nails and stones was thrown at the marchers. Then a middle-aged man with a catapult aimed a glass marble at them. 'From this small beginning developed a riot, enveloping the city for two days and nights,' the Scarman tribunal later reported. Indeed it said that since the rioting in July 'the ability to maintain public order in the city had slipped out of police control: peace depended not upon the will of the lawfully constituted authority but upon the whim of the youngsters of the Bogside'.

The 'Battle of the Bogside', as it came to be known, proved to be the breaking of the RUC. The ill-prepared force, overwhelmed by months of constant civil disturbance, finally reached the point of collapse. So too did the Catholic community in their already uneasy relationship with the force. In the words of a local priest, Fr Anthony Mulvey, to Scarman: 'There was what I would call an apparently complete unanimity in opposition to the police force.' He went on to say that he regarded the situation 'as a community in revolt rather than just a street disturbance or a riot'. By evening, so desperate and disorganised had the police become that many abandoned efforts to separate the rival crowds and took to returning stones at the Catholic crowds. Others slumped to the ground exhausted and slept in doorways. Graham Shillington, then deputy inspector-general, remembers travelling from Belfast to the city that evening.

> It really was a very disturbing sight. Half the city seemed to be in flames and there was rioting. My men had been out on duty all day and were exhausted on their feet and, of course, accepting an awful lot of casualties from bottles, stones and so on. But there was great spirit. I mean the injured chaps were coming in for first aid treatment and insisting on going out on duty again.

Despite such bravery, with buildings burning all around the city centre and police strength being steadily eroded by injuries, including from petrol bombs, the senior officers on the spot told Shillington they were unanimous that the time had come to use CS gas. Indeed, several of the local police commanders were already of the view that only the military could now restore order. During his journey from Belfast, Shillington had been informed by radio that the home affairs minister had authorised the use of gas, if necessary, fulfilling the first condition. Having seen the situation for himself, Shillington telephoned the minister and then, for the first time in the United Kingdom, ordered it to be fired after an appropriate loudspeaker warning. Respirators were quickly handed out to the police but such was the lack of preparation and training for the eventuality that many were nearly suffocated after failing to remove a cardboard packing disc from the filter. Over the next two days waves of gas were fired, interrupting but not suppressing the continuous rioting.

As disturbances spread and erupted throughout Northern Ireland, stretching the hard-pressed police even more, Chichester-Clark broadcast on radio and television in the evening to announce the Government was mobilising 8,500 members of the Special Constabulary to relieve the regular police and enable them to concentrate on the public disorder, a necessary step in the process that had been agreed with London for use of troops. It was now only a matter of time before the Army went in and a forward detachment, two companies of the First Battalion Prince of Wales Own Regiment, was already positioned at the Sea Eagle Naval Base, a few minutes drive from the epicentre of the rioting.

Up to this point Belfast had remained comparatively quiet, but some hours after Chichester-Clark's broadcast, Jack Lynch, the Irish prime minister, announced that his government was to request the United Nations to send a peace-keeping force immediately. It was evident, he said, that the Stormont government was no longer in control of the situation, and he had arranged for military field hospitals to be made ready along the border. At that time, the bedraggled Irish Army could not have mounted any significant presence on the frontier without taking the buses off the streets of Dublin, but the broadcast considerably raised tension and eyewitnesses reported that almost immediately afterwards there was a distinct upsurge in the ongoing violence at many locations in Belfast. Militant Catholics were working to this end in a bid to stretch the police and prevent them from concentrating their efforts in Londonderry. By now, apart from the debilitating events there, the police and Specials were coping with disturbances in many parts of Belfast and a number of outlying towns such as Armagh, Newry, Dungiven, Coalisland and Dungannon. Such was the pressure on police resources that they had withdrawn several Commer armoured personnel carriers from 'mothball' storage. These vehicles, designed for border patrolling, were put on the streets in the Falls area of west Belfast where, around 11 p.m., in two separate incidents, they came under small-arms fire and a vintage hand grenade was thrown. All vehicles were temporarily withdrawn before being replaced by Shorland armoured cars, which normally carry a .30 Browning machine gun capable of firing 500 to 600 rounds a minute, but which were initially unarmed because there had not been enough time to fit the weapons to the turrets.

These escalatory incidents instantly assumed an importance well beyond their actual ferocity and by the next morning, 14 August, the government and police were convinced they were facing an armed IRA uprising. Given the closed mindsets of those concerned there was no other conclusion they were capable of drawing. For years, at the government's insistence, they had portrayed the IRA as the enemy, waiting to swoop down from the hills at a suitable opportunity, and in the midst of the turmoil now engulfing them they could conceive of no other circumstances or causes for the extent of the civil disturbance that were raging. At a political level there was still no appreciation of the deep sense of the grievance among Catholics, intensified by the slow and graceless pace of reform. There was also a gross intelligence failure in objectively identifying that, despite some capacity for agitation, the IRA threat to the state was non-existent and that the dissent came from the deep-seated resentment of the majority of Catholics who had simply run out of patience with those they saw as their oppressors. Stormont also remained blissfully unaware of the depths of hostility that had now been aroused against the police as a result of the events which had begun at Caledon and intensified thereafter. The blame lay with successive generations of inadequate political leaders and many senior police officers, who were either partisan or complacent enough happily to provide 'intelligence' to feed the fears of their political manipulators and justify their repressive and discriminatory policies. A minority of more visionary and hard-headed officers had tried to warn that the conflagration was coming and that when it did the government and the police would be unprepared and unable to cope with it. They were ignored as alarmist, but they were right, and that point had now been reached. As the Scarman Tribunal later pointed out, while some of his senior officers had quickly learned the lesson of their inadequacy from ongoing events, Peacocke blindly refused to appreciate the real situation and continued to act as if police strength and capability was sufficient to maintain the public peace.

During the day of 14 August, the police grip in Londonderry slipped further by the hour. With the number still on their feet in the city now halved from the 700 originally deployed and no reinforcements available from elsewhere, Specials were brought in to help hold the existing police lines. Their presence inevitably angered the Catholic side and by lunchtime the police were driven back to the point where they were all but besieged in Victoria Barracks in the centre of the city and talking of being able to hold it only by force of arms. Defending the police station was vital, for without its wireless and communications links, command and control of the police on the ground and contact with headquarters in Belfast would be severed. More importantly, television pictures of rioters overrunning it would signal a complete and humiliating collapse of law and order. But it was only as the crowds milled ever more dangerously in the proximity of the police station that Peacocke, confronted with the reality of the sheer physical exhaustion of the police in Londonderry, was finally persuaded of the need to make the call for the Army to move in.

Unofficially, final preparations for the Army to be deployed were already well under way. During the late morning, Lieutenant-General Sir Ian Freeland, who had only taken up the post of General Officer

Commanding on 9 July, had crisply outlined his approach to the Ministry of Defence. His troops would go in, surround and secure the station and evacuate the weary RUC personnel through a secure channel. If the rival crowds could not be peacefully separated, the soldiers would do so with CS gas, fired on the ground and dropped by helicopters. In the last resort, the general, who was widely known in the Army as 'smiling death', warned he would order them to open fire. In no circumstances would he send his forces into the Bogside. Stormont was kept fully in the picture and at 2.45 p.m., with Porter's approval, Harold Black, the cabinet secretary, telephoned his counterpart at the Home Office in London to advise that the situation would soon be reached in Londonderry where the police would be unable to contain the situation and the RUC would then make a formal request for Army assistance. The reason would be to enable the police to hold Victoria Barracks and to prevent 'occupation of the city centre by a riotous mob with the prospect of arson, looting, extensive damage to property and injury to the populace'. Peacocke signed and made the formal request to Freeland at 4.30 p.m.: 'In view of the continuing worsening of the situation in Londonderry City, I now request the assistance of forces under your command in Londonderry City.'

By this time, Wilson, Callaghan and Roy Hattersley, standing in for the defence secretary, Denis Healey, had all agreed that the GOC should be authorised to comply. The arrival of the soldiers had an immediate calming effect on the situation in Londonderry but, now that they were involved, Callaghan no longer needed to observe the polite fiction that Northern Ireland was responsible for its own security. He had made his plans for the moment and wasted no time muscling in. In a telephone conversation with Chichester-Clark at 7.45 that evening he said he had decided that since the new GOC would clearly have little experience in police matters, an inspector of constabulary, John McKay, was to be sent to Northern Ireland to act as a liaison officer. He also revealed he was sending two police 'consultants', who would report back to him. The prime minister agreed that the title 'consultants' was better than any alternative word, such as 'advisers', and after some discussion it was agreed that they would leave for Northern Ireland the next morning.

In another indication that the creaking policing order was to be independently scrutinised as never before, the home secretary raised the possibility of creating a separate police force for the area under the control of the recently appointed Londonderry Development Commissioners, who had assumed the functions of the local council. He suggested the new force might consist of former RUC members and some policemen recruited from England and Wales with new recruits to police work from the Catholic elements in the city. Chichester-Clark readily agreed that this was an idea well worth studying and promised to do so immediately.

Overnight, while Derry remained tense but peaceful, under military protection, the first deaths of the conflict took place as Belfast experienced the most serious night of unrest for generations. During the day of 14 August, the five Shorland vehicles available to the police in Belfast were parked at Musgrave Street station, where each was fitted with its customary machine gun and loaded with 500 rounds of ammunition. Three-man crews, a driver, a gunner and an observer, were selected for each of the vehicles but so dangerously improvised had police operations become that none of these crews had ever trained or worked together before. Indeed one of the men had never even seen a vehicle of this type. They were deployed from the city centre station at 5 p.m.: three to Tennent Street in the Shankill area and two to Crumlin Road. Soon after midnight, after Herbert Roy, a twenty-six-year-old Protestant civilian, was killed and three policemen received gunshot injuries, three Shorlands were directed to patrol Divis Street where, soon after 1 a.m., one or more of them opened fire, killing nine-year-old Patrick Rooney in bed at his home in the St Brendan's block of the Divis Flats complex where thirteen dwellings were struck by bullets. Almost immediately after this firing, police marksmen on the roof of nearby Hastings Street station, believing that gunfire was coming from the roof of the in the flats, returned fire, killing Hugh McCabe, a soldier home on leave. At about 2 a.m., with clashes continuing, a cadre of IRA members fired automatic weapons into Percy Street, inflicting a number of casualties. This fire was returned from a Shorland, and afterwards most of the homes in the Catholic-occupied part of the street were destroyed by fire.

Meanwhile across in the north of the city, where rival, hostile crowds, 'spoiling for a fight' as Scarman later concluded, roamed the streets, Samuel McLarnon, aged twenty-seven, and Michael Lynch, twenty-eight, both Catholics, died in separate incidents as a result of heavy police firing in which at least ten others were wounded. Looking back on the night's events in the area, one of the police commanders described them as 'absolutely frightening'. Of the five deaths in Belfast overnight, the police were responsible for four.

The Scarman tribunal later decided that the police operation had been seriously at fault and singled out several aspects for criticism. The 'heavy and indiscriminate' Browning machine guns used in Belfast were 'a menace to the innocent as well as the guilty' and should never have been used in an urban area. Firing them into the block of flats, 'was wholly unjustifiable'. There was also culpable failure on the part of the police to prevent Protestant mobs from burning down Catholic houses at Conway Street, where members of the RUC who were present declined to take effective action.

Away from Belfast, the County Inspector in Armagh, T Hedley Buchanon, who later testified that he 'believed there was incipient civil war', decided to reinforce his sparse resources by deploying armed B Specials in the city. During a night of running battles with rioters in the town centre, a heavily armed platoon of seventeen Specials, from the village of Tynan twelve miles away, travelling in four private cars, encountered a hostile crowd behind a blazing car at Cathedral Road. Believing they were isolated in an ambush, they jumped out and instantly opened fire on the crowd, killing thirty-year-old John Gallagher, a Catholic, who was shot in the back. The platoon then drove to an RUC station where they cleaned their weapons. Despite an RUC arms check they made no initial report of the shooting and subsequently denied all involvement in it. After sifting a mass of conflicting evidence about the incident, the tribunal decided that the conduct of the Tynan party afterwards was 'indicative of a state of panic among them and is certainly consistent with a state of guilt. Grave as was the misconduct of the USC [Ulster Special Constabulary] in firing into the crowd, the Tribunal considers that a measure of responsibility rests with the County Inspector, who put an untrained but armed party of USC, drawn from a country area, into an alarming town riot without briefing or leadership.'

Back in Belfast, daybreak on the morning of 15 August brought no respite from conflict. In the Falls–Shankill area, an exodus had begun from streets littered with debris and blanketed by smoke from burning buildings, houses and vehicles. Families were piling their belongings into vans, cars and even handcarts and soon, lorries and other vehicles were being hijacked to speed the moves. Many of the 1,505 Catholic and 315 Protestant households displaced by intimidation or fear during July and August moved during these hate-filled hours. Similarly the bulk of the onslaught on Catholic-owned licensed premises occurred at this time: altogether seventy-six of some 480 licensed premises in the city were either destroyed, damaged or looted during the violent summer. But the violence and killing was still not concluded. During the afternoon more trouble erupted at several points in the Falls–Shankill battleground, the most serious incident coming near Clonard Monastery at about 3.45 p.m. when Gerald McAuley, a fifteen-year-old Catholic who was later acknowledged as a member of the IRA, was shot dead by a Protestant sniper.

According to Scarman's criticism, the police took no action during the day to restrain or disperse the mobs on the streets or to protect lives and property. Apart from limited patrolling by the five Shorlands, the remaining numbers of police were taken off the streets and ordered to defend their stations against the IRA uprising many of their most senior commanders were convinced was now under way. Another reason the police pulled back was that they expected the Army to be on the streets in Belfast by 10 or 11 a.m. The decision to ask for the Army in the city had been taken by Wolseley and Bradley at 4.30 a.m. when they realised the enormity of the crisis that had developed and that it was absolutely beyond police control. Such was the confusion that night, however, that there also seemed to be no effective control over the police, at least from headquarters. In his memoir, *Stormont in Crisis*, Ken Bloomfield, who was soon to succeed Black as cabinet secretary, recalls how 'the information coming in was extraordinarily confused. Over this chaos there presided, at times in his silk dressing gown, the rather languid Noel Cowardesque figure of Tony Peacocke.' It took, in fact, seven hours for Peacocke to convey his Belfast commanders' decision to Porter, which he did only when they met around 11.30 a.m., shortly before a scheduled cabinet meeting. The written request for Army assistance in Belfast was cleared promptly by Porter who then presented it to the cabinet at a meeting delayed until noon. After twenty-five minutes' discussion, a copy of the formal and, it must be said, distinctly hysterical request for military aid in Belfast was transmitted to the Home Office in London:

From Inspector-General, Royal Ulster Constabulary to the General Officer Commanding, Northern Ireland:

I have to inform you that, following the violence in the City of Belfast last night, renewed clashes are occurring at this time, 11.30 am, 15 August 1969. The Commissioner has informed me that all immediately available police have been committed but that he is unable to separate the rioting crowds and has had to fall back to defend his police stations. In the circumstances outlined, I now request further assistance of forces under your command in Belfast City. Information is to hand from a reliable source that an infiltration of members of the Irish Republican Army is about to commence from Eire into Northern

Ireland. It is the intention to escalate the degree of control over inward-bound traffic and to this end assistance in the form of patrols by armoured cars is also requested. The information indicates that the infiltrators will be armed and the support of mobile armoured units, which I cannot supply, would be of material assistance in countering these subversive activities against the Government and people of Northern Ireland.

London was now desperately trying to get sufficient numbers of troops into Northern Ireland to meet the rapidly increasing demand for them and United Kingdom ministerial approval for the deployment of troops in Belfast was not officially given until 3.10 p.m. However, since midday the commanding officers of the two battalions already in position, 2 Battalion Queen's Regiment and the Royal Regiment of Wales, together with the Commander of 39 Brigade, Brigadier Hudson, had been in conference with Wolseley and Bradley at Castlereagh. Against a background of totally unfounded rumour about the IRA takeover, it was eventually decided that because he did not have sufficient men to occupy the twisted path of the invisible 'Orange-Green' line which divided the communities in west Belfast the Brigadier would put his available men initially on the main Falls Road and Divis Street. They were not however in position on the streets until early evening, well after more rioting had broken out. Their arrival, as in Londonderry, had an immediate calming effect but serious rioting recurred in the Ardoyne and other areas, and another man died in a shooting incident before troops were sent there the following day when reinforcements arrived.

Meanwhile in London, early on 15 August, Callaghan had a meeting at the Home Office with McKay, Freeland's police adviser, and another official who was being sent to Lisburn as political adviser. They were told there were no rules for the job, they would have to judge for themselves what role they would play. Later he briefed his police consultants, Sir Douglas Osmond and Robert Mark, on their task in Belfast. Osmond was Chief Constable of Hampshire and current president of the Association of Chief Police Officers. Mark, formerly Chief Constable of Leicestershire, had recently been appointed Deputy Commissioner of the Metropolitan Police with a brief from Callaghan to root out the legendary corruption in its ranks. Their terms of reference charged them to act as consultants 'on all police matters' to the Northern Ireland government and inspector-general and as 'observers', to report back to the home secretary the way in which the RUC and Specials were deployed and the tactics they employed in dealing with disturbances. Most significantly of all they were asked to make recommendations for the long-term improvement of the police organisation in Northern Ireland. They were also told to wear plain clothes and advised that they had no official authority. That afternoon they were flown to Belfast by the RAF, Mark departing from Northolt and picking up Osmond from an airfield in Hampshire on the way.

In his autobiography, *In the Office of Constable*, Mark described what they saw on their way into the city from the airport as being like 'Dante's *Inferno*'. 'We were taken on a circular tour by the RUC in which we counted something in the order of 100 fires, none of which was being attended by the fire brigade for fear of reprisals.' Their first call was to police headquarters at Knock where, according to the series of situation bulletins filed to Callaghan over the next couple of days and the report they compiled on their return, they found the same appalling state of disarray noted by Ken Bloomfield. A makeshift operations room had been set up in the communications centre but it was so inadequate the inspector-general could not give them 'any information as to the disposition of his manpower or of the frequency and magnitude of incidents. In spite of the situation . . . none of the senior officers at the headquarters apparently thought it worthwhile to don uniform.' Most business, they found, was transacted by Peacocke, who 'held court' in his office 'making sensational and emotional statements' to impress a 'very tired' minister of home affairs, 'who seemed to take second place' to him. Soon after their arrival, in Porter's presence, Peacocke refused to let the two senior British policemen go out into the troubled areas of Belfast to see the situation for themselves. 'We did, however, subsequently penetrate these areas and found nothing like the extreme situation which he presented.'

A day later, again with the minister present, Peacocke referred to intelligence that more serious trouble would take place. 'There's going to be a massacre tonight,' he said. 'This was clearly based on the flimsiest of information and in the event his forecast was not substantiated in the slightest degree,' Osmond and Mark reported. After an incident at a police station in Armagh, they were also unimpressed when Peacocke ordered the formation of three armoured columns to patrol the border. This was consistent with what they described as the RUC being 'traditionally obsessed by the threat from the IRA'. In their judgement, they believed the violence could equally well be attributed to other factors, 'including the penetration of sensitive areas by the B Specials'.

The organisation for gathering intelligence was anyway what they described as 'woefully inadequate' and they found that the way the Special Branch was structured did not provide for 'proper collation, evaluation or dissemination of intelligence'. MI5, which was observing an 'uneasy truce' with the RUC after the 'personality clash' between its man and the inspector-general a month earlier, told Osmond and Mark that IRA intelligence was played 'close to the chest' by the RUC, but the two officers doubted 'whether the intelligence gathering organisation is such as to ensure a great deal of valuable intelligence being forthcoming'. Only thirty extremists out of a planned 150 had been detained in an arrest operation on the very morning of their arrival.

In his first report on 18 August, an obviously astonished Mark noted: 'So far as I can see no senior officer contemplates any eventual change in the status or constitutional position of the police. They see this operation as a short-term military exercise to prolong indefinitely a status quo which they find unremarkable.' He went on to say that it was 'urgently necessary to reduce the melodrama and tension' and that 'thanks to the presence of troops in adequate numbers', the first moves ought to be an immediate reduction in the visible use of firearms except for the protection of police stations and fixed vulnerable points or for special purposes. In particular, he recommended the B Special Constabulary should be disarmed altogether and only carry arms when on duty under the command of a regular police officer. Evidently an instant mutual antipathy developed between them and Peacocke, for Mark reported it was 'already clear that the Inspector-General has no intention of consulting us on police matters', and further suggested:

> The foregoing changes might not be capable of implementation without a change of command of the force. That might be advantageous if for no other reason than that the present IG has been familiarized with a unique degree of autocratic control and would be unlikely to implement them with enthusiasm. He would argue, probably correctly, that such a change would result in the virtual disintegration of the B Specials. Provided there is a prospect of military assistance, even on a reducing scale, that is an eventuality which should not cause dismay.

Over the next few days, as the two consultants extended their observation of the RUC beyond the Knock headquarters, they found officers at all levels affected by 'extreme fatigue' and a prevailing atmosphere of 'emotion, exaggeration and rumour'. The lower ranks were typical policemen, some of them perhaps of rather lower standard than in England and Wales but basically sound, they said, although they had the impression that 'the Force was defeated and depressed. The men genuinely feel that they have done their impartial best and are bewildered at the public and press reaction. They accept that they are discredited but feel (probably rightly) they have been done an injustice.' Osmond and Mark were impressed by Graham Shillington, who, unlike Peacocke, had visited areas of special difficulty during the troubles and was 'more rational and unemotional. He gave us several indications that he differed with the Inspector-General on matters of policy but he was nevertheless essentially loyal'. With individual exceptions, they found the force leadership 'by no means impressive', but Wolseley and Bradley, the commissioner and deputy commissioner responsible for Belfast, were praised for giving 'more positive leadership, being out on the ground in uniform with their men and remaining in touch with the situation'.

> The Commissioner was desperately tired and clearly feeling the strain; he was of a gentle personality but was steeped in the traditions of the RUC, and, being unable to visualise any different system of policing, was depressed at the thought that the RUC in its present form was unlikely to continue to exist. The Deputy Commissioner was of a different type; of impressive physique, he was a sound, practical policeman anxious to be up and doing, and he was clearly competent in any local operational situation. He is probably at his ceiling but is none the worse for that in his existing appointment.

At Londonderry they said the wrong men were in command. The county inspector, Gerry Mahon, only promoted in July, was 'weak and ineffectual' and was overwhelmed by County Inspector (Traffic) Mickey Magill, 'a pompous, self-important and dogmatic personality sent temporarily to assist him. The two individuals were quite unsuited for dealing with what is probably the most intractable problem with which any police force has ever been faced,' said the consultants, who added that they were, however, supported by one or two good policemen and 'a particularly useful' district inspector Michael McAtamney. (He would later become deputy chief constable.) In areas of Belfast, Londonderry and elsewhere, they found the police almost entirely on the defensive:

> Police stations were bolted and barred. Sentries armed with machine guns were on duty. Large numbers of men were sitting about in

inadequate accommodation waiting for something to happen. There seemed to be a 'stable door' policy.

At the Rosemount Police Station in Londonderry, situated on the perimeter of the Bogside area, still bearing signs of recent attacks, all doors were locked and the windows were barred and shuttered.

> The station was filled with policemen waiting about, all fully armed, and no police patrolling was going on. The station was described to us as 'under siege' and had to be held because of the wireless mast in the grounds. In spite of the men having nothing to do, the whole place was in a filthy, untidy condition and vehicles recently used in operations had not been cleaned up or serviced.

There was a similar atmosphere at the headquarters in Londonderry where they had to wait for the gate to be unlocked by an armed sentry to allow access to their car. There they discovered the district inspector's office had been taken over by the soldiers who were holding a conference without any police officers being present. At Dungiven, twenty-five miles away, a ninety per cent Catholic village with a population of about 1,500, they found the police station completely shuttered, bolted and barred with all the front windows broken and the constable's house, which was part of the station, bearing the scorch marks from a petrol bomb attack a few nights earlier. Inside some eight or ten police officers under the command of a sergeant were sitting about, fully armed, and, according to the observers, 'waiting for they knew not what'.

> Outside on a warm, summer afternoon it would have been difficult to imagine a more peaceful scene. The men were playing cards or sleeping and their morale was very low. They were almost pathetically grateful to us for having visited them. The Sergeant, quite a good type, told us that the local people had on the whole been well disposed towards the police, but that following the attack they would no longer have anything to do with them for fear of reprisals.

In and around the sensitive areas in Belfast, with troops now fanning out widely, what positive police action there was seemed to be limited to 'probes' in armoured cars which bristled with machine guns and rifles. The local police explained the necessity for this form of action because of the numerous reports of snipers, yet, in the course of several patrols with them neither Mark nor Osmond saw any 'evidence of the incidence of such a menace'. Their belief that the police could have been doing more about the 'no-go' areas was compounded by the sight of groups of 'stewards', sometimes equipped with white armbands, but for the most part boys aged sixteen to twenty sometimes armed with sticks, to ensure no infiltration by Protestants. The district inspector in Bogside pointed out two groups of youths standing about in the street whom he described as 'typical troublemakers in the area'. The observers concluded: 'These youths have their counterparts in every town in England and were the sort of groups of layabouts which the normal English policeman would recognise as requiring breaking up by firm handling.'

At the end of their tour they concluded that apart from the political and religious disputes, basic police problems seemed to be comparatively light. 'The total population, at rather less than 1.5 million, is about the same as that of Hampshire but the crime rate is about one-half and traffic is immeasurably less,' they reported. Urging London to act in the period of comparative quiet that had been won by the deployment of troops and 'before a state of civil war could become inevitable', they advised of the need for 'the presentation of clear, unmistakable evidence of a determination to de-militarise the police, of an intention to re-establish the rule of law by the restrained and well-founded English police methods depending on public support and sense of responsibility [which] could, in the emotional atmosphere prevailing, well result in a sense of public relief and relaxation of tension'.

> The RUC is an isolated police force, inbred and inward looking, and until now well satisfied with its paramilitary role. It must be made to feel less isolated, to have its spirit and morale lifted out of its present despondency and to have the confidence and pride in itself and its proper civilian role that will in time inspire the confidence of the public. To do this internal changes are not enough, for they would be bound to be regarded with scepticism. There need to be changes at the top, in the constitutional relationship between police and Government and there must be a removal of any suspicion that the police are influenced by local political and sectarian considerations. While fully appreciating the existing political difficulties, in our view the ultimate responsibility for the maintenance of law and order in Northern Ireland should be removed from the Northern Ireland Government and placed in the hands of the Home Secretary. If this is ever to be achieved, now is the time.

Turning to their views of the Ulster Special Constabulary, they were highly critical. In the Protestant Shankill Road area of Belfast they had three times been stopped by B Specials, unaccompanied by regular police and unequipped with the red lights they were supposed to use for road checks. The Englishmen were shocked to find that from the inspector-general down 'nothing dangerous is seen in the fact that failure of a car to stop is ample justification for the occupants to be fired on'. The 8,000 Specials, they said, were exclusively Protestant, all armed and 'mostly of a poor type. There is little doubt that they are inflaming the present situation.'

> Supporters of the organisation claim that it is an essential part of the internal defence of Ulster, that its members are well disciplined and are impartial in the exercise of their duties. We had little doubt that at least some members have not recently been as restrained as their supporters would suggest. Although Catholic areas are barred to the Specials, some have undoubtedly found their way there and may well have been an aggravating feature of the more serious rioting, if not the instigators. The fact remains, however, that the USC can only be seen as a Protestant reserve army designed to protect the Northern Protestant against the Catholics and the threat from the South. As such its continued existence in its present form can only aggravate the internal differences that exist.

They suggested the Special Constabulary should either openly become a military reserve with recruitment from all religions or that it should be disbanded altogether and replaced by a new body within the English concept of a special constabulary to assist the police.

As a result of these exchanges, which began immediately after Osmond and Mark had reached Belfast, dealing with the Specials became the priority and Callaghan initiated contact with Chichester-Clark and asked him to listen to Osmond's advice carefully. As the senior man, Osmond was instructed to apply 'strong and urgent pressure' to have the armed Specials removed from street duty to avoid any possibility that they would become involved in any rioting. Over the weekend the pressure continued, and by late Sunday night resistance in Belfast had been worn down. Callaghan and Chichester-Clark reached a deal whereby the Specials would be withdrawn from the streets and, along with six battalions who were already in transit, two additional battalions would go to Northern Ireland immediately to provide more support for the police.

London's real aim remained to disarm the Specials altogether, though they could be allowed to retain their arms on duties inside police stations and in protection of certain key installations, but Callaghan feared the exercise might well give rise to something approaching mutiny on the part of the Specials or that some would defect or pass arms to the illegal Ulster Volunteer Force. In discussion with officials, he said the question was whether these were greater evils than the evil of allowing the B Specials to continue in their present form.

Osmond and Faulkner, Freeland's political adviser, were temporarily called back to London for consultations at the Home Office on the evening of 18 August. What they had to say was in stark contrast to the semi-hysterical utterances by the government and police in Belfast that the IRA was on the march and Ulster was in peril. (Over the weekend Chichester-Clark had once again publicly blamed the disorder on 'extreme Republican elements and others determined to overthrow our state'.) The causes of the disturbances, Faulkner reported, were 'part hooligans, part revolutionary socialists, part IRA and the more responsible civil rights workers who aimed to discredit the Unionist Party but not to destroy Northern Ireland itself'. IRA influence, he said, was greater in Belfast than Londonderry but if one had to allocate the degrees of responsibility for the damage he would attribute three quarters of it to hooliganism, both Protestant and Catholic.

Faulkner also told Callaghan that he had been greatly struck by the political blindness shown by both sides and the ugliness of the physical environment. The current situation was quiet but uneasy, he said, but Freeland, who called it the high point of the honeymoon, was pressing ahead with plans to open up the situation, encourage people to take down the barricades around their areas and to send out patrols, first of soldiers but gradually introducing police officers, and eventually handing over to the police. Osmond reported that the police had lost the confidence of both Catholics and Protestants and said that 'given half a chance the RUC turns itself into an army, cuts itself off from society and makes no real effort in public relations'. He described the level of recruits as mediocre and morale as low, and said that the force had lost control and 'given up thinking of doing anything constructive to regain it'.

That could certainly not be said of what was going on in London, where hasty work over five hectic days was aimed at enabling the cabinet to endorse the policies and machinery that had been put in place to manage the dramatically changed relationship between Belfast and London. For the first time since the 1920s the Irish issue, for so long concealed in the mundane depths of the General Department of the Home Office alongside such matters as the regulation of London taxi cabs, was now at the very forefront of British politics and heavily taxing the time and ingenuity of the nation's most senior politicians, diplomats, police, military and mandarins. Apart from the future management of the RUC, the long-running question of obtaining more reliable intelligence had become much more important now that British troops were actually on the ground in considerable and growing numbers.

By now, Callaghan had received a report from the Ulster Intelligence Working Group which had been created in April. After four meetings it had concluded little could be done in the way of 'predicting or fore-stalling acts of disorganised violence carried out by sectarian hooligans; nothing but observation on the streets can provide coverage of the activities of a leaderless mob'. The group also concluded, as Callaghan told Wilson in a lengthy minute earlier in the month, that 'there are practical and constitutional difficulties' in recruiting independent sources. He continued: 'I accept the conclusion that it would be right to concentrate on developing the maximum intelligence coverage primarily by training and supporting the RUC rather than by attempting to establish any independent and undeclared intelligence operations in Northern Ireland.' An Army suggestion that the RUC would come under military control for this purpose was assigned to a military staff officer for evaluation. The question arose again at a joint meeting between Army commanders and officials from the Foreign Office soon after the troops went in, but while these deliberations were taking place, over in Belfast General Freeland, in his own no-nonsense way, had raised the thorny topic with Chichester-Clark and made progress. As a result the military immediately took over most of the responsibility for the co-ordination and collation of information and a number of lieutenant-colonels were posted into police headquarters for the purpose. Freeland's real game-plan, though, was to have a Director of Intelligence for Northern Ireland, answerable to him. But despite these moves, the lack of good intelligence would all too soon have adverse consequences.

Chapter Five
'The Cinderella Service'

The sorry state of the RUC, so vividly portrayed by Osmond and Mark, convinced Callaghan that swift and sweeping changes were vital. So he tasked his officials to come up with the names of a dozen or so capable British police officers who would go to Belfast to replace the most senior men in the RUC. Their aim would be to transform it into the effective and professional organisation it ought to be, with a new-found confidence in itself and enjoying a high level of public esteem among both Catholics and Protestants. Given that the Osmond–Mark report amounted to the blueprint for the necessary changes, Callaghan earmarked Osmond to replace Peacocke in Belfast. Mark was ruled out because of his ongoing work tackling corruption in the Metropolitan Police. At the same time, the Home Office compiled a shortlist of suitable high-flying assistant chief constables which included a Scottish nominee, listed because he 'may have really valuable experience of Irish sectarian trouble'. It was also envisaged that someone from Scotland Yard with the relevant expertise would take over the Special Branch.

Callaghan intended to telephone Chichester-Clark about his plans late on the evening of 18 August, but before he could do so, the Northern Ireland prime minister called with a suggestion of his own. With public confidence in the police having ebbed away, he felt the need for an inquiry into the RUC and suggested Mark or Osmond might undertake the work. Although Peacocke had been assured that the idea was not directed at him personally, he had reacted 'unfavourably' and threatened that if it were set up, he and his deputy might have to step down and there would be mass resignations from the force. (In the event this proved to be an empty threat.) Callaghan confided to Chichester-Clark that Osmond judged Peacocke 'not up to the job' and that the top leadership of the RUC was poor, though the middle rank included many good men. What he had in mind, he went on, was that a British chief constable, perhaps Osmond, should take charge for six months or a year, but he would now look favourably on the idea of an inquiry. Chichester-Clark, who was under considerable pressure from uncompromising elements within his own government and party, wanted to announce the inquiry that very night to avoid the impression that it had been imposed on him by London but Callaghan, in the light of his own unfolding plan, dissuaded him until it had been fully considered in London the next day, at what would amount to the first ever joint meeting between the British and Northern Ireland cabinets. This encounter, chaired by Harold Wilson, was intended formally to define the terms of the new relationship between Northern Ireland and the rest of the United Kingdom now that large numbers of troops were directly involved in maintaining law and order. The seven-point 'Downing Street Declaration', which emerged from the joint meeting affirmed that 'nothing which has happened in recent weeks' compromised or affected Northern Ireland's position within the United Kingdom and stated firmly that 'the border is not an issue'. It also renewed the joint commitment to the reform programme designed to ensure that every citizen of Northern Ireland, irrespective of political views or religion, was treated on a par with the rest of the United Kingdom.

But one of the most important, far-reaching and indeed controversial developments was not embedded in the text. During the meeting Chichester-Clark, in a bid to anticipate Whitehall's well-signposted concerns about the constitutional implications of the military involvement and head off a more drastic pruning of Belfast's devolved powers, had pre-emptively offered a formula whereby, for the time being, the Army's General Officer Commanding would be appointed Director of Operations and assume supreme responsibility for security. While there would still be a local home affairs minister, a security committee and the inspector-general as head of the RUC and Specials, for all practical purposes those forces would now do what the Army told them. With the GOC exclusively accountable to Whitehall, Chichester-Clark had effectively ceded control of Northern Ireland's internal security, the provision so resolutely guarded by Craig and Bates in the formative days of the state and so rigorously abused and exploited ever since in the Unionist interest.

As if this was not a tough enough concession for Chichester-Clark to sell to his right-wingers, Wilson considerably raised the stakes when, speaking immediately after the London meeting, he referred to the 'phasing out' of the B Specials in a television interview. Whether a slip or not, the remark was an unfortunate one for Chichester-Clark, who always believed it was deliberate 'treachery'. By the time his private plane landed back at Sydenham airfield in Belfast a full-scale political row had broken out, with his government and party divided as to whether he had conceded far too much. Bill Craig, now his principal tormenter, was calling for the resignation of the government: 'Stormont is responsible to the people of Northern Ireland for the rule of law and internal security of the state. Control of that important field has passed to a person not responsible to the Government of Northern Ireland. This is a constitutional change we cannot accept.'

The Army's 3,000-strong pre-Troubles garrison had soared by 4,000, the reinforcements flown in within four days of the soldiers first being committed, and was set to increase by another 2,000 within the week. A flotilla of troop-ships was converging on the ports of Belfast and Derry bringing in the extra men, their vehicles and equipment. Signals from Lisburn to the Ministry of Defence had asked for large quantities of barbed wire, wooden chicanes and corrugated iron to build 'peace lines' at the flashpoint intersections between Catholic and Protestant enclaves. While the build-up accelerated, Freeland wasted little time in exercising his new authority over the police. Two days later he issued an Order of the Day to the inspector-general confirming that he had been given the task of commanding and controlling all forces employed on security duties in Northern Ireland and saying: 'I am sure that I can count on your loyal support and on that of your constabulary . . . who have been working under very great pressure and strain during the past months.' The general then announced that the Special Constabulary had been relieved of all riot control duties and would be given the task of guarding vital installations. Later in the day, with the support of the chief of the General Staff who travelled to Belfast for the purpose, he laid out for the Northern Ireland Security Committee the way he proposed to call in the firearms the Specials had historically kept in their homes.

Given the political passions that had been aroused about security and the future of the Specials, Freeland knew that he must move very cautiously to minimise a backlash which would have the potential to bring down the Northern Ireland government. He further feared that if the morale of the Specials was seriously shaken, it was possible that they could conceivably mutiny, give their arms to extremists or become such themselves. He was also afraid of causing friction with the regular police because of their close relationship with the Specials. By now, a week after the height of the disturbances when 4,000 Specials had been on the streets, the nightly deployment had fallen to 500, with 200 guarding Vital Points and 300 patrolling border areas. Freeland decided to maintain this commitment for the time being and present the planned disarming as being a centralisation of arms for security purposes. As a further sign that what was happening was not a complete Army takeover, he also proposed that the guns should be held in police armouries in Belfast and Londonderry and that rural-based B Specials would continue to hold weapons at home in case they were called out for 'crash action'. This was all announced at a news conference on 22 August. Turning to the RUC, the general ordered them to remove the Browning machine guns from their ten Shorland armoured vehicles. He also put in hand plans for training them in crowd control, starting with the eight Reserve force platoons, who would be redesignated the Special Patrol Group, bringing the name into line with the terminology used to denote similar groups in the British police.

Another important initiative, arising from the London summit, was also launched during this period. Mr Justice Leslie Scarman and two prominent local businessmen, George Lavery, a Catholic, and William Marshall, a Protestant, were asked to conduct a judicial investigation into the chain of disturbances from March until August 1969. Following the Callaghan–Chichester-Clark conversation, it was also decided there would be an Advisory Committee on Policing in Northern Ireland, chaired by Lord Hunt of Llanfairwaterdine, the leader of the first mountaineering expedition to conquer Mount Everest in 1953. Its other members were Sir James Robertson, the Chief Constable of Glasgow, whom the Northern Ireland government had requested, and Robert Mark. Announcement of the inquiry had been slightly delayed because Peacocke tried to veto Mark's appointment.

Callaghan's draconian plan to replace the highest echelon of the RUC with British police officers was thus abandoned, giving Chichester-Clark something with which to placate his critics. The committee was his idea, he could truthfully say, and both London and Belfast publicly stressed that the inquiry would be as responsible to the British government as to the Northern Ireland government. But when Hunt was briefed on the delicacies of his task at the Home Office on 26 August by Callaghan, he was left in no doubt about the outcome London wanted: a paramilitary border security force and a conventional constabulary which would recruit Catholics as well as Protestants and 'result in the Northern Ireland province not having to depend for its security on an armed citizenry' like the B Specials. Mindful of the historic prohibition on Northern Ireland raising a military formation, such a force, Callaghan said, would have to be staffed full-time and professionally and 'be strong enough to control potential IRA gun-running but not powerful enough to challenge British forces' or 'in any way provoke the Republic [of Ireland] Government'. His attitude was in stark contrast to that of his predecessors who had bowed to the Unionists in the 1920s and authorised the creation of the swollen constabulary. When Hunt raised the possibility that the inquiry might conceivably recommend things which could be unacceptable to the Northern Ireland government he was told not shrink from it but to 'recommend it in as tactful a way as possible'. There were better opportunities for getting changes made now than hitherto, said Callaghan, ushering in a fundamental change in attitude: the Belfast administration would no longer benefit from a disinterested London turning a blind eye to its activities. At the end of the discussion, Hunt said that he would leave for Belfast the next day and aim to produce a report within five weeks. Paisley greeted him in Belfast as 'the man sent by Whitehall to write the obituary of the B Specials' and led a motorcade to Stormont to protest about the 'military dictatorship' that had been imposed.

Over in Northern Ireland, Hunt and his small team established a base at the Ballygally Castle Hotel on the picturesque Antrim coast, just north of the ferry port of Larne, from where they travelled out to visit police establishments and conduct informal interviews. The Governor of Northern Ireland, Lord Grey, told them it was 'necessary to reform the police for professional reasons and desirable to reform them for political reasons'. The dilemma, he suggested, was that some changes that would be welcome to one section of the community could be achieved only at the cost of antagonising another section and possibly of gravely damaging the RUC itself. 'The RUC is the only police force that there is; and it is not possible to conjure another into being at short notice.'

Although it was taken in private and never published until now, the body of evidence gathered by the Hunt team provides a frank and intimate snapshot of the state and mindset of the RUC in the late 1960s when reticence and discretion in public were abiding characteristics of the profession. The RUC Code, for instance, expressly forbade all contact with the press. It reveals the pent-up frustrations about the partisan political role the RUC was required to play, the chronic lack of investment in its personnel, capacity and facilities and the nadir to which it had been driven. A Londonderry officer complained that things had reached such a low point that 'we cannot even go into the Bogside to collect evidence for a Coroner's Inquest'. Another complained: 'The RUC was the Cinderella service'.

Hunt encountered widespread criticism of the lack of leadership and organisation in the RUC, especially during recent events, and he had to listen to a long litany of complaints about the working conditions they had to endure. Sir Richard Pim, inspector-general from 1945 until 1961, accused the current leadership of lacking concern for the men. During the months of trouble there had been, for instance, poor provision for meals even though some mobile canteens had been provided. 'The chuck wagons system is not working,' moaned one officer. The most common demands were for the police to be relieved of menial duties such as cleaning, gardening and cutting hedges around their stations. They also wanted an end to the 'archaic charades' of ten annual inspections of each station, which required five days' preparation with the station party having to polish floors, practise drill, ensure all the records were up to date and even whitewash the buildings. Vehicles were being retained dangerously long after the end of their useful lives and the delays in replacing them were becoming intolerable, Hunt was told. The lack of clerical assistance was another widespread grievance. 'A constable who is a poor typist spends more time reporting an event than investigating it,' one sergeant complained. Moderate expenditure on copying machines would result in a great saving of manpower throughout the force. One Belfast station said they could manage with one typist fewer if they had a copier. Sir Albert Kennedy, inspector-general from 1961 to 1969, revealed there was just one photocopier in the entire headquarters. Officers also complained that they had to buy the RUC Manual after the ministry prevented the inspector-general from making a free issue. The cost was 19s. 6d. but when it was published in August 1969, after six years in preparation, it was already out of date.

There was also much carping about the location and condition of stations. Downpatrick, Lurgan and Victoria Barracks, Londonderry, were singled out as the worst but the wasteful case of a new station built at Magilligan and then closed was also mentioned. Kennedy said that some stations were kept open mainly because 'the locals like to see the bricks and mortar' and, in a widely shared criticism, said that border stations were a liability, maintained only for political reasons because the 'Government sees them as showing the flag'. Guarding them was a major commitment with, for instance, a sergeant and thirteen constables at Rosslea County Fermanagh. Brigadier Tony Dyball, the Army's Chief of Staff, also criticised the concentration of men and the virtual paranoia about the border. 'There are much easier ways of importing arms into Northern Ireland than the use of unapproved roads and attacks have been carried out on police stations in border areas which stand out like something of a sore thumb. It is a matter for consideration whether there is a real police need for such stations as Crossmaglen and Forkhill,' he said.

Following many adverse comments about the state of the Training Depot at Enniskillen, Hunt commented, after going to see for himself, that while the external appearance of the building was impressive, the interior dormitory and other facilities were sub-standard and more appropriate for Victorian soldiery. Some officers calculated that the accommodation had not been renovated since it was taken over in the 1930s. 'We have been complaining for a long time about living conditions in the Depot and some stations and all we get is promises and the stock excuse of the present economic crisis,' said a member of the Central Representative Body, which looked after the interests of the rank-and-file police officers. Its procedures and remit were also sources of dissatisfaction. Allowed to meet only once a year, the members complained that in the interim there was a tendency for the inspector-general arbitrarily to turn proposals down because they were 'not in the interests of the force'. They wanted a right of appeal to the minister. Equality of treatment for the fifty-odd female officers was another issue. They wanted full-time representation on the committee, not just when matters affecting only female officers were being discussed. They were highly dissatisfied that they had not even been consulted about their uniform design and that many male sergeants regarded them as mere clerks or typists.

Hunt found conflicting views about whether or not the RUC should continue to be permanently armed. For some time beforehand there had been a policy that police would go without guns by day, but earlier in 1969, after an armed bank raid in Newry, attributed to the IRA, two constables caught up in the episode said being without weapons had probably saved them from being shot. Others took the view that if the constables had been armed, the robbers might well have been apprehended. As a result of the incident, however, the experiment was quietly abandoned. Hunt found Peacocke 'unrepentant' on the need for an armed force as a deterrent to criminals; an unarmed force would not work because one of the consequences would be a need for greater numbers. Nevertheless there was a pretty general cry of 'few have used them' and 'we would love to get rid of our arms'. The Fermanagh Constables' Body said that if the paramilitary image was to change 'the gun will have to go from the belt'. Some officers suggested that a localised policy might be the best option while others believed they should follow the example of the Garda Siochana and just arm the Special Branch.

Inaugurating a demand that would hang over the force for decades ahead, Cardinal Conway, the head of the Catholic Church in Ireland, wanted the name of the force to change but recognised that the choice of a replacement would be difficult. Some officers, also in favour, suggested the 'Northern Ireland Constabulary'. A district inspector in Armagh said: 'The "Royal" is anathema to many Catholics who, as a whole, still have a great respect for the RUC but don't like to reveal it.' But Pim was opposed to any change and a group of officers in Antrim said: 'We are proud of the name and wish to keep it.' While some were not opposed to changing the uniform colour to British police blue, possibly to distinguish them from the Specials, there was an overwhelming wish to preserve the green uniform. Speaking on behalf of the whole organisation, the Central Representative Body said it was opposed to any name or uniform change. Underlining the strength of feeling on these points, Kennedy warned perceptively: 'Some would defend the uniform down to the very buttons.'

The most intractable policing problem, Hunt was told, was the handling of processions. Ministers of home affairs had not always acted impartially and had made the police appear to be the tool of the government, Unionist Party and Orange Order, one senior man complained. Wolseley said the most difficult task was enforcing wholly impracticable political decisions and specifically referred to the requirement for the police in Londonderry to enforce a ban 15,000 people were determined to break. The Newry District Inspector reported that he had been against re-routing the civil rights procession on 11 January but had been overruled. Trouble then resulted. Kennedy recalled that during the spasmodic outbreaks of trouble in Northern Ireland the politicians always stirred up 'extremists' on both sides with the police caught in the middle. 'There has been little or no change in outlook of the opposing sides in my lifetime and there is unfortunately no sign of any improvement. The difference now is world-wide publicity,' he said. In fact, many officers complained how strongly they resented being cast as scapegoats and strenuously denied they were partial. In its lengthy submission to Hunt, the Central Representative Body claimed there had been a barrage of one-sided propaganda in an attempt to discredit the force and that it was confident that Hunt would find the calibre of its members comparable with any other force in the United Kingdom. Hunt was told that while a public relations officer had recently been appointed he had, so far, made little difference. There was particular concern about effectively countering the frequent allegations of police brutality. Officers wanted the internal disciplinary investigation procedure for handling complaints from members of the public used in England, Wales and Scotland to be extended to the RUC and said any citizen who had a legitimate complaint against the police had a further remedy through either the Criminal or Civil Courts. Nevertheless there were reservations on the part of some officers. 'People will not make written statements because they see police as judge and jury,' said one who favoured a system of outside scrutiny.

Increasing the proportion of Catholics in the RUC was another fundamental problem to be solved. Peacocke complained that Catholic-owned and published newspapers would not accept advertisements and recruiting officers could not get into Catholic schools. A sergeant in County Down reported some priests were very bitter and had indeed refused them entry to schools. Another officer said it was seen as an honour for a Catholic family to have a priest among its number but a disgrace to have a policeman. Cardinal Conway said it was highly exaggerated to say Catholics in the police were accused of treachery by their co-religionists but he told Hunt that the RUC had never been popular with Catholics because it was linked in their minds with the enforcement of the separation of the north from the rest of Ireland, although practically all of them, 99.9 per cent he reckoned, opposed the idea of union by force. 'In the minds of Roman Catholics the RUC is also remembered for acts of partiality in favour of Protestants, for allegations of brutality and for such activities as the midnight arrests, in the 1930s, of persons suspected of IRA activities. Since 5 October 1968, Catholic feeling towards the RUC had hardened greatly,' the cardinal said.

Some of the police officers interviewed blamed the RUC's own recruiting system for deterring some Catholics from joining. People were excluded for distant Republican connections. One policeman told of an applicant turned down because his uncle, whom he had never met, had been the election agent for a Republican candidate. Another, from a different county, knew of a man who had been accepted although his relatives had openly carried Republican banners. In more anecdotal evidence, there were stories of young men being rejected after the local police made the mandatory home visit to assess suitability for the job because there was a picture of a prominent nationalist or Republican figure hanging on the wall. The Hunt team discovered that about 900 officers, one third of the entire RUC, were ex-Specials who had bypassed the basic educational and suitability tests and training by enlisting after being mobilised full-time for security duty. 'The B Specials were an easy source of recruits with many getting in by the back door but there was no such back door for Catholics,' one officer said. A sergeant in County Down suggested potential officers should not have to state their religion on the application form as 'rumour gets round that men are being rejected by their local sergeant on religious grounds which is prejudicial'. So that there would be fairness and consistency, many officers expressed a need to centralise and standardise recruiting.

Among the more senior officers there was discontent that some postings were regarded unofficially as either Catholic or Protestant and a feeling that Catholics had to wait longer for promotion, especially the nearer they got to the top. At that point it was estimated that two of the twelve men holding county inspector rank and some nine of the fifty district inspectors were Catholics. A head constable said many of the plum jobs were not open to Catholics. Another head constable, a Catholic, alleged that he had had to wait four years for promotion after attending the police staff college at Bramshill in Hampshire yet three others who had attended at the same time were promoted at once. Apart from the religious factor, a number of officers expressed concern that there was unfairness about marking written examinations and favouritism, with some people being promoted without even passing the exams. (It is interesting to note that nowhere in their evidence does any of these officers refer to or complain about either Orange Order or Masonic influences being a factor.)

The Hunt team also elicited new information about the creaking state of the RUC's intelligence gathering capacity. Major DV Wright, a military intelligence liaison officer with eight years' experience posted to Northern Ireland in May, stated the RUC had been looking at everything through 'IRA-tinted spectacles'. Knowledge of what was going on behind the barricades was nil: that was where the sources were and the Special Branch had lost touch with them, especially in Londonderry. He put IRA strength at no more than forty or fifty compared with the RUC estimates of 400 in the north and 1,200 in the south. In his view, Peacocke slanted his intelligence reports to the government. (Hunt's record of this interview interestingly contains the caveat: 'Major Wright's knowledge appears to be superficial.') Brigadier Dyball said the IRA was not capable of making a frontal assault; their capability was limited to small raids on key points.' His view was that much of the recent trouble resulted from ill-founded fear but it existed on both sides and, whether justified or not, was nonetheless genuinely held, but fanned for political motive by extremists.

All the direct evidence they heard was of Special Branch offices understaffed, poorly equipped and untrained in the necessary expertise. The Fermanagh Special Branch sergeant had to use his own camera for work purposes and the only specialised training he had was a short course on the shadowing of suspects. The Belfast Special Branch office had £4,000 a year to pay informants and was so understaffed that there was a year's backlog of unprocessed paper. The Down County Representative Board wanted a proper undercover branch set up along the lines of MI5. 'The SB let us down at the start of the IRA campaign in 1956 and it is apparent that they have never been in touch with the causes of the present disturbances,' they said. Pim felt that Crime Special and MI5 should 'get stuck into' Queen's University, Belfast and perhaps plant a woman lecturer to provide intelligence. He thought retention of the Special Powers Act was vital, but Peacocke warned, 'Repeal was a hot political potato.'

Turning to the future of the Specials, the cardinal told Hunt that the threat from the IRA was greatly exaggerated in Northern Ireland, particularly by the Special Constabulary and its supporters, and it would be very satisfactory if the defence of the frontier could be made the responsibility of the British armed forces and if the USC could be disbanded. 'A security force based on the Territorial Army for the defence of the frontier and of key points might be acceptable, particularly if its officers were British,' he ventured. Predictably, some police were supportive of the Specials. 'They're very willing chaps who know their townlands like the back of their hands,' said an officer in Tyrone. 'Although they might contain a few hotheads, in the main recruits to the USC are first class,' said another. 'In some places they are controllable but not in other places,' was another honest view. 'Their sectarian image rubs off on the RUC,' according to one officer, who added, 'Love them or hate them, the police have a high dependency on the USC.' It was put at fifty per cent in Fermanagh, for instance.

Former inspector-general Pim feared that if the B men were taken away from the Ministry of Home Affairs it would be a gift to the Paisleyites and would tumble the government of Northern Ireland. They were also defended by Peacocke, who revealed that thirty had been detected as belonging to the Ulster Protestant Volunteers (an unofficial Loyalist group) but no action had been taken. He felt it safer to keep them in the Specials where they could be watched. Peacocke favoured a two-tier force, helping police in cities, armed with revolvers and, in rural areas, with rifles and sub-machine guns, conducting checkpoints and guarding the border and Vital Points.

When the committee conducted direct interviews, they found a highly militant mood among the Specials themselves. 'If we hand in our arms we hand in our uniforms', said some County Antrim members. The USC was 'an essential shield for Ulster' and many would join unofficial forces if it was disbanded, Hunt was told by another group. The Specials defended the need to retain their arms and the Antrim men boasted they had lost only one revolver in twenty-six years. McKay, the GOC's police adviser, reported on views expressed at a recent conference of county commandants. The Specials were the main deterrent to the IRA and any move to disband them would be surrendering to the enemy, was one widely held sentiment. Feelings were so strong that one county commandant reported he would need time to consult his men about any changes or 'there could be a bloodbath'.

Looking to the future, Peacocke was pessimistic and opposed to change: 'The sectarian threat is a continuing thread running right through police work whether just a pub row, a football match or whatever.' Wolseley, who was having to work eighteen-hour days for months, thought the job would be less interesting if the RUC was not a 'gendarmerie'. But these were minority views. What the clear majority wanted was closer integration with the British police service, parity on pay and conditions and, through the well-established principles of mutual aid, the prospect of mainland officers coming to Northern Ireland to back up the RUC at times of pressure. There was also a very broad consensus in support of separating the conventional policing role from that of defending the state. A group in Downpatrick all strongly favoured having a single, civil, unarmed policing role with a separate security force to back them up. 'When crowd control developed into a riot they should intervene,' said one officer, who thought they should wear a khaki uniform. Most officers wanted to be policemen, not soldiers. 'We are robber-catchers at heart,' said a district inspector in Antrim. This viewpoint was reinforced in the submission of the Central Representative Body, whose one major aim was:

> [. . .] to establish the Royal Ulster Constabulary in the role which all its members wish to see it occupying: that of a civilian law enforcement agency carrying out recognised police duties only. The paramilitary image which has been given to the force arises from the requirement to perform a dual function as a police force and a state security body. In the past there were historical reasons for this situation, but we feel that the quasi-military duties still undertaken by the Royal Ulster

Constabulary are now totally out of keeping with the modern understanding of police functions.

Brigadier Dyball, also called for a very clear distinction between the police and military roles and was certain that defence of the border was the responsibility of the British government and therefore of the British Army. So that Vital Points could be guarded in time of unrest, he suggested a 'home guard' be created. By multiplying the number of VPs by a factor of thirty, he calculated a force of 3,500 would be sufficient, far fewer than the 8,000 enlisted Specials.

The committee was left in no doubt that the police were united on the need for an independent oversight body to act as a 'buffer' between them and the politicians. Peacocke said the present system 'boiled down to a battle of wills between the Inspector-General and the Minister'. A group of officers in County Down said that 'too much depended on the attitude of the Minister of Home Affairs of the day. Some have been too amenable to direct right-wing pressure if they didn't like what the local District Inspector was doing.' A district inspector among them said they were inhibited in doing their job because 'they had to look at police implications then political implications. The root cause of our bad image is that we are seen as the tool of the government.' In Fermanagh, a group of three officers, including a Catholic, said they were embarrassed whenever they were involved in disputes arising from political mismanagement. Another County Down district inspector said, 'If the RUC see a rabble coming down the street, who produce a Union Jack, they are reduced to a jelly because of the political implications of standing up to them.' A delegation of Antrim officers said the RUC suffered from its close association with the government and would be more acceptable to the public if it was seen to be controlled by some public body other than the Ministry of Home Affairs. Cardinal Conway said that he was in favour of a single Police Authority, as did Peacocke and many others. John Greeves, the permanent secretary at the ministry, said that the selection and composition of such a 'buffer body' would be very important and 'it would have to have an adequate representation of Roman Catholics'.

While this evidence-gathering process was going on, Callaghan had published the report of the Cameron Commission on 12 September. The previous March, Lord Cameron and two local men, Professor Sir Henry Biggart and James Campbell, had been asked by O'Neill to investigate the causes and circumstances of the violent disturbances in Londonderry on 5 October 1968 and thereafter. They concluded the RUC's inept handling of events provoked serious hostility, particularly among the Catholic population of Londonderry, and an increasing disbelief in its impartiality towards non-Unionists. Cameron compiled a private memorandum for Hunt which graphically underlined the need for reform. He thought the mishandling of the civil rights marches 'suggest[ed] that the staff work in the higher echelons lacks something and is less satisfactory than it should be. There does appear to have been a poverty of ideas in how to suppress disorders at an early stage and how to disperse crowds before they got to the stage of being a menace to peace and good order.' Similarly he expressed reservations about 'the wide variety of competence within the Special Branch' and the impression left that 'intelligence enquiries were not always directed or pressed with the same skill and zeal'.

All through September 1969, while Hunt and his associates were still at work, Callaghan was taking his own political soundings through Oliver Wright, a first-division Foreign Office diplomat, who had been sent to an unusual 'home' posting in Belfast on 22 August to operate both as a 'political' intelligence gatherer for London, independent of the Stormont government, and as a trouble-shooter. Following a direct approach to Callaghan from John Hume, about the possibility of using 'London bobbies' to restore policing and law and order in the Bogside, Wright was immediately asked to go and see him. Hume, who would become one of the most influential political figures in Ireland in the late twentieth century, had first come to prominence as a civil rights leader in Londonderry which helped win him the local seat in the Stormont parliament earlier in the year. During an hour-long conversation with Wright, Hume, who was and would remain completely hostile to the RUC, outlined a radical agenda for policing reform which he would pursue relentlessly for the next thirty years until it was achieved in almost totality. He hoped that when Hunt reported, 'the police would have a new name, a new uniform, a new leadership, a new function, a new body to be responsible to, and would be disarmed'. Wright tried to scale down his expectations. 'I said he might well get most of the substance of what he wanted, but in return he might have to concede some of the shadow, like the name "Royal Ulster Constabulary",' Wright reported back to Callaghan in a telex.

A good part of the discussion centred on Hume's proposal for 'London bobbies' in the Bogside, which he was certain the people would accept. Wright asked why they would tolerate them but not the military police,

Callaghan had been trying hard to introduce. The military police could only hand over suspected offenders to the RUC for prosecution, whereas if 'bobbies' took over the whole business they would also be responsible for preferring charges themselves, explained Hume. In fact, regardless of anything Hunt might soon say, the idea of using British police officers was actually under active consideration in London and the practicalities of two different approaches were being discussed inside the Home Office. One involved sending a party of between 500 and 1,000 officers to re-establish 'normal' policing along 'British' lines, especially in the 'difficult' areas of Londonderry and Belfast. They would be volunteers, but in a note on 10 September a senior Home Office official, JH Waddell, said it would be necessary to get the best kind of volunteer, 'this being a job that may make more appeal to policemen whose outlook is a bit aggressive than to the best elements in the police service'. The other option was to put in a training group of about 120 to rapidly transform the policing style and calibre of the RUC. Both proposals required new interlocking legislation to be passed at both Westminster and Stormont. There would also be parallel provision for some RUC officers to transfer to Britain 'to break down the isolation of the RUC and the "chip on the shoulder" attitude of some of its members', as McKay had put it in one of his reports to Callaghan, who was still personally in favour of replacing the entire RUC command with senior officers persuaded to transfer permanently to the RUC.

Officials were therefore ordered to consult the Police Federation, whose members would be involved, but not before getting 'an express guarantee of confidence'. Callaghan said it would be 'disastrous if rumours about any of this started flying around before it was possible to present a decision within the context of the Hunt report'. Dick Pamplin, the secretary of the federation, was therefore called to a meeting on 19 September. He immediately adopted a negative stance; there would be complications over pay, pensions and other conditions if a large-scale transfer of police to Northern Ireland was contemplated. He was equally unenthusiastic about the prospect of seconding a party of 500 or so for a temporary period: RUC morale would suffer another blow; the British police had no knowledge of the intercommunal tensions; and he doubted if even 500 would be enough. There was, however, much merit, he thought, in putting in up to 200 British officers to help redevelop the RUC along British lines and he thought the right sort of volunteers would easily be attracted.

By now the home secretary's favoured option had become the despatch of 500 to 1,000 officers and at another meeting on 22 September, attended by Sir John Waldron, the Commissioner of the Metropolitan Police, who was expected to provide a large proportion of any contingent, more considered reservations on the part of the police began to surface when they got down to the practical detail. Waldron thought British officers would not work happily under RUC command and did not like the idea at all. Osmond, who was also present, thought the best way to retake the enclaves was with British police but he was worried about getting enough of them and providing accommodation for them in Northern Ireland. While officers from all over Britain could be invited to volunteer, there should be some reservation about drawing officers from Glasgow and Liverpool, cities where the expatriate Irish communities preserved the old hatreds exported from their homeland. The possible reaction of the troops if the police got better conditions, such as weekend home leave, was also raised. At the end of the meeting Waddell suggested a compromise: sending a substantial number of police to be formed into units to patrol the Belfast 'NoGoland' and Bogside areas.

As the month wore on, although careful not to actually pre-empt Hunt, the home office continued its planning, now refocused on raising a more modest mission. However, Freeland, became increasingly keen on the assembly of a major police task force, which made it all the more difficult for the Home Office to retreat from the idea. Events played into their hands though, and the idea was dropped after fresh violence erupted on the streets of Belfast over the weekend of 27/28 September. During prolonged clashes, troops had to fire large quantities of CS gas against rival crowds, who injured fifty-four police and forty-eight soldiers before they were subdued. Writing up the situation for his permanent secretary the next day, Waddell wrote: 'In view of the disturbances in Belfast yesterday it is plain that we cannot send policemen from this country for some time; and as the possible time comes nearer there may be a bigger measure of agreement on what is needed.'

With its more ambitious plans now shelved, Home Office attention was sharply focused on the narrower objective of who should be put in charge of the RUC. After all they had heard and seen of him, opinion in London was unanimous that Peacocke must go, and, using the persuasive powers of Wright on the spot, Callaghan was already trying to bring Belfast round to the same viewpoint and offering help in finding a successor. Chichester-Clark and Porter actually favoured someone from Scotland but, with Osmond having firmly ruled himself out, Callaghan had already chosen another man: Sir Arthur Young. An avuncular old roué with an unrivalled record of colonial police service, he was presently Commissioner of the City of London Police, but from time to time in the past he had undertaken overseas police assignments for the government. On 1 October, Callaghan wrote to Chichester-Clark urging him to agree to Young's early appointment and advising that he had informally approached him about the move. At the end of the letter, he added an extensive handwritten note:

> I hope this will help. Arthur Young could be in Belfast to take over next Friday week by breaking his holiday. He is ready to move at a moment's notice. How lucky we are to have so many people with such a sense of duty. He is a tremendous leader of men. I do hope you can agree because I am sure we can get no one better.

The small secretariat supporting the Hunt committee had been giving the Home Office regular informed insights as to its final form while the report was being fashioned over at Ballygally. Given Chichester-Clark's precarious political position, officials in London became increasingly anxious about the timing of its publication, fearing a serious backlash of Protestant opinion against the planned disbandment of the B Specials. The sensitivities were outlined at a meeting on 17 September, where it was agreed that the public presentation of the report should be by Northern Ireland ministers, who must be seen to welcome it. In the event, after a discussion with Hunt about his conclusions, Callaghan opted for publication on 10 October during a four-day visit he would make to Northern Ireland. The plan was for him to meet Chichester-Clark immediately after his arrival on the Wednesday and conclude an agreement about the report, which would go to the printers next day and be published on Friday, when Peacocke's resignation would be announced and his replacement, Young, introduced. However, on the eve of the visit, at 11 a.m. on 7 October, Callaghan was forced to engage in a spot of eleventh-hour firefighting after receiving a telephone call from the beleaguered prime minister in Belfast. With his cabinet about to meet to discuss an advance copy of the completed Hunt report, Chichester-Clark said there was considerable opposition to Young becoming inspector-general since he was older than the current holder of that post. Hunt's committee had suggested two other names: Frank Williamson, an inspector of constabulary, and Peter Brodie, an assistant commissioner at New Scotland Yard, and the Belfast ministers wanted both of them to be considered. Callaghan immediately said that he could not release Brodie, who was doing an indispensable job in tackling serious crime in London, and while Williamson was good, he was probably not as suitable as Young. Callaghan doubted whether Young's age would count against him and insisted they press ahead with the appointment at the same time as the Hunt report was published. Chichester-Clark said he would telephone the home secretary again after the meeting but added that he would not be seeing Peacocke to sack him until a firm decision had been taken about his successor.

When the two next spoke by telephone at about seven that evening, Chichester-Clark was now more troubled about another issue arising from the report and Callaghan had to go into firefighting mode once again. The draft Hunt report had proposed that there should be a new British Army regiment, comprised of part-time soldiers, recruited and trained wholly in Northern Ireland and subject to military command and discipline, to replace the B Specials. Chichester-Clark said he wanted one crucial qualifying word added to the forthcoming report so that the force would be under the 'operational' control of the GOC. Callaghan firmly replied that if the force was on the Ministry of Defence budget, as planned, control must rest with the United Kingdom parliament. Anyway, said Callaghan, the British cabinet had grave doubts about the very existence of such an armed force at all and had only come round to accepting it on the condition that as it was responsible for creating it, so it must also control it. If the word 'operational' were added, Callaghan said, the implication could only be that ultimate control of policy did not remain with Westminster.

Chichester-Clark then remarked that the problem would not arise if the Ulster Special Constabulary remained and threatened that if the report was published unamended he would be bound to state that his government disagreed with it. The backwoodsmen in Belfast, already angered by the ceding of security control, were now using opposition to the winding-up of the B Specials as a ploy to regain at least some of the ground they accused their prime minister of losing and had put him under severe pressure. Turning to the Peacocke question, Chichester-Clark said that he would be sacked either that evening or next morning after which time the way would be clear for Callaghan to approach Young. Belfast had decided to fight for the Specials rather than the inspector-general. Although Callaghan had already talked to Young and, indeed, approved obtaining £50,000 life insurance cover for him in the City of London, he told Chichester-Clark that he was not prepared to take any decision on Young while the whole question of an armed civilian force remained unresolved. Police reforms and assistance from the British police had to be considered as a whole. At that junction, the conversation ended and they agreed to consider their positions before taking matters any further.

When Callaghan flew to Belfast the next day, accompanied by a posse of Scotland Yard bodyguards, he immediately went into a series of arm-twisting sessions with members of the Northern Ireland government to overcome opposition and clear the way for the scheduled publication of Hunt. With no real sanctions at their disposal, they succumbed without serious protest and forty-eight hours later, on Friday 10 October, as planned, Chichester-Clark announced that Peacocke would stand down and be replaced by Young. Gentlemanly as he was despite his other failings, Peacocke had immediately written out his resignation after he had been called to Stormont and asked for it. He was the last inspector-general of the RUC and Young became the first chief constable.

Revising the old rank structure inherited from the RIC and bringing it into line with that used by the British police was one of the key elements in the Hunt report, which was published later that morning. It was an improbable bestseller. There were queues outside the Stationery Office in Belfast before it went on sale and 7,000 copies were purchased in the first couple of hours. Among its forty-seven recommendations were the abolition of the B Specials, the creation of a Police Authority, the end of military-style duties by the RUC, the setting up of an RUC Reserve, the disarming of the force, an increase in numbers from 3,000 to 3,500, the establishment of a central recruiting system and closer links and interchanges with the rest of the British police service, which included changing the colour of the RUC rifle-green uniform to blue. There was also to be a separate 4,000-strong 'home guard', the Ulster Defence Regiment, which would be a fully-fledged, locally recruited regiment of the British Army under the exclusive command of the GOC. The changes, the most radical since the establishment of the RUC, closely mirrored the recommendations originally made by Osmond and Mark a few weeks earlier.

In introducing Young at a news conference, Chichester-Clark said he had been entrusted with the task 'of carrying out these great changes and of seeing to it that law and order is fairly, firmly and impartially enforced in all parts – I repeat all parts – of Northern Ireland'. So that there was no misunderstanding about the political priority of the task in soothing Unionists and protecting the prime minister from his ever more vociferous critics, Callaghan said the police would be back in the Bogside 'within a matter of days'. To underline the point he took Young with him to Londonderry for what Wright later described as 'a ceremonial entry' when he visited the Bogside to round off his four-day visit. Cheering crowds greeted them as Callaghan and Young shook hands with well-wishers. 'I believe that we are now at the beginning of a new era for everybody in Northern Ireland,' said a beaming Callaghan. However, there was a sobering reminder that there were two sides to the Northern Ireland problem when the two men visited the Fountain, a Protestant area on the other side of the city across the River Foyle. There people remained indoors behind drawn curtains in protest at the Hunt report. 'Fenian lover. You have sold us out to Rome,' shouted a woman, one of the few people on the streets as they walked through.

Indeed hopes that the report would bring an end to what Callaghan had described as 'this nonsense in the streets' were quickly dashed. While nationalists generally acclaimed the reforms, hardline Unionists were angered and called even more angrily for the government to resign. On that Friday night angry crowds gathered on Belfast's Shankill Road, jeering at the police and taunting them: 'You can't go into the Bogside', 'You can't go on to the Falls.' The next evening they gathered again and the police were unable to contain the rioting, which soon developed into a full-scale gun battle with the Army, who returned fire for the first time since arriving on the streets of Northern Ireland. Hundreds of shots were exchanged that night and Constable Victor Arbuckle, ironically a Protestant, was killed by a volley of shots aimed at his police party by Protestants allegedly defending 'their' police force. He was the first police fatality for eight years. Two other people died in the overnight gun battle which left a further sixty-six people injured, including police and troops. Many of them had gunshot wounds. Next day, as soldiers searched for the guns that had been used against them, they were jeered: 'Englishmen go home – we don't need you.' Craig demanded the RUC and Army withdraw from the Shankill in favour of the B Specials, a proposition contemptuously dismissed by Sam Bradley. It was a very bad start to Callaghan's 'new era' and an omen of much, much worse to come.

Chapter Six
'Softly, Softly'

An ebullient Young, clad in his London police uniform, with RUC epaulettes attached and a peaked RUC hat hastily commandeered from Peacocke, set off for Londonderry by helicopter on the morning of 14 October with high hopes that a party of his officers would be going into the Bogside with the Royal Military Police that very day. Over the weekend, despite the violence in Belfast, the Military Police, with their distinctive bright-red caps, had commenced patrolling what had now become known as 'Free Derry'. However, the new chief constable's optimism that the way was clear for the RUC to join them proved to be hopelessly premature. Despite the welcome and assurances given to Callaghan some forty-eight hours earlier, the Bogsiders were still not ready to accept the RUC. 'The opposition was both emotional and political,' observed a civil servant at the Home Office. Young was therefore forced to back down and announce he was not thinking in terms of RUC re-entry for another five days at least, a decision that, according to Oliver Wright's account, 'blew the [Belfast] government's top'.

They were faced with a political backlash against Hunt not only from angry right-wingers, like Craig, but from the very grass-roots of the Protestant community offended by more concessions to the Catholics, which they saw as a double standard in law enforcement and a reward for violence. There had actually been rumblings of discontent for weeks. William Fyffe, a Unionist MP who was strongly opposed to the civil rights movement, wrote to Chichester-Clark in mid-September, warning that any diminution of the status of the B Specials would be greatly resented and resisted in the border areas and lead to the government having to deal with an illegal organisation (the UVF) rather than 'disciplined men'. In Fermanagh, the retired prime minister Lord Brookeborough, the 'father' of the Specials, had stepped in to reassure the local members that the new arrangements would be satisfactory, but another attempt to placate Armagh platoons erupted into 'a flaming row'.

With 100 or so B Specials at Newtownards having handed in their kit and equipment on Monday evening, and the Belfast government seriously fearing a chain reaction, it was absolutely crucial that the 'Queen's writ' was seen to run again in the Catholic areas of Belfast and Londonderry if the administration was to maintain any credibility. So a very wobbly Chichester-Clark hurriedly summoned a meeting of the Joint Security Committee in his room at Stormont where, according to Wright's subsequent report to London, Porter said, with his 'typical air of tortured anguish': 'I am rapidly losing my self-respect'. Brian Faulkner, the development minister, said, 'I shall resign this evening unless action is taken.' Captain William Long, education minister, said: 'I agree. I am only in this government to support Jimmy [Chichester-Clark].' From this wretchedness, the committee pulled itself together and ordered Young to visit both the Falls and Bogside the next day, together with the military commanders, to inform the communities that police would accompany the military on joint patrols in both areas starting on Friday and that, to start with, the joint patrols would be in daylight hours only.

To calm his critics, Chichester-Clark planned to make an announcement to that effect in the evening. However, according to Wright, after Young had moved in Belfast, 'the Falls mob' forced the government's hand by leaking their agreement with him in time for the BBC's lunchtime news bulletin. Chichester-Clark had to bring his statement to parliament forward to 2.40 p.m., before Young had time to travel on to Londonderry and establish contact there. In the event the police, unarmed, did go into the Bogside on the designated day, where they were jeered and teased but otherwise unmolested. Two days later, they resumed patrolling the Falls when District Inspector Frank Lagan, a Catholic, and two policewomen, accompanied by two military police officers, took to the streets. Reporting these developments to London, Wright said: 'The net result is that we have taken this fence in tolerably good order.'

As the programme to disarm both the RUC and Specials gathered pace, with one or two further localised outbreaks of discontent, and the situation on the streets settled down, a week later Wright felt able to say the re-entry operations had been 'achieved with condign success':

> Opposition to the Hunt report may be now past its peak. The B Specials of Newtownards who resigned last week have changed their minds this week. I have no reason to suppose that there is anything sinister about this, or that they have received private assurances beyond what has already been said in public. Let us just assume that they are Irish, acted

without thinking on the spur of the moment and have subsequently regretted their action.

Ending on a cynical note he said: 'Maybe they heard that it was planned that the new force should be paid.'

Wright was right. Apart from opposing the planned change of uniform colour (which the government soon abandoned), the RUC itself was supportive of Hunt and proved enthusiastic about putting the recommendations into practice. However, Wright was far more concerned about the deteriorating political situation, reporting, 'We are now in the crisis of the reforms'. He continued, 'I fear that the Northern Ireland Government may have underestimated the determination of their own right wing to oppose reform and overestimated their capacity to carry their supporters in the reforms to which they have, in good faith, put their signature.' Having consulted various political figures from different standpoints, he reported a widely held view that Chichester-Clark would be lucky to last another six weeks. Robin Bailie, an up-and-coming Unionist MP, agreed, warning that 'HMG should seriously consider the possibility that pressure on the Northern Ireland Government would be such that the country would become incapable of political government.' In his report to Callaghan, Wright went on:

Northern Ireland is, of course, Ireland; opinions and tempers and moods are therefore volatile. One hesitates to register and report a mood that may be evanescent. But the one fairly constant factor in the equation is the pressure under which Northern Ireland Ministers, and in particular the Prime Minister and the Minister of Home Affairs, have now been working for months and the barely repressible desire of Brian Faulkner to take control. The pressure is cumulative and it is beginning to take its toll. You yourself saw the Prime Minister on television on Sunday. He was doing his level best; but the broadcast inevitably raised doubts whether his best is good enough. Already there is public discussion, encouraged by Craig and publicised by the 'News Letter', casting doubts upon the durability of the Chichester-Clark Government. Again there is talk about direct rule from Westminster.

In these circumstances, I think we still have no alternative but to pursue, for as long as we can, the present policies: to stick by the programme of reforms and to rely on the Northern Ireland Government as the instrument for putting them into effect. The Chichester-Clark Government is clearly in danger of losing both the desire and the will

to govern. A few weeks of calm, as opposed to successful suppression
of violence, may halt this erosion of confidence but I wouldn't like to
bet on it.

Despite this turbulent and uncertain political background, Young was
going about his new task with impressive vigour. He was soon known as
'"Softly, Softly" Young', the phrase he coined to describe how the
reformed RUC was to be permanently re-established in the Catholic 'no-
go' areas. He cultivated an air of affable pragmatism, appearing to listen
and learn from all around him. By 10 November, he was confident
enough to appear at an upbeat news conference declaring there were no
more 'no-go' areas for the RUC; the force was now generally unarmed; a
recruiting drive was imminent; a new building programme was being
planned; and four police stations had been reopened in Belfast to ensure
affinity between the force and the public. Young pointed to the issuing of
sixteen fixed penalty tickets for traffic offences in the Falls over the
previous few days as a sign that normal policing had been restored.

The reality was, however, not quite so rosy. Individual officers were
wary about their new unarmed role and felt vulnerable to attack when out
on the beat. A constable operating from one of the new police outposts,
established in an abandoned house at New Barnsley, came up with a
novel solution to provide a modicum of cover from stone-throwers. He
correctly calculated that by giving sweets to children he met on the
streets, causing others to surround him, he could create a confectionery
cordon sanitaire to deter attacks. Any impression that 'normal' policing
had been restored was therefore erroneous. At that point police in Belfast
were unable to execute 224 warrants or serve sixty-two summonses on
people residing in the 'barricaded' areas nor were they able to interview
146 persons in connection with a variety of offences. The position in
Londonderry was similar. There ninety-four warrants and twenty
summonses were outstanding and twelve persons were wanted for
interview. Before long the token police–Army patrols became less
frequent and soon stopped, but with the Army so evidently usurping
many police duties, such as traffic control, there was a rapidly spreading
acrimony between the two forces.

Young's view of the Army was no more positive and he quickly set off
a spell of bruising infighting which would engulf both organisations and
Whitehall for months to come. Its origins lay in the turning-point London
summit on 19 August when the Northern Ireland government had
surrendered its exclusive control of internal security. Shortly afterwards,

General Freeland hosted a 'study day' at his Lisburn headquarters for senior officers from both sides to chew over the uncharted implications of police and soldiers operating together in what remained officially peacetime. The morning session did not go well and by lunchtime in the officers' mess, one Army officer who had been present updated a colleague, saying: 'All that's become clear so far is that the Army don't like the RUC and the feeling is mutual.'

The first phase of the battle centred on the words 'full control' of the deployment and tasking of the RUC, contained in the GOC's directive from London. Despite the fact that it was the Northern Ireland government which had made the concession, Young approached the Home Office complaining that it was wrong in principle for the Army to control the police: he wanted all of this made public to raise the morale of the RUC and said it would be a resigning matter if he did not get his way. The division of Army–police responsibility was an area that Whitehall had long foreseen as being littered with problems and it had therefore grabbed at Chichester-Clark's concession with both hands. So, Callaghan, for one, cannot have been best pleased that Young, his own man in Belfast, was seeking to pick the delicate issue open again in such a confrontational fashion.

Young's threat was raised when the cabinet met in London the next day, 14 October, prompting a lengthy missive from Healey who insisted the GOC must remain director of security operations. 'I have no reason to believe that relations between [them] are anything but good at present, but the new situation obviously leaves some scope for friction which we must do our best to prevent,' he added. To help achieve this Healey arranged for John McKay, the inspector of constabulary already seconded to the RUC in Belfast, to be reassigned to the GOC's staff as a police adviser. Meanwhile, in a remarkable letter to the Home Office on 17 October, Young appeared to have 'gone native' and completely sided with the Northern Ireland government in having the GOC's role downgraded and winning back for them from London the security responsibility they had voluntarily surrendered. The GOC's responsibility was 'unconstitutional and at best an expedient', fumed Young:

> My advice is that [Freeland's] proper role is that of GOC without the embarrassment of additional responsibility which he cannot discharge and which puts him in a false position and subject to unreasonable and needless public and political pressures and criticisms. My views are shared, and strongly held, by the Prime Minister and the Minister of Home Affairs, but they have both agreed to leave all initiative in

bringing about the necessary change to me. The peace and stability of
the future of Northern Ireland. must be built upon an effective Police
Force, there can be no substitute. To win self-respect and the
confidence of the disputing political and religious factions the Police
must be manifestly seen to be free of political influence and
independent of Military or any other external control.

Young, now plainly suffering from delusions of grandeur and
significantly underestimating the extent of the crisis that had occurred,
met Sir Philip Allen, permanent under secretary at the Home Office, on
23 October 1969 to further advance his case and declared that in his
opinion 'the future of Northern Ireland largely depended on the efforts of
the RUC' and that the RUC largely depended on himself. Young, who
said he wished to ensure the RUC's loyalty and restore its morale,
explained that Freeland had agreed not to issue orders to him and that he
had issued orders to his local RUC men to 'co-operate' with the military
rather than 'obey' them. What he now wanted was for the directive to be
scrapped without delay and a public announcement made of this change
and the date on which the RUC would be unequivocally released from
military control. Allen pointed out that Freeland had suggested replacing
the word 'control' with 'co-ordinating' to help meet his concerns but that
the directive could not be amended without the approval of the home and
defence secretaries and, indeed, the prime minister. Young eventually
agreed that, for the moment, he would accept the position. Early the next
morning, Young had a chat with Baker, the chief of the General Staff, at
which the differences, while not resolved, were distilled into a working
accord.

The official notes understated the gravity of the constitutional
confrontation that was developing, essentially between the police and the
Army, and the irony of it. The RUC, having just been freed from political
control, was once more being fought over. Young was defending the
time-honoured principle that the British police – which evolving government policy now intended should embrace the RUC – were accountable
to the law and, unlike the military, exempt from direct political control.
Indeed he had threatened to resign, an event that would have seriously
exacerbated what was an already fraught and fragile situation in Northern
Ireland. These dangers were well appreciated by all in Whitehall, where
conciliation efforts to head off an outright clash had reached the highest
level. After his meetings in London, Young wrote again to Allen
reporting that, 'as a result of General Baker's personal invitation' and

'most cordial discussion' he accepted the directive would stand and on the basis of 'a personal understanding between the GOC and myself . . . I would make special efforts to see that the Police at all levels co-operated with the Army fully and willingly.' But Young ended his letter with an important caveat which confirmed the matter was still far from settled:

> I must, however, make it clear that the present position of the GOC as Director of Operations is not entirely satisfactory to me and although I do not anticipate trouble arising from it, it could give rise both to difficulties and to dangers which would be better avoided by taking a Constitutional assessment of the present situation.

What had been formally agreed was that, at Freeland's pragmatic suggestion, the word 'co-ordinate' would be substituted for 'full control' with the instruction to the GOC now to read: 'In accordance with your overall responsibility as Director of Operations you will co-ordinate the tasking of the RUC in relation to security operations.' In the Home Office and at the Ministry of Defence, on the opposite side of Whitehall, the compromise was, however, cynically regarded as nothing more than a sop to Young: 'a distinction of form rather than substance', as one Home Office mandarin described it. Nevertheless, on the back of it, a draft letter was prepared for the home secretary conveying Young's views as requested, but by the time it was ready events had overtaken it and it was never sent. A new problem had blown up: how to tell the Northern Ireland government.

As we have seen, ever since the eruption of the Northern Ireland crisis the previous autumn, layers of concealment and duplicity had been embedded in many aspects of the London–Belfast relationship. Although protocols covering the deployment of the Army had been agreed on 19 August, the Northern Ireland government had not been copied in on a Ministry of Defence letter to the GOC outlining the legal position of troops in Northern Ireland engaged on internal security duties. The impetus for deceit had come from Downing Street where a prime-ministerial aide had discouraged disclosure of the document because of a potentially conflicting interpretation of the military's obligations under common law. The legal advice stated that where they were summoned, the military had an inescapable duty to come to aid of the civil power. With the legal opinion leaving open precisely which civil power – London or Belfast – could call for assistance, Downing Street opted for non-disclosure because 'it raises the fundamental problem of the relationship between Westminster and Stormont on these matters', an ambiguity it preferred to be to be left for clarification in what the official described as 'more propitious circumstances'. Similarly the GOC's operational directive had not been openly disclosed to the Stormont authorities, although a copy had found its way into the Ministry of Home Affairs either through an oversight or some unofficial back channel. Thus, in October, on the back of the Young–Freeland clash, when Harold Black was advised of the amendment to the GOC's directive, he asked, 'What directive?' and refused to accept notice of the amendment without being given formal disclosure of the original.

With the main dispute patched up, however temporarily, these subsidiary tensions were now smoothed over in carefully drafted letters from the Home Office. To Black in Belfast they wrote: 'A purist would say that the amendment is obscure but as, in fact, it is meaningful to the two men concerned it has been approved by Ministers and I have no doubt that it will prove in practice successful in operation.'

There was another letter to the Ministry of Defence in similar terms, but in an element of back-covering this letter also stated: 'If there were to be any failure in co-ordination between the Army and the RUC as a result of our abandoning the overall control of the GOC it would be severely criticised.' But recognising that the issue, unresolved, could all too easily flare up again to the detriment of both parties, the Home Office went on to float a possible mechanism for reaching a more durable settlement. 'So long as there are men prepared to fight it out in the streets the Army will have to remain responsible for law and order,' the Home Office intoned, but 'we should at this moment of time ask the GOC, Mr Wright and the IG for their assessment of the conditions that must prevail before the IG can have the announcement he wishes [that the Army relinquished control of the police] and relations between the police and military can be restored to normal.' In a final tidying-up of the immediate confrontation, it was decided not to tell the British prime minister of the situation: 'in view of the happy way in which the GOC and the IG are working at present it would not seem to be necessary to do so'. As some feared, the truce was short-lived.

Within weeks, on 18 November 1969, Chichester-Clark, who was newly emboldened by a strong vote of confidence from the Ulster Unionist Council, his party's governing body, revisited the issue with Wilson and Callaghan during a visit to London. Northern Ireland's newly bullish ministers now supported the concept of having even the army's 'co-ordination' role removed and, with a recent reduction in street violence, were pushing to get the troops off the streets. Indeed Young wanted a full review of the GOC's position on the grounds that a gradual withdrawal of troops could begin as, he claimed, the policing of the Falls and Bogside was returning to normal. Whitehall was just as anxious to see the troops at least into their local barracks if not back to their normal postings in Britain, Germany and elsewhere as soon as feasible. So, on the back of the original Home Office suggestion, the idea of commissioning a full-scale 'appreciation' of the present and future situation in Northern Ireland had gained considerable ground within the Joint Security Committee at Stormont and the two London ministries. While this study was taking place, the standing directive would remain in place: Healey would not consider any 'emancipation' of the RUC from the GOC until the situation on the ground had radically changed. He was strongly of the view that 'it might lead to muddle and even bad feeling if the directive were discussed prematurely'. At meetings the next day terms of reference for the proposed study were approved and circulated to Freeland, Young and Porter:

> The GOC and the IG are requested to prepare an appreciation of the stages by which, and the time scales within which, the internal security situation in Northern Ireland may reasonably be expected to return to a state of normality; and a phased plan for a return to such a state, in which the regular garrison of Northern Ireland (whatever its size) will have returned to its customary duties, tasks, and roles, it being understood that its common law duty to aid the civil power if required to do so will remain.

Baker signalled Freeland to table the terms of reference at the next meeting of the Joint Security Committee in Belfast and to propose that work on preparing the joint appreciation be put in hand. The text went on to outline some broad, but not prescriptive, guidance for the study to follow. 'Normality', a concept that would haunt the military for years to come, was defined as the point where the troops were in their barracks carrying out normal duties but available for aid to the civil power under common-law obligation if required. The guidance said account should be taken of the effects of the increase in police strength and re-organisation and the coming into being of the Ulster Defence Regiment (the name assigned to the locally recruited 'home guard' force suggested by Hunt) as a military force which would relieve the Army of responsibilities for guarding key points and protecting the border.

Whatever hopes Whitehall had for a quiet winter on the Northern Ireland front, while the police and Army conducted their appreciation, were very quickly dashed. The first point of friction arose when the Army suggested that firearms issued to the new regiment should be safely stored in convenient police stations when the soldiers were not on duty. (There had been considerable determination in London that, unlike the B Specials, the UDR would not take their arms home save in the most exceptional circumstances.) Young was sympathetic to the practicalities of the situation but immediately decided that storing the weapons would impose a major burden on the police and compromise the very concept of an unarmed force which he was trying to establish.

This row was, however, of mere brush-fire proportions when compared with the firestorm that erupted over whether, and how, police or soldiers should in future deal with public disorder on the streets. The opening salvo came from Young in a letter to Freeland on 8 December 1969 when he attempted to lay down the basic principle that the the police should no longer be employed in indiscriminate or aggressive baton charges to disperse unruly crowds and must rely entirely on passive measures of a similar nature to those used by police in the United Kingdom. 'Such duties will be undertaken by police manifestly unarmed and almost certainly outnumbered. We shall have to learn new techniques in crowd control and be prepared, if necessary, to suffer individual casualties in demonstrating our new role', said Young, adding that the RUC Special Patrol Group would no longer carry riot shields or protective headgear. 'If tear-smoke should be necessary I recommend that this should be employed by the military force with the agreement of the police commander and if sterner measures, such as the use of firearms become imperative, I hope that the military commander would first consult the senior police officer,' he concluded.

Freeland received Young's letter the next morning and responded immediately in an outspoken confidential letter to Baker. He began by stressing the urgency of clarifying policy because 'the strength and tactics of the police are essential factors for the appreciation and until ministers in London can agree exactly where the soldiers stand in relation to any new police policy in dealing with riots, our appreciation would be of very limited value'. He was also worried about Young's plans for the RUC not to use riot-control aids, such as water cannon, batons and tear smoke but to call upon soldiers and instruct them when to do so whenever things got difficult.

This is an impossible situation because it virtually places the soldiers under the police command which, in turn, places the soldiers under command of Stormont – a thing that no British Government would agree to. Unless the British Army is going to be involved on every weekend the police force must be increased very substantially and special patrol groups must be equipped with every modern type of equipment to deal with the tough Irish rioters who do not hesitate to use any weapon at hand.

Freeland said he would tell the next Security Committee meeting at Stormont of the need for clarification of police capabilities in riot situations 'which have much significance for the Army, not only in Northern Ireland but probably elsewhere in the UK in the future'. It now transpired that neither the Home Office nor the Ministry of Home Affairs had provided Young with a copy of the agreed guidance designed to inform the preparation of the planned appreciation. The omission, whether deliberate or accidental, was an indicator of the scale of the infighting, rivalries and personal tensions swirling around in the constitutional vacuum that had been created, with London, Belfast, the police and the Army all defending their own corners and promoting their own standpoints on the issues. Freeland had copied his letter to Wright, who provided a caustic commentary on the situation in an epistle to the Home Office on 11 December after the Security Committee gave the go-ahead for work on the appreciation:

[. . .] the position has been somewhat complicated by the Inspector-General's desire to move as swiftly as he can – and to my mind probably rather more swiftly than is wise – to a completely civilianised police force. His objective in placing the RUC on all fours with the British police is admirable and no-one could possibly object to it. But he envisages the police not only being disarmed, but also not being trained in or equipped for riot control with anything beyond the individual policeman's personal fourteen stone. He doesn't want them to carry batons or shields, and he doesn't want them to be responsible for the first use of tear smoke. In other words, the Army would have to come in at the very first scale of escalation if the flesh and bone breaks. Moreover (but this, I think, is more a problem of high horses than of real substance) the Inspector-General appears to be wanting to get into a position where the police summon the Army, to do the initial dirty work for them under police control. That is perhaps putting it a bit too strong, but you see the general drift.

Naturally, the GOC has reacted quite strongly to this. It is his belief that, in Irish conditions, flesh and bone are not enough, and that the RUC, whilst remaining disarmed, shouldn't rely on flesh and bone alone. There is also the question of numbers. Whatever the quality of the RUC, it is common ground that the quantity is altogether insufficient. The target establishment of 3,500 has not yet been reached, and clearly the establishment should be considerably larger. You can't expect 3,000 policemen working an 8-hour day five days a week to replace 7,000-plus soldiers working, if necessary, round the clock.

So you see there are several inter-related problems here. I have indicated to the GOC the undesirability of giving the Northern Ireland authorities scope for going back on the complete civilianisation of the RUC. He takes the point; but says equally that he doesn't much care for his soldiers being liable to be called in as soon as the Irish crowd gets out of control because the police have nothing but flesh and bone to offer. He thinks the soldiers should only come in when the shooting has to start, because that is what soldiers are trained for and are good at.

Wright hoped the differences would sort themselves out once the soldiers and police got down to work together but warned that with 'personalities as well as principles involved, not to mention cash [for expanding the RUC]', it was 'not going to be an easy exercise. We shall be very lucky indeed if we can get through without a certain amount of argument between the Home Secretary and the Defence Secretary,' he concluded. Over in London, the nascent rivalries on the opposite sides of Whitehall were indeed heating up. Although the Home Office thought that Young's last letter 'was not very happily phrased against the background of the review', a minute for senior officials talked of the GOC's 'umbrageous' letter and correctly offered the view that they did not think 'Freeland or the Secretary of State for Defence will acquiesce in a police officer being in command of a situation that the police cannot control'.

These latest differences were smoothed over by officials in Whitehall, well practised in bridging differences. They simply amended the memorandum of guidance, taking account of all the sensitivities that had been expressed. Relationships improved sufficiently quickly after that for Young to be able to report to the Home Office on 23 December, before his departure from Belfast for Christmas, that through their staff officers, Freeland and he were making 'useful progress with our joint appreciation of the phasing-out of the army operations in Northern Ireland'. The work

Sir James Craig, Prime Minister of
Northern Ireland, 1921–40.

Sir Richard Dawson Bates, Minister
of Home Affairs, 1921–43.

Royal Irish Constabulary crest.

Royal Ulster Constabulary crest.

Sir Charles Wickham, Inspector-General,
Royal Ulster Constabulary, 1922–45.

Special Constabulary at Newtownbutler, Co. Fermanagh, 1922.

RUC officers operating a checkpoint on the border during the IRA's 1956–62 terrorist campaign.

Sir Richard Pim, Inspector-General,
Royal Ulster Constabulary, 1945–61.

Captain Terence O'Neill,
Prime Minister of Northern Ireland, 1963–9.

An RUC Shorland armoured patrol vehicle.

Major James Chichester-Clark, Prime Minister of Northern Ireland, 1969–71, and members of his Cabinet.

Police and army on joint patrol in Belfast in 1978.

Anthony Peacocke,
Inspector-General, Royal Ulster
Constabulary, 1969.

William Craig, Minister of Home
Affairs, 1963–4 and 1966–8.

Sir Robert Porter, Minister of
Home Affairs, 1969–70

Sir Arthur Young, Chief Constable,
Royal Ulster Constabulary, 1969–70.

Lord Grey, Governor of
Northern Ireland, 1968–73.

Brian Faulkner, Prime Minister
of Northern Ireland, 1971–2.

Sir Kenneth Newman, Chief Constable, Royal Ulster Constabulary 1976–9.

Sir John Hermon, Chief Constable, Royal Ulster Constabulary 1980–9.

An armed policeman protects a colleague on patrol in Newry, Christmas 1985.

Sir Hugh Annesley, Chief Constable,
Royal Ulster Constabulary 1989–96.

Sir Ronnie Flanagan, Chief Constable,
Royal Ulster Constabulary 1996–2002.

HM the Queen presents the George Cross to Constable Paul Slaine
at Hillsborough on 12 April 2000. Looking on are Assistant Chief
Constable Bill Stewart and Constable Susan Wright.

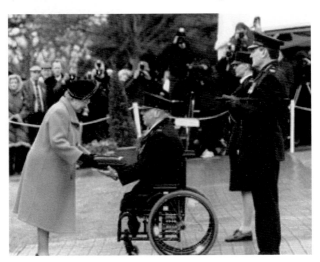

Disband the RUC poster, Belfast 2001.

Hugh Orde, Chief Constable,
Police Service of Northern Ireland, 2002.

Police Service of
Northern Ireland crest.

was actually in third-draft form and over the Christmas period General Tony Dyball, one of Freeland's staff officers, intended to produce a fourth, incorporating a series of modifications suggested by the RUC.

In his 'end of term' report to the Home Office Wright provided a sobering overview of the mood at the end of a momentous year:

> The security situation has been tolerably quiet ever since the week-end of 11–12 October when the Protestant mob took to the streets and registered their protest against the Hunt Report by shooting a Protestant policeman. Many sophisticated reasons have been given for this uneasy calm, but I think the simplest and most straightforward is the best. The security forces shot and killed two rioters. Irish irregulars quite enjoy shooting in the back and in the dark, but are not so keen on open confrontation with the experts. This proof that the British regulars meant business registered; that and the arrest and imprisonment of the ring-leaders have given us a quiet autumn on the Shankill.
>
> Politically, Major Chichester-Clark and his Government have been as good as their word and have put Stage One of their reform programme on the statute book by Christmas. The Stage Two reforms – principally the implementation of the Hunt Report and the creation of a central housing authority – are also making good progress both at Westminster and at Stormont. By the spring, the police should have been civilianised and removed from direct political control; the B Specials should have been finally phased out and the Ulster Defence Regiment, under Westminster control and Army command, put in their place. The tans will replace the black.
>
> As the events of the past twelve months fade from memory, a return to normal has meant a return to the old animosities. The ancient wrongs are too deep-seated for overnight reform to bring instant reconciliation. Although more has been done for the eradication of injustice in the last fifty days than for the last fifty years, there is too much religion in this country for Christianity to prevail. The reforms must be carried through because they are good in themselves, because it is right that common standards of justice should prevail throughout the United Kingdom and because they will ease the immediate tensions, not because they promise any final solution to the Irish problem.

Young caught influenza over the Christmas 1969 break and, in his absence, it was left to Shillington to comment on Dyball's draft of the appreciation early in January. In a letter to the Home Office, signed in the green ink habitually used by senior RUC men, he asked for an insertion stating that the GOC had now 'relinquished his command of the RUC' and suggested including another sentence: 'There is also a building up of Protestant impatience at the slow return to normal policing in some Catholic areas. This could lead to a re-action against both army and police in Protestant areas.' Shillington also sought to add clarification that while the police strength would increase by well in excess of 1,000, the estimate of doing so at the rate of 350 to 400 a year was over-optimistic because of the lack of instructors and accommodation. He further wanted to add text emphasising that while the police envisaged creating a Special Riot Control Unit, Young's doctrine that it would use nothing other than 'traditional British tactics' was paramount.

Young's unyielding views on this point had come to be seen as utterly impractical and obstructive by Freeland and the Army. Over Christmas, the GOC had discussed his frustrations with the governor, Lord Grey, describing the inspector-general's interpretation of 'civilianisation' as 'jolly red-faced policemen with linked arms' being hopelessly inappropriate. The governor, while careful to record that he had not talked directly with Young, was moved to write to the Home Office on 8 January 1970 urging them to resolve what had now become a matter of fundamental policy.

The joint appreciation was completed and circulated towards the end of January. Classified Secret, the fifteen-page document analysed the current 'threat' in Northern Ireland at the beginning of 1970:

> Sectarian division of the population is as deep as ever and will take a long time to break down. On the Protestant side there is resentment at what they believe to be the Government's weakness in yielding to pressure from Westminster; and from Roman Catholic and left-wing agitators; at the continuing delay in re-establishing police authority in the troubled areas in Belfast; and at the fate of the Ulster Special Constabulary.
>
> On the other side, although moderates are prepared to wait and see how the government's reform programme is implemented there are militant elements among the Republicans and IRA, in the People's Democracy and in the Civil Rights Association itself which will not be satisfied with what is being done and which will continue to demonstrate against authority and seek further causes for action. The IRA and Sinn Fein are divided doctrinally; the left-wing leadership and its followers will continue to follow the subversive line of penetrating

and getting control of Civil Rights organisations while the breakaway
groups will endeavour to assert themselves by a more militant policy
which may lead to acts of violence on both sides of the border.

In a section of the report dealing with the police, the study noted that
'even with the use of paramilitary methods, RUC numbers had been
proved inadequate' during the previous year and, however gallantly they
had acted, they had always been outnumbered. Noting the perennial
problem of handling parades and demonstrations, the report said such
events were quite different to those from England. 'In England it is
generally one side against the police; in Northern Ireland it is the two
sides against each other and the two sides against the police.'
Recognising that a programme to train the RUC's 230-strong Special
Patrol Group in London-type public-order policing had 'produced a new
confidence' and that similar training would soon enable it to put 1,000
officers into confrontational situations, the study expressed concern that
it would be April 1975 at least before the RUC would be fully expanded
to its new 4,940 establishment. This was the number of officers it was
calculated would be needed to deter and prevent a repeat of the 1969
experience without calling on military assistance.

In its main conclusions, the report stated that the elusive 'state of
normality' would not be reached until the RUC was capable of maintaining law and order without the involvement of the military, except as
a last resort. With the aim of reaching 'normality' by 1 December 1970,
the study set out an all too optimistic timetable. From January to March,
the Army would provide support for the police and protection for the
community while the RUC would progressively return to all areas of the
province. From April to June, this process would be consolidated while
the Army gradually withdrew to its barracks and dismantled the Peace
Line in Belfast, which would be capable of being put back at short notice
if required. Over the summer, without day-to-day military protection but
with cover at critical times, the police would conduct business as normal.
By November, the Army role would shrink to providing a small
emergency reserve with most troops engaged in normal duties and
training in their barracks. On 1 December, a formal 'state of normality'
would be declared, the post of Director of Operations would be abolished
and all troops would resume peacetime duties.

This rosy appreciation was not accepted uncritically at the Home
Office. A hard-nosed, but unsigned, comment scrawled on the margin
said: 'This says what police won't do. It should say what they will do.

Surely they must in the end be prepared to be more than passive?' At the Ministry of Defence the study was more warmly, but still cautiously, received. A commentary prepared for the chief of the General Staff described it as 'a very much more acceptable and sound paper' because the police input was fuller and more clearly stated, but, as in the Home Office, they harboured doubts about the viability of the proposals for the police to deal with public disorder. Noting that 'it is not the intention to equip the RUC SPG with any riot control equipment', the memorandum continues:

> While this puts them into line with UK police it does, of course, mean that military forces may well be called in earlier than they would be otherwise if the group had CS gas. It should also be noted that the paper seems quite clear that as the RUC have now learned UK police methods for dealing with disturbances 'there can be no doubt that police efficiency to deal with public disorder should have improved immeasurably.' Irish crowds are not however English crowds and [we] have some reservations about this statement.

Meanwhile, throughout that spectacularly busy autumn of 1969, while Young was fighting with the Army, the Home Office was still wrestling with the task of integrating the RUC more closely into the network of British police forces. After the Hunt report was published, they convened a high-powered group on 30 October 1969 to consider the implications. The meeting was chaired by the senior Home Office official HW Stotesbury and the twenty-three other participants included Colonel Sir Eric St Johnson, the Chief Inspector of Constabulary, the Metropolitan Police Commissioner Sir John Waldron and representatives of the police staff associations. Local government organisations from England, Wales and Scotland, whose police authorities paid the bills for policing, also took part. The RUC itself was not represented and the only absentee, from whom an apology was received, was Chief Constable Sir Arthur Young.

Stotesbury began by outlining the government's intention to remodel the RUC to make it more civilian in character, by assimilating British policing traditions through closer links with British forces, especially through training and mutual aid. There was still little enthusiasm for the mutual aid proposition. Dick Pamplin, the Police Federation delegate, again said his members could not be expected to support the RUC until it was doing a similar job of work without firearms. Other delegates expressed disquiet that the compulsory powers inherent in mutual aid removed the decision to serve in Northern Ireland from the individual and could lead to British policemen being subordinated to RUC officers. Stotesbury concluded the meeting by saying the home secretary had authorised him to state that no action would be taken without further consultation and until the RUC had been reorganised and disarmed. The Home Office, although perturbed by the uncooperative tone of the meeting, remained committed to the principle of mutual aid. In a minute next day, an official said: 'The whole object . . . is to ensure that the RUC became as British a police force as any other in the United Kingdom. It would not be acceptable therefore to have . . . special reservations on mutual aid which applied to the special political circumstances of Northern Ireland.'

While the Police Bill, implementing the Hunt report, started its passage through parliament in London that November, the reservations about its far-reaching implications for the mainland police intensified as news of its provisions spread through the national police constituency. The County Councils Association asked who would pay in the event of a dispute with the Police Authority in Northern Ireland and pressed for an arbitration clause like the one in the Police Act 1964 which provided for the home secretary to settle financial disputes. More problematically, the Police Federation and some MPs raised concerns about the possibility of British police officers being required to operate within the framework of Northern Ireland's repressive Special Powers Act or enforce the controversial flags and emblems legislation. Although Chichester-Clark and his Belfast administration had been ready to repeal the Special Powers Act earlier in 1969, the sabotage attacks on public utility installations in March caused them to balk until a period of calm was assured. So, for the moment, they had given assurances to the home secretary that it was not their intention to ask British police to act under the legislation. Nevertheless, Callaghan was still in favour of adding a clause to the legislation specifically to protect British police officers from having to enforce what he described as 'odious' legislation. But the defence secretary, Denis Healey, had serious reservations about the concept of such a partial protection which he frankly expressed in a minute to Callaghan on 21 November 1969. Healey argued that as the Army, and the incoming Ulster Defence Regiment, relied on provisions of the act, but not 'the most repugnant' of them, he would come under pressure to bring in a similar immunisation which would leave the armed forces powerless. He summed up by saying that he was in favour of maintaining 'the utmost pressure upon Northern Ireland Ministers to repeal the Special Powers Acts while retaining those powers which are essential and reasonable within a more acceptable legislative framework'.

In the event, the concept of large-scale mutual aid for the RUC was quietly forgotten as being far too problematic. Some time later, in a letter to the home secretary, Chichester-Clark finally killed the idea off: 'I believe it is vain to imagine that the conditions of the Bogside will within any reasonable period be assimilated to those of Surbiton.' Instead, links with the British police service were widened and deepened. RUC officers increasingly visited other forces to listen and learn and bring back techniques and ideas to Belfast. They took part in national police training courses, acquiring greater expertise, and from time to time experienced senior detectives and other officers were seconded to Belfast to assist them. For the first time the RUC was officially part of the British police family, but, like all troublesome relatives, it was kept politely at arm's length.

Chapter Seven
A Grand Confrontation

'IRA – I Ran Away' was the taunting message daubed on the gable walls of west Belfast in the autumn of 1969 as the Republican movement took stock of its credibility amidst the post-riots upheaval. Old-timers in Belfast, who ranked the defence of the city's Catholics as sacred a duty as the achievement of a united Ireland, were horrified by the lack of arms available from the Dublin leadership, who, in the belief that social agitation rather than urban guerrilla warfare would more effectively attain their aims, had earlier sold much of their arsenal to the self-styled 'Free Wales Army'. By the end of 1969 the northern old-timers had decided to go their own way and resume the fight for a united Ireland, so, in January 1970, they effected a formal split from the 'Official' IRA by forming a breakaway 'Provisional' IRA with a 'Provisional' Sinn Fein as its political shop-front. The move was to have violent and far-reaching consequences for the people of Ireland.

The first sign of new Republican militancy was not long in coming when Northern Ireland's seasonal irritant, the marching season, came round again at Easter 1970. Given its significance for Republicans, who hold a series of events to commemorate the 1916 Rising, and for the Loyalist marching orders who step out on the first parades of the year, Easter was traditionally a testing time for the police. Young prudently cancelled all police leave and called for restraint in a public message a few days before. Initial concern was focused on Armagh, where 600 troops were deployed to seal off the Catholic area while Paisley led a 3,000-strong parade through the town. That night there were sighs of relief and doubles all round at police and Army headquarters as they toasted an incident-free day. There were a series of minor disturbances, but no serious incidents, on Easter Sunday.

Ronnie Burroughs, another British diplomat, who had just succeeded Wright, reported to London that 'the generally satisfactory outcome was however only achieved by working all the security forces very hard'. The RUC's new image as a 'non-retaliatory, non-aggressive' service was enhanced, he reported, but without the Army backing they would not have been able to restrain the marchers, whether Protestant or Catholic:

> Public order was at risk throughout the whole period in a number of widely separated areas, necessitating constant re-deployment of police and army units to potential trouble spots. Liaison between the two forces worked very smoothly, and this can also be regarded as one of the more satisfactory features. Indeed by the afternoon of Tuesday, 31 March, there seemed to be every reason for congratulation and relief.

But that evening, soon after Burroughs's teleprinter had stopped clattering out the encouraging message to London, events took an unexpectedly violent turn as one of the last Orange marches of the weekend returned to an obscure Orange Hall adjacent to the predominantly Catholic area of Ballymurphy in west Belfast. In a premeditated attack, Catholic youths stoned the Orangemen, and once members of the Royal Scots Regiment moved in to separate the two sides the disturbances quickly metamorphosed into a direct confrontation between the Catholics and the military, which seems to have been the primary intention. Over the next five hours, as vehicles were hijacked and set alight to block roads, the soldiers came under sustained attack from petrol bombs and other missiles and twenty were injured. Similar orchestrated trouble continued for two more nights and was only brought to a distinctly uneasy end by what was later described to London as 'very firm military action' on the night of 2/3 April when a large quantity of CS gas was fired. That night, the ongoing trouble was aggravated by mobs of Protestants who gathered in the nearby Woodvale area and threatened to invade the Catholic suburb. The clashes were a dangerous turning-point in that, for the first time, well prepared, stone-throwing, teenage male Catholic rioters formed highly elusive gangs and aggressively attacked soldiers. Soon afterwards, it became clear that the trouble had been carefully stage-managed to mark the violent debut of the Provisional IRA.

The scale of violence prompted renewed calls for a crackdown to restore law and order from Chichester-Clark's critics. Their uncompromising mood since the disbandment of the B Specials had been exacerbated by the continued rolling-out of a reform programme they regarded as rewarding the Catholics for lawlessness. So clashes like those at Ballymurphy further fuelled Protestant discontent and helped swell hostility to the Belfast government. With imminent Stormont by-elections at South Antrim and Bannside, where Paisley was challenging to take the seat of the departed prime minister, Terence O'Neill, and win elected office for the first time, Chichester-Clark, O'Neill's equally embattled successor, was eager to bolster his own unconvincing position and boost his apparently impotent security policies. So, two days before a meeting with Callaghan in London on 10 April, he acted in the time-honoured way of Unionist leaders under political pressure. General Freeland was summoned to Stormont, where the prime minister pushed for much tougher action on the streets. What he wanted was a British government declaration that the RUC in its new civilianised guise would at once re-assume full policing responsibility in all areas and that the Army would use all the muscle that was necessary to enable them to do so.

The next day, at another meeting attended by Freeland, the draft of a statement the Belfast government wanted published was circulated for discussion. When the general read it, he denounced it instantly as 'ridiculous' and added that the police did not have enough men to carry out the proposed task. Young, on the other hand, was less critical but, significantly, did not contradict what the GOC had said. There was further discussion, which revolved around the capability of the police for the task rather than their acceptability in the Catholic enclaves and the effect such a crass initiative would have on opinion there. What the Northern Ireland government intended to do was yet again to play politics with the police for their own Unionist ends by enforcing a high-visibility RUC presence, with the military remaining close in the background to come to their rescue if disturbances took place. The Belfast administration still did not understand that the days when the RUC had done the party's bidding were at an end.

Over in London, where both the Ministry of Defence and the Home Office had got wind of the demand, stiff briefings had been prepared for their respective ministers to counter it. Officials at Defence were unambiguous in their advice: 'The Northern Ireland Government proposal was impracticable, doomed to failure, and, if persisted in, conducive to a major worsening of the security situation.' They took the opportunity to have a sideswipe at Young, citing 'the intermittent character of the Inspector-General's grip on affairs (due to his frequent absences from the Province)'. When the strength of the hostility in London was relayed back to Belfast there was an immediate retreat. A Home Office minute on 9 April records:

> These doubts seemed to shake Stormont Castle. We then told Sir
> Harold Black that the Secretary of State [Callaghan] could not possibly

subscribe to a communiqué indicating dramatic measures to re-impose police control where it did not now exist: or indeed to any statement about the position from which such an intention could be inferred. We said that the Secretary of State thought to announce such an intention would not only cause violence, but would do political harm which might exceed the harm done by the loss of the Bannside election.

When they arrived in London next morning, a chastened Chichester-Clark and Porter had significantly scaled down their demands and the statement that came out after their two-hour discussion with Callaghan was considerably more anodyne. It merely restated the British government's view that there would have to be a considerable period of peace before troops could be taken off the streets. What did not figure in the statement, but which occupied much of the meeting, was the ongoing bickering between Young and Freeland over the future role of the RUC. The Army, whose low opinion of Young was now barely concealed, used the summit as a forum to reopen its campaign for the RUC to assume some of the responsibility for tackling riots if the Army were to be even partially relieved of its growing entrenchment in Northern Ireland. In its background paper for the meeting the Ministry of Defence said that part of the process of examining how progress could be made 'towards a state of greater normality might well consist in reviewing the Joint Appreciation prepared by the GOC and the Inspector-General in January'. This, of course, had been shelved because 'conditions did not appear propitious for proceeding with it', but the Ministry of Defence was still determined to dilute the standing doctrine that the RUC should operate on a strict par with mainland British forces and overturn Young's unyielding stand on the point, the key issue that had so soured his personal relationship with Freeland. Their alternative was for Belfast to recognise 'the virtual inevitability that under Northern Irish conditions the RUC would have to operate rather differently in some respects from a normal English police force' and that 'in dealing with riotous situations they must make use of batons, water cannon or CS, before troops could be called on'. For this reason, the ministry wanted the Joint Appreciation quickly revisited to lay down the principle that while the RUC was a 'British' police force, in many important respects, it was and would be different.

The Home Office was entirely sympathetic to the aim of ensuring the RUC could more adequately deal with trouble without routine recourse to the army but was very clear that the force was not going to be re-licensed to engage in 'the excessive and wanton use of force that has characterised some previous operations'. Young's stand to the contrary was now as unwelcome in the Home Office as it was in Defence and was increasingly being disowned by his host department: 'His view that "normality" can be achieved only when there is no danger of violent disorder . . . may be exceedingly far ahead. It seems to us to carry the doctrine of parity of police practice much too far to say that the RUC should never exceed the measures used by the police in this country.'

The Home Office had managed to persuade Belfast that strict parity was not the way ahead and the point had already been partially conceded when they agreed a new protocol for the RUC to use CS gas in certain circumstances. In a move to further outflank Young, they next suggested drawing a new operational baseline for the RUC where they would adopt only the same sort of measures that the British police would use if they were faced with the kind of disorders that must be foreseen in Northern Ireland. To tease out the precise meaning of this sophistry, they proposed forming a working party of RUC officers, assisted by the Army and members of British forces, to review the type of disorder that occurs in Northern Ireland and produce a report to assist the Northern Ireland government 'in convincing Young of the principles which must be followed'.

While these exchanges to undermine him were taking place, Young submitted to the Home Office a lengthy account of his stewardship to date, bizarrely headed: 'For the eyes only of those for whom it is expressly intended'. Recalling his unheralded arrival in Belfast eight months earlier, Young said he had found the force in a state of shock and trauma after the sacking of Peacocke. Many of the senior officers were unresponsive and, worse, seemed to be out of touch with their commands, and he feared that his first personal contact with the rank and file could easily have resulted in an undisciplined revolt. 'My first objective was to change the attitude of the RUC and to steer them away from the use of indiscriminate, escalating and retaliatory force.' But, he complained, the lack of firm decision on the part of the Northern Ireland government and civil service to proceed with the Hunt recommendations in a decisive and expeditious way had handicapped him. Expressing gratitude to the Army and the GOC, whose parallel control from Westminster and liaison with Stormont made his task 'at times near impossible to achieve', Young remarked that the presence of the Army was both appreciated and resented, often simultaneously, by the same individuals.

Of the RUC, Young believed that morale was sound and that the majority of its members were confident their future would be an improving one. 'Understandably there are those whose political sympathies accord with politicians who resent the changes which are taking place and declare that we shall go back to the days before Hunt. Evidence of this lack of loyalty has not embarrassed me but it has had the insidious effect of making the Government less sure of itself and less firm in decisions which directly affect the police.' On a personal note Young referred to the direct abuse he encountered from those of extreme Protestant views and said he had to be 'at least a little careful when I am away from the office and in public places'. Despite this, he suggested, his secondment to the RUC should not be extended beyond March 1971 when someone else should be drafted in to continue the reform of the RUC, which he estimated would take ten years to complete.

On other communications at this time, Young asked his mentor, Callaghan, to conceal his correspondence from the military, but with the Ministry of Defence and Home Office now united in opposition, he seemed to be unaware of the extent of the hostility gathering force against him. Lieutenant-General Sir Victor FitzGeorge Balfour, the vice-chief of the General Staff, added a postscript to a letter to Freeland specifically instructing him not to discuss its contents with Young. In Belfast, Young's poor relations with the military were mirrored by a deteriorating relationship with Porter, whom he accused of reneging on a decision to dispose of RUC arms stored at the Sprucefield depot near Belfast. (The RUC's arsenal amounted to over 15,000 rifles, a similar number of revolvers, pistols and shotguns, 3,000 automatic weapons, 117 mortars, 970 mortar bombs, 27,000 illuminating cartridges and 3,000 miscellaneous flares and detonators as well as 8,000,000 rounds of ammunition and forty-one armoured vehicles. One astonished Army officer remarked there were 'third world armies not as well armed as the RUC'.)

When Young called to see Callaghan in London on 21 April he confided that he feared the Belfast government and Army were trying to provoke his resignation but insisted he would carry on until the limit of his term a year hence. With frequent violent deaths, sporadic trouble continuing on the streets, shootings and bombings becoming a nightly occurrence and the potentially volatile 1970 marching season looming on the horizon, Callaghan asked him when he would have the 500 men newly trained in public-order tactics whom the Army were pushing for. Young said he might have 200 soon and was aiming for 1,000 in six months.

At this point it was clear that, despite all his confident public pronouncements, Young was floundering. The RUC's future role was uncertain, largely because of his ongoing feud with the Army; political instability and events on the ground continued to fracture every timetable for getting the troops off the streets and, as a report from one of the British diplomats attached to Burroughs underlined, normal policing was far from restored and RUC morale was still at rock bottom. After a visit to Londonderry, the diplomat wrote: 'The police have yet to regain an adequate measure of confidence in their ability to discharge a normal police role in the city.' As a result, unaccompanied military patrols, increasing in scope and frequency, were the principal demonstration of law and order being maintained. He also reported on an unlikely troublemaker the Army discovered in the city and the unorthodox means they adopted to deal with him. The culprit was Trooper McGarrigal of the Royal Irish Hussars, stationed at Bovington Camp, Dorset, a man of supposed Paisleyite views, whose regular visits to a Catholic girlfriend in the Bogside when home on leave invariably stimulated trouble. 'The army are aware of the need to do something about the activities of this man and I gather that arrangements are in hand for him to be posted to the Far East,' said the official.

There were too few light-hearted episodes, however, as the despatches to Callaghan from Burroughs became increasingly gloomy. As Chichester-Clark and Porter feared, Paisley and his deputy, the Reverend William Beattie, convincingly won the two by-elections, administering what Burroughs called a 'severe shock' to the Unionist party and giving a 'shot in the arm' to the hardliners who were now 'serving notice the Protestant community was going to fight to preserve its privileges'. Burroughs continued:

> The prime minister is almost at the end of his tether and last week was privately, but I believe sincerely, threatening resignation. If he goes, it is vain to think there can be a reshuffle of personalities and a retention of the reform programme. Any successor government must be substantially to the right of the present one and the inevitable consequences will be demonstrations on the streets and public disorder, possibly on a very serious scale.

Stating his belief that the British government should offer unequivocal support to ensure Chichester-Clark's survival, which was essential to the safety of Northern Ireland, Burroughs spelled out the implications if:

> Any administration which included people such as Mr William Craig would be unacceptable to the minority and would lead to a serious

breakdown in law and order. In any case, a Government of this complexion would seek to revert to practices which are surely unacceptable
within this Kingdom. I would not expect the right wing to put forward
one of the more notorious extremists as Prime Minister. It is more
likely that they would propose a man of straw such as Captain [John]
Brooke, the present Minister for Information and the son of Lord
Brookeborough, one of the archetypal figureheads of the Protestant
ascendancy. To permit the establishment of any such an administration
would create a situation for which only too many unfortunate parallels
can be found in colonial history. Even a 'compromise candidate' such
as Captain Brooke could only rest on British bayonets. No amount of
military force could prevent disorders and it is by no means fanciful to
envisage civil war.

If, therefore, Major Chichester-Clark's administration were to be
defeated, it would be necessary for HM Government seriously to
consider the suspension of the Constitution and direct intervention by
Westminster. But this itself would create or revive almost as many
problems as it solved. Although it would go far towards guaranteeing
the rights of the minority, I cannot see the Republican movement
accepting without demur the re-imposition of direct rule. On the other
flank, the extremist Protestants against whom such a move would be
aimed, would certainly fight, if only with gelignite and snipers' rifles
in the dark.

There were good grounds for identifying such a threat. When the
Specials were finally 'stood down' and replaced by a part-time RUC
Reserve and the Ulster Defence Regiment on 30 April, thousands of them
formed legal gun clubs, raising fears among the Catholic minority that
they would become the cutting edge of the backlash against the continued
erosion of Protestant supremacy. There was also much anxiety about the
security of the police arsenal, still held at Sprucefield. Although under
heavy guard, there was no absolute guarantee it would not fall into the
hands of hardliners like Craig, who was increasingly talking about a
'unilateral declaration of independence' if the British government
changed the constitutional position and interfered with Stormont.

The British general election on 18 June showed a significant erosion of
support for Chichester-Clark's moderate stance and a corresponding
surge in hardline Unionism in Northern Ireland. Nationally it brought
about a change of government in London. Edward Heath, the Conservative Party leader, ousted Harold Wilson's Labour administration and

became prime minister while Reginald Maudling replaced Callaghan as home secretary. In a secret 'first day brief', the security situation in Northern Ireland was summarised for him as follows:

> The Army have continued to deal completely successfully with the situation and retain a generally untarnished image, though there is antagonism against them in the Shankill Road. Their ready acceptance by the Roman Catholics could, however, be imperilled at any time by a violent incident. There could also be a worsening of relations if the Army are put in the position of controlling many processions that commanded popular support. There are real signs that the RUC are gaining both in morale and expertise, but the Army presence is always visible behind the police. We cannot expect the RUC alone to maintain law and order for a long time yet.
>
> The RUC's weakness is most manifest in the continued lack of full policing in the Falls Road and the Bogside. There is now some police presence in these areas 24-hours a day, but it falls far short of the policing to be expected in a normal situation, and this fact provokes increasing protest from the Shankill Road, Mr. Paisley and right-wing Unionist MP's, who are ready to forget that normal policing did not exist even before the troubles of last August. The RUC, however, are bound to go slowly in restoring full policing to these areas and we can expect the right-wing to make more capital out of this as time goes on.

How volatile it all was became clear very quickly. Bernadette Devlin, the fiery young civil rights activist, who had retained her Mid-Ulster seat in the election, was arrested a week later on Friday 26 June on the outskirts of Londonderry and taken to Armagh prison to serve a six-month term for offences committed during the 'Battle of the Bogside'. Catholics as a whole saw this as a sign of renewed one-sided repression and rioting erupted almost immediately in Londonderry and several parts of Belfast. By the time it had subsided on Sunday evening, five people had been shot dead, 200 civilians were injured (fifty-four with gunshot wounds, of whom two died later) and ten soldiers were in hospital. In a symbol of the very grave escalation of disorder, the Army calculated 2,000 rounds had been fired in running gun battles, the fiercest of them on the Saturday night around St Matthew's Catholic Church in east Belfast, where two of the fatalities occurred. The handling of this incident, which, for the record, was the first armed engagement by the 'Provos', demonstrated the operational gulf that existed between the police and Army. When the gunfire started the unarmed police could not intervene and, despite their call for military assistance, it was several hours before there was an effective intervention because the two battalions available in the city that night were dealing with trouble elsewhere.

This conflict between the police and Army aggravated tensions arising from a street clash at Strabane a few days earlier. Young had taken exception to the vigour with which local police there had taken on a rioting crowd and promptly issued a force order forbidding baton charges or any other form of direct force to subdue an unruly crowd because it was 'inimical to a relationship with the public in which a police service could flourish'. Apart from further antagonising the Army, Young's decision caused widespread unrest within the RUC itself, where many frustrated officers knew they ought to be taking a more active role in tackling riots. The Unionist Party shared this view and, as news of Young's order spread, he was summoned to Stormont on 2 July where Chichester-Clark, Black and two other civil servants urged him, as he later put it, 'to give public reassurance that the police were not entirely pusillanimous'.

A couple of days later, Lord Carrington told a ministerial meeting in London that Freeland was feeling 'lonely' because of similar criticism and needling from the Northern Ireland government. Carrington thought the RUC should be expected to do more, especially in dealing with street disorder, to take some of the burden off Freeland's shoulders. Whitehall then came up with the idea of a 'grand confrontation' between the GOC and the chief constable as a way of clearing the air between them and resolving their fundamental differences, but the idea foundered instantly when Young refused to take part because he could not talk 'freely' in the presence of the GOC. The bad feeling between the security chiefs was all too evident when Maudling arrived in Belfast later in the week for a two-day introductory visit, during which he met politicians and toured the front lines where the police and Army were struggling to defend an increasingly brittle peace. Maudling was shocked by what he saw and heard during his visit. 'What a bloody awful country. Bring me a large scotch,' he ordered as soon as the doors of his aircraft closed for departure.

The following Friday afternoon, a senior police officer in west Belfast obtained information about an arms cache in a house at Balkan Street off the Falls Road. Fearing another weekend of uncontrollable gunfire and violence, the Army arrived at about 4.30 p.m. to search the house. An hour later, when the empty-handed soldiers tried to leave, they were cornered by an angry crowd and attacked with stones. As heavier rioting started, with grenades and petrol bombs being thrown, the soldiers fired CS gas while hundreds of reinforcements in lorries and armoured vehicles were rushed to the area, which was sealed off. Troops were later fired on. Unable to bring the situation under control, Freeland imposed a 'curfew' at around 10.15, and orders were given for everyone in the sealed area to get off the streets. A helicopter equipped with a loudspeaker flew low overhead ordering people into their houses. Large quantities of CS gas were again fired in the narrow streets of red-brick, back-to-back houses to disperse crowds despite protests by priests and others about its effect on elderly people and children. The curfew was maintained during the night and next day while troops conducted a none-too-gentle house-to-house search of the area.

After an outcry from local politicians, including the local MPs, Gerry Fitt and Paddy Devlin, the movement restrictions were lifted for two hours from 5 p.m. to enable families to shop for food and other essentials, and then reimposed until nine on Sunday morning. Three civilians were killed during the unprecedented Army led operation, one being run over by an armoured car, while fifteen soldiers and sixty civilians were injured. Later the Army said they had seized over 100 firearms, 100 home-made bombs, a grenade, 250 pounds of explosives, some 21,000 rounds of ammunition and eight two-way radio sets.

The episode brought the honeymoon between Catholics and the Army to an end. There would be no more cups of tea and buns for the patrolling soldiers and thereafter the Provisional IRA campaign would steadily escalate. The cost of the operation in terms of loss of Catholic confidence was, however, incalculable and the Army would never again resort to anything like it.

Back at his desk in London, Maudling had meanwhile been pondering the handling of the Orange marches over the coming Twelfth of July period. 'Very thorough military assessments have been made and the GOC states that he could not enforce a prohibition on account of the disorder that would inevitably follow,' one of his briefings had said. In line with the Hunt dispensation, the Ministry of Home Affairs in Belfast had actually requested the despatch of 1,500 British policemen for the weekend of 11–13 July, a suggestion that found no favour in London where the concept of mutual aid was deemed obsolete. Officials took the view that London should not press to ban the Orange marches and that additional soldiers should be provided. Maudling did appeal for the marches to be called off as an act of 'humanity and magnanimity to avoid possible bloodshed', but the call was predictably ignored and so two infantry battalions and an armoured-car squadron were sent to reinforce the garrison, with three further battalions standing by to go in if necessary. In the end some 40,000 Orangemen paraded uneventfully in Belfast and sixteen other locations, watched over by a force of 18,000 police and troops. On 23 July, with the Twelfth safely out of the way, the government announced a six-month ban on all marches except church parades and those on Remembrance Sunday in November.

Five days later, Harold Black, the cabinet secretary in Belfast, telephoned the Home Office to say that the ban had been badly received and 'a good deal of gloom is descending over Stormont Castle'. Resolutions of no confidence in the government were flying about, he said. Moreover, hardline Unionists were not impressed with the efforts to reintroduce police into the Bogside and the Falls and regarded the whole affair as 'a villainous package of appeasement. They seem to be beyond the reach of rational argument,' he said. The political danger, he advised London, would be if the Standing Council of the Unionist party were convened and then passed a vote of no confidence in Chichester-Clark. Such a meeting was unlikely before August but, in the meantime, he judged, not even an effective build-up of policing in the Bogside would be enough to take the edge off it.

The growing political turmoil was being aggravated by sharpening Catholic fury, directly aimed at the Army, whose tactics and conduct were becoming tougher by the day. In more street trouble on 31 July, for the first time, soldiers shot someone dead: a nineteen-year-old petrol-bomber, during clashes at Belfast's New Lodge Road. The shooting was the inevitable consequence of worsening street trouble in which the continued use of CS gas, water cannon and a new weapon, rubber bullets, designed to avoid having to fire real bullets, proved ever more ineffective in helping to break up progressively more uncontrollable crowds. An angry Paddy Devlin accused the soldiers of 'behaving like a conquering army of mediaeval times. With the restraining hand of James Callaghan gone from the Home Office, General Freeland is reverting to the type of general that Irish people read about in their history books,' he said.

After the gun battle at St Matthew's, the Provisional IRA's remorseless terrorist campaign had steadily gathered pace and it launched a frightening new mode of urban guerrilla warfare, an indiscriminate bombing campaign aimed at wrecking the economy, with a no-warning attack on a bank at High Street in Belfast on 16 July, which injured thirty people, two of them seriously. A wave of explosions followed. The targets in one week alone included telephone exchanges, an electricity board showroom, several public houses, bus depots, customs posts, a Gospel Hall and the homes of a judge, a barrister and the Grand Master of the Orange Order. The government announced that the reward for information leading to conviction of bombers would be increased from £10,000 to £50,000, another sign of the continuing lack of hard intelligence. The rising tide of violence and explosions fuelled the discontent inside the Unionist community, especially about security. From leading figures and constituency associations came repeated calls to lift the ban on parades (which had anyway been widely defied), recall the B Specials, re-arm the RUC and – the old reliable – intern the IRA, an option that was now firmly on the agenda.

In the midst of this turmoil, the Home Office was frantically trying to smother an effort by Young to have the three members of the Hunt committee return for a public visit with a view to their endorsing his work with the RUC. 'To say that they were transformed would at best state the obvious and at worst provoke those who think they have been too much transformed,' wrote an official in the Home Office, in a minute strongly discouraging a visit that could only have stimulated further and unwelcome controversy, especially among the disenchanted Unionist community. On the morning of 5 August, Burroughs telexed the Home office to say that right-wing Unionists were demanding tough measures 'to put an end to the situation', including the introduction of internment which was even supported by 'liberal members of the cabinet such as [Roy] Bradford, [Herbert] Kirk and [Phelim] O'Neill. Up and down the country, constituency associations and cabals continued passing motions of no confidence in the government and attention centred on what Bill Craig, who had signalled a return to active politics after a break, would do. On Thursday 6 August he pronounced that the 'days of the Chichester-Clark administration are numbered', and the following Saturday, speaking at a rally in his Larne stronghold, he blamed the government for damaging police morale and called for their re-arming and the introduction of internment. Harry West, his hardline ally, hailed him as prime minister designate.

Alarm bells were now ringing loudly in London. Maudling moved to shore up Chichester-Clark by warning that Stormont would be shut down and replaced by direct rule if there was any backtracking on the reform programme. Craig airily dismissed the threat. With his government now clearly trembling, Chichester-Clark and his divided ministers reviewed the situation at a two-hour cabinet meeting on 11 August. Afterwards their growing differences and rivalries were concealed in a statement pledging 'pursuance of policies to which we are collectively committed and for which we have the continuing mandate of the Unionist parliamentary party'. The prime minister was now at the head of a government hanging by the most slender of threads, a vulnerability intensified that afternoon by the murder of two RUC officers in a carefully planned attack at Crossmaglen, County Armagh. Constables Samuel Donaldson and Robert Millar were examining a stolen car when an explosive device concealed inside it detonated without warning.

In a radio interview the following Sunday, Craig openly declared his intention to bring down the government, then turned his fire directly on Young: 'I feel very strongly indeed that Sir Arthur will have to go, not because I hold him responsible for the drastic decision of disarming the RUC, but because I believe his whole approach and attitude to our difficulties has been wrong.' Twice-widowed Young had married for the third time the previous day in London, and despite being officially absent on honeymoon, he gave a follow-up radio interview replying to Craig. As long as he was chief constable, he said, the RUC would not be generally re-armed. More pointedly he called for 'something more adequate' than the controversial Special Powers Act which had been the traditional cutting edge of the Stormont government's security policy. His remarks were the final straw for an increasingly embattled Chichester-Clark, who, too, had been growing steadily more hostile to Young. At 4.30 p.m. on 19 August he telephoned Maudling at the Home Office to ask for Young to be replaced without delay, not in February or March 1971 as intended. Young was away from Belfast too much, gave an impression of lacking urgency and might in future be able to spend even less time in Northern Ireland now that he had married and his wife was to stay in Great Britain, the prime minister complained. He was also unhappy about Young's retort to Craig. That should have been left to the government. What Chichester-Clark did not say was that he was afraid that the Ulster Unionist Council would shortly call for Young's resignation, thus making it virtually impossible to sack him without being seen to be responding to hardline pressure. Lord Grey provided a penetrating commentary on the situation in his account of an extensive conversation with Chichester-Clark on 25 August 1970:

> The PM shares my view that, as we have presented Sir Arthur Young to the world at large in a particular way we must, so long as he is here and so long as possible after he leaves, sustain the image we have so presented even though we know Sir Arthur is complex rather than

simple and does not in all ways measure up to his image. But the PM thinks – and there is probably a lot in this – that unless Sir Arthur relinquishes command soon, he will not be able to do so with credit and he quite takes my point that we must avoid any appearance of disowning Sir Arthur's policies. Not only are most of them sound in themselves but Craig and Paisley & Co would seize on any appearance of the Government's resiling from them to say 'We told you so months ago and you failed to act responsibly'. We have enough problems that we cannot solve without adding new ones.

Faced with this situation and Chichester-Clark's view, Maudling did not demur. Young was not his man, so he owed him no allegiance. Indeed, he was well aware that Young had long lost even Callaghan's ear. So his only anxiety was to have the change made in a way that would cause the least trouble. The two then agreed on an early announcement revealing that both the chief constable and the GOC would soon be replaced, the latter in February. To avoid the two key posts changing hands at the same time, Maudling said the new chief constable could be 'eased into the saddle' well before the departure of the general, who was retiring on a long-plotted schedule after a distinguished Army career. Chichester-Clark agreed and said he would alert the Police Authority to the need to appoint a replacement. The current deputy, Graham Shillington, was immediately mentioned. Again Maudling did not demur.

During their chat the governor had tried to persuade Chichester-Clark that Shillington was not the best man for the job. He told him he had 'sadly' come to the conclusion that unless they could get a 'miracle worker' as chief constable 'no great improvement in the RUC is likely to result from having one man rather than another. There is a sad lack of officer quality that will take years to remedy.' The governor believed Unionists should not be bound by what he regarded as the 'illogicality' that only an Ulsterman could lead the RUC. He favoured appointing an ex-colonial officer or someone with command experience in the military. A number of names were bandied about between them, including that of Field Marshal Sir Gerard Templer, who had fought insurgents in Malaya and was said to be anxious to 'get his hands on Ulster'. However, the two agreed that, vastly distinguished as the Irish-born former Chief of the Imperial General Staff was, he 'may not be as capable of fixing Ulster as he seems to think. We concluded that he is a vast, gorgeous and immensely distinguished red herring,' said Grey.

They then discussed Grey's idea of having County Down-born General

Sir John Anderson (later the first colonel commandant of the UDR) as a government minister – they would find him a safe Stormont seat within six months – to work with Shillington. That way, Grey thought, they could ride out the storm of criticism he foresaw from Catholics opposed to the advancement of Shillington. Grey told London he thought the prime minister underestimated the opposition the appointment might stimulate as a return to 'papist-bashing'. Chichester-Clark confided that he was 'growing a bit hardline' about 'the RC's [Roman Catholics]. Much had been done for them and they had done nothing in return.' He confessed he was fearful of 'insupportable trouble among his back-benchers' and defections to Craig if the Ulsterman was passed by. 'It is emotion, not reason, to which I must have regard,' he told the governor. Nevertheless he agreed to sound out his deputy, John Andrews, about the Anderson proposition, but he telephoned Grey within a couple of hours to say it would be 'politically quite impossible'.

Young appears to have got some inkling of this discussion for, in a letter to Maudling soon afterwards, he warned against the appointment of anyone from an armed services background lest he adopt 'military methods of peace-keeping'. Such an appointment, he continued, even of an officer of already high distinction, 'would be regarded as an affront to the dignity of the RUC. If he were an Englishman, may God help him, for he would be wise to spend considerable time on his knees in the hope of divine support which he would find conspicuously lacking elsewhere.' Young advised that with no practical alternative, the best option was to appoint Shillington.

At 4 p.m. on 20 August, during a general discussion of the Irish situation with Edward Heath, Maudling outlined the Shillington succession strategy and was given approval to proceed. On the role of the police in Northern Ireland, he said that it was necessary to get them to play a larger part, but it had to be remembered that they were a very small force. The official note of the meeting reveals the real concern was about the continued vulnerability of Chichester-Clark to right-wing Unionists, although Maudling judged his position was now stronger. Heath was told that with Maudling's support, because of the difficulty of finding a moderate replacement, Chichester-Clark was proposing to take over the highly sensitive portfolio of home affairs himself. Porter, who had borne the brunt of events for some fifteen exhausting months, wished to retire and resume his practice at the bar. (Oliver Wright had described him as a man of great fundamental decency and liberality of view who had borne the brunt of the battle in recent months.)

With Chichester-Clark's survival having to be assessed on a virtually daily basis, London was now seriously exercised about the danger of someone like Craig taking over, whose first action would be to re-arm the police and bring back the B Specials, thus plunging the two governments into a constitutional confrontation. At this point Craig was talking ever more openly about Northern Ireland opting for independence and even forecasting a British Army mutiny along the lines of that at the Curragh in 1914 when some officers said they would not be prepared to 'coerce' the Ulster Unionists into accepting Home Rule. The two British ministers agreed that a Craig coup would be quite unacceptable and it was very important that they should have a precautionary plan ready. The Army was therefore asked to prepare a detailed contingency plan for the introduction of direct rule.

Burroughs offered what he called 'certain observations on the question' in a lengthy despatch to Maudling on 27 August. The political analysis was self-evident, but what he had to say about the potential reaction of the police and the other security forces, in the event of direct rule being imposed provides a revealing insight as to how they were regarded at that time by their British overseers. Discussing what reliance could be laid upon 'Protestant Ulstermen' to operate the government machinery on the orders of an administration which in their eyes had so treacherously let them down, he said he expected the Civil Service of Northern Ireland to perform its duties honourably.

> But other bodies would be likely to take a very different attitude. In particular, the Royal Ulster Constabulary would have to be regarded with suspicion. A proportion of its members would certainly give active assistance to Protestant 'rebels'. Even more would avert their eyes, and much of the Special Branch intelligence would be valueless. In assessing force levels to meet the security situation, little heed should be given to the numbers which could be fielded by the RUC. The allegiances of the members of the UDR will be more mixed. Out of the present enrolled strength of 3,700, 2,950 are Protestants and of these 1,900 are former B Specials. On the other hand, the Force is under direct military command and in some areas, particularly east of the Bann, units have a relatively high Catholic content. The UDR might therefore perform a number of useful services but could not wholly be counted upon.

Equally revealing was Burroughs's diagnosis and remedy for what lay more immediately ahead. Asking the question what could be done to prevent a situation developing where direct rule would have to be contemplated, he said:

> I can offer no readymade solutions. The security authorities look to the politicians for a solution to ease their burdensome task, but I fear there is relatively little the politicians can offer. The first priority is to maintain the fragile peace which has lasted now for a matter of two weeks or so. The longer it persists the less chance there is of spontaneous violence. We must all therefore be extremely vigilant not to make or permit any errors which could imperil the peace. We must recognise that at the present time it is the minority who are most likely to break this peace. As I have pointed out, they have a vested interest in violence, however lacking in impartiality such an attitude may be. The Protestants can, at this stage, be pushed around more without endangering public order. Once a reasonable amount of scar-tissue has grown over the wounds caused by the recent violence, it will become less necessary to draw any such distinctions, and Catholic toes may have to be trodden upon, equally with those belonging to the Reformed Faith.

None of these highly tendentious opinions had been shared with Cardinal Conway, who had urgently summoned Burroughs to lunch a few days earlier on Saturday 22 August. What transpired was a reminder of the continuing sensitivity about policing and the potentially explosive consequences flowing from every aspect of RUC conduct. In a coded message to the Home Office immediately afterwards, the diplomat reported how the cardinal feared that Young's removal, being precisely what Craig and Paisley had been calling for, would confirm Catholic belief that the Conservative government in Westminster, linked as it was to the Unionist party, was susceptible to right-wing pressures. 'His resignation and replacement would be a tremendous feather in their caps and reinforce their position as men of influence who could bend not only Stormont but also Westminster to their will,' the cardinal said. Because of that, he went on, it was absolutely essential that Young's successor should also be an Englishman:

> No member of the RUC, whatever his personality or record, would be accepted as chief constable by the minority and the situation would not be met by the appointment of an English deputy. The present peace is

extremely fragile. The minority have conceived a distrust, however ill-deserved, of the army. To restore the leadership of the RUC to an Ulsterman would finally convince the Catholics that Westminster had abandoned impartiality for the support of Unionism and Protestantism.

Burroughs reported that during the five-hour lunch, a measure of the cardinal's anxieties, he confided that Young himself was anxious to return to London because of his many commitments there. 'While he [Conway] is far more broad-minded and susceptible to reason than most of his subordinates, he harbours some deep prejudices, but allowing for this, I take his advice about an English successor to Young very seriously,' Burroughs wrote, particularly since the cardinal had given it as his considered view that the appointment of an RUC man 'would bring the hooligans on to the streets, and that in such an event they would have the support of a far larger number of the Catholic population than has recently been the case.'

The cardinal's fears and the diplomat's advice were immediately raised with Maudling, who proved highly amenable, and Burroughs was authorised to advise Chichester-Clark that the home secretary was reconsidering his position about Young's replacement. At the same time, officials were instructed to identify possible candidates from English forces. As news of the impending change spread through the Catholic political grapevine it raised similar concern in Dublin, where despite paying public obeisance to the cause of Irish unity, the government, headed by Jack Lynch, was fervently hoping that continued pressure from Westminster, which they were actively encouraging, would deliver enough meaningful reform in Northern Ireland to keep the larger issue from erupting. A British diplomatic telegram from Dublin around this time stated that the Irish had largely written off Chichester-Clark's hopes of survival and were relying on the British government to deliver.

Burroughs also received another influential representation about the RUC vacancy. Major Tom McDowell, a northern Protestant with service in the British Army, who was managing director of the *Irish Times*, confirmed the unease of the minority about appointing Shillington when he visited Burroughs at his Belfast base on 4 September. After a series of visits north from his Dublin office, the major was of the opinion that 'if the new chief constable is not an Englishman they will view it as a sign that the British are prepared to sell out to the right-wing all along the line'. Burroughs, reporting this conversation to London, added, 'I reiterate my own view, even at this late date, that the appointment of an

RUC man to the job will shake the confidence of the minority in both Westminster and the Chichester-Clark administration. Hardly a shred of the credit which has been built up by the reform programme will remain.'

Apart from the hostility to the very idea of an RUC man having the post, there was particular personal opposition to Shillington because of his Unionist family background. His father was Major David Shillington, a prosperous agricultural and builders merchant, who went on to become a long-serving Unionist MP for Armagh and one-time minister of labour at Stormont. Graham Shillington joined the RUC as a cadet officer in 1933 and rose through the ranks. When Albert Kennedy stood down early in 1969, he moved to RUC headquarters as deputy to Anthony Peacocke, the post he retained when Young arrived.

As acting home affairs minister as well as prime minister, it was up to Chichester-Clark personally to approve Young's replacement once the new, independent Police Authority had made its choice. Despite nudges from Maudling and his officials, who had now come round to the strong necessity of another outsider replacing Young, the Belfast cabinet was concerned that an outside appointment would 'provoke fresh strains within the Unionist party'. In the end, neither the government nor the Police Authority in Belfast could see any reason for disowning Shillington, so they both confirmed his succession. Despite misgivings, London decided to put the best possible face on the situation and issued detailed instructions to Burroughs and the Dublin embassy as to how to present the changes in giving advance notice to Cardinal Conway, Jack Lynch and others. To mitigate adverse sentiments towards the appointment of Shillington they were instructed to emphasise that Jamie Flanagan, an assistant chief constable of the RUC and a Catholic, was to be his deputy and that Chichester-Clark had also agreed to London's suggestion that he should appoint one of the inspectors of constabulary for England and Wales to perform a similar task for Northern Ireland. Very conveniently, John McKay, the GOC's police adviser, also happened to be a Catholic and had previously been seconded to the RUC, so he got the job. To reassure the minority community, the inspector would check on continued adherence to the Hunt reforms. Chichester-Clark was also to state publicly that there was no going back on them: no RUC re-arming, and no revival of the B Specials.

The British ambassador, Sir John Peck, conveyed this news to Lynch in Dublin at 3 p.m. on 23 September, shortly in advance of the formal announcement in Belfast. Lynch thought that the appointment was 'a risky act' but appreciated that it was too late to suggest reconsideration now the appointment had been made. In his view, a new kind of RUC could be brought into being in the course of a year or so but the general public feeling was that it was still the 'old RUC'. Soon afterwards in Belfast, the Shillington appointment was confirmed in a carefully choreographed sequence of meetings and gentlemanly public statements designed to conceal the fact that Young had been unceremoniously ousted. The Police Authority had gathered in the morning, passed a unanimous vote of confidence in Young, expressed appreciation of the services he had rendered to Northern Ireland and the RUC and discharged him to resume his duties as Chief Police Officer of the City of London. Equally unanimously the authority came to the 'view' that the present deputy chief constable, Graham Shillington, an officer, as they put it, 'possessed of the qualities of leadership, integrity and fairness and dedicated unreservedly to the concept of a civilianised and normally unarmed police service', was uniquely qualified to succeed Young. Later in the day, Chichester-Clark formally approved the appointment and confirmed the Authority's secondary decision to appoint Flanagan as the new deputy. In a statement Shillington said it was 'a great privilege to take over command of the RUC' and that despite 'the difficulties of the task . . . I hope I will be able to make a useful contribution to the future of the force and to the community as a whole.' For his part, Young, who was presented with an inscribed silver salver by the chief officers of the RUC, politely preserved the fiction of amicability:

Now that the Hunt recommendations have virtually been accomplished I believe that my purpose in joining the ranks of the RUC has been fulfilled. Since I am due to retire from the police service at the end of 1971 the consequential consolidation and development of the force, which will necessarily take several years to complete, will obviously have to be undertaken by my successor. I am delighted that Mr Shillington has been chosen to do this.

The fact that the Hunt recommendations have been implemented in less than a year since the publication of the report is great credit to the endeavours of all ranks of the RUC, who notwithstanding their onerous preoccupation in keeping the peace, have undertaken these fundamental and involved changes in a spirit of such willing enthusiasm. I am confident that the RUC will remain a non-aggressive police service progressively winning the respect and esteem of the people of Northern Ireland.

These were fine sentiments for parting words but they are also a measure of just how out of touch Young really was. Craig, one of his most persistent critics, described him in a parting shot as 'a good policeman sent to the wrong place'. The reality was that as fast as he could stitch it, the post-Hunt tapestry Young had started to weave was unravelling, and before long all hope of civilianising the RUC would have to be abandoned indefinitely. In any case, while he adopted a highly visible profile when he was in Northern Ireland, he spent a good deal of his time writing romantic doggerel to the woman who was to become his third wife and was frequently absent in London wooing her. Young also compromised his previously high standing with Callaghan by setting himself, and the RUC, at odds with the Army and refusing to accept that Northern Ireland never was and never would be a tranquil shire. He had anyway been reluctant to go to Northern Ireland and only accepted the assignment on the understanding that he would get the peerage he craved. He never did, to his lasting disappointment. In his unpublished memoir Sir Richard Pim states it was always his unyielding belief that 'an Ulsterman, understanding his country's people and problems, would be in a far better position to take charge of police administration in his area than would be an Englishman, Scotsman or Welshman. The obvious truth of my words was amply demonstrated . . . on the publication of the Hunt report and the seconding of an English chief constable to implement its findings. It will be a long time before our fine force recovers.'

For its part, the RUC had little time to ponder the traumatic days of Young. Still tossed by its 1969 ordeal and turned by the speed of change since, it was thrown into fresh turmoil by the double murder at Crossmaglen. The next day, 17 August, police officers from three stations in Belfast voted fifty-four to six to be re-armed and twenty-four hours later the government announced that while the policy of the RUC being unarmed would remain, guns would be deposited at selected stations for issue when required. In line with Hunt, Young had also set up an internal standing advisory committee on arms, headed by a chief superintendent. The issue was put to a force-wide vote in September. One third of the membership abstained and the policy of remaining unarmed was only narrowly upheld by 1196 to 1185, a majority of eleven. The same month, in a sign of the increasing threat to the safety of officers, the six unmarked traffic Q-cars, which had been at the cutting edge of enforcing road safety measures, were withdrawn and widespread training in the use of new Walther PPK personal protection pistols commenced. The old .38 revolvers were finally phased out as obsolete. The policy of totally disarming the RUC was now compromised before it had even been completed.

Despite this setback, Graham Shillington renewed the commitment to Hunt when he officially took over the RUC on 16 November. In just over two years since the fateful clash at Duke Street which sparked off the disorder, three RUC officers had been murdered and 1,195 injured, a third of the 3,700-strong force. More worryingly, the pace and intensity of violence was quickening despite the commitment of 7,000 soldiers and 3,000 members of the UDR to help the RUC. By the end of the year 1970, with the Army openly talking for the first time about gearing up to meet a prolonged IRA campaign, there had been twenty-five killings, 213 shooting incidents and 153 explosions. More than three thousand houses had been searched and some 87,000 lbs of explosives recovered as well as 324 firearms and a large quantity of ammunition. Not surprisingly, with Chichester-Clark's fundamentally divided administration clinging ever more unconvincingly to power, the clamour for the introduction of internment without trial to meet the IRA threat was growing ever louder.

It was something of a foundation of Unionist belief that internment was the most effective weapon for getting to grips with the IRA. From their perspective, the historical evidence was that IRA activity promptly ceased once the activists were locked up indefinitely and they pointed to the collapse of IRA unrest every decade as justification for the view. It was another article of Unionist faith that the tactic was all the more effective when the southern authorities locked IRA men up at the same time. Craig and others of a similar stance had frequently called for internment in the preceding months but the demand was consistently rejected. However, in a significant change of tack, the possibility was now no longer being ruled out. On 10 December, speaking as minister of home affairs, Chichester-Clark ambiguously said: 'I reserve the right to do whatever may be necessary to protect the security of Northern Ireland.'

Although he was not yet fully persuaded that large-scale swoops would do anything other than exacerbate the situation, in a bid to keep his ministers united after the 5 August cabinet discussion Chichester-Clark had ordered the RUC to begin planning for internment and, in great secrecy, a target list of 300 suspects had already been compiled. With the province's only prisons, at Belfast and Armagh, crowded to capacity holding public-order offenders, a discreet hunt was on for a place to hold the internees if and when they were arrested. An empty factory complex at Antrim, formerly used by the Army for emergency accommodation, had already been surveyed and rejected as unsuitable and attention had turned to the possibility of using HMS *Maidstone*, a former Royal Navy submarine support ship, which had recently been taken out of mothballs at Rosyth and towed to the port of Belfast, where it was currently moored to provide accommodation for 1,500 soldiers.

The plan was for Northern Ireland prison officers to guard the internees, with the Navy providing 'hotel services' on board ship and the Army maintaining perimeter security. When this possibility was raised with Army headquarters in December, they passed the matter to the Ministry of Defence and the Home Office, where, at this time, British ministers regarded the introduction of internment as 'a remote contingency' and any involvement in it as a 'source of potential embarrassment'. So when the plan reached Whitehall there was surprise at the number of names on the wanted list, a marked lack of enthusiasm for the entire operation and an imperative to discourage the Northern Ireland government from using its powers of internment. Whitehall thought that if arrests had to be made, it would be much better to prefer specific charges such as membership of an illegal organisation. There were also fears that, in some circumstances, Belfast might 'go it alone' so there was some support for the view that the offer of military facilities for detention, such as the ship, would give the British government a measure of sanction, although they were concerned about 'headline-mongering on the lines of back to the hulks' if the offer was ever taken up. So a message went back to Belfast saying that, while 'Ministers appreciate[d] the Northern Ireland Government may wish to think about the contingency of internment', they felt the examination should be carried out in considerably more depth, and that the alternatives must be much more fully analysed before they could 'consider the possibility of agreeing to the Maidstone proposal'.

However, by January 1971, with violence still surging, the British government was forced to the view that both internment and direct rule were becoming inevitable and might soon have to be introduced either individually, or, in some scenarios, together. So, in prudent Whitehall fashion, serious contingency planning began for each of what were highly unfavoured options. Ministers commissioned draft legislation to be used to suspend the Northern Ireland government. There was no fixed idea of an alternative: the first thought was to empower the governor to rule with the advice of civil servants in the Northern Ireland departments. In its own thorough way, the Army also produced a complementary Top Secret plan for the eventuality, which stated that the precise circumstances in which direct rule might be imposed were unpredictable and hypothesised a number of possible scenarios which could cause the British government to act. These included various permutations of right-wing Unionist takeovers, Catholic uprisings or a disastrous deterioration in the security situation.

Should the British government find itself with the governance of Northern Ireland in its own hands, the Army plan provided for a very wide range of contingencies and a potentially draconian military regime. A security secretariat would be established at Stormont Castle, to enable the GOC, as director of operations, to work with the governor and his advisers to maintain security through the Navy, RAF, Army and the RUC and co-ordinate measures to combat smuggling, infiltration and incursion along the land frontier and by sea. It was also considered necessary to introduce screening of all persons and commercial traffic entering Northern Ireland and provide a highly visible military presence to demonstrate control of the situation. Because of fears that civilian staff would strike in protest and close airfields and sea ports, there was a plan for the military to secure port facilities at the Royal Navy Air Yard at Sydenham as a means of entry for additional troops and stores. Special measures would be taken to protect key civilian and military points and there was particular concern about the safety of the RAF's £200,000,000 worth of key installations in case 'the UK's national tactical and strategic capability' was affected by sabotage. The RAF had made its own plans to protect the installations and to fly out valuable Phantom aircraft if the need arose. At this time there were a number of US military installations in Northern Ireland and they had been advised that the UK government would adhere to its responsibility for their external security.

There were also plans to ensure the safety of British service and UK-based civil service families by concentrating them in married quarters in military bases as a first step and then evacuating them from Northern Ireland, by sea and air, if necessary. Communication between Whitehall and Stormont in a period of crisis was another aspect taken into account. Post Office cables were vulnerable to sabotage, suffered from frequent technical failures and would be inadequate in the situation under review, the plan stated. Similarly, it said, the secure teleprinter links were routed over landlines and would be liable to interruption. However, alternative secure radio teleprinter links, which could be connected with Whitehall, were considered satisfactory and would be activated. As to secure telephone links, the plan pointed out that the Stormont system was manned by local operators. 'Under conditions of direct rule these operators would have to be replaced by appropriately cleared Great Britain personnel and the system would possibly need to be augmented.'

Turning to the courts, the paper articulated a fear that 'under direct rule, a breakdown could occur through disaffection among the local judiciary and magistrates' and urged that 'the functioning of courts needed to be included in contingency plans in view of its impact on the security situation'. Other measures foreshadowed included controls on the news media, an increased public relations effort and the use of psychological operations to influence public opinion. There were also anxieties about the position the UDR might take. The plan stated:

> The reliability of the UDR could vary from area to area, depending on the political circumstances. However, any evident withdrawal of confidence regarding the loyalty of the regiment could have a damaging effect and should be avoided. It is not possible to discount disaffection spreading within the UDR as the situation worsens. This would increase the need for Regular Army reinforcements. Plans for psychological operations to counteract this should be made.

With regard to the possible use of the Territorial Army after the declaration of direct rule, the contingency planners judged that 'the doubts about the reliability of the UDR apply with greater force to the Territorial Army Volunteer Reserve. The Home Office have advised us that they cannot envisage a situation in which it would be politically acceptable to use them.' Noting that legislation had been enacted to enable British police to support the RUC on specific short-term occasions, the plan noted, 'present circumstances are such that reinforcement by British policemen cannot be realistically contemplated'.

In a parallel planning operation, similar military research was taking place into the problems and practicalities of introducing internment. Their 'wanted list', produced in early 1971, envisaged 'lifting' up to 450 people, 150 more than the RUC's.

For obvious reasons, all of this planning work was taking place without the knowledge of the Northern Ireland government, which had become little more than a hypnotised witness to the accelerating disintegration of what, for many years to come, would be fondly remembered as 'normality'. During the early months of 1971, apart from the persistent street rioting, there were arson and bomb outrages, and police and Army posts came under repeated attack. This prompted a fresh row between the two organisations about whose responsibility it was to guard police stations. The army finally won the battle but at the cost of yet another reverse to the principles of Hunt: the police were provided with shotguns and many were issued with bullet-proof body armour for the first time. The police and soldiers had a low opinion of its effectiveness: one said it was only designed to hold you together if you were shot or blown up so that you could be buried in one piece. On 6 February, another grim milestone was passed with the first murder of a soldier, Gunner Robert Curtis, shot while patrolling the New Lodge Road in Belfast in an effort to keep rival crowds from rioting. Three days later five BBC engineers were killed when their Land Rover was blown up by a device intended for a security force patrol on a remote mountain road near a transmitter station, the worst single incident to date in terms of casualties.

On 26 February the RUC suffered a resounding blow when two officers were shot dead by gunmen who opened fire with automatic weapons during rioting at Alliance Avenue in north Belfast. They were Constable Robert Buckley and Detective Inspector Cecil Patterson, the latter a particular loss to the RUC for, as a long-established Special Branch officer, he was reputed to be something of a 'walking filing cabinet' for his encyclopaedic knowledge of IRA personalities. Within an hour, Shillington ordered that all officers going out on duty should once again be armed, bringing a decisive end to another of the central Hunt recommendations. After these double killings, the Police Federation representatives met on two consecutive nights preparing a lengthy memorandum for Chichester-Clark which asked for even tougher measures to ensure their protection and safety. Earlier in the month, on 9 February, Lord Carrington had given the cabinet in London a grim warning that 'the disorder was no longer an inter-communal matter and a situation approaching armed conflict was developing'. In a highly perceptive analysis, which would prove all too accurate in the months and years ahead, the cabinet minutes record:

> Although it might eventually prove necessary to adopt a policy of internment in Ulster, this course should be approached with great caution. It could succeed only if the terrorist leaders could be identified and arrested; and it would be liable not only to exacerbate communal relations afresh but also to create a category of political prisoners whose arbitrary treatment might be held to justify reprisals in the form of kidnapping and the seizing of hostages.

On 2 March, in response to the worsening violence, Chichester-Clark announced unspecified new security measures, though not a general re-arming of the RUC 'as armed combat is a military task', and that 600 additional troops were coming in to bring the Army garrison up to 8,000. Three days later, with the toll of death, injury and violence mounting by the day, Craig called for the Hunt measures to be completely reversed and said changes to the screening of police applicants had allowed the IRA to infiltrate the RUC. It was a false and mischievous intervention by a man with an appalling track record. Stripping him of his status as a privy councillor had recently been considered in London (but rejected for lack of precedent) after he, as the minister who ordered the RUC into action, then refused to co-operate with the Cameron commission. Lord Grey, the governor, who recommended 'defrocking' him, told the Home Office, 'He has or did have quite a good brain but he has long since lost the capacity of sensible judgement and this may be due, at least in part, to physical defects.'

General Sir Michael Carver, the vice-chief of the General Staff, attended a cabinet meeting in Belfast during this period where he had to endure criticism of the Army's far too passive response to events instead of the scheduled discussion about the merits of introducing internment. The situation in Londonderry, where the Bogside and Creggan estates remained sealed off to the security forces with elaborate barricades at the mouth of every street, was a particular affront to Unionists, who saw the repeated television reports from 'Free Derry' as an added provocation. Their demand for the 'Queen's writ' to run in every part of Northern Ireland was becoming ever more strident and was playing into the hands of Unionist extremists like Craig. Unless the Army was seen to 'take the gloves off', Carver, who would soon replace Baker as the senior soldier in Britain, was told, there was an increasing danger of a violent Protestant backlash. On his return to London Carver reported: 'The [Northern Ireland] Cabinet met in a grim, last-ditch atmosphere dominated by the hope of some military panacea.'

The final blow which toppled Chichester-Clark came on 10 March after three unarmed, off-duty soldiers, aged seventeen, eighteen and twenty-three, drinking in a Belfast city-centre public house, were recognised, lured by the promise of a party and taken to the northern outskirts of the city, where they were shot dead. In a community not yet hardened to the inhuman excesses of terrorism, the sheer brutality of the triple murder, carried out by Provisional IRA killers, caused widespread shock and was condemned in highly emotional terms on all sides in Northern Ireland. The fact that the three victims were Scottish, members of the Royal

Highland Fusiliers, exacerbated the reaction, given the close ties across the North Channel, and two days after the killings thousands of shipyard workers downed tools and marched on the Unionist party headquarters at Glengall Street demanding the immediate introduction of internment. The call was taken up by other hitherto moderate Unionists and brought to a head the disquiet in the population and the deepening divisions within Chichester-Clark's cabinet. With his back now completely to the wall, Chichester-Clark demanded a meeting with Heath to press for tougher security action and flew to London on 16 March to make his case.

Like Carver, Maudling had also witnessed for himself the growing frustration of the Northern Ireland ministers during a recent visit. 'The picture that he will paint will be one of gloom,' said a subsequent note prepared in advance of a meeting of the British cabinet's Northern Ireland committee. Maudling, who feared the continuing pressure and the militant mood of some of his ministers could wreck Chichester-Clark's determination to keep governing, had been visibly shocked when one of the Northern Ireland ministers told him he would not mind seeing the Army mow down a Catholic crowd in which a gunman had taken refuge. Whitehall refused to accept the view, shared by several members of the Belfast cabinet, that the main body of Catholics was the enemy and should be treated as such. 'The view of the Westminster Government, which the military authorities reflect, is that while we do not shrink from ruthless measures against gunmen and terrorists, we recognise the main bulk of all sections of the community as citizens of the United Kingdom', a ministerial briefing document declared on 10 March. 'Ministers will not wish to change their view that the security forces should continue to seek to isolate the gunmen and the terrorists, and should not resort to indiscriminate measures which might foster sympathy with the IRA among moderate persons with a sentimental attachment to the idea of a united Republic of Ireland.'

As we know from his earlier remarks to the governor, Chichester-Clark, completely isolated by his own extremists, was impatient with Catholic demands and resentful of the lack of any gesture from them to help him through his difficulties. So when he arrived at Downing Street, looking drained and flagging under the pressure, he had reverted to the traditional Unionist stereotype. What he outlined to Heath, Maudling, Carrington, Baker and Lieutenant-General Harry Tuzo, appointed GOC for Northern Ireland a week earlier, was a series of repressive, one-sided anti-Catholic measures. He wanted a huge influx of troops to take up positions in IRA areas and 'dominate' them, making greater use of cordons and curfews and providing far more muscle to back up the police. Such drastic measures were necessary, the official note of the meeting records, because there had been a panic reaction to the murder of the three young Scottish soldiers and he felt that those, like the shipyard workers, who felt so strongly about the IRA's activities might take the law into their own hands and bring about a general uprising.

Heath said the Army's activities had not been made too obtrusive because the policy had been to try to isolate the IRA from the more moderate elements in the Catholic community. The aim had been to create the impression that such problems as remained were limited and that the bulk of the population could be left to pursue a normal life. Baker added that there were certain obvious disadvantages to establishing units within IRA areas. Moderate Catholic opinion might be antagonised. The unit would be vulnerable to attack and, if trouble arose, reinforcements would probably have to be brought in from outside. It might then be difficult to extricate the unit without some loss of prestige and credibility. Playing for time, he conceded that the application of the proposal to particular areas might be studied and the risks assessed.

The plain truth was that London, committed to being even-handed, had been shaken by the hostile reaction to the so-called 'Falls Road curfew' and, unlike the Unionists, now considered such operations to be entirely counter-productive. The Army believed they not only alienated moderate Catholic opinion but threatened bipartisan support for the Northern Ireland campaign in Britain and provided fodder for pro-IRA propaganda, especially in the United States, where, as we will see later, much of the IRA's firepower was being acquired.

Chichester-Clark said he felt that time was fast running out. Unless he got five more battalions of troops, he feared that within the next few days there might be some violent reaction from the Protestants. Indeed, as he was speaking large numbers of workers had again walked out and were taking part in protest marches in Northern Ireland to coincide with the funerals of the soldiers in Scotland and Paisley was laying a wreath on the cenotaph at Belfast City Hall. Heath replied it was unrealistic to suppose that if the communities were indeed bent on civil war the provision of British troops could effectively prevent them. Carrington added there was no military justification for sending additional troops, and, while there might be a political reason now, this could recur in a few weeks' time and there would then be renewed pressure for still further reinforcements. Tuzo, the new GOC, said that an additional five battalions would certainly enable the Army to be more obtrusive but it was unrealistic to suppose that this would have a significant effect on the effort against the IRA, where the main constraint was lack of intelligence. The reaction to Chichester-Clark's demands was remarkable, for here was a British Conservative administration refusing to yield to the threat of a 'Protestant backlash', however subtly it was conveyed.

Chichester-Clark had travelled to London confident that Heath would 'cave in' to his demands but, out-manoeuvred, he was forced to admit that, in purely military terms, there would be little advantage from reinforcements. Making a plea for his political life, he said it would be in danger unless he could produce 'something to show' in a statement due in the Northern Ireland parliament in forty-eight hours. Heath said he was not clear about the aims of those in the Unionist party who were trying to bring about the fall of the Northern Ireland government. 'They ought not to suppose that by this means they could bring about a change of policy,' he warned. According to the official note, Chichester-Clark said it would be helpful if the prime minister could get this message through to the Ulster Unionists before he faced a censure vote at the Unionist Council meeting on 29 March and suggested he might address the meeting. Heath was non-committal. He could not promise to visit Northern Ireland or to address any particular function but said he would consider how he might bring home the facts of life to the dissident elements in the party.

Chichester-Clark returned to Belfast that night in a very depressed state. For almost two years he had done his duty and defied the backwoodsmen in his own party and pushed ahead with the reform programme. Much good it had done him. Catholics regarded the changes as overdue and grudging. His own party saw them as unnecessary. Now, facing almost certain defeat, he felt that London had grievously misunderstood and underestimated the situation in Northern Ireland and, above all, that he had been betrayed, first by Wilson, now by Heath. Having conceded political control of the RUC, unlike his predecessors, he could not manufacture an 'IRA invasion' scare and set the police on the Catholics to placate his critics. Instead he had to go begging to London for help. By the time he got to his feet in Stormont on 18 March, with 3,000 people demonstrating outside for tougher security measures, Heath had given him only the feather-duster of 1,300 extra troops rather than the rod of iron he wanted to wield. That morning in London, Heath told his cabinet the troops were being sent to help keep Chichester-Clark in power, not for essential military reasons.

Predictably, the deployment failed to please anyone and, after an acrimonious debate, Chichester-Clark decided the time had come to resign.

During a long talk on the Friday morning, General Tuzo tried but failed to dissuade him and after a cabinet meeting that afternoon, he wrote out his resignation and communicated his decision to the governor and then to Heath, who was decidedly frosty when he telephoned him that afternoon.

According to Downing Street's transcription of the conversation, Chichester-Clark said he wanted some initiative to stage a confrontation and 'either kill or capture IRA'. He told Heath all his ideas had been ruled out by the Army because they were 'oppressive and might upset the minority, but I really think we are past the stage of worrying about who we upset'.

Heath retorted, 'You don't want General Tuzo to shoot women and children in the streets.'

Chichester-Clark replied, 'No indeed. I am not asking for that. I am simply saying that at the moment we simply sit and wait, we then have a period of feverish activity and we then have to wait again till there is another incident. This is what has brought about the political situation here, what has made it impossible.'

Pressed by Heath, however, Chichester-Clark could not give a single example of a case where IRA members could have been apprehended had not the Army failed to take action. He continued: 'The plain fact of the matter is that I simply cannot see any way of carrying on unless we do produce some dramatic change. Frankly I don't think we're able to do it. I'm the first to admit that the situation here is not entirely rational. I can't hold it. It's not that I'm not willing to try. I reckon that I've exhausted every possibility.'

An increasingly exasperated Heath said, 'Well, I'm perfectly prepared to consider irrational solutions if you would tell me what those are which are going to improve the situation.'

Chichester-Clark replied, 'Well, I mean, the irrational situation is to move into some of these [Catholic] areas and stay there. I can see no other way that will show anyone that we mean business.'

It emerged during the conversation that Chichester-Clark was opposed to internment and instead wanted the Army to mount extensive cordoning and curfew operations in Belfast, not for military reasons but so that he could tell the country and his party that something was being done. Otherwise, he said again, he would be unable to carry on. Heath asked what reasons he would give for his resignation. Chichester-Clark answered, 'I would propose to say that I went to London on Tuesday and made certain proposals for the intensification of the campaign against the IRA. That I felt the action was not adequate and that I am now faced with supporting methods with which I can no longer agree and therefore I don't feel that I can continue.'

Heath replied: 'Well all I can say is that I consider that to be absolutely unjustifiable. I shall make it quite clear from here that it is absolutely unjustifiable. In fact, it bears very little relation to the truth. I think it is doing immense harm to Northern Ireland and I think it makes the position of any successor of yours absolutely impossible. Absolutely impossible.' After berating Chichester-Clark for leaking news of his intended resignation, Heath then asked why it was necessary to resign on a Friday afternoon, with a dangerous weekend ahead, leaving Northern Ireland without a prime minister. In the end Chichester-Clark agreed to reconsider what he would say as being the reasons for his resignation and would delay it for 'twenty-four hours or so'.

In a bid to calm the situation, Heath sent Carrington and Baker to Belfast the following morning to talk to him again, but with nothing new on offer, Chichester-Clark finally resigned that night, two months short of two years in office. He was essentially a liberal man with the right instincts who was handicapped in living up to his old-fashioned concepts of honour and duty by the lack of an inspiring personality and an inability to persuade either his supporters or his critics to look to the future rather than the past. In the end, however, he reverted to the anti-Catholic Unionist stereotype. Brian Faulkner, one of his ministers, who had missed becoming prime minister instead of Chichester-Clark by a single vote, said he had 'done his duty as an officer and a gentleman [in a job] which I doubt if he ever really wanted'.

When nominations for the vacancy closed on the Monday, Faulkner and Craig were the only candidates. Next day, Faulkner emerged the victor by a margin of twenty-six to four and became prime minister. If Craig had won, or if the party divisions had triggered a general election, London would have moved at once to abolish Stormont and introduce direct rule. The cabinet had agreed as much at its 18 March meeting, but Faulkner came highly recommended to London: 'the ablest politician in Northern Ireland', according to Oliver Wright, who had earlier reported on Faulkner's passionate desire to be prime minister and remarked that as long as Britain wanted to continue to govern Northern Ireland at arm's length, Faulkner would be preferable to direct rule.

Thus Faulkner was given a chance but not allowed a honeymoon. A few days afterwards, as he was announcing the members of his cabinet, two bombs went off at the Unionist Party headquarters in central Belfast, the latest in a steadily increasing wave of explosions: sixteen in January, thirty-eight in February, thirty-one in March, thirty-eight in April and forty-three in May. By the end of that month there had been twenty-three violent deaths, among them that of Sergeant Michael Willets, a twenty-seven-year-old member of the Parachute Regiment killed in a bomb attack at Springfield Road Police Station in Belfast on 25 May. When a suitcase containing thirty pounds of explosive was hurled into the crowded reception area of the station, he immediately pushed two young children into a corner and shielded them from the blast with his own body. He was rushed to hospital but died from his injuries and was later posthumously awarded the George Cross for his bravery.

Despite his tough reputation, attributable to his effective crack-down on the IRA during a stint as home affairs minister from 1959 to 1963, the escalating violence more rapidly undermined Faulkner than it had his predecessor and by June Burroughs was including critical reports about his 'short-term thinking' in his regular despatches to London. Praising some of Faulkner's hard work in a despatch on 10 June, the diplomat went on:

> But all this is of small avail unless he can show that he is determined to bridge the tribal gap; that he is not simply the leader (some would say the captive leader) of a Unionist party permanently in power. I suspect that Mr Faulkner could be more efficiently served by parts of his own government machine and I have already indicated that some of his ministers are not sufficiently house-trained. If this is so it is a reflection on Mr Faulkner himself. It begins to look as if he lacks that authority, combined with a hint of menace, which a leader needs. It suggests to me that he is not the tough man we hoped to see. Whether or not Mr Faulkner is up to scratch, we have to make the best we can of him, and I think he can be got to do a tolerable job if we handle him right.

Faulkner firmly believed in the effectiveness of internment, having had first-hand ministerial experience of the issue during the IRA's abortive 1956–62 campaign. By the time he became prime minister, the preparations for introducing it again were well advanced and the RUC Special Branch and government in Belfast was now aware of and at one in the planning. Whatever scruples there had originally been in London about the potential embarrassment of being associated with internment had dissolved. London's position had gradually moved from one where the Army might simply round internees up, providing an internment facility and guarding them, to one supporting wholehearted military participation in the enterprise, having concluded that it seemed worthwhile to try this option before being forced to take the more drastic step of direct rule.

First thoughts of holding the internees in a British prison or on board ship in a British anchorage were abandoned when officials found out prisoners could not be removed from Northern Ireland jurisdiction without Westminster passing specific legislation. The Isle of Man, which had been used to detain people during the Second World War, was also ruled out because of the need for legislation in Stormont and the Tynwald and because Whitehall judged the government in Douglas would be unlikely to agree. Consideration was then given to the use of ships, following the precedent set by the *Argenta* in the early 1920s and the *Al Rawdah* in the 1940s. Apart from the *Maidstone*, which was already on the spot, two other 'mothballed' vessels were identified: the *Manxman* and the veteran Second World War cruiser *Belfast*, named after the city in which it was built. While these ships could accommodate large numbers in bunks – 500 on the *Belfast* alone – they were ruled out on security grounds because electrical mains and firehose and water pipes ran along the gangways. To protect these vital services from interference, wire grilles would have to be built to enclose the inmates, conversion work which would take several weeks and delay the vessels being towed to Belfast. Other disadvantages included the lack of space for exercise and the difficulty of ensuring external security while berthed alongside a quay in Belfast, which would be necessary to provide the ships with power, water and other services.

Attention then turned to possible locations on land in Northern Ireland. The specification the Army set for an ideal site was one both secure enough to prevent escape from inside and also secure and preferably remote enough to reduce the chances of an attack or liberation raid from outside. It should also be away from politically sensitive areas, both to avoid aggravating public feeling and to reduce the chance of large-scale demonstrations. Because preparations had to be kept secret, for obvious political and operational reasons, they also wanted a site that would lend itself to a cover story once the actual construction stage was reached.

By far the most suitable location was an existing prison, but, after detailed study, shortage of staff and lack of alternative accommodation for sentenced prisoners ruled out the existing cellular establishments in Belfast and Armagh. Rathlin Island, off the north Antrim coast, and the Copeland Islands, at the mouth of Belfast Lough, were then reconnoitred but ruled out on account of the amount of building work required and the fact that it could not be kept secret. The visit to sparsely populated Rathlin, first mooted as a possible location by Chichester-Clark when he visited Heath at Chequers in February 1971, in fact sparked off a wave of unwelcome public speculation about internment. The next best options were military locations and sites at Magilligan, Long Kesh and Ballykinler were surveyed, the last the location of what James Craig called a 'concentration camp' in the 1920s. In the end, after a ten-day feasibility study by military experts and a British Prison Service adviser, the choice came down to Long Kesh, a wartime airfield, as best meeting all the criteria. It was not in a sensitive area and its position, close to the M1 and some ten miles west of Belfast, made it highly accessible. Furthermore, given that it was already partly used by the Army as a vehicle park, the cover story that accommodation was being built for extra troops would hold up. The watchtowers and fences would be the last things to go up, to preserve the secrecy to the last possible moment. Construction of hutted living quarters and associated facilities for up to 450 inmates and 100 custodians, it was estimated, would take a party of Royal Engineers four months.

The RUC Special Branch was again fully consulted about this top-secret planning and approved it. They were also taking the lead, within a much beefed-up intelligence-gathering operation, in refining the lists of those to be detained. In a bid to overcome the personality clashes which had dogged earlier attempts to foster co-operation and to improve the quality of the 'product', there had been a major reorganisation at the end of 1970, personally ordered by Heath. Now a Director of Intelligence, based at RUC headquarters, was in place to provide central direction and co-ordinate all sources of information. The number of military intelligence liaison officers positioned alongside the Special Branch in police headquarters and elsewhere had also been doubled. Over at Lisburn, General Tuzo had an enlarged intelligence team at his disposal, some of whom had attended specialised training at the School of Service Intelligence. The Joint Security Committee had also set up a sub-committee on the subject, where material was discussed and decisions taken. Because of the issue's central importance to the entire campaign in Northern Ireland, Heath was getting monthly progress reports.

Insights into the working of the intelligence machinery at this time come from evidence provided to the Bloody Sunday inquiry by Dr Robert Ramsay, who was Faulkner's private secretary. The Northern Ireland government's oversight of the security situation was organised through the Joint Security Committee (JSC), which was chaired by Faulkner, the prime minister (whose deputy on the committee was John Taylor, the junior minister of home affairs) and attended by senior Army and police officers, including Tuzo and Shillington, and senior civil servants. 'The committee was a constitutional anomaly, in that, ultimately, the GOC, whose forces had the lion's share of operational responsibility, was answerable, not to the Prime Minister of Northern Ireland, but to the Secretary of State for Defence in London,' said Ramsey. The fact that Faulkner enjoyed good personal relations with the GOC, Sir Harry Tuzo, who was an unusually diplomatic soldier, helped to obscure this lacuna in the chain of command and accountability.'

He recalls that JSC discussions were almost always of a generalised, strategic nature. 'Operational details were never dealt with before the event, beyond, for example, the GOC's informing the committee that he was devoting a particular level of manpower to handling an anticipated protest march. As the security situation deteriorated, the Army, on account of the manpower, reinforcement capability and equipment at their disposal, came to be, by far, the dominant security force, sidelining the police to a large extent.' But he cites elements of the Army's policies and practices which, from time to time, caused concern to the civil power. 'Their intelligence material often appeared to both the police and the local civil servants as naïve and the gap between their concept of "intelligence" and the police concept of "evidence" was frequently a problem in the fight to bring "known terrorists" before the courts.' In his evidence to the inquiry, Ken Bloomfield, then deputy cabinet secretary, said of the JSC: 'It was a forum for the exchange of views rather than an executive decision-making body, a very necessary talking shop. My recollection . . . is that the serious decisions were taken privately by, for example, the Prime Minister, the GOC and the Chief-Constable.'

A Top Secret intelligence brief dated 26 April 1971 demonstrates that, however cordial and constructive the intercourse was said to be, there was continued tension and rivalry between the various arms of the security and intelligence community, an ongoing fragility in personal relationships and uncertainty about the legal framework within which they operated. The new director of intelligence had established 'a very close relationship' with the head of Special Branch, Assistant Chief Constable David Johnston, the document records, and there was a high degree of co-operation with the senior military intelligence officer, 'who had gained the complete confidence of the RUC' and, as a result, complete access to all their records and reports. The quality of the joint intelligence assessments being produced by this triumvirate was therefore 'steadily rising. It cannot be said that the Director has the constitutional right to direct and control Special Branch, which is what would be needed in an ideal organisation, but he is in practice achieving a large measure of control by these informal means,' according to the report, which continued: 'It is extremely important that nothing should be done, either here in Whitehall or in Ulster, to upset this hard-won relationship. Any attempt either to introduce an expert Englishman into the Special Branch hierarchy at the top level, or to give the Director formal command over the HSB, would under current conditions be not only doomed to failure but also a very unwise step that would undo all the good work of the last two months.'

The document also reveals that in the previous four months over 100 weapons had been recovered as a result of operations stemming from intelligence leads, compared with 258 in the whole of 1970. Another report from the time reveals that in the same period wanted men or explosives were found in only ten of over 200,000 cars searched. However, operational Army commanders on the ground were increasingly frustrated by the lack of even basic intelligence at their disposal and the way their hands were tied in obtaining it. In some cases, where relationships with the RUC officers were good, the Army benefited from their local knowledge, avoided making blunders and often scored successes against the terrorists. In many cases, however, Army commanders regarded and treated the RUC as 'Paddies' and both ignored and sidelined them. Some, out of frustration, even established their own intelligence cells to work to fill the gap by unorthodox and legally borderline means. A lieutenant-colonel commanding a battalion in Belfast at this period recalls the often elastic way the soldiers interpreted their remit:

> Most of the vital arrests and. identifications of terrorist locations were achieved by plainclothes Army operations but because of legal uncertainty about the control of such operations and. the estimated political price of stepping them up, the Army were denied this highly effective mode of operation. Another vital inhibition was the lack of population control records and the absence of powers to take a census to compile them. For political reasons again these powers were denied us and the Army were forced to compile records 'sub rosa' without open lawful authority. It was done by stretching statutory authorities to an extent that had never been envisaged and by assuming that the Army had rights which it possibly did not have.

With internment becoming ever more inevitable, Sir Dick White, the head of MI5, was sent over in Belfast in March 1971 to cast his expert eye over the new machinery. About the same time, a very important secret decision, with far-reaching consequences for the RUC, was taken within the intelligence community: in order to gain high-grade information, some of those on the suspect list would be subjected to 'interrogation in depth' before being interned. In preparation for this, as the British government later disclosed to the European Court of Human Rights, officers from the Joint Services Interrogation Wing of the School of Intelligence conducted a seminar for RUC officers in April 1971 to teach them the required techniques, whose morality and legality was so doubtful that they had never been written in a directive, order, syllabus or training manual. These provided for suspects to be hooded, deprived of sleep, fed only bread and water, be subjected to constant 'white' noise and made to lean at an angle against a wall for prolonged periods, supported only by their toes and fingertips. All of this was designed to dislocate all sense of time and location and impose fatigue.

The techniques had been employed and developed, as the subsequent Compton report into their use records, by the government departments and agencies concerned in the light of experience gained in the various internal security operations in which Britain had been involved since the war, including Cyprus and Malaysia. Rules were issued in 1965 and revised in 1967 to provide for daily inspection by a medical officer, after complaints about the treatment of suspects during the Aden emergency. They said that subjects must be treated humanely but with strict discipline and the British government said they followed the broad principles for the treatment of persons under arrest or detention during civil disturbances as laid down in Article 3 of the 1949 Geneva Convention on the Treatment of Prisoners of War. From time to time pilots and members of the special forces, as well as undercover agents who might fall into enemy hands behind the lines, had submitted themselves to the interrogation ordeal for training purposes.

At first, ministerial approval was not sought, in either London or Belfast, for this extraordinary interrogation initiative. Some senior police officers expressed reservations about the proposed methods, which went well beyond anything even the paramilitary RUC had ever been permitted to do. Their objections were brushed aside with assurances that the police officers concerned would be protected and not held responsible if the methods were subsequently criticised. The British cabinet was later told, on 18 October 1971, that accounts of this discussion 'varied as to whether, in ultimately adopting [the interrogation techniques]', the RUC 'acted under pressure from the Army or were convinced of their efficacy by argument'. In any case, during the spring of 1971, as the plans for Long Kesh Internment Centre were being developed, parallel arrangements were being made to construct a purpose-built brick-walled interrogation centre inside a fenced compound at the RAF airfield at Ballykelly. The financial go-ahead for this project was given at the same time as that for building Long Kesh, but the costs and purpose were concealed within those for the larger project. The scene was being set for internment.

Meanwhile the mainstream RUC was essentially sidelined. Thanks to a massive recruiting campaign its numbers had risen from 3,000 to 4,000, but the intake of new recruits was accompanied by a worrying exodus of young officers with under two years' service. 'I can only conclude that the continual unrest is contributing to this drain,' wrote Shillington in his annual report for 1971. More and more operational officers were tied up guarding their police stations and, increasingly, providing protection and escorts for vulnerable government and public figures such as ministers, judges, magistrates and some MPs. When going about even the most routine tasks on the streets, the police now had to deploy in numbers, frequently with armed soldiers to protect them, because of the constant threat of violence and disorder. Breathalyser checks were abandoned and traffic enforcement halted to avoid exposing officers to danger. With more and more explosions taking place, many police were concentrated in Belfast city centre and the larger towns to try and deter the bombers and ensure areas were cleared safely in response to bomb warnings. As these were averaging twenty a day in Belfast alone, and all warnings had to be treated as live in the first instance, this posed an increasing burden, requiring the police to show great composure and, more frequently, exemplary courage in getting people out of the danger zones. After the explosions, police often had to guard damaged buildings to prevent looting.

With normal policing virtually suspended and despite the heavy military presence, the police recorded 158,651 indictable crimes in 1970, breaking all previous records. The following year they soared again by 24.3 per cent and the detection rate collapsed from 40.6 per cent to 31.9 per cent. 'I am afraid that this is proof, if proof were needed, that riot and civil commotion, in which law enforcement is challenged, inevitably leads to a lowering of moral standards,' said Shillington in his first annual report. He could not have foreseen how much higher crime would rise, or how far and for how long standards would further drop.

Chapter Eight
A State of Open War

In the early hours of 8 July 1971, a soldier had his helmet knocked off by a stone-thrower during a fourth successive night of rioting in Londonderry. As two men dashed forward to claim it as a trophy, another soldier nearby opened fire hitting one of them. By the time he reached Letterkenny hospital, some twenty miles away across the border, twenty-eight-year-old Seamus Cusack, had bled to death. Later the Army claimed that Cusack, armed with a rifle, had been ordered to 'stand fast' by a soldier and was shot when he ignored the call. Whatever the truth, his death gave fresh impetus to the trouble and later in the day, after a series of explosions in the Lecky Road area, another young man was shot dead. The soldier who killed Desmond Beattie, aged ninteen, testified that he was about to ignite a nail bomb and throw it. John Hume, the local MP, immediately called for an impartial investigation into the disputed circumstances of both deaths. When this was not conceded, Hume and other opposition MPs withdrew from the Stormont parliament in protest, derailing an all too brief effort by Faulkner and Nationalist politicians to work more harmoniously together.

The killings and the walkout intensified the sense of despair during a month when there were three more violent deaths, two soldiers ambushed by gunmen in Belfast and a civilian who suffered a heart attack after an explosion close to his home. The worsening violence united extremists and hitherto more moderate voices in calling for internment, curfew and other repressive measures to halt the increasingly provocative terrorists. On 16 July gunmen, disguised in white medical coats held up two armed RUC guards and removed a wounded comrade from the Royal Victoria Hospital in Belfast. Late the next afternoon, as the *Sunday Mirror* newspaper was being 'put to bed', staff were ordered out of the building by armed men and an explosion and fire put the printing presses out of action. Altogether there were ninety-four explosions that July, more than double the total for June. Writing from the Ministry of Defence on 21 July to Heath's private secretary, a senior official passed on General

Tuzo's view that the IRA was 'getting better organised and more efficient in its methods'. Maudling reacted to the worsening situation by saying a state of 'open war' now existed between the IRA and the Army. From Faulkner's perspective the time had come for internment and, as a sign of reassurance, he gave scantily concealed hints that it was a live option: there would be no advance notice of internment if it was decided to arrest people. In fact, the military rehearsals were already under way.

At first light on Friday 23 July, the Army, with police mainly acting as guides, mounted raids on 100 addresses in Belfast and nine other towns, taking forty-eight people into custody. This was the first of a series of what Tuzo called 'disruptive operations', designed to harass the known main IRA leaders and demonstrate to the two communities that the security forces knew the identity of the IRA members in their midst. A minute prepared for Lord Carrington the previous day said:

> The searches will be specific and will be conducted in minute detail. They can in no way be interpreted as block or speculative searches. One consequence of the operations may well be that the IRA conclude that internment is about to take place. If so they may put their contingency plans into operation, in which case this dummy run should yield useful information.

With Young and Freeland now gone and their feuding ended, RUC–Army relations had settled on a plateau of practical cordiality. Chief Constable Shillington was content to play a passive role and let the Army bear the brunt of the deteriorating situation and Faulkner's demands. Police officers, now as much disillusioned as demoralised, watched Hunt's bold vision of a brave new world splinter around them as sandbags went up around their stations and they became the target of terrorism on and off duty. Despite their demoralised state, day after day there were many acts of bravery and quick, sensible thinking as they coped with the dangers.

By contrast to the lowered police profile, Army visibility on the roads and streets in Northern Ireland had become all-pervading with the average soldier working intensively up to twenty hours a day. The objective, in formal military language, was to reassure ordinary law-abiding people by their presence and deter illegal movement with a minimum of inconvenience and delay to normal commercial and tourist traffic. This entailed a mixture of patrolling on foot and in vehicles, aerial surveillance from helicopters and establishing covert observation points to monitor traffic using the main roads, especially those leading to and from the border with the Republic. Well over 1,000 vehicles a day were being checked. From time to time they imposed major crackdowns, triggering pre-planned operations with mysterious codenames such as 'Spondon', which involved 1,522 soldiers putting 101 blocks on cross-border roads. Another, codenamed 'Knocker', sealed Belfast off with 396 soldiers deployed at thirty-three checkpoints, and 'Fury' imposed control on all east–west movement within Northern Ireland by using 1,832 soldiers at 229 roadblocks at bridges and other points along the lines of the rivers Bann and Blackwater. The Army also gained useful local knowledge and low-level intelligence from these extensive operations which was now being fed into the greatly expanded intelligence-gathering and analysis apparatus.

Despite all the bold claims that had been made about its greater efficiency in recent months, a teleprinter signal from Lisburn to the Ministry of Defence in London on 2 August revealed that harmony within the security and intelligence community was still decidedly fragile. The courts were granting bail too readily and sentencing was erratic, Tuzo complained, at the head of a litany of shortcomings. 'The RUC, in refusing to carry riot guns for discharging rubber bullets, is still insisting on a far too narrow interpretation of Hunt and organisational change, to align police command structures more closely with those of the Army, is far too slow.' With regard to the holding and interrogation of suspects, the signal said 'there is an honest difference of opinion' between the Army and the police, the latter believing, after long experience, that the IRA were well aware that forty-eight-hours was the maximum legal holding period. 'They are conditioned to sweat this out in the certainty of release. When let out they return to their terrorist activities with enhanced reputations.' The Army wanted the police to use the power of indefinite detention which, they thought, might prove far more effective. 'It is suggested that this should be discussed with Mr Faulkner in the terms of a problem to be solved rather than in the terms of a complaint,' advised Tuzo. In a bid to avoid fracturing the delicate intelligence relationships, the GOC's missive ended on a cautionary note:

> On reflection and after lengthy discussion with the Chief Constable on army/police operations in general, [I] would advise against the prime minister raising any specific complaints in the field of army/police co-operation. It is perhaps true to say that relations are now better than they have ever been. This essential degree of mutual trust could be

destroyed at a stroke if it were thought that we were going behind anyone's back. The GOC has in the past discussed these matters quite frankly with Mr Faulkner and feels that the latter would also have a right to feel aggrieved if he were confronted with detailed complaints with which he has already expressed an intention to deal.

Such concern was founded on the fact that, after the months of secret planning, as the 'disruptive operations' indicated, a decision on full-scale internment was now imminent. Although the construction work at Long Kesh would not be complete for at least another month, the countdown to 'Operation Demetrius', as it was designated, had actually begun and, subject to final political approval, it would go ahead in mid-August. A joint police–Army security group had been working constantly updating and compiling files on the people to be arrested and the list had swollen to 500. Reinforcements were already on their way to help with the round-up and deal with the aftermath: one battalion was to fly in from Germany on 9 August and another was due forty-eight hours later.

As the early summer violence had escalated so too had the familiar Unionist clamour to end the soft-pedalling and take 'tough action against the terrorists', Unionist code for internment. It had worked before, the Unionist argument ran, so the time had come to make it work again. With the gunmen and bombers able to strike at will and with virtual immunity, as evidenced by the scarcity of arrests and the soaring incidence of serious outrages, Faulkner, under phenomenal political pressure to roll back the rising tide of violence and death, was without effective options. Dr Robert Ramsay, his private secretary at the time, told the Bloody Sunday inquiry that while 'Faulkner admired the professionalism of the Army as a fighting force he regarded it as a blunt instrument in a civil setting'. Faulkner also realised that the more deeply the Army became involved in the security situation in Northern Ireland, the more likely it was that what he called 'constitutional awkwardness' with London might arise. Faulkner, a critic of the policing territory Chichester-Clark had surrendered, was therefore reluctant to risk any more. So, despite all his political instincts to the contrary and the price he knew London would exact if it failed, internment became his only option, a last desperate throw of the dice to head off the growing anarchy and avert, what was now widely feared to be, the inevitability of outright civil war. In his statement for the Bloody Sunday inquiry, Bloomfield, Faulkner's deputy cabinet secretary, recalled:

One view of Brian Faulkner is that because he had been the Minister for Home Affairs he was a law and order man and that he was itching all throughout Chichester-Clark's reign to introduce internment. I don't think that was the case. I think Brian Faulkner was backed into a political corner and that he didn't come to the decision about internment with any enthusiasm or conviction that it would work. It was just that no one came along with any alternative and people kept saying that it had worked in the past.

Another person who was forced along the same path, despite his better judgement, was Tuzo, 'a thoughtful and diplomatic man who seemed to be at home in the politics of it all', according to Bloomfield. Despite the planning, Tuzo remained consistently doubtful about the wisdom of going ahead with internment. He felt it would do more harm than good and, instead, still strongly favoured a more robust policy of short-term interrogations utilising the existing provisions of the Special Powers Act. During the afternoon of 2 August, the limitations on what the Army could actually do in such an intractable situation became clear when Tuzo spoke by telephone to General Carver, now chief of the General Staff in London. The most pressing concern that day was whether or not the Apprentice Boys' annual parade through Londonderry should go ahead. Tuzo, who had a good personal relationship with Faulkner, considered it morally wrong not to ban it because of the risk of bloodshed, as portrayed in the many appeals the local prime minister had received, even from moderate Protestants. Carver then suggested a number of possible methods of improving security for the event, including further reinforcements. Tuzo was dismissive. The area affected by the march was so small, he said, that even if more troops were sent over, he could not deploy them. He did not see any way of improving his existing plans.

At this point, with Downing Street poised to give the go-ahead for internment within days, there was talk of linking the swoops with a general ban on parades as a make-weight to blunt the anticipated fury of the minority community. Two days later, in another call to Carver, Tuzo made his views explicitly clear: he did not favour internment on military grounds. Carver recorded his views in a minute for Carrington:

> On those grounds he regards it as unnecessary. But there is no other military step which would have the same political impact. There are other military steps which could be taken, which would give the impression of greater activity, but they would oppress the population in

an indiscriminate way and cause justifiable resentment by innocent people. Internment would at least concentrate on the guilty.

Tuzo added that he was in favour of letting the 12 August march go ahead and was against a package deal. A ban on 'all marches' after 12 August does not mean much, he pointed out, for the Twelfth is effectively the last trial of the annual summer marching season.

That morning troops and police had carried out the eighth of their 'disruptive operations' in both Belfast and Londonderry and there was now a widespread expectation that internment was indeed imminent. Sporadic rioting continued with clashes in Newry, Portadown and elsewhere, as did the explosions. In the first week of August another series of attacks took place, among them blasts damaging the home of a resident magistrate in Omagh and devastating an office block in central Belfast. A number of police and Army posts also came under attack. In Belfast, terrorists hijacked a bus and opened fire on Springfield Road Police Station. By far the most damaging incident was a three-bomb assault on an electricity power station near Larne. A saboteur climbed to a lofty cat-walk and planted high explosive devices against the three main oil-fired boilers, knocking them out and slashing a quarter of Northern Ireland's generating capacity. (Only emergency repairs removed the fear that widespread power cuts during the approaching winter would further destabilise the situation.)

The London cabinet had heard from Maudling on 22 July that, with Faulkner's once firm grip diminishing by the day, the situation in Northern Ireland, in masterful understatement, 'gave serious cause for concern'. After discussion, ministers decided it would be better to give internment a try rather than risk Faulkner being overthrown, forcing them to institute direct rule, which it was affirmed should be a policy of only last resort. In a bid to make the gamble more effective, the government also decided to see if the Irish government could be persuaded to adopt a similar policy despite the political pressures Lynch would face. A secret approach was made to him a few days later, on 31 July, by Sir John Peck, the ambassador in Dublin. Putting out the cover story that they were discussing details of his forthcoming visit to London, Lynch was asked simultaneously to arrest IRA activists in the Republic. He replied there were no grounds for doing so and that any Irish government who tried would not survive. Lynch was all too aware of his vulnerability on the question, having recently had to confront senior figures in his own government and party who had been closely identified with the resuscitation of the IRA and with dubious efforts to finance and arm them, abusing the official cover of the Irish state and using Irish taxpayers' money. Lynch was so strongly concerned about the Catholic reaction to internment that during the ninety-minute meeting he repeatedly urged Britain against the step, fearing 'it would produce an explosion it would be impossible to contain'.

With Heath about to set off on a sailing holiday on his ocean-racing yacht *Morning Cloud*, a tense gathering took place in Downing Street at 6 p.m. on Thursday 5 August to make the critical internment decision. Faulkner opened the proceedings, with only British and Northern Ireland ministers present, by saying internment was now the only option: public confidence was in decline, there were increasingly serious implications for industry and commerce and the security forces could suggest no other initiative to make an early impact. The British ministers – Carrington, Maudling and Sir Alec Douglas-Home, the foreign secretary – were concerned at the lack of military enthusiasm and, with the wanted list overwhelmingly dominated by alleged Republicans, insistent that there must be 'balancing action' in the form of an indefinite ban on parades and the curtailment of the largely Protestant-run gun clubs. Heath commented that if internment was tried and failed there would be no option but to introduce direct rule.

Shillington, Carver and Tuzo then joined the meeting. 'The time for internment has arrived', said Shillington, but the soldiers were still opposed. In their view it was not 'an essential measure in military terms' and they were confident they could defeat the IRA by present methods 'but whether the likely time-scale was acceptable was essentially a political question and thus not one for determination by them'. After some discussion, Heath indicated that the government would give the Army the necessary instructions to introduce internment but he wanted 'a corresponding act of discipline' against Protestants by having some of them interned, the imposition of an indefinite ban on marches in Northern Ireland and the prohibition of rifle clubs, which it was feared were a 'front' for Loyalist activity. It was essential that the policy should be seen to be impartial in its application, he told his colleagues. Heath also laid down that the action should be publicly justified as providing an opportunity for fresh initiatives to promote political reconciliation and to carry forward the economic development of the province.

Faulkner, who was stoically battling to hold his divided party together, retreated to Unionist basics and would not accept that those interned should include a certain number of Protestants. He said that, whatever their involvement in past acts, there was no intelligence indicating 'an imminent or potential Protestant threat. The present threat was from the IRA.' He also opposed the indefinite ban on marches as impracticable. How, he asked, could they enforce a ban on the Twelfth of July march the following year? He warned that if the Republican faction reacted to internment by wholesale demonstrations, it would be impossible to restrain Protestants for long from counter-demonstrations. He also opposed restricting the rifle clubs because, as the RUC would attest, most of their members were respectable and responsible citizens and prohibition would be liable to provoke unnecessary ill-feeling. He went on to point out that Protestants in Northern Ireland would regard internment as no more than a merited punishment for the violence of the IRA and that not all Roman Catholics would see it as something which required a corresponding gesture on their part. 'Playing the Orange card', as it was described in Northern Ireland, Faulkner said the British government would need full Protestant support for any new initiatives on political reconciliation which they might be able to undertake, so it would be foolish to alienate them.

Heath replied that the Northern Ireland government must clearly understand that the British cabinet would not be prepared to acquiesce in internment unless there was a ban on marches without specific limit of time. They would not be prepared to have this card played against them again when the Northern Ireland government next found themselves under pressure. Internment was a major decision, which could not be said – as Tuzo had earlier made clear – to be justified by any military necessity. It must therefore be regarded as a political act, which would be thought to be directed against one faction and must accordingly be matched by some political action which would represent its counterpart in relation to the other faction. With surprise being of the essence in catching the potential internees, there was no statement after the meeting other than an announcement of more troops being sent.

Maudling, who was now in charge with Heath having gone sailing, again mulled over the rationale for internment with his own officials at the Home Office the next morning, Friday. Given the constitutional limbo they were working in, London was very clearly apprehensive about what Faulkner might do next. After this discussion, a message was telexed to Belfast just before lunchtime saying that the home secretary wanted to know who was on the arrest list. The message went on to say that Maudling was insistent the list must include a number of Protestants and must not include any Westminster or Stormont MPs. 'If the view is taken that a particular MP should be put on the list, he would wish to consider it most carefully.' At that point, there were in fact two Stormont MPs targeted for arrest. Paddy Devlin, the MP for Falls, had been interned during the Second World War but had long since renounced his Irish Republican associations and become a prominent figure in the Labour and Trade Union movement. As a founder member of the Social Democratic and Labour Party, the moderate nationalist party, the previous year, he was at that point very much working for a peaceful solution and publicly opposed to the growing wave of IRA violence. Paddy Kennedy, elected to Stormont on the back of the civil rights campaign, was the other MP, but his position was much more ambiguous. He had declined to link with all the other elected 'civil rights' figures to launch the SDLP and was keeping public company with people openly associated with the rapidly expanding Provisional IRA.

Early the next morning, tension reached new levels in Belfast after an Army sentry shot dead a man driving a van past Springfield Road Police Station. The sentry said he had heard shots. Amidst calls for an independent investigation of the incident, rioting developed and continued all day. Late the next evening, Sunday, after Faulkner had brought the operation forward twenty-four hours from the time agreed at Downing Street, the arrest teams gathered to be briefed on their individual targets. They were told to go in simultaneously at 4.30 the next morning to avoid other suspects being tipped off that the swoops were finally on. Speed was also a prime consideration to avoid the chance of hostile crowds gathering, even at that early hour. Over the weekend, London's interest caused the two MPs' names to be dropped from the arrest list but the insistence on Protestants being included was ignored.

By breakfast time on the morning of the swoops, as the prisoners were being processed at three holding centres, Girdwood Barracks in Belfast, Ballykinler and Magilligan, a head count showed that 354 of the 452 targets had been detained. Within forty-eight hours, 104 were freed and the remainder lodged in either Belfast prison or the *Maidstone*. Twelve of those captured had however been singled out for special treatment and were handed over to the teams of police and Army interrogators who had been specially trained the previous April. In the words of the subsequent official report by Sir Edmund Compton into allegations against the security forces of physical brutality arising from these events, 'they were believed to possess information of a kind which it was operationally necessary to obtain as rapidly as possible in the interest of saving lives'.

From 11 to 17 August these men, clad in boiler suits, were subjected to the five interrogation-in-depth techniques involving degrees of physical and psychological deprivation. Apart from periods of interrogation and solitary confinement they were kept hooded. They were subjected to continuous and monotonous 'white noise' designed to disorientate and isolate them. During the early days of the process they were deprived of sleep and sustenance, being given only a round of bread and a pint of water at six-hourly intervals. They were also made to stand against a wall with legs apart and hands raised above their heads against the wall. If they attempted to rest or sleep by propping their heads against the wall they were prevented from doing so and if they collapsed on the floor they were picked up by the armpits and forced to resume the posture. The detainees were each subjected to this regime for periods totalling from nine to forty-three hours during the five days. (In a second episode, two men were later subjected to similar treatment between 11 and 18 October.) Some of those involved later claimed that they had been denied toilet facilities, suffered assaults and other abuse and experienced hallucinations, thirst and blood circulation problems.

In the immediate aftermath of the internment operation, the authorities maintained it had been an overwhelming success. Seven hours after the swoops, Faulkner presided at a news conference in the main hall of the Stormont parliament building, where he gave the first official confirmation that the powers to intern had been activated and presented the swoops as a bold and daring strike at the terrorists for the good of all.

> The outrages to which we have been subjected now threaten our economic life and create every day deeper divisions and antagonism within our community. Every means has been tried to make terrorists amenable to the law. But the terrorist campaign continues at an unacceptable level, and I have had to conclude that the ordinary law cannot deal comprehensively or quickly enough with such ruthlessness and viciousness. The main target of the present operation is the Irish Republican Army which has been responsible for recent acts of terrorism and whose victims have included Roman Catholic and Protestant alike. They are the present threat; but we will not hesitate to take strong action against any other individual or organisations who may present such a threat in future.

The security forces quickly embellished Faulkner's bullish tone about the success of their operation, declaring that a high proportion of the IRA leadership had been picked up. They were later to justify the move, and especially the in-depth interrogations, by saying that for the first time they had been able to gain new detailed information about the IRA. The Parker report into the efficacy of the interrogation procedures, published in March 1972, said that as a direct result, they had identified a further 700 IRA members and their positions in the organisation, gleaned forty pages of information about organisation and structure, uncovered details of possible operations, arms caches, safe houses, communication and supply routes and locations of wanted persons as well as details of morale, operational directives, propaganda techniques and future plans, and discovered responsibility for eighty-five incidents recorded on police files which had previously been unexplained.

But on that first morning, from the steps outside Stormont, just a few yards away from where Faulkner was speaking in the main hall, the thick clouds of black smoke swirling into the sky over the entire city already called into question the effectiveness of the operation and signalled the dashing of hopes that internment would rapidly quell the trouble. Bloomfield recalls driving to work that morning and seeing the many fires: 'It was a sobering sight.' Thirteen people were killed in the first twenty-four hours as widespread rioting, shooting, arson and disorder erupted throughout Northern Ireland on a more widespread and intense scale than in August 1969. Two hundred and forty houses were destroyed by fire in the Ardoyne district of Belfast alone and once again, on both sides of the ironically named Army Peace Lines, people could be seen fleeing their homes, their belongings piled high in lorries, vans and cars. The violent reaction, on a scale totally unforeseen in even the most pessimistic assessments by the security forces, caused the authorities to drop plans for a second swoop on a further 200 suspects. Heath pressed Faulkner to go ahead with it and step up interrogations to gain intelligence but Faulkner replied that 'Special Branch was fully stretched' conducting interviews and processing the 'unexpectedly good' information they had obtained. Efforts in London to bring in British police interrogators to help were brought to a swift end when the Police Federation objected.

Within hours, however, the IRA leadership in Belfast dealt Faulkner's bullishness a devastating propaganda blow when the veteran Republican Joe Cahill, who had been reprieved from a death sentence in 1942 for his part in the murder of RUC Constable Patrick Murphy, held a news conference in a Belfast school and boasted that, because of a tip-off about the impending arrests, only thirty of their members had been captured. Two days later an IRA statement from Dublin admitted to fifty-six members being held.

The IRA quickly demonstrated that it had been far from neutered by Faulkner's gamble. In the pre-internment months from January 1971, the number of explosions had reached well over 250. Up to that time twenty-seven people had lost their lives: two policemen, ten soldiers and fifteen civilians, of whom four had been shot by the security forces. Injuries had been inflicted on 454 civilians, 71 policemen and 110 soldiers. In the remaining five months of 1971, after the introduction of internment, the death toll for the year jumped from twenty-seven to 173; explosions increased to 131 in August, 196 in September and 117 in October before reaching a year-end total of 1,022. Shooting incidents soared from 213 in 1970 to 1,756 in 1971, the vast majority of them after 9 August. By the end of the year, the RUC had suffered nine more deaths.

Far from taking the IRA activists and leaders out of circulation, as Faulkner and the politicians suggested had happened, the devastating escalation of violence after internment exposed the abysmal quality of the outdated intelligence on which the arrests were based and called into question the accuracy and value of the information extracted by 'deep interrogation'. Many of the persons detained were arrested on the basis of inadequate and inaccurate information. In some cases fathers and sons with the same names had been confused. Many of those 'lifted' were traditionalist, well-known Republicans who were no longer active in the movement. Others were peaceful civil rights activists with no Republican antecedents. The identity of the cadres of new, younger activists, who had first taken to the streets during the protest marches and then become involved in more sinister and threatening violence, would take the authorities several more years to identify with any certainty and in any numbers.

One of the strongest proponents of internment had been John Taylor, the hawkish junior minister for home affairs. (His appointment, with its attendant elevation to the Privy Council, had alarmed Lord Grey, who considered him 'an unreliable man who talks off the top of his head'. In a report to the Home Office in London he said: 'I thought I should not admit John Taylor to the Privy Council without some words about the need for loyalty by Ministers to the Prime Minister and about the need for discretion in public utterances. As I could hardly single him out for a curtain lecture, I preached to such as were present.') Taylor, who would survive a hail of gunfire in a determined IRA assassination attempt some six months later, had departed to Spain on holiday and only learned internment had started when he saw the smoke from burning tyres as he was driving home a day or so later. In a statement for the Bloody Sunday

Inquiry he revealed that the first doubts about the effectiveness of internment emerged in the secret privacy of a Joint Security Committee meeting at Stormont on 26 August, almost three weeks after the operation.

> I do recall the JSC feeling that key players in the Republican movement had not been interned and it appeared that the intelligence upon which the policy of internment had been based had not been as good as one would have hoped. My recollection is that the RUC and the Army had separate and almost rival intelligence services and one had the impression that the Army did not fully rely on the RUC and the intelligence that it had. I do not recall any discussions prior to my summer holiday about the state of intelligence or its quality prior to internment being introduced.

A much rosier picture was however still being painted for the cabinet in London. At a meeting in Downing Street, at noon on 12 August, Carrington reported that the leaders of the IRA had been put out of action and the terrorist organisation severely disrupted. Six days later a briefing paper prepared in advance of a meeting between Heath and Faulkner provided a more level-headed assessment:

> The internment operation has been a considerable success technically [. . .] the evidence is that both wings [the so-called 'Official' and 'Provisional' factions] of the IRA have been more seriously disrupted than statements from IRA sources suggest and, while they will undoubtedly give trouble, there is reasonable hope that with increased vigilance at the border, terrorist activity will now be at a lower level than in the weeks before internment. But internment is only a means to an end and the political and social consequences have been serious – more serious than many people in Northern Ireland expected. It is too soon to reach conclusions about the permanence of public reaction, but there has undoubtedly been a greater polarisation between the two communities.

However, in reporting to the cabinet, Heath was still being highly optimistic. The arrests had achieved a large measure of success and about half the leaders of the IRA had been apprehended, he told ministers. Although Carrington stated the security situation was 'discouraging' at a subsequent meeting on 21 September, and advised ministers that IRA recruitment was rising and that the task of the troops was becoming increasingly difficult, he did insist that it was still too early to say that internment had failed. The anecdotal evidence from the ground was not so encouraging. Colonel Harry Dalzell-Payne, who ran the new MO4 branch in the Ministry of Defence which had recently been set up to co-ordinate the growing volume of Northern Ireland-related political, legal and military work, reported that he had been able to travel in a Land Rover on a pre-internment visit to Northern Ireland, but by the time of his next visit two months later, he was forced to travel in an armoured personnel carrier because of the deterioration in the situation.

The one-sided implementation of internment, with no Loyalists or Protestants arrested, did however justify the warning by nationalist critics that internment was the best recruiting sergeant the IRA could ever have hoped for. Indeed, there is ample evidence that internment caused many people to become directly or indirectly involved with the IRA and set off the uncontrollable explosion that Jack Lynch correctly predicted. In the coming twenty-five years, the Provisional IRA would cause carnage in the name of Irish Republicanism that was without precedent, even by the bloody standards of Irish history, and fight the might of the British state and Army to the point where all talk of victory had long vanished and Britain would eventually negotiate for peace.

Despite Maudling's specific insistence that Protestants must be included on the arrest list, they were finally excluded at the last minute. A draft of a message prepared for the British ambassador to deliver to Lynch in Dublin, advising him of the imminent internment arrests, contains the phrase 'the measures taken do not discriminate between the different sections of the community' and the sentence: 'Protestants as well as Catholic and IRA extremists will be liable to internment.' This sentence was struck out and not included in the final version of the message. David Bleakley, the Labour outsider brought in by Faulkner as minister for community relations, reminded ministerial colleagues of his doubts about the policy at a cabinet meeting in Belfast on 17 August and expressed his concern about its divisive effect. In reply, Faulkner emphasised that the operation applied to anyone, regardless of political or religious affiliation, against whom there was information. At present he was advised, he said, that there was no case to justify the detention of Protestants. The attorney-general, Basil Kelly, confirmed that the police had been genuinely unable to furnish them with any information suggesting that a subversive organisation existed in the Protestant community.

This was plainly myopic. One of the first signs of resurgent violence had come in May 1966 when Protestant extremists, designating themselves 'the Ulster Volunteer Force', declared war against the IRA and its splinter groups. The warning was dismissed as the work of cranks until a month later, on 26 June, when a Catholic barman was shot dead and two companions wounded as they left a bar on the Shankill Road in Belfast. Two days later the UVF – 'this evil thing in our midst', said O'Neill – was proscribed. The first bombings of the Troubles, the attacks on the public utilities in early 1969, had been the work of Loyalists, who also claimed the first police life during the protests about the Hunt report. With Craig and Paisley consistently threatening to 'resist' the British government and 'liquidate' the enemies of Northern Ireland, all sorts of shadowy Loyalist organisations had been formed and were wheeling in the background, so Basil Kelly's remark was disingenuous in the extreme. In an equally incredible intervention at another cabinet meeting three days later, Taylor suggested that in view of criticism that the application of detention was one-sided, it might be made known that one or two Protestants were among those 'arrested for suspected IRA activities'. There were, in fact, two non-Catholics among those arrested but both were decidedly and publicly acknowledged civil rights activists.

The omission of any Protestant subversives was a bigoted and costly blunder. Catholics regarded the decision as a renunciation of the new, even-handed RUC they had been promised. Once again, as far as they were concerned, the RUC was being used as an instrument of repression by Unionists only interested in their own political survival. More damagingly, the Loyalists who would have been on a properly balanced internment list would soon launch a campaign of brutal sectarian assassination, randomly targeting victims who would be done to death for no reason other than their Catholicism. 'I think that for whatever reason, Special Branch had got behind the game by this point,' recalls Bloomfield. 'The re-introduction of internment exposed flaws in the police surveillance system in that the police picked up too many of the wrong type of people and failed to pick up anyone really nasty from the other side of the community. And when the Irish Republic didn't implement similar internment legislation it made it impossible to deal with the problem in isolation.'

Robert Ramsay identifies several reasons for the failure of internment:

> It had become so obviously 'inevitable' that many of its intended prisoners had already fled; the intelligence on which arrests were made

proved to be sadly out of date, so that many inactive Republicans were interned, whilst the new generation of PIRA [Provisional IRA] volunteers had been only patchily identified; the Irish Republic took a cynically opportunist view of the situation, both providing a safe haven for men on the run and adding a loud condemnatory voice against the measure in the forum of world opinion; the to-be-expected bad press of the operation was exacerbated by revelations about the Army's use, without the knowledge of the Northern Ireland government, of quasi-torture techniques during interrogations, involving, for example, the use of 'white sound' and other elements of sensory deprivation; and it was seen as one-sided. The arrest of some Loyalist paramilitaries, who had been active a few years previously, was considered at political level in both Belfast and London, but on the advice of the security forces had not been carried out.

He believes that in the months following the introduction of internment 'community polarisation increased dangerously'.

The protest marches which had started out some three years previously under such civil rights banners as 'One man, one vote' now had the internment issue to give them a new and menacing impulse. Almost every weekend, despite a blanket ban on marches, there were illegal protests, which would frequently degenerate into serious violence. Sometimes there would be counter-demonstrations, mounted by Loyalists, which added to the increasing disorder. PIRA's bombing campaign, which targeted more and more towns and villages across Northern Ireland, added to the general atmosphere of crisis.

Bloomfield reckons that 'in the six months following the introduction of internment Brian Faulkner's government was going down the tube in terms of the security situation':

[A senior colleague] said that the ability to maintain law and order is a mark of true government and that if you don't have that you are not a government but a local authority. People were looking to their Prime Minister to sort the security situation out. I think it was clear to Brian Faulkner and to most of us who worked for him that security measures weren't going to work but that political measures were needed. The puzzle here was whether the existing Northern Ireland government would make any significant changes. It had become apparent to many

of us that there were real grievances amongst the Catholic community
and some of us felt a sense of shame that more hadn't been done to
address the imbalance.

In retrospect, internment turned out to be a disastrous and defining
episode with other far-reaching political and security consequences. In
the first instance, the courts declared all the arrests had been invalid and
therefore illegal. As a result of a test case, all 340 internees in due course
received a compensation payment. In respect of the 'hooded men', as they
became known, the Compton report, hastily commissioned by Heath once
the episode was exposed, concluded in November 1971 that they had
indeed been ill-treated. The cabinet took the cynical view that it had been
justified in the circumstances. With the lives of British soldiers and
innocent civilians depending on intelligence, the cabinet minutes of 18
October record, 'We were dealing with an enemy who had no scruples
and we should not be unduly squeamish over methods of interrogation in
these circumstances.' The minutes also disclose that contrary to
Ramsay's recollection, the candidates for interrogation were selected by
Faulkner after Carrington and Maudling had given political approval for
the practice on 10 August.

Britain ended up in the dock at the European Court of Human Rights
after the internment and interrogation operations, facing complaints of
torture made by those affected with the active support of the Irish
government. After the failure of the two governments to achieve a
friendly settlement, the court ruled in January 1976 that 'the interrogation
techniques did not occasion suffering of the particular intensity and
cruelty implied by the word torture' but did amount to 'inhuman and
degrading treatment'. In June 1974, one of the claimants was paid
£10,000 in an out-of-court settlement before claims for unlawful arrest,
false imprisonment and assault and battery were brought before a judge.
In December that year, six others received awards totalling £76,000.
Meanwhile, new legislation and other measures had been put in place to
protect suspects while in custody and to put the arrest and detention
process on a sound legal footing.

Internment was a more costly débâcle in other ways. Catholics pulled
out of parliament, councils and public life in protest at the brutality and
partiality of the operation. Thousands embarked on a campaign of civil
disobedience, refusing to pay rent and rates until internment ended. It
seemed to them that the clock had been turned back to the bad old days of
discrimination and repression and that the reforms only grudgingly

promised were now being denied. This was the point at which Northern Ireland's partial independence was finally doomed. On 4 December 1971, the senior civil servant, Dr John Oliver, chairing a meeting of the advisory committee on relations with the Catholic community, said, according to the minutes: 'The government needs to decide upon its basic philosophy in relation to the minority. Did it consider itself at war with the minority or did it believe in treating it fairly, firmly and openly? At present, the government's attitude was not clear.'

But it was the consequences of an apparently innocuous military arrest on the streets of Londonderry a few days after internment that had the greatest impact, for it demonstrated that all Army operations in Northern Ireland since 1969 had been mounted from a legally flawed standpoint. On 8 September 1971, John Hume and Ivan Cooper, both Stormont MPs, and Michael Canavan, Hugh Logue and William Gallagher were convicted at the Magistrates' Court in Londonderry, charged that on 18 August 1971 they 'did remain in an assembly of three or more persons after the persons constituting that assembly had been ordered to disperse by a commissioned officer of Her Majesty's forces then on duty, contrary to regulation 38(1) of the regulations under the Civil Authorities (Special Powers) Act (Northern Ireland) 1922–43'. Each was fined £20 and sentenced to three months' imprisonment in default. However, two Belfast barristers, Jim McSparran QC and Charlie Hill, took up the case and, citing obscure Canadian, Australian and other precedents, successfully argued all the way to the Appeal Court in Belfast that the convictions were unlawful because the regulations under the Special Powers Acts, containing provisions relating to the Army, were beyond the scope of the Northern Ireland parliament and therefore invalid. Their case was that having regard to the Government of Ireland Act 1920, it was outside the competence of the Northern Ireland parliament or of the minister to confer powers on 'any member of . . . Her Majesty's Forces on duty acting on his behalf' and that the regulation under which the men were convicted did not conform to the powers of the northern parliament or executive under the 1920 Act. When the Appeal Court unanimously ruled in their favour on 23 February 1972, and ordered the quashing of the convictions, the case of Regina (Hume and others) *v* the Londonderry Justices took on a startling legal significance.

The British government had been made aware of the likelihood of an adverse judgment a few days earlier by John McDermott QC, legal adviser to the ministry of home affairs in Belfast. 'I have heard on the grapevine that after the judgement in the Hume case . . . if it goes against the Crown, and I fear it will, the Army is going to be out on a limb. Powers of arrest, search and anything of a quasi-police nature will probably be unlawful; in short the Army becomes impotent as an aid to the civil authority', he wrote. Heath convened a meeting at Chequers on 20 February to consider how best to navigate the legal consequences. 'Past activities by army personnel under the Special Powers Act . . . have been so widespread that the possibilities of litigation [for] irregular usage would be endless,' said an Army briefing paper. It was quickly decided not to take the case to the House of Lords because there was no guarantee it would reverse the Belfast court's decision and, for reasons of time, Heath also decided the decision could not be exploited as a bargaining counter with Faulkner to achieve constitutional change, especially exclusive control of security.

The Army had already considered the operational implications of the ruling and had come to the conclusion that, without a change in the law in their favour, they would be rendered impotent unless an RUC officer was present to give legal justification for every search of a person, car, building and other actions necessary to maintain law and order. This was impracticable, for there were simply not enough police available. An alternative proposition, that members of the armed forces be sworn in as constables, was also rejected; the offices of soldier and special constable were legally incompatible and there would be the vexed question of whose orders they obeyed – the GOC's or the chief constable's.

In the end it was agreed to move at once after the court had ruled and bring forward a short bill to regularise the anomaly. Heath briefed Wilson on the situation in the House of Commons on the afternoon of 22 February. The former prime minister was 'flabbergasted' but agreed to co-operate so that legislation could become law within hours. Thus the Northern Ireland Act 1972 was rushed through every legislative stage in parliament at Westminster, including the Royal Assent, the next day to ensure, as Maudling put it, 'that the law as far as the armed forces are concerned is and always has been what it has hitherto been believed to be'. Despite all the concerns about the Army's legal standing while conducting internal security operations in Northern Ireland, first expressed by Wilson himself in late 1968, and the legal research carried out afterwards, nobody had spotted the fundamental flaw. The new act not only regularised the Army's future legal standing but, in a highly rare and unusual move, retrospectively authorised all its actions, including arrests made, and indemnified soldiers from the first moment they had stepped from their barracks on to the streets in August 1969.

For the increasingly embattled RUC, the aftermath of internment was another crucial turning point. The modernisation steps that had been taken in the wake of Hunt were abandoned as the police retreated into fortified stations and patrolled only in armoured vehicles and in strength, usually accompanied by a force of soldiers. A military appreciation of the security situation in October 1971 described morale in the under-strength force as 'very low':

> There is some confusion of aim, a lack of will and leadership – particularly at intermediate levels – and a tendency to rely too much on the Army. Its attitude is passive and its contribution to the security situation minimal. This does not apply at present to the Special Branch but there are ominous signs of some weakening there. Meanwhile the Army must continue to bear the brunt of the security burden until the RUC can play a more effective part, which may not be for some years.

Within the Catholic community anti-RUC feeling was rampant. The force was blamed for resorting to old prejudices in its choice of people for internment and moderate people who had been willing to give it a fresh start after Hunt felt betrayed and exposed and withdrew their support. The one-sided nature of internment confirmed Catholic perceptions of partisan control of the police by the Unionists. The tentative efforts to build links with the Catholic community were finally severed as Republicans turned on the police and from that point there was no close-contact, community policing. An officer visiting relatives in Londonderry was besieged in their house by a crowd of 300 and three priests moved in to protect him before he was removed by the IRA across the border to Letterkenny, dropped off at the hospital for treatment and then allowed to go free. As the violence surged, in September a new row blew up over whose responsibility it was to protect police stations. Shillington called for Army guards rather than police with shotguns. On 27 October there was a concerted attack on the homes of several Catholic police officers in the Finaghy, Dunmurry and the Andersonstown areas of Belfast. The incidents triggered an exodus of Catholic police families from similar Catholic-populated areas, a segregation that would last another thirty years and even then look indefinite. In another manifestation of how dangerous life was becoming for the RUC, off duty as well as on, a party of police from Armagh attending a function across the border in a Monaghan hotel were confronted by two gunmen demanding to know their identities. One of three unarmed women police officers in the party bravely tackled one of the gunmen, who fired several shots as they fled.

On 12 November there was a call for a police strike because of the lack of urgency in arming and protecting them after two more officers were killed in an ambush at a shop on the Oldpark Road in Belfast. In the final departure from Hunt's recommendations, the Police Authority called for all 4,000 police officers to be armed for their own protection and that of life and property, but not before British officials had fought hard to prevent the Catholic members of the body resigning in protest about the abandonment of Hunt and the one-sided imposition of internment. Events over the weekend of 27/28 November, when two people were shot dead and a wave of twenty-two explosions occurred across Northern Ireland, were accompanied by an IRA statement saying the attacks gave the lie to government claims that they were on the run.

At a cabinet meeting in London a few days later the British government took the view that the large-scale violence 'had been something of a propaganda victory for the IRA, since [it] appeared to belie the relatively optimistic assessments emanating from official sources. It would be most important in future to avoid any statements which might afterwards be shown to be rash prophecies.' However, on 15 December, during a visit to Belfast, the increasingly hapless Maudling made the crass remark that he could foresee a time when IRA violence, while not eliminated, would be reduced to 'an acceptable level'. It was a phrase that would haunt British policy for years to come, with its implication that the people of Northern Ireland would have to tolerate terrorism in a way that was not expected of citizens elsewhere in the United Kingdom where, the cabinet was told, there was a growing feeling that Northern Ireland should be left to its fate.

Apart from the impression that the government had given up on pacifying Northern Ireland, the additional inference that terrorism could not be defeated caused general dismay. The death of fifteen people in an explosion at McGurk's bar in Belfast on 4 December, the work of Loyalists, deepened anxieties all round and underlined the folly in excluding them from the internment process. By the end of 1971, the murder rate in Northern Ireland had soared by 900 per cent as, after internment, the Troubles escalated to unthinkable levels. Faulkner's last throw had failed tragically and much worse was to come. During January 1972, in which there were 156 explosions and 336 shootings, twenty-six people died. Two of them were police officers, Sergeant Peter Gilgunn and Constable David Montgomery, ambushed and shot dead when their patrol car was fired on and hit seventeen times at Creggan Road while approaching the RUC station at Rosemount. Two other officers in the car escaped injury. Years later, Constable Robert Black, who was a colleague of the dead officers and a scenes-of-crime officer for twenty-two years, recalled the aftermath of the incident, the first killing of RUC officers in the city:

> It was a big shock to us all, particularly in a police station like Rosemount. We were a very small group and there was a great feeling of comradeship amongst the men. It was well known that the IRA had done the shooting. Personally, I was petrified when I found out. I drove up that road nearly every day and it could have been me. It was a traumatic time for me although, terribly, I got hardened to death as time went on.

A few days later, on 30 January, there was an even more traumatic incident in the city when soldiers from the Parachute Regiment shot dead thirteen civil rights marchers taking part in a banned parade and fatally wounded a fourteenth. Two days later, angry crowds stormed the British Embassy in Dublin and burned it to the ground, while there was another convulsion of protest violence in Northern Ireland similar to that after internment. The event has become indelibly inscribed in British-Irish history as 'Bloody Sunday', but there were equally tragic though less well remembered events to come. On 22 February the violence was exported to the British mainland for the first time when seven people, including five women canteen staff, a gardener and a Catholic padre, died in an explosion at the headquarters of the Parachute Regiment in Aldershot, Hampshire. The attack was a reprisal for the shootings by the regiment in Londonderry. Three days later John Taylor survived an assassination attempt although gravely wounded.

Saturday 4 March was another ignominious day. Late that afternoon a bomb exploded without warning in the Abercorn restaurant in central Belfast, killing two women and injuring another 130 people. In the middle of the month the IRA staged a seventy-two-hour truce to coincide with a visit to Dublin by Harold Wilson, but it rapidly fizzled out and the incessant cycle of shootings, bombings and deaths resumed. On 20 March, a 999 call was received by the police stating that a bomb had been placed in Church Street, Belfast. While the security forces were evacuating the area further telephone calls indicated that the bomb was in adjoining Donegall Street. Before that area could be cleared a device in a car, estimated to contain 100lbs of explosives, was detonated, resulting in the deaths of seven people, including two members of the RUC, and causing injuries to 146 others.

In the meantime, with Bill Craig taking salutes from ranks of masked Loyalists in military uniforms at weekly Nazi-style rallies and making ever more outrageous threats to confront the British government, London's appalled tolerance of the sectarian carnage finally ran out and Faulkner was called to London. At a meeting which lasted for nine hours he was told to agree to the transfer of responsibility for Northern Ireland's internal security to London or there would be direct rule. After another forty-eight hours of crisis talks in both London and Belfast, Faulkner still refused and signalled he and his entire government would resign. Heath did not attempt to dissuade them and, on 24 March 1972, prorogued the Northern Ireland parliament after fifty years and introduced direct rule from Westminster. The next day William Whitelaw, the leader of the House of Commons, arrived in Belfast as the first Secretary of State for Northern Ireland. As a full member of the British cabinet, he created the Northern Ireland Office, modelled on the existing Welsh and Scottish Offices, with twinned secretariats in Belfast and London.

With the control of security now firmly in British hands, a summit to set out policy took place at the Ministry of Defence in London on 14 April. Whitelaw said that, from many of the cases he had examined, grounds for internment were not strong enough and that the collection of intelligence must not become an end in itself, at the risk of alienating moderate Catholic opinion. Carrington said the government would be 'politically vulnerable' if the security situation deteriorated further and that this must not be allowed to happen, but 1972 turned out to be by far the worst of what would prove to be thirty years of unrelenting terrorism. The death toll reached 467 over the twelve months, with 10,628 shooting incidents, while 1,382 bombs exploded and another 471 were defused. Some of these were car-bombs, packed with explosives and usually left to explode without warning in city streets or town centres. Those close by were slaughtered or maimed indiscriminately and damage to property by blast and fire was invariably devastating.

Friday 21 July, or 'Bloody Friday' as it is remembered, was a singularly violent day when the IRA exploded nineteen devices during a two-hour period in the early afternoon, killing nine people and injuring hundreds. Loyalists intensified their own campaign of random sectarian assassination, contributing to the ninety-five deaths that month attributed to the security situation. At that point the intelligence community calculated that, despite the continued internment of some 350 suspects and the release of some 500 since direct rule, active Provisional IRA membership had only dropped from 1,300 to 1,170. The campaign of violence was substantially fuelled by the proceeds of armed robberies which increased fourfold in a year to 19,031, raising at least £800,000, a figure almost certainly understated by the authorities. What was extorted through intimidation and the payment of 'protection money' cannot be calculated.

Inevitably it was a devastating year for the fifty-year-old RUC and unarguably the most demanding in its history. Apart from riot situations, police personnel came under attack on more than 3,000 occasions, 600 of the incidents involving firearms or explosives. Another 269 attacks, four-fifths of them involving rockets or firearms, were made on police stations. Seventeen RUC officers were murdered and 745 injured, on and off duty, as they became constant targets for the gunmen and bombers. 'The seemingly endless spiral of death, destruction and human suffering tends to make all but the most resolute despair of restoring peace to our strife-torn community,' wrote Shillington in his annual report. The Army's analysis was equally bleak: 'It is unrealistic to think in terms of total elimination [of the IRA]. Complete demoralisation and surrender is the best we can hope for,' said one intelligence assessment soon after direct rule.

But in other, more positive ways, 1972 was a highly significant year. Whitelaw drew the IRA into a short-lived truce, establishing a secret channel to negotiate with the politically blinkered organisation through intermediaries, but that, as we shall see, would not bear full fruit for over twenty years. Recognising that any enduring solution to the problem would be a political rather than a military one, he cajoled the reluctant politicians into engaging with each other. He also launched 'Operation Motorman', the Army's largest ever deployment in Northern Ireland, fnally opening up the enclaves in the Bogside and Creggan in Londonderry that had been barricaded since 1969, and at the same time reimposing the presence of the military and police throughout all parts of Northern Ireland. 'Motorman' marked the start of a period of high-intensity military domination of Northern Ireland while the RUC continued quietly to regroup and expand despite the pressures of the terrorist onslaught.

All of this represented the most complete reappraisal of the British government's attitude to Northern Ireland since partition and there was now complete, though private, disenchantment with the Unionists and their disgraceful record. The new approach was articulated by ministers early in 1972, in advance of direct rule, after the effects of the ill-judged policy of internment had become clear and the government was shaken by the gross military misjudgement which resulted in the events of Bloody Sunday. It was summarised in a minute for the cabinet committee dealing with Northern Ireland: '[a] solution demands far-reaching changes, designed both to re-assure the Roman Catholic minority and to prevent us again being saddled with troubles of this sort as a result of Ulster Unionist incompetence and intransigence. The essential point is . . . the Protestants must not be allowed to revert to the *status quo*.'

Soon after his arrival in Belfast, Whitelaw published the Scarman report on 6 April. It provided a dispassionate, intricate minute-by-minute analysis of the searing events of 1969 that had dragged Northern Ireland to the very edge of complete anarchy on the streets. The report justified Whitehall's new hard-nosed perspective on the Unionists. There had indeed been no IRA plot or armed insurrection to overthrow the Unionist government, although there had been planned acts of violence on both sides to discredit it. What had happened, the tribunal concluded, were 'communal disturbances without plan or premeditation' resulting from 'a complex political, social and economic' situation and culminating in 'an eruption of violence which neither the political leaders or the forces available to the Northern Ireland government could prevent or suppress'.

> On one side people saw themselves, never 'the others', charged by a police force which they regarded as partisan; on the other side, police and people saw a violent challenge to the authority of the State. These attitudes were the creature of recent events. Their own interpretations of the events of 1968 and early 1969 had encouraged the belief amongst the minority that demonstrations did secure concessions, and that the police were their enemy and the main obstacle to a continuing programme of demonstrations, while the same events had convinced a large number of Protestants that a determined attempt, already gaining a measure of success, was being made to undermine the constitutional position of Northern Ireland within the United Kingdom. In so tense a situation it needed very little to set going a major disturbance.

Of the police, caught in the middle, the report concluded:

> Undoubtedly mistakes were made and certain individual officers acted wrongly on occasions. But the general case of a partisan force co-operating with Protestant mobs to attack Catholic people is devoid of

substance, and we reject it utterly. We are satisfied that the great majority of the members of the RUC was concerned to do its duty, which, so far as concerned the disturbances, was to maintain order on the streets, using no more force than was reasonably necessary to suppress rioting and protect life and limb. Inevitably, however, this meant confrontation and on occasions conflict with disorderly mobs. Moreover, since most of the rioting developed from action on the streets started by Catholic crowds, the RUC were more often than not facing Catholics who, as a result, came to feel that the police were always going for them, baton-charging them – never 'the others'.

In fact the RUC faced and, if necessary, charged those who appeared to them to be challenging, defying, or attacking them. We are satisfied that, though they did not expect to be attacked by Protestants, they were ready to deal with them in the same way, if it became necessary. The Shankill riots of the 2/4 August [1969] establish beyond doubt the readiness of the police to do their duty against Protestant mobs, when they were the disturbers of the public peace.

But it is painfully clear from the evidence adduced before us that by July the Catholic minority no longer believed that the RUC was impartial and that Catholic and civil rights activists were publicly asserting this loss of confidence. Understandably these resentments affected the thinking and feeling of the young and the irresponsible, and induced the jeering and throwing of stones which were the small beginnings of most of the disturbances. The effect of this hostility on the RUC themselves was unfortunate. They came to treat as their enemies, and accordingly also as the enemies of the public peace, those who persisted in displaying hostility and distrust towards them.

Thus there developed the fateful split between the Catholic community and the police. Faced with the distrust of a substantial proportion of the whole population and short of numbers, the RUC had (as some senior officers appreciated) lost the capacity to control a major riot. Their difficulties naturally led them, when the emergency arose, to have recourse to methods such as baton charges, CS gas and gunfire, which were sure ultimately to stoke even higher the fires of resentment and hatred.

There were, in the judgement of the tribunal, six specific occasions in the course of the disturbances 'when the police, by act or omission, were seriously at fault'.

The report did little to assuage the Catholic community's virtually irreversible hostility to the RUC and prompted fresh calls for reform and renewed rumours: the Special Branch was to go and be replaced by the Royal Military Police and Army Intelligence; splitting the RUC into three forces, Belfast, Londonderry and the rest, was again suggested; 300 British 'bobbies' were to be brought in. Whitelaw quickly scotched the speculation: there would be no major change. These were baseless assertions. But changing the RUC to make it completely acceptable to both sides in Northern Ireland was now, and would remain, a conspicuous element of British policy, although, like an accommodation with the IRA and a durable political settlement, it would take far longer to achieve than even the direst pessimist would have thought.

A key element of Whitelaw's political strategy was to foster a more constructive relationship with Dublin. After internment Heath had succeeded in bringing Lynch and Faulkner face to face at Chequers, a notable achievement given the icy relationship and lack of real north–south intercourse right back to the days of Craig and Collins. A change of government in Dublin, bringing a coalition led by Fine Gael to power, significantly improved the working relationship to the point where, in December 1973, all sides gathered at the Civil Service Staff College at Sunningdale, Berkshire in a bid to thrash out a new deal for Northern Ireland. It was a groundbreaking moment, for ever since the 1922 settlement Britain had pointedly discouraged any interest from Dublin in events in the north. Now that had changed and their attention was being actively encouraged. Apart from the two governments, those present included Ulster Unionists, led by Brian Faulkner, and a delegation of the SDLP with Gerry Fitt at its head. Over a long weekend and during many hours of talks in the proverbial smoke-filled rooms, they agreed a landmark deal. The Sunningdale Agreement, signed on Sunday 9 December after a final fifty-hour negotiating session, provided for a new Assembly at Stormont and a power-sharing executive, with Unionists and Nationalists holding ministerial appointments and running Northern Ireland together for the first time. There would also be a Council of Ireland, where matters of mutual north–south interest would be considered, and the creation of a Common Law Enforcement area embracing the entire island of Ireland.

But the talks nearly foundered on the issue of policing. On the Saturday morning, at the start of the third day of the negotiations, the sub-committee on policing was solidly deadlocked. The SDLP believed, and was urging strenuously, that police forces on both sides of the border should ultimately be the responsibility of the Council of Ireland. A declaration to this effect would enable the SDLP to identify with and support a reformed police service in the north, working in the context of a common law-enforcement policy for the entire island. The Unionists were resolutely opposed to this approach. Indeed, their position was that reform or change of any sort was not necessary. Faulkner, fighting for his political life under severe pressure from extremists on his own side, was already on public record as wanting control of the police and security policy to be returned to the Stormont administration, a standpoint he resolutely maintained in the course of long and often heated exchanges.

In the early hours of Sunday morning, as the other committees completed their agendas and agreed their input to the final communiqué, the impasse over policing threatened the entire outcome of the conference. Around 5 a.m. Heath tried to mediate by holding individual talks with each party in their private rooms. In *Straight Left*, Paddy Devlin recalls: 'He found no joy, and gloom descended when it was reported that Faulkner was threatening to walk out of the talks. Our side of the policing sub-committee were proving intractable, especially when Hume had joined them.' At breakfast, Dr Garret FitzGerald, the Irish foreign minister, and Conor Cruise O'Brien, a former UN diplomat who was responsible for Posts and Telegraphs, pulled Devlin to the side of the room, confirmed that Faulkner was indeed on the verge of going home and asked him to use his old trade-union negotiating skills to see if he could broker a deal.

'I found Faulkner and went for a walk round the grounds with him. I asked what he needed to get the talks going again,' says Devlin. 'He said he needed the SDLP, his potential partners in government, to recognise and publicly support the RUC . . . It did not make sense that we should be sharing administrative responsibility with him yet refusing to consent to the means of maintaining law and order.' After the walk, Devlin called a meeting of the SDLP delegation in the party room. 'There were emotional and fierce exchanges before we agreed to a more accommodating stance,' he writes, describing how he confronted the brooding hostility that John Hume, in particular, harboured towards the RUC. When the sub-committee meeting resumed, the British and Irish delegations were asked to leave the northerners on their own for a time, and after a series of laborious exchanges which brought about a breakthrough, a statement was drafted setting out a radical, visionary and far-reaching blueprint for an all-Ireland policing regime, which was incorporated in the overall Sunningdale Agreement.

It was recognised that the two parts of Ireland were interdependent in the whole field of law and order, and that the problems of political violence could not be solved without taking account of that fact. The accord provided for the British government to return responsibility for normal policing to the Northern Ireland executive as soon as the security problems were resolved and the new institutions working effectively. The umbrella institution was to be a Council of Ireland and it was envisaged that after consultations with it two Police Authorities, one in each jurisdiction, would be created to spearhead the new era of cross-border police co-operation. In Northern Ireland, in a bid to boost confidence in the police, especially among the historically alienated Catholics, an all-party committee from the Assembly would examine how best to introduce effective policing throughout Northern Ireland and an independent organisation to oversee the investigation of complaints against the police would be set up.

Brian Faulkner, the architect of internment, who faced grave problems in convincing Unionists of the merits of the deal, hailed the policing dimension as 'an achievement missing for generations: respect and support for the RUC from the whole community in Northern Ireland and the Irish government. If that had happened four years ago, we could have stemmed the violence at the start and avoided the need to send for the Army. We might have saved hundreds of lives.' However, as with Hunt, the visionary reform programme was scuttled before it ever had a chance to work. Barely five months after taking office, the power-sharing executive was brought down by a general strike organised by the Ulster Workers Council, a hardline Loyalist group who paralysed Northern Ireland in May 1974 by using sympathisers in the power stations to run down electricity supplies. They had applied pressure to the most vulnerable point in a modern, developed society, for those who did not necessarily agree with the protest were forced to acquiesce. As shops and factories closed, farm animals were slaughtered and masked gangs roamed the streets enforcing the strike.

The Loyalists, and indeed a very large number of Unionists, were not opposed to power-sharing. What they all feared was the Council of Ireland, which a prominent member of the SDLP had rashly described as the 'Trojan horse' which would trundle them into a united Ireland. On 28 May, with John Hume and others in the SDLP refusing to shelve the all-Ireland dimension for a time to break the strike and save power-sharing, the pioneering executive collapsed and with it the far-reaching proposals for police reform.

In the years ahead, as the hard-pressed RUC became ever more preoccupied with policing the conflict, for the thwarted SDLP and Hume in particular, fundamental police reform remained an obsession as unfinished political business. The consequences for policing from the collapse of the Sunningdale Agreement were lasting, according to FitzGerald, later prime minister of the Irish Republic and one of those who conceived the police reform agenda.

> I felt then and still feel that however difficult and even risky such a radical transition might have been, failure to attempt such a reform in 1973 almost inevitably condemned Northern Ireland to continuing violence and insecurity. [. . .] without the kind of radical changes I then proposed, the police could not within any foreseeable future become an acceptable force in the areas that had suffered most intensely from the old RUC, in particular the nationalist 'ghetto' areas of Belfast and Derry. This is certainly one of the major lost opportunities of the prolonged Northern Ireland tragedy.

Part Three

The Point of No Return

Part Three

The Rout of No Return

Chapter Nine
Police Primacy

Around the same time as the Sunningdale Agreement was being planned in late 1973, Eileen Newman spotted an advertisement in the weekly trade journal, *Police Review*, inviting applications from suitably qualified officers to be Deputy Chief Constable of the RUC. 'What kind of nut would take that job?' she asked. 'I might,' replied her husband Ken sheepishly, not having told her that his application for a move to Belfast from his present job as a commander at Scotland Yard was already in the post.

The origins of the search for outside officers to beef up the command of the RUC lay in a wide-ranging conversation about events in Northern Ireland between Heath and Tuzo a year earlier. The effectiveness of the RUC still varied markedly from area to area and the part-time Reserve had not proved to be as useful as hoped, said the GOC. The main problem, he suggested, was inadequate leadership, and more cross-posting with the British police forces would help. There was also dissatisfaction with Shillington. Carrington told the Bloody Sunday inquiry years later: 'He was considered to be a relic of the past and not a very dynamic figure. He was not a bad man but inadequate to the circumstances and rather tarred with the Protestant/B Specials brush.' General Carver shared this view and was pushing for a 'non-Irish deputy to be appointed as heir apparent'. So it was that the highly experienced Newman, who had early first-hand experience of counter-terrorism from his three years in the Palestine Police before joining the Metropolitan Police in 1948, applied successfully for the job and arrived in Belfast towards the end of the year. Shillington had just retired and been replaced by his deputy, Jamie Flanagan, the first and only Catholic to serve as chief constable. The game-plan was for him to hold the fort and show that a Catholic could go all the way to the top in the new RUC while Newman got on with the real work of reorganisation.

By this point, RUC strength had reached 4,391 but was still 1,000 short of its interim establishment and well under the new longer-term target of

7,000 officers. Although recruiting was going well, too many were retiring prematurely because of the ongoing violence, thus slowing the annual gain. Not surprisingly, Newman also found a force overwhelmed by its accelerating workload. There were, for instance, about 500 unsolved murders, more than one for each of the member of the 400-strong CID. Consequently, relatively inexperienced detective constables were virtually single-handedly conducting investigations that anywhere else would have been carried out by a large murder squad, commanded by a very senior officer. Theoretically, every one of the 3,578 shooting incidents and 1,007 explosions required thorough investigation, but in practice, even when somebody was killed or injured, only the most superficial inquiries were made. Some murder files from the time consisted of only three or four pages.

This neglect was forced on the RUC because the officers and forensic experts, and those required to protect them, were greatly exposed to the danger of booby-trapped explosive devices and sniper fire, so the ideal of protracted 'inch by inch' evidence-gathering on the ground had necessarily to be curtailed. What material was collected piled up in a huge backlog of fingerprint impressions, ballistic samples and other scene-of-crime detritus waiting to be processed because the sheer volume of work overwhelmed the forensic capacity. Similarly, lack of administrative support for the front-line detectives meant there were mounds of documentation waiting to be evaluated in every CID office. On more than one occasion suspects slipped through the net, vital information was not processed and crucial evidence was missed. Not surprisingly in 1973, the murder 'clearance' rate was just eighteen per cent, forty-six out of 255 violent deaths, though this was up from thirty-two out of 375 (8.5 per cent) the previous year. A senior detective serving at the time recalls the reality:

> With killings and multiple killings taking place on a regular, even daily, basis you would find yourself dropping one case to deal with the next before you had even done the basics on the first one. The few typists and clerks we had were stretched to the limit and you must remember there was none of the computer assisted technology and little scientific back-up in those days. Everything was manual and an awful lot depended on the sharp memories of detectives being able to piece vital information together.

Ken Newman's primary task therefore was to accelerate the expansion and transformation of the RUC into a far more professional, skilled, effective and capable police force. After his preparatory spell as deputy chief constable, he was duly promoted to the top post in May 1976 when Flanagan retired. By the end of that year, Newman's strategy was clear: the RUC was striving for 'effective' law enforcement by professional means and 'enlightened' law enforcement by forging a close and harmonious relationship with the community in which the force would come to be seen as 'reassuring, helpful and benevolent'. His aim was to restore credible policing throughout Northern Ireland by pushing a highly trained and properly equipped police force to the forefront of the fight against terrorism and progressively diminishing reliance on the Army.

Newman masterminded an extensive shake-up of the RUC's detective force to turn it into the cutting edge of his campaign to bring terrorists before the no-jury courts and secure convictions. Adopting what he called a 'high-risk profile', he dramatically increased police visibility on the streets, deploying a series of Mobile Support Units equipped with heavily armoured Land Rovers, consisting of uniform officers trained to patrol troubled areas extensively and handle public order situations intensively with plastic baton rounds and batons. They were also armed with Ruger revolvers, Sterling sub-machine guns and M1 carbines to enable them to engage armed terrorists on equal terms without the constant support of the Army. 'The intention was that the RUC should stand on its on two feet for the first time since 1969,' recalls one senior police officer. There were early signs of success. The death toll from the violence had declined from its 1972 high point of 470 to 247 in 1975, although it did rise again to 297, including sixteen RUC officers, in 1976. Nevertheless, at the end of that year Newman reported the number of IRA members charged with offences had doubled from 320 in 1975 to 708, and the total number of persons charged with terrorist offences was 1,276. Similarly, explosives seizures had soared from 8,500 lbs to some 20,500 lbs and the capture of weapons increased by fifty per cent and ammunition by thirty per cent. On 1 January 1977, Newman, dapper and pipe-smoking, who was affectionately known as 'the wee man' throughout the RUC, signed a new joint directive between the police and Army, finally stripping the GOC of his role as director of operations and ushering in a new era of 'police primacy' with the RUC in the driving seat.

The new policing order faced its first substantial test a few months later. At about 8 a.m. on 3 May 1977, Andy Tyrie, the burly Supreme Commander of the Ulster Defence Association, mug of tea in hand, was directing a mob of pickets outside his headquarters on the Newtownards

Road in east Belfast. They were trying to discourage thousands of workers from going to the nearby Belfast shipyard and aircraft works in support of a 'constitutional stoppage' called by Paisley to protest at the failure of the British government's security policy and the unchecked onward rampage of IRA terrorism. Paisley had no difficulty accepting the muscular support of Tyrie and his henchmen despite their own equally brutal campaign of sectarian killing involving, in Tyrie's words, the use of violence to 'terrorise the terrorists'.

As masked men rolled looted beer kegs from a nearby pub out across the road to halt rush-hour traffic and obstruct patrolling police Land Rovers, one vehicle halted and an officer alighted to warn Tyrie to clear the road and disperse his men. Angry words followed, stones started to fly through the air and the officer retreated to the safety of his vehicle and drove away. However, a few minutes later, having regrouped further along the road, a phalanx of police on foot, clad in riot gear and wielding batons, charged the crowd of men, who scurried in all directions. A posse of troops held in reserve a couple of hundred yards away were not needed. The incident was a decisive turning point, for it showed a new RUC in the making, one that was prepared and competent to deal energetically with trouble on the streets, whether the culprits were Catholic or Protestant. More perceptive Catholics noticed the signal change from the way the police, and indeed the Army, had failed to confront the mobs on the streets during the Ulster Workers Council strike three years earlier. For his part, Newman hoped that this demonstration of strictly impartial policing would begin a process of healing the long fractured relationship with the Catholic community.

A cornerstone of Newman's anti-terrorist policy was to subject terrorist suspects to intensive police questioning over several days by isolating them in police holding centres and encouraging them to make statements admitting their crimes. Intelligence gleaned from well-placed informers in terrorist ranks, undercover surveillance and the questioning of other suspects was used to confront them with their guilt. However, thanks to a mixture of skilful propaganda, principally by the IRA, and a spate of well-documented instances of 'wall-to-wall interrogation' by over-zealous detectives, many notorious terrorist figures were able to allege inhuman or degrading treatment and walk free. Newman's considerable achievement in turning the tide back against the terrorists was therefore overshadowed when an official investigation into allegations of torture and brutal treatment concluded that a small number of detectives had indeed resorted to assault and recommended a series of safeguards for suspects in police custody. In spite of this hullabaloo, at the end of his tenure Newman, who went off to be Commandant of the Police Staff College at Bramshill and later Commissioner of the Metropolitan Police, left behind him a revitalised RUC with immeasurably improved confidence and capability and, for the first time in its history, a philosophy and a commitment to impartial, even-handed policing in a deeply divided society, although there was yet no universal understanding of the concept among the vast majority of the rank-and-file police officers whose priority, risking their lives on a daily basis, was simply to survive.

Jack Hermon, a Protestant, who succeeded Newman as chief constable in 1980 after rising through the ranks of the RUC, was another enlightened police leader who deplored the sectarian nature of Northern Ireland society and abhorred the one-sided and politically controlled nature of policing in the past. In his first annual report, he set the promotion of reconciliation and trust between all sections of the community and between the community and the police as an aim, but the effects of the IRA hunger strikes in 1981, when ten prisoners starved themselves to death in pursuit of a demand to be recognised as political prisoners, wiped out the faltering progress that had been made and polarised inter-community and police community relations as never before. In addition, after a brief respite in 1980, which despite seventy-six deaths (including those of nine RUC officers) was the least violent year for a decade, 1981 saw a nasty resurgence of terrorism and 101 people, including thirteen RUC officers, lost their lives. With forty-seven of those murders having taken place in the final three months of the year, the RUC deployed a number of SAS-trained undercover units to act with 'firepower, speed and aggression', as one senior policeman described it, in a bid to apprehend terrorists red-handed. Briefing one of the new units about their task, another senior man put it more graphically: 'The people of Northern Ireland want bacon for their breakfast. It's your job to cut the pig's throat.'

There followed, in rapid succession, three murky incidents in the Armagh area during which six Republican terrorist suspects were shot dead. The first took place on 11 November 1982 when three men died in a hail of police gunfire after crashing through a roadblock. When the car and bodies were examined there was no trace of any firearms or explosives. In the second incident, on 24 November, one man was shot dead and another wounded during a carefully planned ambush at a supposed terrorist arms dump. However, again when the police moved in all that was recovered were three ancient rifles not capable of being fired, although there was evidence that a considerable amount of explosive had recently been stored there. (Despite the surveillance, it had been removed and used to set a landmine ambush in which three police officers were killed.) Two more people with known terrorist connections died in a third shooting on 12 December and, yet again, they were found to be unarmed. The trilogy of shootings and another recent case where a man painting slogans on a wall had also been shot dead by police – his brush was mistaken for a gun – prompted an outcry that the RUC was operating a 'shoot-to-kill' policy.

What happened afterwards became known as the Stalker affair and remains one of the darkest clouds of controversy hanging over the reputation of the RUC. Four of the police officers concerned in the shootings were put on trial and during the proceedings there emerged a grubby tale of false cover stories, police officers being ordered to change and falsify evidence and illegal incursions across the Irish border. All the officers were acquitted and at the conclusion of one trial the judge, Lord Justice Maurice Gibson, even congratulated them for despatching the terrorists to what he called 'the final court of justice'. (He and his wife were later murdered in a carefully laid IRA ambush at the border in May 1987.) There was more disquiet when a coroner subsequently refused to open inquests because of 'grave irregularities' in the police files submitted to him.

Predictably, these disclosures prompted an almighty political and diplomatic row and in May 1984, in a bid to allay widespread concern, John Stalker, Deputy Chief Constable of Greater Manchester Police, was appointed to conduct an independent inquiry. He reported in September 1985 but far from resolving the issue, his abrupt suspension from duty and removal as head of the RUC inquiry, amidst what ultimately proved to be trumped-up allegations of close links with criminals in Manchester, simply created more cover-up controversy. Although he was later cleared and reinstated to his post in Manchester, Stalker resigned in some disgust in March 1987 and published an excoriating memoir in 1988, which became a bestseller. The book revealed Stalker's opinion that while there had not been any 'shoot-to-kill' policy, the RUC had handled the cases badly and, with the help of MI5, obstructed his investigation and conspired to have him removed from it. In his own memoir, *Holding the Line*, Hermon describes how he flung Stalker's book across the room when he first read it, 'so incensed was I by its innuendoes and false statements'. Whatever the absolute truth of the 'shoot-to-kill' affair, the controversy it generated indelibly stained the soul of the RUC, confirmed its critics in their hostility and fatally compromised Hermon's genuine efforts to improve Catholic perceptions of the force.

While these events were unfolding, the RUC was sucked into fresh turmoil after the signing of the Anglo-Irish Agreement on 15 November 1985, the first successful political initiative since Sunningdale. The treaty, which provided for an unprecedented level of Irish co-operation in the governance of Northern Ireland, was inevitably regarded as a 'sell-out' by a broad sweep of Unionist opinion and sparked off angry protests which had, of course, to be policed by the RUC. Eight days after the signing ceremony, an unprecedented crowd of at least 100,000 people gathered at Belfast City Hall to demonstrate that 'Ulster Says No'. Some of those opposed to what had been agreed criticised the RUC for 'enforcing' the Agreement and even called on the police to mutiny, causing Hermon to issue a statement saying that politics was no business of the police, who would simply uphold the law of the land. But over the next few months, Unionist protest frequently degenerated into violence, drawing the police into often bruising conflict with disorderly Protestant crowds. A spate of attacks on police homes, which began in Cookstown and Portadown, rapidly became an epidemic and by the time it was halted, late in 1986, there had been 564 incidents, which included slogans being daubed on houses as well as more serious attacks with bricks, petrol bombs and firearms. On one notorious occasion, Hermon's wife, Jean, who was visiting some victimised police families in Lurgan, was subjected to a barrage of eggs and tomatoes by a crowd of their hostile neighbours. The threat was so worrying that the Association of Chief Police Officers in London arranged for police houses throughout Britain to be made available for evacuees, but, in the event, none were needed. The experience had a lasting effect on police morale. For so long isolated from the Catholic community, mainly because of the IRA threat, which had accounted for some 200 police lives at that point, the wider RUC family soon came to see itself as a third community in divided Northern Ireland Virtual police 'ghettos' developed in some parts of the Lagan valley and north Down where officers and their families clustered together for mutual security.

A contributory cause to this unparalleled wave of disaffection between the Protestant community and the RUC was Hermon's simultaneous initiative to tackle, once and for all, the long-running tensions arising from the annual marching season which not only blighted any chance of achieving wholesale community reconciliation but imposed an increasingly intolerable financial and operational burden on the police every summer. Hermon believed an independent public tribunal should relieve the police of the duty of deciding whether a particular march should be banned or re-routed and remove the conflict of interest involved in both making and enforcing the decision. Pending such a reform, he turned his attention to the most troublesome parade flashpoint of all: the 'Tunnel' in Portadown. In so doing, he could not have foreseen that he was marking out the parameters of a crisis which would ultimately ignite with such ferocity that it would lead directly to the RUC's demise. By the time it ran its course, however, Hermon was long retired and the final culpability would lie with Hugh Annesley, who succeeded him in mid-1989.

As a young man, Dublin-born Annesley chose to join the Metropolitan Police rather than the Garda Siochana, because it provided more scope for his ambitions. During thirty years' service in London he achieved the senior rank of assistant commissioner before leaving to command the RUC. His departure was not universally mourned at Scotland Yard. At a bibulous gathering of senior officers soon afterwards a toast was proposed: 'To the RUC . . . for relieving us of Hugh Annesley.' The new chief was, however, given an open-minded welcome in Belfast where he had an opportunity to consolidate the great operational and organisational gains made by Newman and Hermon and embark on the heavy spadework necessary to bridge the widened gulf between the RUC and the communities it served.

Despite the stains of scandal and controversy on its record, the RUC was now widely applauded for its outstanding courage and recognised as a world-class exponent of conflict policing. The accolade had been achieved at great cost to the force and its interface with the community. Using the death rate as a crude barometer, the overall situation had substantially improved during the Hermon years and in 1985, with fifty-five deaths, it reached its lowest point since the Troubles began. Although it surged again to a peak of ninety-five in 1987, the deaths and violence steadily declined thereafter (although there were a number of continuing attacks and atrocities), reflecting the yearning of an ever more war-weary community for peace and a more 'normal' society.

After an upsurge of bombing and shooting in the early 1990s, the years of intermittent secret talks between the British government and the IRA which had begun in 1972 climaxed in the late summer of 1994 when the organisation called an indefinite ceasefire. Loyalist paramilitaries followed a few weeks later, transforming the situation for everyone in Northern Ireland. Before long, as the political debate focused on how to consolidate the uneasy peace, policing emerged as a major issue and the RUC was required to consider how it would adapt. The circumstances were therefore entirely favourable for Annesley to embark on the challenging business of transforming the RUC, above all by changing its internal culture and philosophy in order more effectively to heal the historic rift with the Catholics. One of the most important weaknesses was the lack of Catholics in the ranks, a problem which had long been acknowledged but always sidestepped. But, to his shame, Annesley failed to act in spite of the compelling political reasons for him to do so. His neglect was all the more reprehensible for it also put him in serious breach of his obligations as an employer.

For some years previously, in a bid to outlaw and reverse years of anti-Catholic discrimination, the British government had introduced legislation to ensure that employment was shared out broadly in line with the sixty–forty Protestant–Catholic proportion in the wider community. It was already clear Catholics were seriously under-represented in police ranks: the proportion had always been claimed by the RUC to be 'around' ten per cent, but when formal religious monitoring began in 1990 it was discovered that the actual number of Catholics was even more disproportionate at only 7.75 per cent – 639 officers out of a total of 7,363. According to the law, such an imbalance required an employer to take practical steps to redress it. In the new post-ceasefire situation, therefore, it was open to Annesley to act in ways that were not previously possible, but he failed to do so.

Another of the cornerstones of the fair employment regime was the requirement that an employer create a 'neutral working environment', and many in the private and public sectors endured great difficulty in ensuring that employees, from whatever political or religious persuasion, felt comfortable while at work. In the official jargon, there should be no 'chill factor'. Thus, under codes of practice, employers were expected to strip factories, rest rooms, offices and the like of any symbols or emblems which could be offensive. In places with overwhelmingly large Protestant workforces, there was a long-standing practice of decorating workshops with Orange and royal regalia, especially around the tense Twelfth of July period. Many flew the Union flag during that period while others actually displayed it all the year round, more to demonstrate 'Britishness' to Catholics than from any patriotic feelings for Britain or the Queen. On the other side of the sectarian divide, Irish tricolours, slogans and emblems were flaunted in a similarly provocative fashion.

In these terms, the working environment within the RUC was far from neutral and one of the clearest breaches was at the training centre at Garnerville, where the Union flag was flown every day in defiance of the RUC's own rules. These provided for the flag to be run up on all police stations on nineteen days of the year, eleven of them marking birthdays or anniversaries of the British royal family. Northern Ireland actually flew the flag on four days more than elsewhere in the United Kingdom: on New Year's Day, Easter Sunday, 12 July and Christmas Day. One could well ask what was the policing reason for flying the Union flag over the RUC outpost in fiercely Republican Crossmaglen in South Armagh on Orange day, a practice which offended virtually the entire local community and soured further the already tentative relations with the police. So it is worth digressing at this point to look at how the policy of official flag-flying in the RUC had actually evolved.

Although the Union flag appears prominently in pictures of events in Northern Ireland in the early 1920s, it was some five years after partition, in early January 1928, before the Unionist administration got round to laying down a policy about the flying of what it saw as the national flag. According to contemporary files, an order was issued from the Ministry of Finance in Belfast specifying eight occasions during the year when the flag should be flown on public buildings. Five marked royal anniversaries; the others were St Patrick's Day, Empire Day and Armistice Day. In addition the flag could be flown on Christmas Day, New Year's Day and Easter Day at local discretion; a note from the Ministry of Home Affairs to Finance dated 21 January interestingly records that 'it would hardly seem necessary to have flags on prisons and police barracks'.

There the matter rested until November and December 1932, when it was debated by the Northern Ireland parliament at a time when serious sectarian trouble had returned to the streets. As a result, instructions were issued to the Inspector-General of the RUC that henceforth flagpoles should be erected on the 209 barracks and buildings under his control and the Union Jack was to be raised on the designated days. About six months later, on 5 April 1933, the cabinet met in Belfast and decided that the Twelfth of July, the anniversary of the Battle of the Boyne, should be added to the list. They were clearly sensitive about the decision for the next day a senior official at the Ministry of Affairs wrote to a counterpart in Finance: 'It remains therefore for us to devise a means whereby effect can be given to the decision without raising too much comment or objection and after discussion with the minister [Bates] it was agreed that your ministry should write to us . . . and intimate that the flag should be flown on all Bank Holidays, in addition to the other stated holidays.' All of these instructions, prescribed by the Unionist government's sleight of hand, were slavishly incorporated into the RUC Code and strictly followed. So, in the vastly changed circumstances of the late 1990s, it was well within the discretion of Annesley to review and change the practice, especially as the modern Police Authority, and not the government, owned the RUC's buildings. Again he ignored the issue.

In the same equality context, another problem that deserved re-examination was the oath of office sworn by RUC constables, which originated in Section 17 of the Constabulary (Ireland) Act 1836 and was carried forward into the Constabulary Act (Northern Ireland) 1922:

> I (name) swear by Almighty God that I will well and truly serve our Sovereign Lady the Queen in the office of (rank) without favour or affection, malice or ill-will; that I will to the best of my power cause the peace to be kept and preserved and that I will prevent to the best of my power all offences against the same; and that, while I shall continue to hold the said office, I will faithfully, according to law, to the best of my skill and knowledge, discharge all the duties of the said office and all such duties as may be attached to such office by law and that I do not now belong to and that I will not, while I shall hold the said office, belong to any association, society, or confederacy formed for or engaged in any seditious purpose, or any purpose tending to disturb the public peace, or in any way disloyal to our Sovereign Lady the Queen and that I will not, while I shall hold the said office, engage or take part in the furthering of any such purpose, or take or administer, or assist or be present at or consent to the administering of, any oath or engagement binding myself or any other person to engage in any such purpose.

For many years the Northern Ireland government had required dustbin collectors, street sweepers and all classes of public servants to swear a similar oath of allegiance to the Crown, in the hope that it would deter Catholics from seeking public employment. The practice had long since been abolished for all but a handful of positions but persisted in the RUC, where the declaration committing them to 'well and truly serve our Sovereign Lady the Queen' was anathema for most Catholics. What was needed to attract them into the police was a simpler formula merely requiring a constable faithfully and impartially to discharge the duties of his office, as was the practice in Scotland. In the way that a jury member or court witness could opt either to swear or to affirm, it was even feasible that future constables could choose which oath of office they would take. Any move on these highly contentious issues would, of course, have attracted great controversy and debate within and outside the RUC.

Annesley was encouraged in his intransigence by those such as Les Rodgers, the chairman of the Police Federation, who was on public record explicitly opposing change designed to ensure the RUC's conformity with fair employment legislation and make it more acceptable to the minority community. 'My members view themselves as British in the main. They are quite happy with the emblems, the flags and the [royal] pictures,' he said. But at a time when the demand for such fundamental reform was gathering force, negotiations backed with the authority of the chief constable could have led to accommodations acceptable to both communities and the police themselves. In the event, Annesley's unwillingness to challenge the prevailing order would turn out to be a costly misjudgement, as would his inept handing of the grim situation at Portadown in 1996, which would prove to be the point of no return for the RUC.

Even before the force was formed in 1922, Orange Order parades were a recurring source of sectarian tension and violence in the northern part of the island, regularly requiring the intervention of the RIC. With the highly active role the Order played in opposing Home Rule in the closing decades of the nineteenth century and clinching partition in the opening decades of the next and its role as midwife in the formation of the all-powerful Ulster Unionist party, there was never any likelihood that it's self-proclaimed 'right to march' would ever be curbed. Indeed all the prime ministers and most ministers of Unionist governments over the years were members of the Order, ensuring that the RUC was unfailingly directed to facilitate it. Marching was therefore a factor in further poisoning relations between the force and the minority community as, time and time again, it was manipulated to push unwelcome marches through nationalist areas.

There was no more long-running or symbolic march for both sides than that in Portadown on the Sunday before the Twelfth of July every year, when the local Orange Lodge marched to and from Drumcree Parish Church for its annual church service. The customary route included Obins Street (the Tunnel), the Catholic quarter of the town, and sectarian tensions between the inhabitants and the marchers fostered a culture of resentment and frequent violence. In the mid-1980s, with population movement and new roads providing an alternative route to the church, Hermon, responding to Catholic lobbying, confronted the marchers and finally succeeded in having them re-routed. Resentment now focused on the traditional return route to the town along Garvaghy Road, once a quiet country lane but now a busy thoroughfare serving several newly built, Catholic-populated housing estates. The issue simmered for several years and came to a head in July 1995, a year after the terrorist ceasefires. On 'Drumcree Sunday' that year, a confrontation developed after police prevented the church parade from returning along the intended route. The resulting 'siege of Drumcree' ended after nearly three days of violence throughout Northern Ireland after the police played a part in negotiating with residents to allow a small march without bands. However, triumphalist behaviour afterwards by the Unionist leaders Trimble and Paisley and the Unionists' claims that there had been no deal soured the atmosphere. By the time the 1996 march was due, a real sense of crisis surrounded the event.

The days when the Orange Order could dictate its will to compliant politicians, who were also members, had long gone and it was now widely accepted that contentious marches could only take place with the consent of the communities affected by them. By this yardstick, with the Garvaghy Road residents not only against the march but still angered by the behaviour of the politicians a year earlier, Annesley had little option but to re-route the parade because of the threat of serious public disorder.

Despite the second prohibition, the Orangemen formed up after the church service on 7 July and when they were prevented from proceeding by a phalanx of police and lines of barbed-wire entanglements across surrounding fields, another stand-off developed. By the time darkness fell that night an angry crowd of up to 5,000 had gathered in front of the line, bombarding police and soldiers with a variety of objects and making repeated attempts to break through. The trouble spread and over the next four days as the confrontation continued there was widespread blocking of roads and rioting throughout Northern Ireland. The most sinister incident was the abduction of Michael McGoldrick, a Catholic taxi driver, who was shot dead by the Loyalist Volunteer Force. Clifford McKeown, the man eventually convicted of the killing, said it had been carried out as a birthday present for the local Loyalist hardman, Billy Wright, leader of the outlawed group.

The murder and worsening situation prompted some serious heart-searching and deep thinking among the police and Army commanders. A senior soldier recalls how the police, as in 1995, had tried to minimise military visibility as much as possible. Getting the troops off the streets remained one of the most tangible achievements of the peace process and the RUC was most reluctant to take what would have been seen as a backward step. 'But they are not as well-equipped to live and operate in the field as we are and by Tuesday night there were clear signs of fatigue and a lack of fresh resources to keep roads open and tackle the large crowds at Drumcree,' he said. So the Army was already preparing to take a far more pro-active role in the fast deteriorating situation, if the call came from the chief constable for help. During the day the police became more and more concerned about the appearance of a heavy excavator and a slurry tanker in the field beside the church, especially when they received intelligence that the plan was to use the excavator, fitted with heavy metal plates to make it bullet-proof, to spearhead an assault on the police lines while the tanker was intended as a flame-thrower to spray police and soldiers with a potentially deadly mix of petrol and sugar.

Every day of the crisis, the Army commander in Northern Ireland, Lieutenant-General Sir Rupert Smith, and other military chiefs flew into the police headquarters at Knock for a meeting with Annesley and his senior commanders to review the situation. When Smith arrived for the Wednesday meeting this threat was top of a long police 'worry list' centred on concerns that the crowds gathering every night, 50,000 and more, would make a determined assault on the police cordons, overrun them by sheer force of numbers and end up on the Garvaghy Road itself with incalculable consequences. Everyone gathering for that meeting knew that it would be the defining moment for the outcome of Drumcree Two, as it had been dubbed, and there was a realisation that Annesley's ban on the march might have to be fundamentally reconsidered. The police were also fearful of being over-stretched during the traditional drunken revelry at the bonfires on the night of 11 July and coping with the demands of the Twelfth itself, when Catholic opposition to another march, along the Ormeau Road in Belfast, was threatened. The full implications of this grim security picture were totted up by the police officers and the soldiers, who brought their own professional philosophies to bear on the possible outcomes. The central dilemma was at Drumcree: could they sustain the effects of continuing the ban or should they back down? Ronnie Flanagan, Annesley's deputy, who had been on the ground in Portadown for most of the preceding days, sums up the terrible dilemma they faced:

> All the options were discussed with the Army. [. . .] We came to the operational conclusion that [. . .] it was actually better to contain people on the hill at Drumcree but the fear then was, what if there are such numbers that we are actually overrun? It was a real fear because we didn't have the physical measures in place. There was some barbed

wire but [. . .] it was lines of Land Rovers basically. And that's when the language began to change, gradually becoming the language of a military operation. Somebody said, 'Do you think if they actually overrun us, were burning houses, if we'd expended every plastic baton round that we had, and that's not enough, do you think they're then going to line up in ranks of three and march in an orderly fashion?' The [Army] answer was: 'I see no problem, I'd shoot them.' And suddenly there was great horror. This can't happen.

The soldiers went on to outline in detail what they would be able to do if the chief constable, whose sole decision it still was under public order legislation, decided to continue the ban and requested much more pro-active Army assistance in ensuring the ultimate safety of Catholics in the Garvaghy Road by preventing any violent breakthrough. The Army had already moved 6,000 plastic batons rounds to Portadown – at the time the entire police stockholding was 2,000. A large quantity of CS gas was also in position – a means of riot control unused for more than twenty years. The planning also provided for a number of fall-back lines of barbed-wire entanglements to cope with any charge by large numbers of demon-strators. The general coolly described, in line with conventional military logic, how the final line would be at the edge of the housing estates and that if any rioters got that far, if all else had failed, they would be shot. Moreover, the Army had already inserted at least two concealed sniper teams with orders to monitor the excavator and slurry tanker and to shoot the operators dead if all other efforts to halt them failed. 'It was well within our capability to have contained the situation but it wouldn't have been a pretty sight,' said one of the senior soldiers involved.

The RUC's most senior officers, having worked closely with the Army for some thirty years, knew better than any other British police force that committing soldiers in such a situation would inevitably result in lethal force being used. 'The proposition was unthinkable,' one said afterwards. 'We were looking at a possible Bloody Sunday for Protestants.' Everyone in the conference room on the third floor at police headquarters in Belfast knew that the decision now had to be changed, that a way had to be found to get a march through quickly. Flanagan says: 'A policing organisation always has as its number one priority the protection of life, so, in a position where holding to a decision is going to lead to the risk of much greater loss of life than changing it, then the police service, however badly its reputation might be damaged, has only one choice to make.'

Annesley therefore reversed his decision and gave the go-ahead to make arrangements to push a parade through on the Thursday morning, so that the situation would be calm by the time the bonfires were lit that evening. A senior man at the Northern Ireland Office remembers the police commanders looking 'tired and beaten' when they came to tell Sir Patrick Mayhew, then Secretary of State, of the decision. When he heard Annesley outline his solution the official, far from impressed by the climbdown, loudly commented: 'Surely a battalion of paratroopers with pickaxe handles would have been more effective?' With the parade making ready to move, Annesely decided to go to Portadown. 'Over the preceding days he had been his usual self-confident and haughty self,' recalls one of his senior colleagues at the time. 'But when I saw him not long after the end of that chilling meeting, going off to Portadown in a helicopter because the roads were all blocked, he looked like the loneliest and saddest man on the planet.'

In line with what Annesley had agreed, shortly before noon, about 1,200 dishevelled Orangemen formed up outside Drumcree Parish Church in readiness to march back to their Orange Hall in the town centre. As they set off, a large force of police in armoured Land Rovers swept into the Catholic area ahead of them. Officers clad in riot gear and swinging batons jumped from the vehicles and lashed into protestors blocking the road. A few minutes later the march went through, hemmed in by a moving corridor of armoured Land Rovers with lines of police holding the jeering residents back along the side of the disputed route. As the parade set off, church leaders who had been trying to mediate for days beforehand were at Seagoe Rectory nearby, listening to radio reports of what was happening. Archbishop Robin Eames, the head of the Church of Ireland, got a call from Annesley. 'He said, "How are you?" I said, "I'm shattered, I'm tired, I'm disillusioned." Annesley said, "That about covers me." I said, "You must have let them down the road, you knew we were still trying." And he said, "All I can say to you is 'I apologise'."'

Those present remember Cardinal Cahal Daly, the Catholic Primate of All-Ireland, sitting with a cup of coffee, hunched deep in thought and very deeply upset.

> I confess I was concerned to get to the Garvaghy Road as quickly as I could to see just what was going on there. I had great difficulty getting past the security cordons and then I got a very angry reception on the Garvaghy Road and this was not from any militant and certainly not from any Sinn Fein quarter. It was a total population which had been tricked and thought that I had been party to the trick played on them.

People were banging on the side and windows of my car and telling me to get out of the area and never come back, that I was a traitor and I had let my whole community down, that they would never come back to mass again and so on. The hostile crowd included people I knew well and people who were regular mass-goers and had no political affiliation with Sinn Fein or that kind. It was quite clear that the whole population was enraged that the march had been allowed to come down, that the police behaved as they had done and that I had been complicit in all this. I would say it was one of the most unpleasant experiences of my life, to have your own parishioners rejecting you. It was quite scary. There was a great air of apprehension but I told them how I felt, that I had been duped, just as the people felt that they had been duped and that I felt it was a very bad day's work and that a very wrong and disastrous decision had been taken by the police and made the situation immeasurably worse.

Annesley, having seen the situation for himself, insisted there was no political interference in his decision and that his original decision had been right at the time. He went on to say that, faced with daily escalating violence and the prospect of thousands of Orangemen facing thousands of police and soldiers and the real risk of fatalities, he was not prepared to risk a single life in such circumstances and, therefore, after the best efforts of the four church leaders failed to get an accommodation, he had had no alternative but to take the decision to let the parade through. The effect of his extraordinary about-turn on the Catholic community throughout Northern Ireland was compounded by the aggressive way the police cleared the road for the marchers. Catholic opinion was shocked by the forceful police action, which contrasted starkly with what was widely seen as their failure for days to take robust action against the Loyalist mobs. One observer was horrified when a police Land Rover halted beside him and the leader of the crew jumped out and shouted, 'Come on, let's get at the fuckers.' The local SDLP representative, Brid Rodgers, rushed to the Garvaghy Road in time to see the march make its six-minute passage. She recalls:

That was one of the worst experiences of my life. The events of that day had the same impact on the nationalist community as Bloody Sunday. People were traumatised by what happened. Even moderate nationalists were outraged. For those who didn't already think so, that was the day the RUC became totally unacceptable.

Cardinal Daly believes the comparison with Bloody Sunday is not exaggerated.

> It was one of a whole series of major blunders, misreading the situation
> – Bloody Sunday, internment – in which there was a strong, strong
> security element and in all cases they proved to be wrong. I don't think
> there's any way in which the decision could have been favourably
> received but the way in which it was executed made it still more
> unfavourably received. It had a devastating effect on the relationship
> between the RUC and the Catholic community.

The next morning the front-page headline on the *Irish News*, the paper which closely articulated the Catholic/Nationalist viewpoint, was simply: 'Betrayed'. The following day the issue came up during Northern Ireland questions in the House of Commons in London. The SDLP deputy leader, Seamus Mallon, expressed Catholic anger:

> This is a government problem and the result rests with this government.
> The marches had not to do with who marched up what road, but whose
> writ runs in Northern Ireland. Your government was asked that
> question and you failed. The other question was asked: who polices
> Northern Ireland? Was it the legitimate police force or was it those
> thugs with sashes who once again imposed their will upon the whole of
> the north of Ireland?

Later on 11 July, the day the march was forced through, further terminal damage was done to the RUC relationship with the Catholic community when the Ormeau Road was flooded with police and vehicles and the area sealed overnight so that protesters could not obstruct the Orange march next morning, the Twelfth. This march was being allowed to stop the massed ranks of the Belfast Orangemen abandoning their usual route and laying siege to the Ormeau Road.

The decisions to permit these marches were bad enough in Catholic eyes, but the way they were enforced was worse, helping to provoke a violent backlash in Catholic areas. The disturbances were at their worst in Londonderry, where the rioting was as prolonged and intense as anything seen in the early 1970s. For two consecutive nights the police were under sustained petrol-bomb attack in the city; each night, they estimated, 2,000 were thrown. As the violence subsided on 16 July, its terrible extent and implications became clear. The police logged 8,000 incidents and calculated that up to 24,000 petrol bombs had been thrown. They had fired 6,000 plastic baton rounds, the most intensive use of the weapon since the week following the death of hunger striker Bobby Sands in May 1981. One man died in the disturbances – a Catholic crushed by a military vehicle in Londonderry; 149 police officers and 192 civilians were injured; thirty-nine police homes were attacked and twenty-eight officers and their families forced to move permanently.

As in 1985–86 the personal allegiance of policemen and women was brought close to breaking point. Some officers were indeed members of the Orange Order or had close family or relatives as members. 'During the stand-off there were people on both sides of that confrontation who were blood relatives,' one senior officer said, and not all RUC officers demonstrated the impartiality that they should have. (During July and August six officers were suspended from duty and a seventh reported for taking part in Orange parades or protest demonstrations. Some subsequently left the force and others were dealt with by internal discipline.)

In retrospect, it is absolutely clear that Annesley's about-turn at Drumcree in July 1996 was the point of no return for the RUC. By surrendering to Orange threats and thuggery, he reinforced the prejudices of those already bitterly critical of the force and brought despair to those who believed that gradual, agreed reform could, in the end, bridge the fateful split and bring about a new era of policing with cross-community consent and co-operation. Now, in order to satisfy even moderate Catholic opinion, there would have to be far more fundamental reform. A couple of months earlier, in May, the Northern Ireland Office had produced the White Paper 'Foundations for Policing', setting out an agenda for reform and proposing new policing structures. It was certainly not as radical a document as could have been expected from some of the ideas and drafts recently floating around the Northern Ireland Office, for it struck a very negative note about some key issues:

> Much attention has focused [. . .] on the issues of the RUC's name, badge, oath and uniform. The Government has noted with interest the outcome of the [recent Police Authority] consultation exercise in relation to these issues. The findings generally reflect a lack of political agreement and no consensus to support potential legislative change in any of these areas. The Government therefore is not minded to propose legislation in these areas, but will reflect on the nature of any political agreements reached in the course of political talks which might impact on these matters.

The secretary of state, Sir Patrick Mayhew, who had already decided to stand down at the forthcoming general election, had decided, like Annesley, to leave such difficult issues to his successor and was merely publishing a road map. In the meantime, as an alibi for the lack of action, the emphasis was put on the Fundamental Review of Policing, announced in June 1995, a jointly conducted study by the government, the RUC and the Police Authority to consider the policing needs of the community and the future organisation and size of the RUC if the transition from conflict to normality took place. It was being led by Ronnie Flanagan.

The general election on 1 May 1997 swept Tony Blair's 'New Labour' party into government with a landslide victory and brought the highly personable Mo Mowlam to Belfast. There could have been no greater contrast than between the sepulchral solemnity of Mayhew and the mischievous informality of Mowlam, who immediately listed policing reform as one of her priorities. Her position was reinforced by Blair, the prime minister, two weeks later when a trip to Belfast became his first official visit outside London. In a wide-ranging address he revealed that he had authorised officials to sound Sinn Fein out about prospects for renewing the IRA ceasefire, which had been unilaterally ended on 9 February 1996 with a carefully planned bombing in the London Docklands which killed two men and caused extensive damage to a number of prestige office blocks. In the context of policing, he added: 'We want to increase public confidence in policing through measured reform [. . .] I am convinced that the time is right finally to put the past behind us and meet the deep thirst of the people of Northern Ireland for peace, normality and prosperity.'

The ceasefire was eventually reinstated on 19 July, although the IRA still refused to contemplate decommissioning even a token proportion of its arsenal of weapons and explosives. It did, however, sign up to the 'Mitchell principles', which committed it to 'democratic and exclusively peaceful means of resolving political issues', enabling it to gain admission to a new round of political negotiations under the chairmanship of the former US senator George Mitchell. When these negotiations got under way in September 1997, there began the most fundamental and far-reaching examination of the Irish question since the early 1920s, seeking to redefine the complex north–south and east–west constitutional and political relationships within Ireland and the British Isles. As at Sunningdale some quarter of a century earlier, the unresolved question of police reform was again high on the agenda. At the same time, the Northern Ireland Select Committee of the House of Commons also turned its attention to the police and embarked on an exhaustive study of the 'Composition, Training and Recruitment of the RUC'.

However, in December 1997, in a pre-emptive strike, Mowlam, working to her own agenda, produced a bill to put in place legislation that would kick-start the massive shake-up in policing that was now clearly unavoidable. On the face of it, the legislation appeared to be the culmination of the slow drift to police reform over the preceding years, but, in reality, it owed much to Mowlam's impatience and personal hostility to the RUC and an unhealthy desire on the part of the Northern Ireland Office to interfere more directly in policing. So while the Police Act (Northern Ireland) 1998, when it became law, rightly tackled a number of the problematic issues that had been sidestepped by Annesley despite growing public debate about the desirability of reviewing them, it was correctly criticised for being premature. Nevertheless it did fracture some sacred precepts. The most important innovation was the intro-duction of a new oath of office. In a bold and praiseworthy break with the past the bill introduced a new declaration merely requiring officers to state: 'I hereby do solemnly and sincerely and truly declare and affirm that I will faithfully discharge the duties of the office of constable,' the requirements of which were more fully spelled out in the body of the legislation.

Among other significant innovations, the bill established 'the Northern Ireland Police Service, to consist of the Royal Ulster Constabulary, the Royal Ulster Constabulary Reserve, traffic wardens and civilian support staff', a formula which paved the way for people to call the police by whatever name suited them: the RUC or the NIPS (Northern Ireland Police Service). This was potentially another important breakthrough, for it had become clear that while most Catholics resented the RUC's 'Royal' prefix, Protestant (and police) opinion steadfastly cherished it and were deeply opposed to any name change for the force. People had become used to talking about 'Londonderry' or 'Derry', depending on individual allegiance, so there was no reason to think that, with a spot of pragmatic generosity, the idea of using both names for the police would not satisfy the conflicting sensitivities concerned.

In another necessary step to winning cross-community confidence in the service, the bill also provided for the new office of Police Ombudsman, bringing in independent investigation of complaints against the police to replace the much-criticised system where they investigated themselves, usually with a high degree of inconclusivity. Amended administrative arrangements, long postponed, whereby the chief constable, not the Police Authority, would be responsible for the police budget and employment of officers and civilian staff, were also included. Through the concept of an annual policing plan, agreed between the authority and the chief constable, a yardstick was established by which to measure clearance rates, the effectiveness of traffic policing and just how satisfactorily the vast sums expended on policing – now almost £1,500,000 a day – were being spent.

The most serious weakness in Mowlam's package was that it side-stepped the fundamental issue of police accountability. The central flaw in the 1970 Police Act was that it did not rigorously define the individual roles and duties of the secretary of state, the Police Authority and the chief constable and the interaction between them. At the time, the Home Office spotted this fundamental flaw in the legislation which was supposed to be revisited in due course. It never was, and therein lay the great weakness which undermined the Authority and handcuffed it from being an effective forum to make the police accountable and involve Catholics in the process of police oversight. This enabled successive chief constables, and the Northern Ireland Office, to ignore and defy the Authority and rendered the notion that the police were effectively accountable to the community as nothing more than a polite fiction. The facts that members of the Authority refused to disclose their names for security reasons and were far too timid in exercising the limited powers they had did nothing for their credibility.

Ever since the process of police reform was heralded in a discussion paper in 1994, it had been common ground that this weakness would be remedied in the long awaited legislation, but it was not. The Mowlam act also contained a remarkable power, unique to Northern Ireland, which empowered the secretary of state to give the chief constable directions over the head of the Police Authority 'as to the exercise of his/her functions'. In the early months of 1998, with the political negotiations dragging on, Mowlam moved again to put her own imprint on the policing discussion when, on 4 March, she published a discussion paper, 'Principles of Policing', setting out her manifesto for reform. It was nothing more than a statement of the obvious.

Soon afterwards, against all expectations, the elusive political agreement became reality. At the beginning of April, Mitchell, convinced a historic breakthrough was possible, announced round-the-clock negotiations and a deadline of 9 April. Tony Blair and Bertie Ahern, the British and Irish prime ministers, flew in for the concluding marathon and on the late afternoon of Good Friday, 10 April, after a final thirty-hour session of petulance, brinkmanship and hard-nosed horse-trading, what became known as the Belfast Agreement was reached. It provided for a power-sharing administration in Belfast, a series of north–south bodies to jointly administer key functions such as health, tourism and agriculture, and a new set of east–west co-operation groups to include England, Wales, Scotland, the Channel Islands and the Isle of Man. In addition there were provisions to enable the early release of prisoners convicted of terrorist offences, integrate human rights legislation into the Northern Ireland system and promote greater equality and mutual recognition of the cultural heritage and traditions of the entire community. The Irish government also agreed to set aside its constitutional claim over Northern Ireland and accepted that Irish unity could only come about if a majority of people there voted for it. On 22 May, the Agreement was over-whelmingly endorsed in simultaneous referendums: in Northern Ireland by 676,966 (71.12 per cent of those who voted); and, in the Irish Republic by 1,442,583 (94.39 per cent).

From the RUC's point of view the most important section of the Belfast Agreement was the one headed 'Policing and Justice', which provided a mandate for the most basic reappraisal of policing and criminal justice since partition.

> The participants recognise that policing is a central issue in any society They equally recognise that Northern Ireland's history of deep divisions has made it highly emotive, with great hurt suffered and sacrifices made by many individuals and their families, including those in the RUC and other public servants. They believe that the agreement provides the opportunity for a new beginning to policing in Northern Ireland with a police service capable of attracting and sustaining support from the community as a whole. They also believe that this agreement offers a unique opportunity to bring about a new political dispensation which will recognise the full and equal legitimacy and worth of the identities, senses of allegiance and ethos of all sections of the community in Northern Ireland. They consider that this opportunity should inform and underpin the development of a police service representative in terms of the make-up of the community as a whole and which, in a peaceful environment, should be routinely unarmed.
>
> The participants believe it essential that policing structures and arrangements are such that the police service is professional, effective and efficient, fair and impartial, free from partisan political control; accountable, both under the law for its actions and to the community it

serves; representative of the society it polices, and operates within a coherent and co-operative criminal justice system, which conforms with human rights norms. The participants also believe that those structures and arrangements must be capable of maintaining law and order including responding effectively to crime and to any terrorist threat and to public order problems. A police service which cannot do so will fail to win public confidence and acceptance. They believe that any such structures and arrangements should be capable of delivering a policing service, in constructive and inclusive partnerships with the community at all levels, and with the maximum delegation of authority and responsibility, consistent with the foregoing principles. These arrangements should be based on principles of protection of human rights and professional integrity and should be unambiguously accepted and actively supported by the entire community.

Policing was always going to be one of the most contentious issues at the Stormont talks and so it proved. Although the years of conflict had heavily ruptured the relationship between the police and sections of the Protestant community, especially working-class Loyalists, there was still a strong tendency to claim the police as 'ours', a mindset that, as we have seen, can be traced all the way back to the 1920s. So, just as Craig and Bates had so sturdily created and defended 'their' constabulary then, their modern Unionist counterparts adopted a highly proprietorial 'hands off the RUC' stance in the talks. Even the most perfunctory change was unnecessary; anything more would amount to appeasement of the IRA, they insisted.

Rigid historical attitudes were equally evident on the other side of the argument. The SDLP, as uncompromising about the police as ever, was determined to achieve root-and-branch reform, fulfilling the agenda Hume had first outlined to Wright at their meeting in Londonderry way back in August 1969. For its part, Sinn Fein, whose IRA masters had inflicted so much on the RUC in the intervening years, wanted the total disbandment of what Martin McGuinness called 'the most discredited police force in western Europe'. Indeed, his organisation had ambitions, first articulated in Republican think-tanks in the Maze prison as far back as the mid-1970s, to control locally recruited police forces in its strong-holds and had controversially experimented with its own ruthless concept of 'community policing' by beating and knee-capping, without the benefit of judge, jury or appeal, those it accused of 'anti-social behaviour'. The prospect of the RUC being replaced by cadres of locally recruited community constabularies, 'putting terrorists and knee-cappers into uniform', as one delegate articulated it, caused apoplexy to sturdy defenders of the RUC.

With the width and depth of the fateful split so evident, some of the participants feared the policing issue could cause the entire talks process to founder. So the idea of remitting consideration of the future of policing to an independent commission was born early in 1998, gained ground as the talks drew to a conclusion and ended up in the terms of the final Agreement in the hope that somebody else might find a solution where they had failed. The task thus fell to Chris Patten, the former Governor of Hong Kong, who had most recently presided over the colony's return to China. He was no stranger to Northern Ireland, having served there as a minister from 1983 to 1985, and was best remembered as the man who forced through the renaming of Londonderry City Council as Derry City Council, a redesignation which infuriated Unionists and pleased nationalists. By this logic, both sides therefore immediately anticipated that Patten would come out for the renaming of the RUC, the symbolic issue which rapidly emerged as the litmus test of whether his eventual report would be acceptable or not. 'Having pulled down the Union flag in Hong Kong, he was now coming to pull it down from RUC stations in Northern Ireland,' moaned one hardline Unionist. On 3 June, Mowlam announced the other seven members of the commission, each contributing a different perspective and expertise. They included former police officers from London and Boston, a Belfast barrister, a retired civil servant, two north American academics and a Northern-Ireland based English businesswoman.

By this time Ronnie Flanagan was well established as chief constable, a subdued Annesley having retired to well-earned obscurity in November 1996. With the appointment of the commission, Flanagan promptly decided to put on hold any implementation of the 189 recommendations of his own fundamental review of policing lest he be accused of pre-empting its findings. He also set up a small team of officers to liaise with the Patten team, making a professional policing case on every issue and providing them with all the material they asked for. In line with his strategy of complete openness, Flanagan even allowed Patten to examine the secret files on the Stalker affair and other equally controversial episodes in the past. More than most in his force, Flanagan recognised the inevitability of change and was committed to it, admitting that the force's culture and outlook was overwhelmingly 'white, male and Protestant'. But Flanagan's head and his heart were not always synchronised on the issue for he was also deeply attached to the RUC and its traditions. On several occasions he publicly defended the 'Royal' prefix and condemned any possibility of its removal as 'tokenism. It's not just a name. It's a title conferred by royal charter. There are very few policing organisations in the world that enjoy that privilege. It makes us proud,' he said. Not everyone agreed. As we have seen, the award had not been earned, merely granted as a sop. He was, however, on stronger ground when he warned repeatedly that ill-considered change would merely swap alienation between the RUC and nationalists for complete alienation from the Unionist community.

Flanagan's emotional defence of the RUC was very much in tune with widespread, but not unanimous, feeling throughout the force. While the ceasefires had been welcomed as a respite from the day-to-day pressures of policing in an environment of constant threat and danger, the subsequent clamour for change and reform generated a new set of fears and uncertainties. The use of the word 'reform' infuriated many, with its implication that all they had endured was somehow dubious or flawed and needed putting right. Officers who had been involved in sensitive events secreted notebooks and other material evidence as insurance against any future witch-hunts. There were many examples around the world, they said, where guerrillas had become governors and turned on those who had recently pursued them. Others who had incessantly risked their lives, health and reputations to serve the community began to worry about their jobs and futures as talk of down-sizing for peace gathered force. Within the wider police family a great sense of grievance and resentment grew. 'Many of us feel hurt that the great sacrifice that was made and the tremendous courage that was shown in dangerous times is being written off, forgotten about. There's not a station entrance without a roll of honour plaque and we will never forget our colleagues who gave their lives,' said one woman officer.

With only a handful of rogue exceptions, it is to the RUC's lasting credit that, despite the murder of 302 of their colleagues since 1969 – 277 at the hands of the IRA, twelve by the INLA/IPLO and eight by Loyalists – and the maiming of another 9,000 – they did not resort to wholesale reprisals or revenge, like their counterparts such as Nixon in the 1920s. To this toll of death and injury, underlining the terrible pressures imposed on the RUC, must be added the seventy officers who took their own lives. From time to time there was evidence of bigotry or sectarian attitudes but the vast majority of officers drew a distinction between ordinary Catholics and those with militant Republican sympathies. This was reflected in how they dealt with people and, as in police–public relations anywhere in the world, somebody oozing hostility or adopting an uncooperative attitude was going to have it reciprocated. But, over the years of the Troubles, with minor exceptions, the police view of the world became more sophisticated and notions of even-handedness and impartiality became more steadily accepted and practised. The growing numbers of women coming into the job with the march of the equality agenda tempered some, but not all, of the male chauvinism. Higher quality recruits, a steadily increasing proportion with university degrees, and encouragement to serving officers to improve their educational attainments helped bring about a situation where the purer police concept of serving the community rather than defending the country gained ground, in turn leading to a perception that policing was a vocational career requiring people with appropriate skills and attitudes.

Nevertheless rumours swirled and morale plummeted as Patten and his team contemplated the future. Hermon had once described the RUC as a mighty oak which would continue to thrive however many branches it lost. Now the feeling grew that, where the IRA had failed, Patten was coming with a giant axe to dismember it. One long-serving veteran of the years of conflict said: 'I joined just after the Hunt report outlined the vision of a civilianised, unarmed police force, but that had to be abandoned virtually before we got started on that road because of the growing violence. I hope this time that peace really does take hold and that the young officers who have just come into the job and others, who will join over the next few years, do not have to live through what we went through.'

Even before Patten had been appointed, one of the foundation stones for the coming change had been put in place. It was an inevitable outcome of the review that there would be a considerable reduction in police numbers. At that point, there was one police officer for every 135 of the population in Northern Ireland, compared with a ratio of 1:256 in London and 1:446 in England and Wales. In the Irish Republic the figure was 1:325. So that officers whose anticipated police service was to be shortened could be helped to find alternative careers for the rest of their working lives, the Police Rehabilitation and Retraining Trust (PRRT) was launched. Pledging £4,500,000 for the programme when he visited RUC Garnerville on 6 May 1998, Blair talked of a day 'where you are able to operate in circumstances and conditions that would be familiar to police officers everywhere' and said the trust would provide counselling for police victims and help for people who are changing their career and ensure that 'past service and the past sacrifice . . . does not go either unrewarded or unnoticed'.

Patten's report was finally completed in August 1999 and Flanagan was given an advance copy at the end of the month. Its contents came as a huge relief. For some time he had feared the recommendations could make his position untenable and he would have to resign. Afterwards, in a letter of reassurance to the force in which he announced its formal publication on 9 September, he said: 'The RUC stands ready for significant change. I could not be more proud to lead you in these challenging times and watch you succeed as you always do.' Inside the RUC, the news was greeted with a huge sigh of relief for finally bringing to an end a period of morale-sapping uncertainty and organisational paralysis. 'At last we'll be able to get on with the job. Everything has been waiting for Patten,' said one senior man. The report, entitled 'A new beginning', made 175 recommendations for police reform. The main points were:

- The RUC should be renamed the Northern Ireland Police Service.
- It should have a new badge, insignia and uniform entirely free from any association with the British and Irish states and the Union flag should no longer fly from police buildings.
- Memorials to RUC casualties should remain in place.
- A new human rights-based approach to policing should be created with a Code of Ethics and an oath of office explicitly committing the police to upholding human rights.
- Policing with the community should be the core function of the police service.
- The policing service should be delivered through a series of District Command Units co-terminous with each of the District Council areas.
- Depending on the security situation, police strength should be reduced to 7,500 officers over ten years.
- The Full-Time Reserve should be abolished and the Part-Time Reserve enhanced.
- Future recruiting should be on a fifty-fifty basis to increase the number of Catholics from under ten per cent to a proportion closer to their forty per cent proportion in the overall population.
- There should be a purpose-built training college.
- The police service should be capable of dealing with public disorder without calling for mutual aid from Britain but the Army should retain the capacity to support the police when necessary.

- The CID and the Special Branch should be amalgamated.
- A new Policing Board made up of political and independent community representatives should replace the Police Authority and hold the chief constable and police service more effectively to account.
- A network of local District Policing Partnerships should be set up.
- Co-operation with the Garda Siochana should be enhanced and put on a more formal basis.
- An eminent person other than from the UK or Ireland should be appointed as Oversight Commissioner to monitor the implementation of the recommendations.

For an official report, it was an unusually articulate and elegantly written document, citing predictable policing authorities such as Sir Robert Peel, Rowan and Mayne and the law lords Scarman and Denning. Less predictably it also quoted Abraham Lincoln, the episcopal father of the poet Louis MacNeice and the Roman poet Juvenal. More than that, it was an intellectually reasoned, logically argued and convincing manifesto to transform the seventy-seven-year-old Royal Ulster Constabulary from a police force into a renamed and rebranded Northern Ireland Police Service. But equally, there was no mincing of words in estimating the enormity of the task or the visionary gains to be made: 'There is no perfect model for us, no example of a country that, to quote one European police officer, "has yet finalised the total transformation from force to service". The commitment to a fresh start gives Northern Ireland the opportunity to take best practice from elsewhere and to lead the way in overcoming some of the toughest challenges of modern policing.' One of the most remarkable features of the report was its penetrating analysis of the fateful split and consequent failure of policing in Northern Ireland for several generations:

> The identification of police and state is contrary to policing practice in the rest of the United Kingdom. It has left the police in an unenviable position. In one political language, they are the custodians of nationhood. In its rhetorical opposite, they are the symbols of oppression. Policing, therefore, goes right to the heart of the sense of security and identity of both communities and, because of the differences between them, this seriously hampers the effectiveness of the police service in Northern Ireland.

Policing cannot be fully effective when the police have to operate from fortified stations in armoured vehicles, and when police officers dare not tell their children what they do for a living for fear of attack from extremists from both sides. We have studied policing in other countries and while we can discover no model that can simply be applied to Northern Ireland, we can find plenty of example of police services wrestling with the same sort of challenges.

Having so succinctly defined the dilemma and its unique factors, the commission went on to set authoritative parameters and the starting points for the way ahead. Setting the most emphatic baseline as the Universal Declaration of Human Rights, the report deplored the fact that in the present RUC training curriculum only two segments out of 700 were dedicated to human rights, compared to forty of drill and sixty-three of firearms training. It prescribed that respect and understanding for human rights should be fully integrated into the ethos of the new police service through training, monitoring, a new code of ethics, the appointment of a specialised legal adviser, and the incorporation of an undertaking to respect and uphold human rights into the oath of office to be taken by all officers in the police service.

Noting that it received many submissions, from all parts of the community and from elsewhere, calling for more 'community policing', the report commented that the term had many definitions and had become somewhat devalued by frequent and indiscriminate use. It suggested the term 'policing with the community' encapsulated better what most people wanted to see: 'the police participating in the community and responding to the needs of that community and the community participating in its own policing and supporting the police. What we emphatically do not mean by "community policing" is vigilante groups policing neighbourhoods with baseball bats, or, at the other extreme, what the Philadelphia police chief, John Timoney, has described as "sitting around the trees, holding hands and singing 'Kumbaya'".'

One of the most important issues the commission grappled with was the central question of delineating the limits of responsibility between the suggested new oversight body, the Northern Ireland Policing Board (to replace the existing Police Authority), and the chief constable. It opted for, by the existing standards, an unthinkable degree of openness: monthly public meetings between the Board, which would consist jointly of elected representatives from the Assembly and independent representatives of the community, and the chief constable, in which the community would be seen to be visibly holding the police to account for its conduct and actions. It further went on to define the scope of the relationship between the 'operationally responsible' chief constable and the requirement for him to account for his decisions afterwards, spelling out the doctrine that he could not be told in advance either by government or the board how he should deploy resources and officers under his independent command and control. This was, of course, one of the most vexed questions at the heart of accountable and open police–public relations for many years.

The management style of the RUC was also severely criticised. It was an 'organisation which is commanded rather than managed', said the report, quoting an operational officer in Newry who told the commission: 'Nobody comes down to discuss policy decisions – we are told.' The commission suggested this 'hierarchical and bureaucratic' style of management must change. Foreshadowing a period of consultation and discussion about its recommendations, the commission concluded: 'We cannot be judge and jury now of the precise timing of implementation. The Government and others responsible should not take our realism as an excuse for footdragging.' To safeguard against the proposals being shelved indefinitely, the commission wisely advised that someone of international standing should be appointed to monitor change, to publish a progress report and to ensure that it took place. In the end this recommendation was to prove the most necessary recommendation of all.

The report was greeted with few informed or intelligent responses. As ever in Northern Ireland, the wider reaction and subsequent debate focused almost entirely on the symbols, not the substance. What followed was an ignoble and frequently ill-informed campaign, concentrating primarily on the name change, in which policing was used as the customary bargaining chip during protracted political haggling. Predictably, Paisley was at the forefront despite his past antics, which had included inciting mutiny or threatening and defying the RUC when it suited him. In an act of the evangelical showmanship for which he is infamous, he led about eighty people in a slow march across the lawn in front of Parliament Buildings at Stormont, where they placed small white crosses, studded with poppies, in memory of the 302 RUC officers killed during the Troubles. During one of his prayers, in which religion and politics are so seamlessly blended, he revealed yet another of his doomsday 'plans of action', this one to stop the Patten recommendations from being implemented. 'We are totally dedicated to the destruction of this report. If this report is not destroyed, the RUC will be destroyed,' he thundered. Soon afterwards, in an act of piracy, he incorporated the RUC's 'harp and crown' in his party literature and on posters. David Trimble, his great rival for the soul of Unionism, meanwhile denounced the report as 'a gratuitous insult to the RUC' and the 'most shoddy piece of work I have seen in my entire life. Patten has allowed himself to be diverted into a gratuitous insult to the RUC and the community by stripping the service of its name and badge and flag.' He said the only change needed was the recruitment of many more Catholic officers to the RUC.

What both Paisley and Trimble were doing, in defiance of the new pluralist political dispensation arising from the Belfast Agreement, was playing an old game, trying to maintain the obsolete concept of proprietorship; that it was 'our' RUC. But perhaps the weirdest and least informed champion of the force was the London *Daily Telegraph*. Reacting to the Patten report on the day after publication, in what marked the start of an ill-considered and hopeless crusade, the paper's editorial said: 'Instead of being rewarded for holding the rifle-green line in the face of tremendous adversity, the RUC is now effectively to be disbanded. Even by the standards of late imperial retreat this is a great betrayal.' Charles Moore, the paper's haughty editor, characterised as 'Lord Snooty' by *Private Eye*, even flew to Belfast and spoke at a 'Save the RUC' rally in the Ulster Hall on Saturday 18 September, where he said people in Britain were disgusted by concessions to terrorism and would support the campaign. To portray the necessary business of police reform in this fashion demonstrated what can be only be described as a 'flat earth' understanding of the real situation in Northern Ireland. The memory and tradition of the RUC, despite its 'bad apples', mistakes and misjudgements, deserved better informed and more realistic allies.

From its professional point of view, the RUC should have been largely satisfied with the report: 165 of its 175 recommendations, the 'nuts and bolts' issues which were universally accepted as necessary, directly mirrored those already identified by Flanagan's frozen fundamental review. Inevitably in such a large organisation drawn so overwhelmingly from the majority community, there were strong and mixed feelings, especially about the loss of the name, uniform, badges and insignia. However, emotion prevailed and reality evaporated as the reactionary Police Federation emerged as one of the most strident and uncompromising critics of the report. Some of the attitudes it publicly expressed about key elements of the report, intentionally or not, identified the RUC with the most die-hard elements of Unionism. There can be no doubt that its attitude encouraged some in the ranks who harboured extreme views to engage in mutinous behaviour. No doubt buoyed by this, a few members of the organisation reacted with significant surliness and, in several cases, senior officers had to defuse confrontational situations. In one station, where there was talk of not going out on patrol in protest, strong leadership smothered the dissent. 'Tell them to go out or go home,' said the commander on the telephone, before rushing down to his base to ensure compliance. By the time he got there the embryonic revolt was over.

The depth of resentment should not be underestimated, and in many cases Flanagan himself intervened, using the sheer force of his personality to maintain discipline.These rumblings, however, concealed the fact that while the overwhelming silent majority of RUC officers regretted the proposed renaming of the force, they welcomed the rest of the report and were quickly resigned to accepting the name change in the interests of freeing them from the handcuffs of history and making a new beginning with a clean slate. The way ahead after Patten, and the challenge of the new beginning, was more succinctly summed up by a long-serving detective in Belfast:

> We can do without the proprietorial attitude unionists take to us and we want to see the SDLP coming off the fence and giving us their full consent and co-operation. This community has a new political opportunity because of the sacrifice of the RUC and the way it thwarted so much of the intended violence. We will embrace change but the mindset of the entire community must change too.

Chapter Ten

A New Beginning

Chris Patten travelled to Washington soon after the publication of his report to perform his final duty as the head of the Independent Commission on Policing for Northern Ireland: addressing a committee of the United States Congress. His journey underlined the importance the British government now attached to winning American support to help consolidate the still fragile peace process in Northern Ireland. Above all they badly wanted to win a Congressional benediction for the new policing arrangements because the RUC had been demonised in a series of critical reports and damaging resolutions from US representatives, many in open sympathy with Sinn Fein, which explicitly criticised the British government's defence of human rights. As winning a complete change in Catholic attitudes to policing was such a vital aim of the Patten process, it was hoped approval from them would have a profound knock-on effect in Northern Ireland itself.

In terms of global affairs and strategic importance, Northern Ireland was, of course, decidedly small beer for the superpower, but its problems had achieved a disproportionate interest inside the Washington beltway for the very good reason that with some forty-eight million of the 281 million United States population claiming Irish descent or origin, Irish-Americans enjoyed considerable political clout and were able to use it to channel some of the vast political influence and economic resources of their affluent nation into helping 'the old country'. Over the previous 200 years, Irish leaders such as Theobald Wolfe Tone, Jeremiah O'Donovan Rossa, Thomas Davis, John Devoy, Charles Stuart Parnell, James Connolly, Padraig Pearse and Eamon de Valera had all crossed the Atlantic at various critical stages to tap into this fountain of succour.

The same happened almost as soon as the civil rights campaign in Northern Ireland evolved into violent disorder from late 1968 onwards. Republican and nationalist activists were quickly on flights to New York and Washington to rekindle dormant links in a new bid to win both spiritual and practical help. With his Irish roots, the glamorous Senator

Edward Kennedy, whose elder brothers had both been assassinated (John while president in 1963 and Bobby while running for the office in 1968), was at that time the virtual monarch of Irish-America and hailed as a future president. He took a vociferous but typically simplistic interest in Irish affairs, frequently calling for immediate British withdrawal and Protestants to be resettled elsewhere. Within a month of Bloody Sunday in January 1972, working with the other pillars of Irish America, Kennedy persuaded the European sub-committee of the Committee on Foreign Affairs to hold a series of hearings in Washington DC. Over three days, a procession of Catholic and Protestant witnesses from Ireland expounded their conflicting views of Irish history, throwing an abundance of heat but little light on how to settle the problem.

Simultaneously, stimulated by the emergence of the Provisional IRA, more sinister efforts to sway events were under way. In 1970, expatriate veterans of the 1920s IRA campaign formed the Irish Northern Aid Committee, soon abbreviated to Noraid, ostensibly to send money to 'feed and clothe the homeless, hungry and naked' victims of the early Troubles. By the mid-1970s this pretence was dropped and the 'welfare' role was openly redefined: to help the families of Provisional IRA prisoners, portrayed as being unjustly incarcerated by British repression in Northern Ireland. Artefacts, such as wooden harps hand-carved by internees in Long Kesh (later the Maze), fetched as much as $10,000 when auctioned at fund-raising events, and in one notorious instance a Russian-made AK47 rifle, apparently used in several murders in Northern Ireland, was smuggled into the US and sold for a similarly large sum. In the twelve months after Bloody Sunday in 1972, Noraid declared remittances to Ireland of $441,099 and was still registering contributions of $300,000 dollars a year by the mid-1980s.

More specific evidence later emerged that these declared amounts heavily understated the true extent of fund-raising and 'welfare' support and that far more substantial sums of undeclared money were being used to exploit the liberal United States gun laws to procure arms, ammunition and other ordnance for the modern 'war' against the British in Northern Ireland. Between 1973 and 1986, for instance, the British security authorities calculated the 'Provos' had obtained 1,250 assorted weapons, many of them traced back to their US origins by their serial numbers after being used in some of the worst terrorist incidents in Northern Ireland. They also acquired vital components for making ever more sophisticated bombs, such as detonators and electrical and radio control devices. There was some embarrassment for the US authorities when it was discovered that Noraid emissaries had even penetrated the US military and were sending stolen material for use against the police and army in Northern Ireland. The US Bureau of Alcohol, Tobacco and Firearms and the FBI contested the central doctrine of British anti-IRA propaganda that the US was overwhelmingly the source of IRA arms but, nevertheless, were sufficiently concerned to obstruct the flow of weaponry.

Whatever the sympathy for the united Ireland cause, the US government did not want to encourage it by violent means and so, despite often vociferous criticism from Irish-Americans, there was close co-operation with the British law enforcement agencies, including the RUC, to thwart arms smuggling, although many consignments of arms and other material predictably evaded detection. Thanks to this intensive transatlantic work, by 1981 the claim that Noraid was merely a welfare organisation had been conclusively exposed as fraudulent after a series of trials in which its activists were directly linked to arms-buying and gun-running activities. After that the pretence was dropped. Speaking during a pilgrimage to trouble spots in Northern Ireland in August 1984, Noraid leader Richard Lawlor said: 'I would not discourage people from sending guns. . . . It's probably the moral duty of every Irish-American to get them American guns to ensure democracy.'

In a bid to articulate the Republican cause more effectively and mobilise support within the US, another organisation, the Irish National Caucus, was founded in 1974. The prime mover was Fr Sean McManus, a Northern Ireland-born priest whose outspoken IRA sympathies were engraved on the public record and who had been a notable proponent of Noraid during its 'welfare' phase. A skilled propagandist with an instinctive feel for the monochrome patriotic nuances of Irish America and sufficient brass-neck and personality to back-slap his way into the corridors of Congress, he quickly established himself and the Troubles as a prominent issue in Washington, despite the press of well-funded lobbyists who besieged every congressman and senator. In no time, McManus and his shoestring organisation had become a constant thorn in the sides of the British diplomats in the US and even the Irish government was forced to buttress its diplomatic work on Capitol Hill to counter the impression that it was the Caucus and not the democratically established government that spoke for Ireland.

McManus's earliest ally was Mario Biaggi, a colourful Italian-American, who had served in the New York Police Department for twenty-three years, becoming one of the most decorated officers in its history. Biaggi first became interested in Ireland while sharing a patrol car in New York's tough 24th District with one of the many city policemen with Irish roots. When he became a Democratic congressman for the city in 1969, to help secure his Bronx political power-base with Irish votes he took an active stance on Northern Ireland affairs. In 1970, with Representative Ben Gilman, a Jewish New York congressman who would also become a long-term Northern Ireland crusader, he signed a letter calling on President Richard Nixon to interest himself in the deprivation of human rights and discrimination against Catholics, a cause pursued during a handful of high-profile trips to Ireland which peaked in a vainglorious effort in 1978 to form a peace forum and act as an 'honest broker' in framing a historic peace deal. The same year, again working closely with McManus, in a move to undermine the predominant influence of Kennedy Biaggi created an Ad Hoc Congressional Committee on Irish Affairs, many of whose adherents wanted the US to call outright for a united Ireland and arm the IRA to achieve it.

By this time, the New Yorker and his fellow travellers were battling for influence on Capitol Hill with a more heavyweight faction who set out to challenge the more simplistic Irish Americans who had been nourished from birth on dubious romantic myths about past rebellions to overcome the perpetual British dictatorship, who saw no harm in running guns for the supposed liberation of 'the old country'. With precision timing, Thomas 'Tip' O'Neill, Speaker of the House of Representatives, Senators Edward Kennedy of Massachusetts and Daniel Patrick Moynihan of New York and Hugh Carey, Governor of the State of New York – quickly designated 'the four horsemen' – chose St Patrick's Day, 17 March 1977, to put their names to an historic statement condemning 'the politics of death' in Northern Ireland: 'We appeal to our fellow Americans to embrace the goal of peace and renounce any action that promotes the current violence or provides support or encouragement for organisations engaged in violence.'

In Dublin a few weeks later, in a deeply passionate lecture, Carey pledged that at a time when 'many minds are frozen shut to the ordinary acts of compromise by which brothers usually settle their political differences', he would 'bend every effort in dealing with other leaders in American life to see that any request of assistance from men of peace and justice in the North shall never go unheeded'. It was not an empty undertaking from a powerless man. The statement and the lecture proved to be landmark points in persuading the United States to take a far more constructive attitude to a small nation whose emigrants had played such a vital role in creating and achieving the American dream. From then on the most powerful and affluent country in the world turned a benevolent eye on Ireland and became a spur for peace-building.

If the 'four horsemen' could be said to have kick-started this important process, then the push that gave it real impetus should be rightly credited to the then President of the United States, Jimmy Carter. In an official policy statement from the White House on 30 August 1977, Carter stated: 'A peaceful settlement would contribute immeasurably to stability in Northern Ireland and so enhance the prospects for increased investment. In the event of such a settlement, the US government would be prepared to join with others to see how additional job-creating investment could be encouraged, to the benefit of all the people of Northern Ireland.'

Hitherto, in deference to the so-called 'special relationship' between the United States and the United Kingdom, its NATO partner and supposedly closest ally, the Americans had loyally maintained a non-interventionist stance towards Northern Ireland. But, to Britain's constant discomfort and the detriment of its standing as a civilised nation, Carter's change of course intensified official US scrutiny of a whole range of difficult issues and events in Northern Ireland, especially in relation to the RUC and policing. Given his profession and his view that the force engaged in 'institutional terrorism', which chimed well with McManus's long-standing aversion to the RUC, it was not surprising that Biaggi interested himself in the topic. With Biaggi in the chair, the Caucus had now 'signed up' 128 out of the 535 members of the House of Representatives, mainly those with a sizeable Irish-American element in their districts, and were seeking to persuade Congress to hold a series of hearings to highlight what were cast as disturbing human rights issues in Northern Ireland.

In 1978, after Amnesty International published a highly critical report about the interrogation procedures at the heart of Newman's anti-terrorist drive, the Caucus swung into action and in February 1979 succeeded in having a summary included in the State Department's 705-page annual review of the state of human rights in 115 countries. It was the first time Northern Ireland had ever been mentioned but the review did stop short of any outright criticism of Britain for the state of affairs, noting, by way of a make-weight, its 'strong commitment to the improvement of human rights practices at home and abroad'. The 'four horsemen', who had taken a considerable political risk in promoting their approach to an Irish settlement, were not handcuffed by any diplomatic niceties and after reading the disturbing review they reacted angrily. Kennedy went so far as to call for a special prosecutor to be appointed to investigate the allegations of police brutality. More importantly, with a British general election looming, it compounded their growing disillusion that neither Jim Callaghan's ruling Labour government, clinging to power only with the help of Ulster Unionist votes, nor Margaret Thatcher's replacement Conservative administration appeared to have any intention of mounting a new initiative to halt the ongoing violence and break the political deadlock as they had hoped. Indeed, during a recent visit to Britain and Ireland, O'Neill, whose power base lay in the Irish-American-dominated city of Boston, had been stung by the vehement 'Mind your own business – you don't know what you're talking about' attitude he had encountered from prominent British politicians. Finding a strong consensus for action among all the political parties in Belfast, O'Neill accused the British government of treating Northern Ireland as a 'political football' and called for the incoming administration to 'get negotiations moving quickly'.

Margaret Thatcher came to power as expected a month later, in May, and settled into Downing Street with the Northern Ireland issue well down her action list. Embittered at the outset of her election campaign by the assassination of the wartime intelligence specialist, Airey Neave, her Northern Ireland minister designate, she believed there was little value in trying to make political progress until the violence was defeated. In any case, Thatcher was a stout defender of the Union and would not countenance any arrangement that smacked of British withdrawal. Not long before, she had told her party's annual conference: 'If you wash your hands of Northern Ireland, you wash them in blood.' This uncompromising Unionist standpoint brought her into conflict with O'Neill, as Speaker of the House of Representatives arguably the most powerful politician in the US after the president, and within weeks of her taking office, they were on a collision course. The RUC was the point of impact.

Since it had been founded by William B. Ruger in a little red barn by the train station in Southport, Connecticut in 1949, Sturm Ruger and Company had produced close to sixteen million weapons and, as the company literature proudly proclaimed, among its range of fifty state-of-the-art models of rifles, shotguns, revolvers and pistols there was a gun for every sporting, personal, defence, military and police purpose. US armed forces, many US government agencies and hundreds of police departments worldwide used Ruger firearms. So in January 1979, with the RUC facing an ever more potent terrorist threat, at Newman's request the Police Authority for Northern Ireland had placed orders with Sturm Ruger for 9,000 handguns and rifles. It was not the first time the force had purchased arms in the United States and, as a legitimate law enforcement agency operating in a friendly country, the State Department, as it had done on the previous occasions, swiftly approved the order. The first tranche was quietly delivered within a few months but in June 1979, just as the second batch of .357 calibre Magnum handguns and M1 carbine .223 rifles was being packed for shipment to Belfast, Fr McManus got wind of what was happening and consulted Biaggi, who speedily announced that when the annual Appropriations Bill for the State Department went to Congress in July he would sponsor an amendment to halt the consignment and prevent the RUC from acquiring US-manufactured guns. By supplying the force, Biaggi argued, the State Department was compromising America's neutrality by supporting one faction in Northern Ireland. Furthermore, citing the European Court ruling on the 1971 interrogation episode and the Amnesty interrogation report, he claimed the Carter administration was violating its own foreign policy to uphold 'human rights' throughout the world by supplying armaments where abuse had been proved. What happened next was beyond the Caucus's wildest dreams.

Instead of using his position as speaker to block what would normally have been sidelined as a nuisance motion, O'Neill threw his considerable political weight behind it in a bid to pressurise the British government on his own concerns over Northern Ireland. While a formal ban was not imposed after a Congressional hearing at the beginning of August, the State Department announced a 'review' of the RUC order as a result of 'pressure from Congress'. The decision, effectively equating the RUC with terrorist organisations, created a predictable storm in Northern Ireland where the Democratic Unionist MP Peter Robinson accused O'Neill of a 'venomous outburst' in equating the RUC with the IRA as a 'faction' in the situation. The *Belfast Telegraph* condemned the sales suspension as 'an outrageous action which demonstrates an ignorance of conditions here as well as the effectiveness of the Irish National Caucus propaganda campaign', while Humphrey Atkins, the recently appointed secretary of state, said, 'I very much regret that a body of men and women who have borne so much of the brunt of the terrorist campaign during the past ten years, should be made the subject of controversy over the provision of modern weapons to defend the community and themselves from attacks by mindless assassins.'

On 2 August, after the 'review' had been put in place and it was clear the shipment was being indefinitely delayed, Atkins attempted to play down what was, by any standard, a most serious snub by one friendly country to another by saying they had 'no information that the United States administration has imposed a ban on any further supplies' and affirming the United States government had been reminded that the RUC was 'the legally constituted police force in Northern Ireland, charged with the task of protecting all its citizens, no matter what their religious persuasion'.

It was a measure of the British government's private concerns about the rift with the US that, in a complete reversal of the manifesto on which it had been elected, the Thatcher government hastily conceived a political initiative, publishing a document entitled 'The government of Northern Ireland – A working paper for a conference' that November. On the back of it, the four main political parties were called into conclave to consider ways in which an elected assembly could be created and given back some measure of local administration. About the same time, an RUC firearms expert was secretly invited to Downing Street to give the prime minister a 'hands-on' demonstration of a number of the weapons they wanted and explain why they were needed. Both exercises were part of Thatcher's preparation for a wide-ranging summit meeting with President Carter on 19 December 1979 at which the guns issue was discussed. On this particular point, Carter referred her to O'Neill, who listened politely to what she had to say but remained unconvinced. With a presidential election looming, Carter, who was much more concerned about securing the release of fifty US diplomats held hostage in Iran, was simply not going to alienate O'Neill and the powerful Irish-Americans over what was a comparatively low-level problem on the Richter scale of the White House.

By contrast, the influential *New York Times* did call the embargo into question in an editorial nearly six months later, on 28 May, remarking that 'while the British passion for law and order did not match up to their zeal to secure a political settlement, there is no basis in law or logic for denying a licence for the export of guns to combat political murder in Northern Ireland'. *The Times* referred to the recent murder of a policeman and the wounding of three colleagues by terrorists using an American-made M60 heavy machine gun, one of seven stolen from a US National Guard armoury in Massachusetts in August 1976 in a haul which also included M16 automatic rifles and other high-grade military equipment.

Despite such embarrassing linkages for the Carter administration, in an election year their line did not change. Writing to the Ulster Unionist MP James Kilfedder in June 1980, Dr Kingman Brewster, the US ambassador in London, reported a fall-off in fund-raising and gun-smuggling and said that 'an important share of the credit belongs to leading Irish-American political figures, like Speaker O'Neill, who have consistently opposed support for terrorist groups, often at a political cost to themselves'. The ambassador went on to report that 'responsible Irish-Americans – the very ones who are keeping the lid on support for the terrorists in the States – have advised us that they believe a decision to supply guns to the RUC could lead to a sharp reaction and a new effort to re-launch the traffic in guns and money'. The 'review' of the order therefore remained in place and was still ongoing in November 1980 when Carter failed to win a second term as president and was replaced by the Governor of California, Ronald Reagan. He took office in January 1981, having signalled a return to a policy not to 'interfere or intervene' in Northern Ireland, but refused to close the door completely on any Irish-American influence on his administration by saying that 'Washington should make it plain that if there is any way we can be helpful, we would be more than eager to do so.' His key aides promptly made it clear, though, that it would be 'premature' to end the ban on arms for the RUC.

Thatcher, carving out what would prove to be a very close relationship with Reagan during his two terms, visited the new president at the end of February, but on her return she surprised the House of Commons by reporting that the arms ban had not been raised because the RUC had no urgent need for the weapons. In reality, well-informed British diplomats had correctly divined that there would be no imminent change in US policy. Their judgement was proved to be correct within days when the White House published a letter from a presidential aide to fifty congressmen who, orchestrated by the Caucus, had written to Reagan in advance of the Thatcher visit, urging him to maintain the arms ban. 'As the situation now stands, the administration is holding to the policy of not approving licensing for the sale of handguns to the RUC,' the White House said. The continued embargo was not publicly referred to on St Patrick's Day, when Reagan delivered a statement condemning terrorist violence as a way of influencing events in Northern Ireland and calling for joint UK and Ireland effort to halt terrorism and find a solution to the conflict.

Thereafter the embargo remained forgotten but still officially in force. It surfaced briefly again in 1984 when Biaggi claimed that an export agency, with offices in Washington DC had supplied 100,000 rounds of ammunition and 266,000 plastic bullets to the RUC. The company concerned refused to comment on the allegation and in a suitably ambiguous statement, the State Department said that it 'had not approved any licence for the export of arms, ammunition or riot control equipment on the US Munitions List where there is evidence the commodities would be used in Northern Ireland'. Although the embargo has never formally been ended, the police in Northern Ireland still acquire and use Rugers and other US-manufactured weapons and ammunition, bought on their behalf by the British police service or the Ministry of Defence, with the US turning a convenient blind eye to the real end user.

In the wake of the RUC guns row, the British government invested considerable effort in trying to 'educate' Irish-American opinion about the complexities of the Northern Ireland situation, but a contribution to the proceedings of the House of Representatives in June 1990, from Congressman Brian Donnelly of Massachusetts, demonstrated how deeply the mythology about Ireland was embedded and how difficult it was to overcome.

> When 'the troubles' flared anew in 1969, children who were under 16 and too young for the IRA rushed to join the Na Fianna Éireann, a group created in the early 1900s as an Irish patriot's answer to Baden-Powell's 'John Bullish' Boy Scouts. Fianna members had their own uniform and the black shirts, berets and sunglasses gave even small children a scary, paramilitary look. The youngsters became a macabre part of the pageantry in every IRA funeral cortège. The IRA broke up the formal structure of the Fianna after the RUC and British intelligence forces had too often managed to squeeze information out of its members. The numbers of Fianna children who were killed, not just in riots or military operations, but in accidents as well, were also bad for public relations. The IRA still has a youth wing [. . .] John, 16, joined when he was 13, and his early years mainly consisted of reading books, learning Gaelic and, to his frustration, painting posters and marching. 'We've been protesting for 20 years against the Brits, and they've never taken any heed,' he says. 'They take heed of war.' John plays drums in a Republican band, the only legal way for kids in Belfast to flaunt their defiance.

The 1981 hunger strikes caused immense interest and protest in the US and boosted IRA fund-raising and support. British diplomatic premises throughout the country were constantly picketed and the RUC's activities remained under close scrutiny but McManus did not pounce again until 1987, when he found that the American Police Foundation had invited Hermon to Washington to take part in a symposium for 300 of its members on 'police methods in areas of tension'. McManus said Hermon should not attend because the RUC was 'the personification of sectarianism and anti-Catholic discrimination' and had been indicted by the State Department and Amnesty International for its notorious record. Thanks to his prompting, the Rev. Jesse Jackson, the black American figurehead, and the mayors of several cities supported McManus and protested to the Foundation as, inevitably, did Biaggi. The Foundation saved face by announcing that it had changed the topic of its seminar and was confining it to US-based officers. This campaign proved to be Biaggi's last, for, the same year, the man who had been elected to the US National Police Hall of Fame suffered a spectacular fall from grace when he was sent to prison for eight years for bribery and corruption.

By the mid-1980s, years of formidable Irish diplomacy, bolstered by the 'four horsemen' and others, had secured major influence in the White House, notwithstanding the closeness of the Reagan–Thatcher relationship. The Irish cashed their goodwill cheque in persuading Reagan to help win the strongly disapproving prime minister round to the continued need for a ground-breaking political deal, which he did during Thatcher's Washington visit in March 1985, when she was given the rare honour of addressing the joint Houses of Congress. This helped clear the way for the Anglo-Irish Agreement later in the year. Immediately afterwards, fulfilling Carter's 1977 pledge, the US government created and generously financed the International Fund for Ireland, which has since poured $350,000,000 into Northern Ireland and the six southern counties along the border to help alleviate the effects of the Troubles. Among the conditions placed on spending by Congress was that none of the money would be used in connection with security policies or the RUC, whose continued imperfections still interested McManus and his allies.

Despite the high-level political rapport and understanding that had been forged between London, Dublin and Washington, the Caucus and the Ad Hoc Committee did not disappear. The lead voice now became that of Republican Congressman Ben Gilman, a Jewish-American, who, like Biaggi (now behind bars), represented a New York district. In spite of his own ethnicity, his Irish credentials were sound: he was co-signatory on Biaggi's 1970 letter to Nixon and had accompanied him on visits to Ireland. Taking its cue from Jimmy Carter, who had first put the protection of human rights at the forefront of the US international policy agenda, the State Department had more rigorously been measuring compliance around the world and Congress had deeply immersed itself in drawing attention to those countries where there were deficits. Northern

Ireland was consistently among them, so, given all these factors, it was inevitable that Gilman, with his long-standing concerns about the place, would turn his attention there once he was re-elected to Congress in 1995 and appointed chairman of one its most powerful committees, that for international relations.

Gilman kicked off his six-year term of office with the first of what would be a series of hearings about the RUC, boasting that it was the first time in twenty years that the situation in Northern Ireland had been fully examined by Congress. The hearings centred on a number of core themes and cases: the 'torture' of terrorist suspects; use of plastic baton rounds; operation of a 'shoot-to-kill' policy; collusion between the police and Loyalist terrorist groups; and the harassment of defence lawyers. The committee also examined a number of cases alleging miscarriage of justice or other abuses of process but homed in on three particular incidents: the murder of the solicitor Pat Finucane in 1989, the death of Robert Hamill in 1997; and the murder of another solicitor, Rosemary Nelson, on 15 March 1999.

The Finucane case had become a major cause for the anti-RUC lobby after it emerged that his Loyalist killers had been working hand in glove with a shadowy undercover military unit and members of the RUC Special Branch. Whether this 'collusion' was co-ordinated or not, the campaigners claimed that Finucane, some members of whose family were steeped in IRA activity, had been targeted and killed on the orders of the security forces and the government. Less than a month earlier, Douglas Hogg, a British junior minister, had visited Northern Ireland and afterwards criticised the number of solicitors 'unduly sympathetic to the IRA'. After a protracted investigation conducted by Sir John Stevens, the Metropolitan Police Commissioner, and a team of non-RUC detectives, a prominent Loyalist, William Stobie, was charged with the murder, but in November 2001 he was acquitted when the principal witness against him was ruled mentally unfit to give evidence. The case took another mysterious twist a few weeks later when Stobie was ambushed and shot dead outside his home in Belfast. A Loyalist group, the Red Hand Defenders, claimed they had carried out the killing but many nationalist politicians and others preferred to believe that Stobie had been murdered as part of what they continued to see as official involvement in a lasting cover-up of Finucane's murder.

Robert Hamill, a twenty-five-year-old Catholic, died on 4 May 1997 from injuries received during a street brawl in Portadown several days earlier. The case became a *cause célèbre* for the RUC's opponents when eyewitnesses claimed that four RUC officers sitting nearby in a Land Rover had observed the brawl and refused to intervene. The credibility of the RUC's version of events was not helped by a series of inconsistent statements made immediately afterwards and conflicting evidence given later at the trial of one of six men charged with murder. Charges against five of the men had to be dropped after key witnesses withdrew their evidence. The sixth man was acquitted of murder but convicted of affray and jailed for four years.

The case did not rest there, for with fresh evidence subsequently unearthed by internal RUC investigation, the Police Ombudsman's office launched its own inquiry, which was still unresolved in the summer of 2003 with criminal proceedings pending.

The murder of Rosemary Nelson made a particularly deep impression in Washington for she had appeared before the Committee on International Operations and Human Rights some months earlier, on 29 September 1998, when she told them she 'feared for her life' because of death threats from the RUC.

> Another reason why RUC officers abuse me in this way is because they are unable to distinguish me as a professional lawyer from the alleged crimes and causes of my clients. This tendency to identify me with my clients has led to accusations by RUC officers that I have been involved in paramilitary activity, which I deeply and bitterly resent [. . .] I believe that my role as a lawyer in defending the rights of my clients is vital. The test of a new society in Northern Ireland will be the extent to which it can recognise and respect that role, and enable me to discharge it without improper interference. I look forward to that day.

One morning the following March, as she was driving away from her home in Lurgan, an under-car booby-trap bomb exploded, killing her instantly. Because of her high-profile role representing the Hamill famly and legally advising the Catholic community opposed to the Drumcree parade, her death prompted claims that there had been RUC collusion in her murder. New York Democratic Congressman Joseph Crowley later praised her 'riveting and chilling testimony' as she alleged the RUC had intimidated her, roughed her up and made death threats against her. 'She was inspiring, courageous and smart,' he said on 5 August 1999.

These cases and the suspicions surrounding them were extensively aired at Congressional hearings which were, in reality, overwhelmingly one-sided affairs. At one, in October 1997, for instance, the witness list consisted of Julia Hall, Northern Ireland Researcher for Human Rights Watch, Jane Winter, Director of British Irish Rights Watch, Martin O'Brien, Director of the Committee on the Administration of Justice, Halya Gowan, Northern Ireland Researcher for Amnesty International and Elisa Massimino, Director of the Washington office of the Lawyers Committee for Human Rights. Their standpoints were far from objective and the submissions they made were long on opinions and views, many of them feeding off each other, but woefully short of hard evidence to back up their assertions. On other occasions the committee heard emotional testimony from a blinded plastic-bullet victim and from the highly articulate sister of Robert Hamill, but, if anything, the cumulative data reinforced their prejudices and decidedly superficial knowledge of the multi-dimensional realities of the conflict in Northern Ireland.

For instance, from the chair, Chris Smith, a New York Republican, introduced a hearing on 24 June 1997 with the words: 'Human rights abuses committed by the members of the Royal Ulster Constabulary, the RUC, Northern Ireland's police force, is a pathetic reality . . . and credible accusations persist that security forces harass citizens and leak names of suspected Republicans to Loyalist paramilitary groups who then carry out the killings.' In what was more a sermon, worthy of a bible-thumping pastor, than a speech, he pointed out that the great butchers of the twentieth century – Hitler, Stalin, Mao Tse-Tung, Pol Pot and others – had all been atheists. Turning to human rights, he said they were 'given by God, not by governments or ideologies, and the most fundamental of these God-given rights is the right to life'.

> When governments resort to methods that are illegal, unjust, or inhumane, even when these methods are seemingly directed against the guilty or the dangerous, the effect is not to preserve law and order but to undermine it. It is particularly shocking that the British Government, America's trusted ally, is the object of serious and credible charges of disrespect for the rule of law in the north of Ireland. Just as the My Lai massacre was especially revolting because it was carried out not by the Viet Cong, but by Americans, freedom-loving people everywhere are outraged to learn that law enforcement officials of the United Kingdom tolerate and even perpetrate some of the gross abuses that have taken place in the north of Ireland.

During the summer of 1997, Smith was a member of a week-long Congressional fact-finding mission to Ireland but what he saw and heard had little impact on his views. On his return, he reported on 9 October 1997:

> My most disappointing sessions were with RUC Chief, Ronnie Flanagan, and Lord Chief Justice, Sir Robert Carswell. Both men head up departments, police and judiciary, respectively, which have been severely criticised by human rights groups the world over. Both men remained in a state of denial, refusing to admit that human rights abuses take place in their agencies. It was easy to see why so few in the Catholic community have any confidence in the ability of the police or the judiciary to make meaningful reforms on their own. Reforms in these departments will have to come from external pressures and sources.

This was precisely the sort of thing McManus wanted to hear. Thanks to his close relationship with Gilman, he had been able to play a leading part in encouraging the influential committees to take up the Irish cause and steer them towards factions in Ireland who would make the case as he saw it. With the Patten commission just getting underway, in a statement on 2 December 1998, marking the twentieth anniversary of the opening of the Caucus office on Capitol Hill, McManus launched a timely campaign: 'One of our top priorities is the creation of an acceptable police service in Northern Ireland. There has never been such a police service in Northern Ireland. Nothing is more central or more pressing.'

Soon afterwards, in the early months of 1999, he generated another bout of anti-RUC feeling when a combined team of RUC and Garda Siochana boxers were due to fly out and take on the New York Police Department. The tournament was intended to help finance medical care for a New York policeman who had been critically injured when he was struck by a drunken driver. 'This is clearly and blatantly an attempt to get the New York Police to condone and cover up the horrible RUC record,' said McManus, firing the opening salvo of a bid to halt the event. There had already been similar charity contests in Dublin and Belfast but this was the first time the joint Irish police team was to fight in New York. After McManus's appeal, New York City's Mayor Rudy Giuliani and the New York State Governor, George Pataki, were urged to cancel the tournament. The Sinn Fein leader, Gerry Adams, wrote to them and Irish-American leaders promised to picket and 'hound the event'. The threat caused the owners of the first-choice Manhattan venue to decline to host the event, and when an alternative arena made the same decision the contest was cancelled. Instead, the Garda and RUC staged the match again in Belfast and raised a total of £11,000 of which $5,000 was donated to the NYPD in October 1999. The row perplexed one of the NYPD organisers: 'It's ironic that they can have a fund-raiser for a New York cop in Ireland, but I can't have one in New York,' he said.

The cumulative effect of this controversy and the prolonged series of hearings in Congress, studded as they were, with talk of 'bungled investigations', 'cover-ups', 'white-washes' and 'sweeping under the carpet', was completely to demonise the RUC. Amidst all the rhetoric about fairness and justice, there was absolutely no equivocation or doubt about the conduct or guilt of the RUC on the part of some elected Representatives. 'Torture, murder of children, intentional killings, intentional maimings. This was all part of the police policy in the north of Ireland,' said New York Congressman Peter King, who enjoyed a close relationship with Adams. Underlying all of this speechifying was a conviction that they were making a real difference and bringing effective pressure to bear on Britain to heed their concerns and make sweeping changes to the institutions for policing and justice, primarily in the interests of the minority community in Northern Ireland.

The official British reaction to this sustained criticism of its security and human rights policy in Northern Ireland was not anger or resentment but haughty indifference. Asked why they mounted no defence, a senior diplomat in Washington exclaimed: 'Her Majesty's Government does not accept summonses from foreign legislatures.' They much preferred to operate behind the scenes at the other end of Pennsylvania Avenue, where the presidential administration, which shared concerns about the efficacy of policing, declined to be drawn into such open criticism but made its contribution to the ongoing peace process in a far more balanced and constructive fashion. The British diplomatic effort was not misplaced, for by the late 1990s White House interest in Irish events had reached a higher level than ever before. President Bill Clinton, who was tickled to be told that he had obscure family origins in County Fermanagh, had committed himself to helping the Irish cause during his first presidential election race in 1992 but, far from it being a ritual undertaking to harness Irish-American votes, he honoured it more fully than could ever have been expected once he was victorious and took office. In fact, as president he would make three official visits to Ireland. Among the first appointments he made was that of Nancy Soderberg to the National Security Council. A former aide to Edward Kennedy, she had become an expert on Irish affairs with open conduits to a spectrum of people north and south, which she fully utilised as the president and his administration became immersed in the secret back-channel diplomacy which helped broker the turning-point 1994 ceasefires. Afterwards, he and several other senior US political figures maintained a close interest in developments and intervened to help at critical moments. In particular, former senator George Mitchell, a presidential envoy in all but name, would chair the forthcoming political negotiations and, with Clinton, play a clinching role in helping achieve the Belfast Agreement.

Although their interest was never publicly articulated, the Clinton administration took the view that the historic deadlock over policing in Northern Ireland was one of the biggest obstacles to a durable peace and must be broken. In the absence of effective policing, they judged, terrorist violence and its associated lucrative criminality could flourish, compromising the chances of any new political institutions surviving and thriving. Despite the embargo on arming the RUC, the Reagan administration had taken a similar view after the Anglo-Irish Agreement in 1985. Fearing that without a more efficient squeeze on those using violence the new deal would be undermined, they offered whatever the British and Irish governments wanted by way of specialist equipment, training or even financial aid. For their own reasons, both governments rejected the proposition. The British were sensitive about how their own police establishment and the Army would feel if they were suddenly bypassed by an influx of US aid for the RUC. Dublin, equally defensive about the prowess of the Garda and the reaction in the country, also declined. Since then, Washington had closely monitored policing events through the eyes and ears of its diplomats on the ground in London and Dublin and especially in its consulate in Belfast, which produced a more factual analysis of the problem than the largely unbalanced and emotion-laden screeds emanating from Congress. For instance, the reports from Belfast about the Drumcree U-turn in 1996 helped inform the 1997 State Department review on international human rights compliance, which said: 'Many observers on both sides of the community perceived the government's reversal, in the face of unlawful Unionist protests, as a victory of might over the rule of law and the incidents damaged the RUC's reputation as an impartial police force.'

While the original offer of large-scale police aid had been rejected, lower-key assistance was offered and accepted. Over the years, several RUC officers, including high-flyer Ronnie Flanagan, participated in joint training with the FBI National Academy at Quantico, Virginia. In the wake of the 1994 ceasefires, five more RUC officers attended and a further twenty-five participated in FBI training courses held in Europe. On the back of the peace process, as the clamour for RUC reform and the debate about the shape of future policing structures gathered force in Northern Ireland, the Clinton administration ignored the anti-RUC stridency elsewhere in Washington and decided to support more substantial initiatives. Funding was thus channelled through the United States Information Agency for an ambitious transatlantic conflict resolution and community relations venture to help condition senior police officers to the challenge of change. The project was led by the Mediation Network, established in 1991 in Belfast, to work as 'an independent third-party encouraging individuals and agencies to develop new ways of living with difference by stimulating more creative responses to the sort of seemingly intractable disputes which so split the Northern Ireland community.'

Work on the three-year Policing Our Divided Society (PODS) project began in October 1997 when a group from the network opened a dialogue with a group of senior police officers designed, in the first instance, to get them to reflect on the past, present and future of the RUC and begin the process of bringing new cultural values and attitudes to bear. As part of this stage, in partnership with the Conflict Management Group from Cambridge, Massachusetts, the initiative widened into an exchange programme between the Citizens Committee for New York City, the NYPD and the RUC. During the second year of the project in 1999, when the implications and mechanism for changing so large an organisation as the RUC were being studied, the team visited Atlanta, Georgia, to see how the Police Department there had made the transition from a segregated force in a segregated society to an integrated force representative of the community it served. There were, of course, clear parallels between the traditional racial tensions in the US and the religious strains in Northern Ireland.

In a separate operation in January 1999, a cadre of fifty officers, drawn equally from the two police services north and south of the border, made a joint visit to Washington and New York sponsored by the Office of Anti-terrorism, run by the State Department and the FBI. A statement from FBI headquarters in Washington said, 'The attendees are considered to be among the future leaders of the law enforcement community in both parts of Ireland.' Their programme of visits was devised, the news release said, to help the police in Ireland address 'the new challenges that societal changes are having on law enforcement in the region'. The study topics included interaction between police and public in the human rights environment, recognition of diversity and anti-terrorism strategies. It was a measure of the importance attached to the visit that two senior figures in the Clinton administration publicly endorsed it. Secretary of State Madeleine Albright said it was an important example of the kind of practical assistance which the United States could offer in the law enforcement area, and 'indicative of US commitment to a system of policing in Northern Ireland which enjoys widespread community support'. Attorney-General Janet Reno said: 'Through joint training, we can improve co-ordination, enhance co-operation and ensure greater understanding between law enforcement officers.' The FBI Director Louis J Freeh, who addressed the group during the week-long programme, said: 'The FBI is proud to provide a forum not only for learning and discussion, but for the development of professional and personal relationships. These "cop-to-cop" relationships provide the foundation of better understanding and greater law enforcement co-operation on both sides of the border.' Both Flanagan and his Garda counterpart, Commissioner Pat Byrne, joined their officers on the training programme.

Despite these forward-looking enterprises, back on Capitol Hill the RUC's Congressional critics quickly manoeuvred to inhibit them. Despite the fact that Flanagan had shrewdly asked Freeh to send FBI consultants to advise on the Nelson murder investigation, Congressmen Chris Smith and Peter King started moves in April to have Congress end the FBI training programme unless President Clinton could certify the British government was conducting 'independent, credible and transparent' investigations into the Finucane and Nelson murders and had set up 'an independent judicial inquiry into allegations that defence attorneys are systematically harassed and intimidated by security forces'. This proposal was still winding its way through the labyrinthine law-making process in the US when Patten arrived in September 1999, just thirteen days after his report was published, to explain it at a hearing of the Committee on International Relations. He told them the aim was 'to take the politics out of policing and to take the police out of politics'.

> We held forty public meetings around Northern Ireland. People said nobody is going to go to a public meeting. Nobody goes to public meetings these days. Well, over ten thousand people came to those public meetings. Over a thousand people spoke at them. I can remember a meeting in a little village cinema in Kilkeel, a fishing village in the shadow of the Mournes. Protestant fishing fleet, Catholic farmers in the hinterland. We had a noisy and quite a good meeting. At

the end of it, I made the sort of speech that we all can make terribly well as politicians about reconciliation and healing and hope. At the end of it, after I had finished, to my consternation I saw a little lady at the back of the cinema getting up to say something. I sat down rather nervously. She said, 'Well, Mr. Patten, I have heard what you say about reconciliation and I voted yes in the referendum campaign, but I hope you will realize how much more difficult that is for us here than it is for you, coming from London. That man there murdered my son.' And it was true. On both sides of the community, that is the reality in Northern Ireland. Two stories, two sets of pain, two sets of anguish.

We had an evening which began on the Garvaghy Road. I remember Robert Hamill's sister talking to us about his murder, and the meeting was chaired with considerable integrity and skill, a difficult meeting, by Rosemary Nelson. We then went down the road to Craigavon, and we had four police widows, one after another, telling us their stories, ending with Mrs Graham whose husband had the back of his head shot off, a community policeman, in 1997. Mrs Graham finished her remarks by saying, 'You know, my husband wasn't a Catholic, but he didn't regard himself as a Protestant. He tried to behave like a Christian.' I have to say that I went back from those two meetings that night and had the largest drink I have ever had in my life.

But Patten's finely judged oratory initially appeared to have fallen on deaf ears. A couple of months later, in December, Congress forced Clinton to sign into law restrictions ending exchange programmes between the FBI and the RUC. The main author of the bill, Congressman Smith, said they were put in place because of the RUC's 'dreadful human rights record. For the first time, the full Congress is taking specific action to spotlight, isolate and mitigate the human rights abuses committed by the RUC.' The real intention of the measure, though, was to ensure that the new beginning for policing, so comprehensively outlined by Patten, which had in reality deeply impressed the listening congressmen, was going to be fully implemented.

There were good grounds for their doubts. In October 1999, within a month of the Patten report being published, Tony Blair relieved Mo Mowlam of the task of implementing it. Despite the triumphant end to the protracted political talks some eighteen months earlier, she was sidelined to a new ministerial post at the Cabinet Office in London and succeeded by Peter Mandelson, grandson of Herbert Morrison, one of the father figures of the British Labour Party. As the principal architect of New

Labour's 1997 election victory, Mandelson was one of the prime minister's most intimate confidants, who was seen to be getting the reward for his loyalty and skill. But the Northern Ireland job was no sinecure, for the entire peace process was deadlocked and police reform was one of the most entrenched obstacles.

Chapter Eleven

'Law and Orde'

Soon after his arrival in Belfast, Mandelson confided to a friend that there was much to do to repair the 'damage' done to the deadlocked peace process by 'that woman Mowlam'. To be fair, it was not all her fault, for lack of trust was the real brake on making progress. Unionists said the IRA was not committed to exclusively peaceful means because it would not consider even a token disarmament gesture, a defiance underscored by the graffiti writers: 'Not a bullet, not an ounce' (of explosive). In response, Unionists devised their own slogan: 'No guns, no government', indicating they would not serve alongside Sinn Fein until the IRA had put itself out of business. Faced with this tangle of distrust and an alarming evaporation of Unionist support for the Agreement, Mandelson, as he recalled when writing in *The Spectator* on 11 May 2002, decided it was important to 'fuel the peace process' by giving 'reassurance to the Unionists that what they were giving up as part of the Agreement was not leading inexorably to the dissolution of the Union'.

Given Unionist hurt and fury about police reform, he decided this would be the best pill to sweeten for them, but in doing so, and in meddling with the detail of the recommendations as he would, Mandelson grievously undermined Patten's central aim 'to take the politics out of policing and to take the police out of politics'. By playing politics with the police he only encouraged the local politicians to exploit the issue themselves and further aggravate the difficult enough process of police reform. He did not even achieve his aim for his interference only managed to multiply the distrust and dissatisfaction among all the political parties, including his intended beneficiaries, and so seriously disrupted and prolonged the entire implementation process of the Belfast Agreement that its durability was put in doubt.

Mandelson's doomed process began a month after he arrived in Belfast. On 23 November 1999, Buckingham Palace announced that the RUC was to be awarded a collective George Cross, a distinction it would share only with the Mediterranean island of Malta, which had been similarly honoured for its communal fortitude in enduring sustained attack at the height of the Second World War. The honour, the highest for which civilians are eligible, takes precedence over all other medals with the sole exception of the Victoria Cross and is normally awarded for acts of the greatest heroism, or of the most conspicuous courage, in circumstances of extreme danger. In the sixty years since its inception by the Queen's father, George VI, the Cross has only been awarded to a select elite of some forty individuals. The RUC's citation says:

> For the past 30 years the Royal Ulster Constabulary has been both the bulwark against, and the main target of, a sustained and brutal terrorist campaign. The Force has suffered heavily in protecting both sides of the community from danger – 302 officers have been killed in the line of duty and thousands more injured, many seriously. Many officers have been ostracised by their own community and others have been forced to leave their homes in the face of threats to them or their families. As Northern Ireland reaches a turning point in its political development this award is made to recognise the collective courage and dedication to duty of all of those who have served in the Royal Ulster Constabulary and who have accepted the danger and stress this has brought to them and their families.

The idea appears to have originated within the Northern Ireland Office before the suggestion was informally floated to the RUC through royal channels to gauge the reaction. There was initial scepticism about the genuineness of the offer, according to a senior officer, and it was only after some debate that the force's command decided to accept it as an apolitical and altruistic tribute to their incomparable ordeal. The award was not without its political value, as Mandelson well knew, and, given his reputation for ruthless political exploitation as the inventor of New Labour 'spin', the sincerity of the award was instantly called into question once it was publicly announced. Indeed, so many commented on what seemed to be the politically convenient timing of the announcement that Downing Street was forced to reject any suggestion that the award was cynically designed to placate Unionists. Nevertheless, it was warmly received by Trimble, who said: 'The rest of the world should recognise today that, had it not been for the RUC, Northern Ireland would not now have the prospect of peace and stability within its grasp.' Paisley said the honour was richly deserved but added the best award the RUC could receive was 'the burial of the Patten proposals'. Inside the RUC, where widespread doubts about the sincerity of the award remained, it was greeted with a measure of black humour. A T-shirt was produced with the words 'RUC GC – for gallantry' on the front while the back showed a bloody dagger being plunged between the shoulder blades.

By contrast, in a vastly encouraging sign that, post-Patten, hostile nationalist attitudes to the police were at last softening, Seamus Mallon, the deputy leader of the SDLP, greeted the honour in notably generous and statesmanlike terms:

> The announcement reflects the reality that, whatever differences exist over the role and conduct of the RUC, many members of the RUC and their families have suffered greatly and demonstrated courage over many years. The award of the George Cross should be seen as recognition that the concerns of those who most value the RUC have been acknowledged and appreciated. The Patten report remains, however, a road map for the future of policing and remains in totality the basis to develop a police service that attracts the allegiance of all.

For Flanagan, the award marked 'a momentous day' in the history of the force: 'Today, we remember all who have served in the RUC – not just the regular officers, full and part-time Reserve officers and civilian colleagues of today's RUC – but we reflect particularly upon the great sacrifice of all officers who have given their lives or have been injured down through our history. They and their families are constantly in our thoughts.' By any standards this collective award was richly deserved by the entire RUC, its 13,000 present and 11,500 former members. Over the years, they had earned 368 individual awards for gallantry and 701 for distinguished service. One officer was awarded the George Cross and fifteen George Medals. Like the other parties to the Northern Ireland conflict, the RUC was an equal victim of its troubled history and, whatever the stains on its soul, the imperfections in its reputation or the mistakes that had been made, recompense was paid many-fold by the aggregate efforts of the vast majority of its individual officers doing their honest best for the entire community.

On 19 January 2000, Mandelson announced the government's response to Patten's recommendations in the House of Commons. The report was the way forward, he said, and he would soon be publishing legislation to bring the changes into effect, but already there were clear signs that he was going to tinker with it. Mandelson had already decided that while the name of the force would indeed change, it would become known as the

Police Service of Northern Ireland (PSNI) rather than the Northern Ireland Police Service (NIPS) as Patten had suggested. This was probably a shrewd move, for the police would undoubtedly have become the 'Nips' in popular argot. As one officer put it at the time, 'I'd rather be a PSNI-ite than a Nip.' But Mandelson also foreshadowed two other significant concessions disowning Patten and aimed at expressed Unionist sensitivities. In a bid to subdue opposition to the loss of the RUC crest he said responsibility for the design of a new badge for the police would go to the envisaged nineteen-member Policing Board. He also proposed downgrading the role of the network of proposed district policing partnerships to a largely consultative one. This was important for the Unionists feared the IRA, and indeed Loyalists, who shared an ambition to run their own militias, would use the partnerships to muscle in and take over local policing with 'vigilantes controlled by terrorists', as one Unionist MP said.

The way the SDLP, for so long hostile to the police, would react to implementing Patten was a key factor and the House of Commons debate exposed for the first time the rift between Mallon and Hume, the twin figureheads of the party, in their personal attitudes to the police. Whereas Mallon had been fulsome in responding to the George Cross award in an ambiguous speech, a notably-grudging Hume avoided giving the new policing dispensation the sort of ringing endorsement the government hoped for. Mandelson roundly rebuked him, saying that it was time for the political and religious leaders of the nationalist community to 'stand up and speak up and back the police and call for people from the nationalist community to support them'.

Although it did not have any formal responsibility for policing, the Assembly at Stormont also debated the Patten report on 24 January and voted fifty to forty-two to reject it. The division, along the well-established political and religious fault-line, reflected the emotional importance of the issue to both sides and underlined that many obstacles still lay ahead. Indeed, holding the debate at all demonstrated that the Northern Ireland politicians could not leave policing alone, that they had not learned from past failures and would continue to play with the police like a kitten with a ball of wool.

Meanwhile, having halted any reorganisation to wait for Patten, Flanagan was now moving to get what was going to be a vast programme of work under way. In deference to the Federation's sensitivity about the word 'reform', he designated Assistant Chief Constable Tim Lewis as 'Change Manager' late in 1999 and put him at the head of a new Change

Management Team in police headquarters to drive the task forward. The 175 recommendations were grouped and allocated to a set of 'account-able officers', assistant chief constables and their civilian equivalents, who set up a series of project boards and action teams to carry out specific tasks: style (policing with the community, uniforms, buildings, vehicles), shared values (developing a new culture of accountable, human rights-based policing), skills (training and building the new police college), staff (recruiting, severance and human resource issues), structures (setting up District Command Units and reorganisation) and systems (information technology and financial management). Another board was responsible for communications, marketing and image. Progress was constantly reviewed and reported to the change manager and the chief constable. The task was complicated by uncertainty about the security and political environment ahead. Consequently all planning was predicated on one of three scenarios: a return to conflict, a complete end of conflict or, the one considered most probable, an uneasy peace. There was also a pressing need to maintain morale and a sense of purpose among officers fearful for their jobs and others anxious to know if they would qualify for the generous severance terms anticipated to be on offer to meet the targets on downsizing. It was one of the ironies of the situation that among the most vociferous and cantankerous critics of change and the transition from the RUC to the new police service were those who were intending to cash in by retiring early and playing no part in it.

With the peace process on hold and the Assembly and executive suspended, policing reform was at the very heart of the efforts of the British and Irish governments to breathe new life into the Belfast Agreement during early 2000. Unionists continued to call for the 'proud name' of the RUC and its symbols to be retained, while increasingly doubtful nationalists reserved their position to see if the promises to implement Patten would be fulfilled when Mandelson produced the necessary legislation, the promised publication of which slipped steadily from the promised February date onwards. Meanwhile there was, however, another encouraging sign that Catholic attitudes to the police were evolving in the right direction when the Archbishop of Armagh, Sean Brady, attended a poignant ceremony in a rainswept Hillsborough Castle on 12 April 2000 where the Queen presented the George Cross in front of 1,500 RUC officers, civilian support staff, family members and guests. The officer chosen to receive the medal was wheelchair-bound Constable Paul Slaine, who had had his legs blown off in an IRA bomb attack in

Newry in 1992, in which one of his colleagues, Constable Colleen McMurray, was murdered. He was accompanied by Assistant Chief Constable Bill Stewart, the longest-serving member of the RUC, and Constable Susan Wright, who had just entered training ten days earlier and has the distinction of being the last ever officer to join the RUC.

A month or so later Mandelson's legislation, the Police (Northern Ireland) Bill, was finally launched on its Westminster parliamentary journey on 16 May. In a clear concession to the Unionists, the bill side-stepped designating the new name for the police and confirmed that a final decision about name, badge and insignia would be made later by regulation by the secretary of state. The RUC's future name and badges had now eclipsed IRA disarmament as the major political issue and, as publication of the bill coincided with another push to restore devolution, the fudge was enough to persuade the Ulster Unionist Council on 27 May to back Trimble 495 to 403 and mandate him to return to power. One of the clinching interventions was that of John Taylor, who waved what he said was a confidential letter from Mandelson indicating that the RUC name would be preserved in the 'title deeds' of the new police service. It was a typical piece of political chicanery by both men, which helped carry that vital vote. Although the fudged legislation and the letter had temporarily assuaged the Unionists it fired what would be lasting suspicions on the nationalist side that Mandelson was going to renege on the most crucial aspects of Patten. The scene was therefore set for a series of confrontational and acrimonious exchanges as the Police Bill continued through parliament.

Meanwhile Mandelson's manoeuvres had also raised anxieties among those in Washington opposed to the RUC and committed to Patten. Soon after becoming secretary of state he flew out on a mission of reassurance and a few months later, in an act of overt obeisance to this watchful lobby, he appointed Tom Constantine, a close New York acquaintance of Congressman Ben Gilman, as Oversight Commissioner, whose job it would be to monitor and report on the efficiency and faithfulness with which the Patten reforms were being implemented. Constantine, formerly chief of the New York State Police, had recently retired as head of the US Drug Enforcement Administration. It was intended that he would visit Northern Ireland for a two-week period every four months and conduct progress review meetings with Northern Ireland Office ministers, the chief constable, the new Policing Board and other interested groups. Afterwards he would produce formal reports highlighting progress and commenting on any delays or failures in driving ahead the reform programme. Soon afterwards the government published its promised Patten implementation plan, outlining in detail the programme of work, who would take it forward, the timescale for doing so and the key 'milestones' for measuring progress.

While Seamus Mallon, a shrewd, old-fashioned nationalist, had been outstandingly constructive in signalling a new attitude to the police, he had become more and more alarmed by Mandelson's departures from the Patten road map. Having fully digested the inadequacies 'right through' Mandelson's proposals, Mallon launched a bombardment against him in the House of Commons on 6 June, accusing him of emasculating, diminishing and reducing the report. Patten was 'the first person in the history of the Northern Ireland state who laid down the foundations with which we may solve policing'. The Patten report did not contain everything the SDLP had wanted, he went on, but it was a blueprint for policing with which everyone could identify and for which everyone could assume responsibility, so the SDLP had indicated it would put people on the Policing Board and encourage young people to join the police – but only on the basis of the full and faithful implementation of the report. Leaving the door open for the bill to be amended, he added, 'Get this bill right and we will do that.' All three SDLP MPs, Hume, Mallon and Eddie McGrady, then voted, helping to approve the second reading of the Police (Northern Ireland) Bill by 329 votes to fourteen.

The goodwill did not last. As the bill moved forward, over the next few months Mandelson continued his efforts to trim and reshape many aspects of the legislation to make them more congenial for the Unionists. Mallon led the nationalist campaign to ensure it remained true to 'the spirit and the detail of Patten'. By mid-July, despite what he described as continued 'political chicanery', Mallon's dogged persistence was rewarded when Mandelson and the Unionists failed in a bid to include the formula 'the Police Service of Northern Ireland incorporating the Royal Ulster Constabulary' in the legislation. This was what Taylor had meant when he claimed the old name would be preserved in the 'title deeds' of the new service. From that point the RUC name was effectively consigned to history. But the parliamentary battle was not yet complete and, in preparation for the final rounds, Mallon vented his deep reservations during a speech in Washington in September. Accusing the British government of taking a 'minimalist approach' to Patten, he said that 'after long and bitter debate' some changes had been reversed and these were welcome. 'But the Bill still does not measure up to Patten.

Serious faults remain; faults that strike at the heart of Patten's proposals; faults that the British government must put right.' In a pointed dig at Mandelson and Trimble, he said the full implementation of the Patten report was more important than the political survival of any individual: 'Patten should not be sacrificed to keep any political party on-side.'

Elsewhere in the US that month, Mallon's stance was considerably reinforced. With Clinton coming to the end of his second term and the election to choose a replacement looming, influential Irish-American interests prevailed on both candidates to give undertakings that, if elected, they would take an interest in Northern Ireland and maintain support for the peace process. Writing as Governor of Texas from Austin on 8 September, the Republican candidate, George W Bush, assured Ahern of his 'personal interest and full commitment to helping move the peace process forward', if necessary, by appointing a special envoy. Bush specifically referred to 'the work of Chris Patten and his Commission in reviewing and recommending reforms of the police authorities in Northern Ireland. I appreciate the importance of tradition and symbols, and the sensitivities of the communities in Northern Ireland on this issue, and support the full implementation of the Commission's recommend-ations.' At the end of September, the outgoing Democratic vice-president, Al Gore, also issued a statement identifying himself with the Clinton administration's role in bolstering the peace process and urging the British government to 'fully and expeditiously implement' the Patten recommendations. There was also a resolution in similar terms tabled in the House of Representatives that month.

Back in London, the bill finally became law in November 2000. During its passage, Mallon had tabled 150 amendments and secured about 100 changes, mainly while the bill was being dissected word by word at the committee stage of the legislative process. Mandelson's pro-Unionist tactics only served to make a demanding journey more gruelling for the Unionists. He had failed to make the fraught and emotional process of overdue and necessary police reform any more palatable for them and only increased their resentment when he failed. At the same time he had forfeited the goodwill and much of the trust of the nationalists and, above all, of an already sceptical Sinn Fein, a development which would have longer-term consequences for the entire peace process. All of this also crucially handicapped efforts to get the new beginning for policing off to a good start. Striking a balance on such a fundamental issue was never going to be easy but, in departing so far from Patten, Mandelson got it completely wrong. Unionists had been saved from having to face up to the full implications of fundamental police reform by the onset of violence in the early 1970s, and though the need for it remained and intensified over the years of conflict, and became inevitable once the 1994 ceasefires were declared and the issue sprang to the top of the political agenda, there was no willingness to reach even a sensible accommodation. Unionists arrogantly assumed ownership of the police and refused to concede the necessity of change. The Patten report, therefore, became the forum to decide fundamental reform and his subsequent, considered, comprehensive report, taking into account all views and ideas that had been submitted, became the template. Mandelson should have seen that and reinforced, not meddled, with it. As Patten himself put it in a newspaper article on 28 November, as the heavily amended bill became law:

> The whole point about the report is that it is not political. It is the work of an independent and international group of people from very different backgrounds, entrusted with a task by the politicians who agreed to the Good Friday agreement precisely because the issue of policing could not be solved by politicians.
>
> [. . .] we said emphatically that we regarded it as impossible to build a bridge between the diametrically opposed political views on policing, that we had therefore rejected that as an approach and instead developed and tested our proposals entirely against policing benchmarks, not political ones. Those benchmarks were effectiveness, efficiency, impartiality, accountability, representativeness and respect for human rights. Get those right and you depoliticise policing in Northern Ireland. Argue about the politics of policing and you remain stuck forever. The 'spirit of Patten' is that everyone should put the politics of policing behind them and get on with building the new beginning for depoliticised policing.

Mandelson, who conducted a flamboyant social life, was not around to oversee the final transition of the RUC to the PSNI. In January 2001, he was forced to resign from the government after allegations that he had abused his ministerial position to sway British passport applications for two Indian-based businessmen, the second personal misconduct scandal to engulf his short ministerial career. Dr John Reid, an affable but tough Scot, replaced him.

Although the police legislation had been formally entered on the statute books in November and Mallon had achieved much of what the SDLP wanted, there were other detailed issues on which the party needed advance assurances before they would make their nominations to the Policing Board and fully activate the new dispensation. Much of the detail was already covered in the published implementation plan but such was the distrust Mandelson had generated, Mallon would not proceed without real guarantees. It would be several more months before he was satisfied but a good part of the delay, it must be said, was the SDLP's own fault. Because of their historic estrangement from the policing process, there was nobody in the party who was familiar with it. Indeed, one of the senior party figures, who regularly commented on policing matters, did not even know the rank structure. What the party needed, and the RUC willingly gave them, was a series of tutorials which demonstrated that many of their concerns were both spurious and unfounded because they were based on lack of basic knowledge. In other cases some criticisms were tempered when they learned the reasons governing one policy position or another.

While transition day could not be finally scheduled because of the political delays, the change programme was pushed ahead and visible traces of the RUC were already beginning to fade. The 500 replacement vehicles which joined the 2,700-strong fleet every year were now going on the road without the customary 'harp and crown' crest. As an interim measure, they were signed instead with the word 'Police'. In February 2001, a campaign to attract the first recruits for the coming Police Service of Northern Ireland was launched. A slick advertising campaign, costing £328,154 and using the slogan 'Towards a true reflection of the whole community', was launched. It prominently featured a young Chinese woman as a subliminal reminder that there were more people than just Catholics and Protestants in Northern Ireland and that the police belonged to everybody. The response was excellent. Over 20,000 requests for information packs were made, resulting in 7,843 applications to join. Among them were 2,745 candidates from Catholic backgrounds, a record response from the minority community. The most recent competition for RUC recruits in 1998 had only attracted twenty-two per cent of Catholic applicants. On behalf of Sinn Fein, Gerry Adams sneered there were no Republicans or nationalists among them: 'Catholics of "a certain kind" had always been members of the RUC.' But a postcode analysis of their addresses showed that young men and women living in all parts of Northern Ireland, including so-called Republican areas, wanted to become police officers. In fact, 7,208 applicants came from Northern Ireland, 332 from the Irish Republic, 262 from Great Britain and forty-one from elsewhere.

Not all would be suitable, however, and the applicants next faced a demanding assessment process to select those who had the personal qualities and skills to do the job. All who survived were then listed on merit. At that point the top scorers were offered posts in the police service and called forward for training on a quota system requiring equal numbers of Catholics and non-Catholics. This controversial affirmative-action measure was designed by Patten to reverse as rapidly as possible the lack of Catholics in the service. It was widely attacked as being discriminatory against Protestants, and so it was, but the gain to be made in terms of having a police service more closely representative of the sixty–forty Protestant–Catholic make-up of the community than ever before in Northern Ireland's troubled history is incalculable. In the first competition the qualified pool numbered 553, 154 of them Catholics. One young Protestant man was rejected purely on the fifty-fifty headcount, though he had scored higher than ten of the Catholics offered jobs. He challenged the formula in court and lost. The judge decided that as the need to correct the imbalance in the police force had been endorsed by the electorate and parliament, other initiatives had failed in the past and no alternative method to redress the imbalance could be suggested by the applicant, his case should fall. It was calculated by Patten that over ten years, this formula would increase the numbers of Catholic police from under eight per cent to 28.9 per cent of the strength. (By early 2003, the proportion of Catholics had already reached thirteen per cent and, with steadily increasing numbers of Catholic applicants, was set to climb even higher and reach the Patten target on time.)

But as many young people were competing to join the police, many long-serving officers were seeking to retire early, attracted by a £220,000,000 fund promising generous severance terms. The first wave of departures took place between January and March 2001, when 483 officers left. 'It was like an extended Christmas party. There was just one going-away do after another,' said one reveller. Sales at the RUC Museum soared as plaques and other artefacts were snapped up as mementoes and few officers left without a clutch of crystal glasses from which to sip nightcaps at the end of the long leisurely days ahead. (By March 2002 another 750 had departed and in the year after that a further 684 stepped down.)

The next stage of the transition took place on 1 April when the new District Command Units (DCUs) came into being. Planning had begun back in January when Flanagan chaired an all-day Sunday meeting of the designate commanders to outline the scope of the change. Out went the twelve Divisions and that thirty-nine subsidiary Sub-Divisions, and in came a new set of twenty-nine DCUs. Because of its size and population concentration, the Belfast City Council area was divided into four DCUs: north, south, east and west. DCUs in the rest of Northern Ireland had their boundaries drawn to match those of the corresponding district councils. This provided a practical framework for the district commander, the pivotal figure in the new-style policing, to forge and build the essential police–community partnerships with elected councillors and a range of community representatives and organisations in each council area through the corresponding District Policing Partnerships, also conceived by Patten. In due course, each DCU commander would be given local autonomy to deploy his or her personnel, set local priorities and allocate his or her budget to meet the specific needs of the locality.

Chief Superintendent Stephen Grange was one of the officers at the cutting edge of the change process. As District Commander for South Belfast, he steered the transformation of the RUC into the PSNI in an urban area which includes the city centre, the notorious Loyalist strong-holds of the Village and Sandy Row, the Lower Ormeau Republican flashpoint, the University bedsitter-land and the affluent leafy suburbs which stretch from the Upper Ormeau across the Lagan to Stranmillis and Malone. The 113,000 resident population is not only made up of Protestants and Catholics but includes the highest concentration of Chinese and Indian residents anywhere in Northern Ireland. There are also thousands of shoppers and workers who commute in and out of the city every day and the similar number who invade it at night, especially at the weekend.

The change for which Grange would be responsible was more than just nominal, for the new beginning envisaged a very different style of policing with respect for human rights and close-contact community policing as its core values. When the situation permitted, the new police service would also be routinely unarmed. Grange divided his territory into five sectors, each under the command of an inspector, with a total of eighty-five officers at their disposal, twice the number committed to similar neighbourhood policing in the past. With only about a fifth of the 4,000 calls they got every month being genuine emergencies, the old routine of switching on the blue light and siren in a vehicle and rushing to respond came to an end. Instead, the police began screening every call to single out the pressing emergencies and switched the emphasis from what was called 'demand-led policing' to problem-solving policing on the ground, working to computer-generated crime-pattern analysis plans to identify the causes of and opportunities for crime and recommend ways to beat them. The innovation started paying off quickly. An auto-crime 'hot-spot' centred on a cinema in the University area was cooled by making announcements about the risk of car thieves in the cinema and distributing leaflets reminding patrons to lock their vehicles and not leave valuables in them. After a spate of house burglaries through the rear alley of a terraced street, every dwelling was visited and the residents were encouraged to make their doors and windows more secure. Police also advised a public house to install security lighting at the rear of the premises after parked cars were taken away and a large quantity of drink stolen from a store.

A major feature of this problem-solving policing was building partnerships with the community and other agencies serving their needs. 'In some circumstances, such as a domestic violence case, there might be a need for social workers, the housing executive and others to be involved as well as the police and we are doing that,' said Grange. For years the city-centre police had had to deal with hundreds of drunken young people emerging from pubs and discos in the early hours of Saturday and Sunday, causing fights, disorder and other problems. So, in a major initiative with the owners of the premises and the city council, who licensed them for entertainment, the level of nuisance was significantly curbed. Street traders selling hot food were subjected to strict controls, taxis were warned to stop hooting their horns and provided with extended ranks to get people away quickly and door staff were told to check departing patrons to prevent them taking bottles of alcohol out to the street on their way home. 'This is the template for the future,' Grange said. 'The police are only one leg of this. We are all sitting like columns, the police, councils, schools, community and voluntary groups, business organisations. We all need to have an integrated, multi-agency approach, then we can get something done.' Despite the encouraging start, he was not complacent about the huge task ahead or the difficulties.

> We have a massive training need within the police to show the new way of delivering our service. We must manage people's expectations of what we can do for them because large numbers of police will not be available. Everybody else must be signed up to their responsibilities. Effective crime prevention and problem-solving policing takes time. We are in a period of transition and there needs to be patience.

In a bid to create contact points for this relationship to flourish, there were a number of other innovations. A newly built station at Moira,

County Down, replacing one devastated by a terrorist car bomb, and a renovation at Greyabbey in the same county unveiled a new look with smart black and gold railings instead of sentry posts or grim fortifications surrounding the buildings. Elsewhere, in a bid to present a more friendly face, sentry posts were left unoccupied, stations' gates were opened in daylight hours and plans were made to open up the front halls with potted plants and civilian receptionists rather than police officers and bullet-proof grilles facing visitors. Police also began to hold 'surgeries' in community and shopping centres away from their stations, and in some areas it became commonplace to see uniformed officers riding on local buses to and from their beats.

The new thinking that was now stimulating the radical reform of policing in Northern Ireland was evident during a ground-breaking two-day international conference examining the fashionable theme of 'Human Rights and Policing' at the Waterfront Hall in Belfast in October 2001. Assistant Chief Constable Sam Kinkaid, a forthright former detective with a law degree who had helped investigate some of the worst atrocities of the Troubles, was responsible for ensuring that, in line with Patten, the 'human rights-based approach to policing' became a reality. He organised the conference to expose both the police and key members of the Northern Ireland criminal justice fraternity to the latest thinking on the topic, inviting experts from Britain and Europe to address them. In his own contribution, using the policing of parades as an example, he said there was the possibility of infringing at least ten of the articles of the European Convention on Human Rights. 'No other profession working within the criminal justice system has the potential to infringe human rights as much as we can,' he said. 'Equally, no other profession has the capacity to protect human rights in a democracy as much as police officers. That is why police services are, quite properly, turning into human rights champions.' Over the next year, through an 'action plan' including a specially designed two-day 'course for all', this message was directly imparted to every police officer and member of the civilian support staff. For Kinkaid, Grange and his twenty-eight district commander colleagues, this change programme was a unique and formidable assignment, made all the more difficult and uncertain by the protracted political wrangling over the future of policing which caused constant slippage in the timing of the steps and the consequent uncertainty about the safety of officers. 'It was always a difficult call between taking a risk to break new ground or playing safe and not exposing our officers to danger,' said Grange.

However, by the summer of 2001 the arguments had finally materialised into a working agreement and a surge of progress took place after the two governments and the pro-Agreement parties conducted six days of crisis negotiations to revitalise the Belfast Agreement at Weston Park, a former stately home in Staffordshire. The major breakthrough on the policing controversies was given strong impetus when Dr Maurice Hayes, a Catholic who was an influential member of the Patten commission, said that despite the police bill being a bad bill by definition, because it had required some 150 amendments, it had now been satisfactorily enacted. He added that if the core Patten objective of acceptable policing, responsible to the community, was to be achieved then many more young Catholics and nationalists must join in numbers and be encouraged and enabled to do so by community and church leaders.

With political consensus and a sturdy bridgehead of the physical and philosophical components of the new beginning for policing now firmly in place, the scene was at last set for the highly symbolic step by which the RUC would become the Police Service of Northern Ireland. So, after publication of a revised Patten implementation plan on 17 August, which contained the specific undertakings that Mallon and his SDLP colleagues had been looking for over the previous ten months or so, Reid set a deadline of noon on Tuesday 21 August for the political parties to sign up to the new policing arrangements.

The first response came from the Catholic bishops. In a truly historic joint statement, carefully balanced to support SDLP affiliates in their flocks without totally alienating those sympathetic to Sinn Fein, they said they shared some of the reservations expressed about the new arrangements but believed 'sufficient grounds now exist to give real hope for a new beginning in policing. We believe the time is now right for all those who sincerely want a police service that is fair, impartial and representative to grasp the opportunity that is presented and to exercise their influence to achieve such a service.' The statement welcomed the emphasis on human rights and said young Catholics must feel 'totally free to choose' whether or not to participate in the new service. In other words, they were telling militant Republicans, still strongly opposed to the police despite Patten, not to threaten or attack them.

Later in the day after a meeting of its Assembly representatives, the SDLP took an equally historic step when it decided to nominate representatives to the new Policing Board and encourage young nationalists to join the new police service. The SDLP said it had identified ninety-four important gains since the Police Bill was published in May 2000.

In view of these changes, we believe that the time is now right for us to play our part in delivering policing change. We believe that this will benefit not only the nationalist community – but all in the community. For it is only through a police service that is accepted by all that we can enjoy true security and peace of mind.

The SDLP justified its change of heart in a lengthy statement, outlining the background:

Ever since 1920, policing has been at the very heart of the political fault-line in our society. No issue has been more difficult, more divisive and more controversial in the history of the north of Ireland. The Good Friday Agreement offered us the chance to break with this bitter legacy of the past. It promised 'a new beginning in policing in Northern Ireland with a police service capable of sustaining support from the community as a whole.' The SDLP has always been determined to realise this new beginning to policing, and to play our part in its creation. We made detailed submissions to the Patten Commission. When its report was published, we welcomed it – recognising in it many of the recommendations for policing change that we had advocated.

The statement went on to recall the party's disappointment at the Police Bill and outline their extensive campaigning to bring about radical policing change despite Mandelson's activities. It concluded with the recommendation that what is now on offer can 'comprehensively deliver the spirit and substance of the Patten report'. In so doing it was over-turning one of the most dogmatic principles of party policy, defended stoutly ever since it was founded in 1970. It was a truly historic turning point. The word 'historic' had become somewhat overworked since the breakthrough ceasefires in 1994, but there was no more appropriate appellation for the situation where, for the first time in the history of the Northern Ireland state, the Catholic Church and the main nationalist party had approved the policing arrangements and intended to fully participate in them. Given the trials of the past, the importance of such a break-through should not be underestimated. But one important leg of the tripod was not yet in position. Sinn Fein chairman Mitchell McLaughlin said the latest policing proposals were only 'half a loaf' and that they would continue campaigning to reverse what they said were remaining departures from Patten. The breakthrough was however applauded at the

White House in Washington, where the official spokesman for the new President Bush said agreement on policing was, 'an essential element of lasting peace. We urge other parties to follow suit.'

Sinn Fein would have been entitled to two of the ten political seats on the new Policing Board, so in their absence, one each was awarded to the Trimble and Paisley Unionist parties. (The proportional allocation was by the d'Hondt process, reflecting the elected party strengths in the Assembly.) This stimulated another bout of inter-party quibbling about who would chair the board. Trimble and Paisley wanted the newly ennobled Lord Kilclooney, the former MP John Taylor, as chairman with an SDLP deputy. To take account of the fact that two additional Unionists had seats on the Board, the SDLP demanded that the chair should be awarded to Tom Kelly, a public relations consultant who, remarkably, was appointed as an independent member despite the fact that he was a party activist and former election agent for Seamus Mallon. (Similarly, the appointment of Viscount Brookeborough, grandson of the former prime minister and a declared Unionist when in the House of Lords, as another independent weighted the political membership of the board.) Reid brought the matter to a conclusion by insisting that two of the board's nine independent members be appointed. Doctor Desmond Rea, Emeritus Professor of Human Resource Management at the University of Ulster, got the £45,000 post of chairman. The £35,000 vice-chairman appointment went to Denis Bradley, a former priest who was for many years the secret mediator feeding the channel between the British government and the IRA, which played such an important backroom role in developing the peace process.

While all this had been going on, the RUC was making preparations for its change of name, now set for midnight on 4 November. It was also decided the first batch of trainee constables would report to Garnerville the next day to commence what had been rebranded 'foundation training'. Flanagan wanted the transition day to be 1 June 2002, the eightieth birthday of the RUC, which would give plenty of time for the new badge and insignia to be prepared, redesigned uniforms procured and replacement signs, stationery and other items to be in place for a clean switch from old to new, but the politicians overruled him. Instead the whole transition process had become 'a bit of a dog's breakfast', in the words of one senior police officer. The delay in getting the board into operation meant that many vital decisions could not be taken, not least those concerning the most difficult and emotive issues of badges, uniforms and flags. At one point it was feared the trainees might have to spend their six months in tracksuits until a new uniform was agreed and that serving officers would have to cut the RUC insignia from their uniforms until the issue was decided by the board. In the end it was agreed that the name would change that night and other elements of the transition would take place progressively afterwards. In the meantime officers would continue to wear their existing clothing and insignia and the trainees would be kitted out in plain police uniform without any RUC emblems. Bigotry about the issue had now become so rampant that some Unionists caused a fuss when they heard the baseball-style caps for the trainees had the word 'Police' embossed on them in gold. Green trousers, white shirts and gold caps equalled the colours of the Irish Republic in their minds.

The week running up to the name change was both a busy and an emotional one. Printing presses at the Lisnasharragh complex were busy churning out thousands of copies of forms headed with the new name but no crest. Nearby they were being loaded into vans for delivery to the 200 or so premises that comprised the police estate. Business cards were also being replaced for senior officers. In the press office at headquarters, the webmaster was redesigning the site to go live at the push of a button at midnight on Saturday. There were, of course, the inevitable 'do's' to mark the passing. During the last Friday afternoon, in many offices and stations, the old force was celebrated and the new service toasted in a heady cocktail of sorrow and anger. A directive about the transition suggested that from now on they should use the word 'service' rather than 'force'.

For the men and women on duty that emotional Saturday night it was very much business as usual. William Britton had said of the 1922 transition, 'You were one day an RIC man and the next day you were an RUC man. You carried on just the same as if nothing had happened.' So it was seventy-nine years later. At midnight, a message of re-assurance and goodwill from Flanagan was read over the police radio channels by the duty officer and a letter from Tony Blair marking the passing of the RUC was published: 'The bravery, dignity and resolve which police officers, their civilian colleagues and their families have displayed in the darkest of times are qualities which I firmly believe will endure into the Police Service of Northern Ireland.'

For many officers, past and present, it was an emotional moment. Chief Inspector Tom Haylett, who was running the South Belfast DCU, said: 'I would sense that the officers, like myself, feel that tonight's a very difficult night. A lot of us have spent the greater parts of our working lives in this organisation, serving the Royal Ulster Constabulary, so the change is a big change for us but we're a professional policing organisation, we're here to serve the community and the community is what we'll serve.' Next morning, Flanagan was up and about early for what was to be another busy day. His first stop was Broadcasting House in Belfast where he was interviewed for a series of radio and television programmes. He was upbeat about the challenges ahead:

Last night at midnight I quite deliberately was at my desk and then went out to meet some of our colleagues. I reminded them that at the stroke of midnight they didn't become different men and women. Their determination to give the people of Northern Ireland, all the people, the very best policing service they can has not diminished. Their ability to do that has not diminished. Yes, it is a poignant day but it is now time to look forward. It is a very exciting day. It marks the dawn of a new era in policing and I am desperately proud to be the Chief Constable of the Police Service of Northern Ireland.

Jimmy Spratt, the chairman of the Police Federation, who was also there, was far less ebullient:

I have to say there's a lot of hurt. People are feeling hurt at the name change but we move on. The Police Service of Northern Ireland is now in existence. The people who were doing their job yesterday as members of the Royal Ulster Constabulary are today the Police Service of Northern Ireland but I think that morale is at an all-time low and management need to pick up the fact and support the officers who will continue to do their job as professionals out there at the coal face tomorrow, next week and the following week.

As they were speaking, teams of workmen were going from station to station in Belfast and elsewhere replacing the RUC crests and signs with simple plates bearing the new name. The old ones, highly prized by collectors, were taken to the police stores at Seapark for safekeeping. Some more elaborate RUC signage, such as etched glass doors at Castlereagh and carved stone impressions there and at other locations, were only saved from the sledge-hammer by Assistant Chief Constable Alan McQuillan, the chairman of the RUC Historical Society, who intervened to have them preserved for future display in the planned RUC museum and a £650,000 memorial garden to be created at police headquarters. He spent the morning in his office at Castlereagh taking down many of the plaques and pictures displayed on his wall in line with long-overdue compliance with the legal obligation for all employers to create a 'neutral working environment'. As we have seen, the RUC had been dilatory in doing so, but it had recently decided that, in the climate of change, the point of transition would be the best opportunity to face up to the difficulties involved. As with the name change itself, there was, of course, much mischievous and misleading propaganda misrepresenting the new regime as one of 'clean walls'. Most of the controversy centred on a poster 'Our murdered colleagues' which contained the names and thumbnail-sized pictures of the 302 murdered RUC officers. In response to rumours that it was to be banned entirely under the new regime, the office distributing it was swamped with orders and multiple copies of it were soon defiantly displayed in the corridors, offices and rooms of every police station.

There was no intention of prohibiting RUC memorabilia, least of all something as sensitive as the poster. Indeed Patten had unambiguously stated that RUC memorials should remain. What the 'neutral working environment' legislation required was the removal of items which would offend people on religious, political, sexual or gender grounds. Thus provocative pin-ups, political or royal portraits and flags or representations of them were banned. The philosophy was that in divided Northern Ireland, rather than have two sets of symbols, each one anathema to adherents of the other tradition, it was more practical to have none. Although the legislation did not specifically prohibit items associated with the British Army, Flanagan and his officers decided it was also timely to bring down the large proliferation of military memorabilia and artefacts displayed on RUC premises and preserve them for eventual display in the RUC museum. So McQuillan took down a plaque commemorating his time in embattled Crossmaglen with the Army and several similar items, including some of his collection of political cartoons:

> These are a part of me, a part of my history, a part of this organisation's history but the time has come to move on, to look to the future. This place has had a long and troubled history for thirty years. If creating a neutral working environment, to make sure that anyone who comes in feels comfortable and feels this is a neutral organisation that is prepared to represent and respect the rights and interests of both sections of the community, is part of the process of putting that behind us then it is a small price for a much greater gain. For a section of the

community the reality is that they feel, or some of them feel, that they object to the RUC crest because of the past history of this organisation. I don't think that's really fair but as a senior officer I've got to take the lead in this and we have got to move forward and got to move on.

While he was doing that, Flanagan had moved from the BBC to Garnerville to greet the first intake of forty-eight new recruits and meet them over coffee. They were the first of a sequence of similar-sized intakes, half of them Catholic and half non-Catholic, who would join the service at five-week intervals over the coming years and commence their forty-week initial training. This group were aged from eighteen to thirty-six and included fourteen women. Before their arrival that morning, Garnerville had been stripped of all signs of the RUC. In deference to what was seen as this strict political correctness, the establishment had already been renamed 'PC World'. Unlike their predecessors in the RUC, and in line with Patten, the PSNI trainees would not be sworn in as constables until the end of their first twenty weeks' training at Garnerville, when they would not 'pass out' but 'graduate' with a Certificate in Police Studies from the University of Ulster. After that they would be attested as police officers, undergo eight weeks of combined operational training (including driving and firearms courses) and, finally, twelve weeks with a tutor constable before going to their first proper posting somewhere in Northern Ireland.

Next morning, Monday, Flanagan was again at work early. His first engagement was to chair the weekly chief constable's policy meeting, where all his senior officers and officials gathered to review the last week's events, preview the week ahead and take whatever decisions were necessary. Flanagan marked the historic transition only briefly:

Good morning, everybody. Obviously the weekend was a very poignant time and a very important time. Truly, a landmark in the history of policing in Northern Ireland and I know it involved a lot of pain for all our members but it is now time to put that pain behind us. It is now time to embrace the future, so, can I thank you all for all that you've done and can I welcome you to our first policy meeting as the Police Service of Northern Ireland. I know that we'll all work together for the benefit of all the people just as we have always done in the past as the Royal Ulster Constabulary. So, without further ado, we will go straight into the content of our meeting. Frank, can I ask you to brief us on recent developments, please.

The first report was from the Drugs Squad commander, who recounted that during the last week they had made the biggest ever seizure of cocaine. 'It was very pleasing, Sir, but, quite obviously, very hard to keep that up every week.' The new beginning had begun.

With the Policing Board now having been appointed and having assumed its powers, attention now focused on its inaugural meeting on 7 November, where the first priority was to settle the designs uniforms and badges. The target date was already set – 5 April, the day the first trainees were scheduled to graduate – but the omens for rapid progress were not encouraging. Both the Ulster Unionists and Democratic Unionists were still opposed to the recommendation that the traditional 'harp and crown' insignia should be replaced. Some Ulster Unionists said that if it had to go, then the crown should be incorporated into the badge, as with every other British constabulary, to signify that Northern Ireland remained firmly within the United Kingdom. At a cost of £41,329.45, the Northern Ireland Office had already commissioned seven potential emblems from a number of locally based graphic designers for the board to consider. The suggestions included neutral emblems based on the unique hexagonal columns at the Giant's Causeway in County Antrim and the flax flower, the neutral symbol adopted by the Northern Ireland Assembly. With echoes of the identical controversy that had surrounded the insignia issue after the RIC–RUC transition some eighty years earlier, the board met on 21 November to consider the designs and decided to remit them to a sub-committee. Meanwhile the *Belfast Telegraph* and *Derry Journal* launched competitions inviting their readers to come up with designs for a badge. The large response to both indicated the great interest in the topic and there was much amusement when the £200 prize on offer from the *Telegraph* was won by a former police officer who had left the RUC six months earlier.

With all the public and political squabbling few expected the board would pass its first major test, but it did and triumphantly. On 12 December it announced a design had been agreed unanimously by the members. Pauline McCabe, who chaired the sub-group, said: 'The emblem, as now agreed by the Board, explores the notion of inclusiveness and parity through the simple stylistic representation of a variety of symbols that reflect diversity, hope and the desire to mutually respect and protect difference through policing.' The sunburst surrounding the roundel represented a new beginning or new dawn for the new police service. The shape was echoed in the central star that provided six areas – one for each county of Northern Ireland – between its rays for a series of equally prominent symbols: the scales of justice, a harp, a torch, an olive branch, a shamrock and a crown. The centre housed the Cross of Saint Patrick, placing all six symbols in the context of Northern Ireland. 'The simple rendering of these symbols in a neutral format of things that both unite and divide reflects an inclusive society where all our values, common interests and differences are recognised, celebrated and protected,' McCabe said. (It must be recorded that the agreed design closely resembled and incorporated elements from some of the entries in the *Telegraph* competition.)

The board passed its recommendation to the secretary of state, who had the final decision under the terms of the Police (Northern Ireland) Act 2000. Although the design was cluttered and provincial and clearly defied the Patten yardstick that it should be free from association with either the British or Irish states, Reid approved it. He reckoned that the unanimity of the board was the telling factor and he wanted to encourage them to approach and settle the other policing problems they would face in the same pragmatic and constructive way.

While the badge controversy was being settled there had been another highly positive breakthrough which further transformed the policing landscape. The Patten commission had said it was high time the Gaelic Athletic Association dropped its Rule 21, which prohibited members of the security forces from playing Gaelic games and members of the Association from serving in the Crown forces. The prohibition dated back to darker days in Irish history but although the issue had been put to a vote several times, the membership always decided to retain the ban until such times as there was acceptable police reform. With the SDLP and the Catholic Church having supported Patten, the GAA put the issue to a vote again at a special Congress in Dublin on 21 November. Despite strenuous Sinn Fein efforts to influence them, the members voted to abolish the rule but five of the six northern counties, with the exception of Down, still voted to retain it. The decision was widely praised and would enable many more young Catholics to consider a police career. For his part, Chief Superintendent Brian McCargo, who had been a GAA player until he was excluded after joining the RUC, set about forming a PSNI Gaelic football team and issued a challenge to the Garda to play them in their first match. (The landmark encounter eventually took place in Dublin on 30 October 2002, when the Garda convincingly beat the PSNI by twenty-one points to fourteen.)

All these developments had been hailed in Washington, both by the White House and the RUC's critics on Capitol Hill, where the process of police reform was still being closely monitored. As a result, on 7 December, now that the policing deadlock had been broken, President Bush approved documents of certification lifting the congressional restrictions on federal law enforcement training for the RUC. Immediately afterwards, the Department of State sponsored an information tour to the United States for eleven members of the new policing board and a cadre of senior PSNI officers to give them 'first-hand exposure to American experiences with community policing, accountability, and management techniques'. The real agenda was to enable them to get to know each other and ignite what their hosts hoped would be constructive working relationships.

When Tom Constantine, the Oversight Commissioner, returned to Belfast in December 2001for his third visit, his progress report praised the 'excellent start' that had been made on implementing 'the largest and most complex [change programme] undertaken by a law enforcement agency', which, he forecast, would take seven to ten years to complete. He praised Chief Constable Sir Ronnie Flanagan and the change management team for being 'totally open and co-operative. There was no resistance. They laid bare the whole agency for us to look at.' But he highlighted a lack of documentary evidence of policies and plans being provided by some parts of the service to help them assess progress. He singled out training and the Special Branch for not providing documentary evidence of progress on the grounds that documents were not made available or not finalised. Such criticism on this and future visits proved to be an important factor in driving the programme forward, sometimes in the teeth of internal resistance or inefficiency.

Having completed five years as chief constable and managed the emotional and challenging transition, Flanagan had decided in September that he would give up the job and leave it to his successor to drive through the details of change. It had been a gruelling tenure. Time and time again since Patten it had fallen to him to soothe and placate police widows and restive officers, angry and resentful at the demise of their beloved RUC. There was also the relentless burden of the farewell speeches he was called to make for lifelong colleagues as the Patten exodus gathered speed. It was a measure of Flanagan's personal strengths that he steered the organisation intact through such an emotional storm. Few others could have succeeded. For his future, he had several options open. He could simply put his feet up and spend more time watching rugby. There had been several offers of high-powered consultancy jobs or lecture tours in the aftermath of the '9/11' terrorist attacks on the World Trade Center in New York, reflecting Flanagan's and the RUC's international reputation in the field. Or, it had been hinted, Blair, who thought highly of him, wanted to benefit from his expertise by appointing him as one of Her Majesty's Inspectors of Constabulary. In October, Flanagan told the board of his intention to resign and left the date open so that they could consider the succession and get a replacement. At that point he had every reason to bask in the glow of all that had been achieved and glide out of his tough job with praise ringing in his ears. There had already been expansive tributes when his resignation had been announced. As ever in Northern Ireland, though, at the end of ladder there turned out to be a snake.

Earlier in the summer, a former police informer known as Kevin Fulton had virtually convinced a British Sunday newspaper that if his advance warning to the RUC had been properly followed up, the horrific Omagh bombing in August 1998 could have been prevented. Twenty-eight people and two unborn twins had died and almost 400 others had been injured when a 300-lb car-borne bomb exploded amidst conflicting telephone warnings about where it had been placed by breakaway IRA terrorists. However, before printing the story and handing over a promised £50,000, the newspaper insisted on one final check. Contact was made with recently retired Chief Superintendent Eric Anderson to check the veracity of the story. The former RUC detective, who had been despatched to the town by Flanagan to lead the investigation into the bombing immediately after the incident and had broken down in tears at a subsequent news conference when describing the carnage, unequivocally dismissed Fulton's claims as untrue. The paper promptly spiked the story, the agent was denied his bounty and a course of events was triggered off that would call into public question the credibility of Flanagan and the Police Ombudsman, Nuala O'Loan, and would shake the fragile edifices of the new beginning for policing in Northern Ireland to their very foundations.

A short time after the collapse of the deal, Fulton went to another national newspaper and in July 2001 its Irish edition carried a front-page story, based on his claim, despite the fact that some three months earlier the same journalist, in the same paper, had described Fulton as a 'notorious double dealer behind a string of dubious hoaxes'. This newspaper report was noted by O'Loan, who decided to use her considerable powers to launch an investigation into Fulton's claim and the RUC's activities before and after the Omagh attack. Her highly critical report, published in December 2001, accused the RUC of a 'failure of leadership, poor judgement and a lack of urgency' for not acting on what she said were vital pieces of intelligence before and after the bombing. The findings prompted a widespread outcry, especially from the relatives of the Omagh victims, and caused Flanagan to remark that he would publicly commit suicide if the report was ultimately proved to be both fair and rigorous. (The unfortunate suicide remark was quickly withdrawn.)

In February, after weeks of round-the-clock work by a hand-picked team of ten officers, Flanagan published a detailed rebuttal. Its most striking feature was the unprecedented way it lifted the veil on the invisible front line of the secret intelligence war in Northern Ireland in order comprehensively to discredit Fulton. From 1992 to 1994, he had provided what the report describes as 'valuable' intelligence to both the Special Branch and another agency, presumably MI5. Although this was not revealed in the report, his information enabled the police to foil the assassination of one of the RUC's most senior and tenacious detectives. However, after two years all contacts with him were severed because 'he was becoming increasingly unreliable and deliberately fabricating information'.

Although Fulton continued to make contact with police officers – CID rather than Special Branch – his 'product' was treated with caution because he was manufacturing information, passing material to the media and taping phone calls with police officers. By August 2000 the police decided to end all contact with him 'because the risks he posed . . . outweighed the gain'. Flanagan concluded that in all of Fulton's contacts with the police in the run-up to the Omagh bombing he had not known of the coming attack and therefore could not in any way have helped to prevent it. He went on to rebut O'Loan's numerous criticisms in similarly factual detail, particularly her charge of 'failure of leadership' which he says would be unsustainable by 'any impartial and objective assessment'. 'Of course, as with any investigation – particularly one of this magnitude – mistakes will have been made. I acknowledge that,' he said, before remarking that 'in the same way that the Police Service has always recognised that it would have lessons to learn from its handling of the Omagh Investigation, it hopes that the Ombudsman will accept that her office has lessons to learn from the way her own investigation was conducted.'

The publication of Flanagan's rebuttal of O'Loan's report sounded the bell for the final trial of the issues between the two. The police staff associations launched a legal challenge to the way the ombudsman had acted by way of judicial review. (It was finally settled out of court early in 2003 but not before an embarrassing series of evidential inconsistencies and shortcomings in the Omagh investigation were disclosed.) The controversy however overshadowed Flanagan's final months in office. The Policing Board, the ultimate arbiter in the confrontation because of its statutory duty to ensure the 'efficiency and effectiveness' of the police service, discussed full copies of both reports and quizzed both O'Loan and Flanagan in detail at a special meeting in February 2002. O'Loan took the public position that there are 'clear disagreements on fundamental matters of fact' and insisted that Flanagan's rebuttal had not made her position untenable or a resignation issue. The board concluded 'on the basis of the information available that the Omagh bombing could not have been prevented', but identified 'a number of issues which require independent review and consideration'. As a result, a senior British police officer was brought in to to provide an overview of the inconclusive but ongoing investigation of the bombing and another was appointed to work alongside a restructured PSNI investigating team. In addition, the inspector of constabulary was asked to review the general conduct of terrorist-linked murder inquiries and to carry out a study into the management and dissemination of intelligence by Special Branch with a view to identifying any weaknesses and applying lessons learned. Reid hailed the Board for 'displaying the wisdom of Solomon' in its handling of this 'very complex and sensitive issue'. But in the summer of 2003 the Omagh cloud still hung dark and threatening over the still fragile policing structures and, with the whiff of scandal since extended to include the Garda Siochana's handling of its side of the affair, there was no telling what the lasting consequences might be for the RUC's already contentious reputation.

With the furore over Omagh at its height, Flanagan formally stepped down on 31 March. The board brusquely rejected his offer to stay in post until a successor had been appointed. With the propriety of the RUC's conduct during the Troubles once again under very public challenge, he knew that, whatever the final outcome of the Omagh controversy, its stain would hang indelibly over his own reputation as surely as the 'shoot-to-kill' episode compromises that of his predecessor Sir John Hermon or the appropriateness of events in the Castlereagh interrogation centre distorts the achievements of Sir Kenneth Newman. Flanagan was, however, given a rousing send-off. Unknown to him, the police band and up to 1,000 officers had been mustered for a 'final salute' and he was visibly moved as he inspected a guard of honour of new trainee officers from Garnerville. After three cheers led by his deputy, Colin Cramphorn, he left police headquarters along the drive lined by the loudly applauding officers.

The last stage of the RUC–PSNI transition took place a few days later on 5 April when the officers of the Police Service of Northern Ireland took to the streets in their new uniforms. These were the result of an extensive consultation and trials to ensure they were smart, comfortable and practical. With the design finally settled, a major logistical exercise began to procure and distribute about 300,000 items to the 10,000 serving officers in time for the target day. Under European legislation, the tenders had to be advertised internationally and, in line with its obligation to obtain best value for public money, the service eventually placed contracts worth £4,500,000 with suppliers in six countries: boots from Italy, hats from the UK and Pakistan, shirts from Bulgaria, trousers from Macedonia, and pullovers from Romania. Arrangements were also made to obtain alternative items of uniform and head-dress for members of minority communities such as female Muslims, Sikhs or Jewish officers. In a spectacular act of obeisance to equality requirements and political correctness, it was even prescribed that any trans-gender officer who might join would be equipped with mixed male and female garments as required. The uniform changeover went off without a serious hitch and shortly before midnight on 4 April officers on duty changed from their RUC uniforms and went back out again in the new kit. At the same time the teams of workers who had taken down the RUC crests some months earlier were back at work putting up the new PSNI 'sunburst' signs, and the first patrol vehicles to be liveried with the new emblem also took to the streets. Overnight the transition was completed and the last vestiges of the RUC consigned to history.

Later in the day at Garnerville the first graduation ceremony for the new trainees took place. Flanagan was there as an honoured guest. He too had a new uniform, in his new role as one of Her Majesty's Inspectors of Constabulary, the career option he had finally chosen. The format of the ceremony had been plagued by controversy for weeks and there were suggestions that some Unionist members of the Policing Board would stay away if the Garda Commissioner was asked to speak. Similarly, it was rumoured, the SDLP might boycott the event if Flanagan was given the role of reviewing officer. The trainees were also involved in a wrangle about whether or not they should maintain the tradition of throwing their hats in the air at the end of the proceedings. In the end they did, and everybody concerned attended what was the first ceremonial occasion for the new service.

At the end of April 2002, another important element of the Patten agenda was put in place when the British and Irish governments signed the North–South Co-Operation on Policing Agreement, which provided the basis for the PSNI and Garda to work together on an enhanced, more formal basis, sharing knowledge and expertise, alternatively hosting a joint annual conference on policing and collaborating in training, disaster planning and investigatory arrangements. Progress on the agreement had been slow and, at one time, had nearly foundered, when the Irish government insisted that any RUC officers seconded to the Garda should have full diplomatic accreditation and be placed via the British embassy as police attachés, a position that was hardly in keeping with the 'spirit of Patten' they were simultaneously demanding on other vital issues. Things changed at Weston Park, the proposal was dropped and, while the full agreement was still being negotiated, the first joint conference had taken place at Templemore, the Garda training college, earlier in April. Fifty officers from each side attended and set work in motion on a wide-ranging co-operative agenda. Soon technical experts from both organisations were jointly planning a new all-Ireland digital communications network to improve links and exchange of data and information. Work had already begun, too, on drafting legislation and regulations to facilitate personnel moving between the two forces either on short, temporary exchange, on a long-term secondment with police powers or by lateral entry, a permanent transfer at the same rank. These propositions raised many practical questions about differing rates of pay and conditions, currency exchange and pension rights which were still being hammered out in the early summer of 2003.

Soon after Flanagan's resignation was announced the Policing Board widely advertised the vacancy. There was ambitious talk from some members of attracting candidates of international standing and persistent rumours that a top man from the Royal Canadian Mounted Police was lined up. The main barrier to appointing someone from outside the British policing elite was removed when the criterion for candidates to have completed the Strategic Command Course at the Bramshill Police Staff College was eased by the addition of the words 'or equivalent', theoretically enabling FBI-trained Americans or others to apply. Cramphorn, the deputy, ruled himself out at once: 'In working with the Northern Ireland Policing Board over the last six months, it has become apparent to me that the Board's aspiration is for a Chief Constable of a style and type that I could never be. I have therefore decided not to burden the Board with an application, which would be in neither my own or the Board's long term best interests.'

In the light of subsequent events it is worth noting that at the same time another statement was issued in the name of the chairman, Des Rea: 'To protect candidate confidentiality, information on the appointment process is not being released.' With all the rumours, one of the potential local candidates mused if there was much point in spending a day or more filling in the lengthy application form if the job was already fixed for an outsider. When another took his form to have the medical questionnaire completed, his doctor flicked it back and forward a couple of times and said there seemed to be a section missing. 'I don't think so,' said the policeman. 'Oh, there is,' said the doctor. 'There should be room for a psychiatric report on why you want the job at all.'

When applications closed, to the great disappointment of the board, there were only five entries, and they had dwindled to four by the time the eight-strong selection panel met for shortlisting on 3 May. The previous day, Maria Wallis, a Northern Ireland-born Catholic who had risen through the ranks of the Metropolitan Police but never served in the RUC, was appointed Chief Constable of Devon and Cornwall and withdrew her application. In the end three candidates were invited for interview: Chris Albiston, the PSNI Assistant Chief Constable (Crime), Alan McQuillan, the Police Commander of Belfast, and the only outsider, Hugh Orde, a forty-three-year-old deputy assistant commissioner in the Metropolitan Police, who had spent a considerable time in Northern Ireland over the previous couple of years running the third phase of the Stevens investigation into alleged collusion between RUC officers and Loyalist terrorists. The fifth candidate, an American, was not called.

Alan McQuillan was the first of the candidates interviewed by the panel on 29 May, followed by Albiston and then Orde. The board had called a news conference for 6 p.m. to announce their choice but, in the first sign that things had not gone as smoothly as intended, it was late in the evening before Orde emerged as the new chief constable. 'I am absolutely delighted to have been given this opportunity to serve the community in Northern Ireland to lead the PSNI in this new era for policing,' he said boldly. The job was 'the ultimate challenge'. But the clouds of controversy were already gathering as he spoke. Two Unionist members of the selection panel were conspicuously absent from the news conference and it emerged during questioning that the choice of Orde, although approved by Reid under the legislation, had not been a unanimous one.

Early next morning, during radio interviews, in defiance of all convention and Rea's specific call, the confidentiality of the selection process was publicly shattered. The two dissenters, Ulster Unionist Fred Cobain and Democratic Unionist Sammy Wilson, said none of the three candidates should have been appointed because they had not reached the threshold of qualification for the post. They claimed this was the view expressed by Dan Crompton, the inspector of constabulary whose role was to advise the panel on the professional competence of the candidates. Soon afterwards, the SDLP member of the panel, Joe Byrne, revealed that he and the five independents had backed Orde. Trimble then joined in, saying, 'We've had two previous chief constables who came highly recommended from the Met. One succeeded, the other failed and it's up to Mr Orde to work out which was which.' It was now clear that the whole process had become entangled in Northern Ireland's murkiest politics and that political yardsticks, rather than vision, merit or capacity had been, disproportionately applied to the selection process. The SDLP would later boast it had used its position on the board to get rid of Flanagan and ensure an outsider was brought in to replace him, a shameful stance given the party's consistent unhappiness at the way Unionists had customarily applied political considerations to the oversight of the police.

For Albiston and McQuillan, clearly disappointed by their failure to get the job, the disgraceful public disclosure that their professional assessor considered they were not even up to it was a hurtful and humiliating blow. Crompton promptly took the highly unusual step of issuing a carefully worded statement saying that Orde would prove to be a chief constable of distinction. The reality was that, as with his decision to support the board on the sunburst badge, Reid decided to go with the majority, who had chosen Orde despite being advised that he was weak on change management skills, unarguably those the new chief constable would need most to bed down the new beginning for policing. Some three weeks later, on 21 June, the Policing Board issued an apology to each of the candidates for the breach in confidentiality. Rea said: 'The recruitment process should have been strictly confidential to the Policing Board and the media comments following completion of the process were completely unacceptable. It was a grudging apology and disingenuous in its implication that it was the media, and not several identifiable members of the board, who were responsible for the débâcle. Despite its commitment to be open and transparent, the board did not reveal whatever recriminations took place after the interviews, nor did it give any fuller explanation which might have fostered greater public confidence in its competence. The episode was a defining one in that it showed the politicians did not understand the apolitical role they should be playing in the new beginning for policing, and it heavily undermined Patten's objective of depoliticising the service.

The affair highlighted what is possibly the only serious weakness in the Patten report. Given the historical entanglement of politics and politics and policing and his stated aim to sunder the connection, it would have been more effective if the politicians had only been given a one-third representation on the board, with the decisive controlling interest residing with independent members, who should be convincingly apolitical. Meanwhile, 'Law and Orde', as he was quickly christened, announced he would be taking up his post at the beginning of September 2002 after he had cleared his desk at Scotland Yard.

The new police service was having to confront the same old problems with a reduced number of officers because of the 'Patten pay-offs'. It was now clear that the severance programme had been badly managed. Too many officers were allowed to depart too quickly and there should have been some filtering, especially of experienced detectives. The power problem was seriously aggravated by a sustained surge of sectarian public disorder in several parts of Belfast which imposed such a level of demand that the police were forced into a greater reliance on Army support, thus reversing the most prized gain of the 1994 ceasefires, that of getting the soldiers off the streets. By February 2001, the aim had been largely achieved, but eighteen months later 600 a day were being deployed and the police had called for public order support from the Army in twenty-four out of the twenty-nine DCUs. Organised crime was now endemic, with some eighty identifiable gangs of terrorists and their frontmen steeped in lucrative protection rackets, cross-border fuel smuggling, currency counterfeiting, video and CD piracy, extortion, blackmail, structured fraud, drug trafficking and money laundering. The Northern Ireland Affairs Committee of MPs calculated the gangs raised about £18,000,000 a year, almost certainly an underestimate, and cost both the British and Irish governments millions of pounds in lost revenue. Their specialist adviser calculated that for every £1 spent by the terrorist organisations on their operations, it cost the two governments £130 to combat them and repair the damage they caused.

Ordinary crime soared on the back of this instability and 104,299 offences were recorded between April and December 2001, almost as many as in the entire fiscal year 1998/1999. The clear-up rate dropped as well, from twenty-nine to 18.5 per cent. In the mid-1990s, despite the Troubles, the clear-up rate in Northern Ireland had always been around thirty-six per cent, at a time when it was running at twenty-six per cent in England and Wales. The result was a serious drop in public confidence in the police.

From their perspective, senior police officers were frustrated that the courts did not appear to be helping. One hardened criminal with ten previous convictions was released after serving three years for robbery. Within days, a police patrol spotted him acting suspiciously and he was put under surveillance. After just four hours, police stopped him in a car following a Securicor van and found he had a balaclava, an imitation firearm and a container of water to smother the smoke cartridge on the cashbox. He was arrested and charged but bailed by the courts, who only remanded him in custody after he was caught setting up a robbery for the third time in twelve weeks. Police ability to maintain law and order was further eroded by record levels of sickness absence. On one day in February 2002, for instance, when the average daily availability should have been 9,445 officers, 1,032 were off sick, 318 from injury on duty. Cramphorn said some of the sickness was a legacy of thirty years of conflict

By the end of 2002, after eight years of ceasefire and four years since the signing of the Belfast Agreement, Northern Ireland was still in security and political turmoil with fears growing that the entire peace process might unravel. While Catholics now openly supported the police, in line with the guidance of their church and the SDLP, there was still some apprehension about doing so openly for Sinn Fein had still not endorsed the new policing structures and made it clear it was safe for young Catholics to enlist. They were pursuing a series of hair-splitting demands, which fell short of the Patten threshold, they said, and could not support the police until they were conceded. In reality, they were withholding support as part of a wider political bargaining process with the British and Irish governments and Trimble's Unionists. At the same time there were fears that a spate of intimidation and attacks on some of the new recruits, including a failed bombing at Garnerville carried out by breakaway Republicans, would undo the gains that had been made.

By early 2003, Unionists were more seriously divided about the merits of the Belfast Agreement. The exposure of IRA efforts to run handguns from Florida in postal packets, the capture of IRA activists with considerable expertise in bomb-making aiding guerrillas in Colombia, the theft of sensitive files from the Special Branch headquarters in Belfast on 17 March 2002 and the subsequent exposure of a spy-ring at the heart of the Northern Ireland Office and Stormont administration had all caused them to doubt the veracity of the ceasefire and fuelled calls for Sinn Fein to be indefinitely excluded from government. The break-in was particularly embarrassing for the police. It dramatically exposed the weak security around the police headquarters building for Belfast which had enabled the raiders to get away with the personal details of over 300 Special Branch officers. As a result, in an operation costing £3,000,000, at least seventy were forced to move house and most of the remainder had to have their homes fortified with bullet-proof glass and other security measures to help protect them and their families.

The trouble and caustic hatred on the streets further destabilised the political process and undermined moderate political leaders. Dissident Republican groups, who had been mounting an attack on the security services every twelve days on average, and Loyalist paramilitaries, who had reverted to carrying out sectarian gun and pipe-bomb attacks on Catholic homes, created further tension. As the RUC had done for so long, the Police Service of Northern Ireland now provided the thin green line between what passed for normality in Northern Ireland and the anarchy which always hovered nearby. However, thanks to the Patten reform process, which was predicated on complete peace and stability rather than the uneasy peace that in fact existed, the force's ability to cope with debilitating conflict had been significantly weakened.

At the end of August 2002 Cramphorn, now acting chief constable, alerted the Policing Board to the fact that the line was almost at breaking point and warned political and community leaders that the police could not hold it indefinitely while they continued with their squabbles. Cumulative pressures on resources left 'little to deliver ordinary day-to-day policing' and 'in many areas we are simply responding to emergency calls and little else', he told them. This, he said, had the effect of reducing policing with the community to an 'unfulfillable aspiration' and reduced the policing plan, and the targets and objectives it set out, to a 'series of exhortations remote from frontline realities'. He said the situation had been brought about by a combination of factors outside the control of police. Wider civic society, which did not see itself directly affected by the disorder, had failed to require its elected representatives to find solutions: 'It has been too easy to label the problem as a policing problem, and to turn away.' The toll of all this on the men and women of the police service, he said, was just not a matter of the high levels of injuries sustained due to public order and security but also the cumulative impact of working excessively long hours week after week, month after month, with little opportunity of rest and recuperation. 'The Police Service has taken all the pain of the new beginning for policing, but has yet to see any of the gain. Such levels of activity cannot be sustained indefinitely,' he declared.

Cramphorn said that the wider community was deceiving itself if it thought that the impact of these circumstances were confined to closely defined geographic areas, mainly in Belfast. 'Wherever you live or work in Northern Ireland, it is affecting you,' he said, calling on society and its representatives to play the part envisaged for them in the Patten report. 'Civic society and the body politic has not yet delivered. As a consequence the benign policing environment envisaged by Patten has never materialised and the over-stretch on the capability of the Police Service to meet the demands made upon it is a direct consequence of this failure.'

Although the Northern Ireland Office paid the additional costs arising from the Patten reforms and maintained the level of the police budget (£620,000,000 in 2002/03), the service was also under severe financial pressure for it had to bear the cost of policing the constant disorder. A long-running sectarian confrontation at a Catholic school cost £1,100,000 for just three months. One of the biggest burdens was policing the large number of parades. The overall number dropped from 3,309 in 2000 to 2,722 the following year but the number at which disorder occurred jumped from six to twenty-seven, all but one of them Loyalist. But even the nominally peaceful majority required a heavy police commitment to prevent disorder. The cost of police deployment in the two villages of Kilkeel and Annalong in County Down, for instance, to cover nineteen parades, seventeen of them Loyalist, between April and September 2001 was a staggering £290,415. The annual confrontation at Drumcree continued to cost up to £10,000,000.

More pressure for the police resulted from the unfinished business of the Troubles. With a vastly expensive and painstaking judicial reconstruction of the events of Bloody Sunday in 1972 already under way in Londonderry and London, the Omagh controversy set off an avalanche of grievances and the police were inundated with requests for information about the progress on unsolved murders or to reopen old cases. There was a vast reservoir of disaffection among families who had been denied justice for the death of a loved one. Official figures demonstrated the problems there had been in getting evidence to bring people to justice for the offences committed during the years of violence. Early in 2003, the police said there were 2,730 unsolved serious crimes, including murders, dating back to 1969. Of the 1,761 murders attributed to Republicans between 1969 and 1998 murder charges had been brought in only 517 cases. Loyalists committed 841 murders in the same period and charges were brought in 421 cases. That left 1,664 unsolved. As the ombudsman reopened other cases and some former members of the security forces engaged in revelations about dubious conduct and unlawful collusion between security force members and terrorists, calls for judicial public inquiries, even a comprehensive truth commission on the South African model, gathered force. For their part the police, who were finding it hard to muster enough detectives for current investigations, were appalled at the prospect of having to look at old cases where the likelihood of getting sufficient evidence to charge anyone was exceedingly remote, even with new scientific advances such as DNA profiling.

So it was against this background, turbulent even by the standards of recurring policing crises in Northern Ireland, that Orde finally took up his post on Monday 2 September 2002. Clad in PSNI uniform, he spent his first day out and about visiting hard-pressed officers on the ground. His first stop was at Newtownabbey during the 7 a.m. changeover, where he listened in on the briefing for officers going out on patrol and talked to others coming off night duty. After that it was off on a whistle-stop tour of stations across Northern Ireland, starting at Lisburn Road in south Belfast and ending late in the evening in Londonderry. On the way he met Rea and the Policing Board, called on Reid at Stormont and gave a succession of radio and television interviews which painted an even more depressing picture than Cramphorn had done. The PSNI he inherited, he said, was a gutted, demoralised and technically inadequate service. Its technology was from the dark ages, its police stations were crumbling and there was a desperate shortage of detectives. In truth, the new police service was as demoralised and neglected as the RUC had been in 1969. However, there was one significant difference. This time, there was a growing feeling on both sides of the deep sectarian divide that the PSNI was 'our' police, and within the force, now more representative of the entire community than it had ever been before, there was a real sense of a new beginning and a commitment to overcoming the difficulties and making it work.

When Orde addressed an SDLP conference on 1 March 2003, accompanied by several of his most senior officers, all in uniform, it was a sign of the profound change that was going on. The ultimate recognition of what had been achieved came on St Patrick's Day 2003 in Washington, when he and two new recruits, one Catholic, the other Protestant, were invited by President Bush to the annual 'shamrock shindig' at the White House. Given Washington's harsh criticism of the RUC in the past, there could have been no more authoritative endorsement.

The final breakthrough, however, remained elusive. After a massive push through the winter and spring of 2002/03, the British and Irish governments believed they had successfully negotiated a 'shared understanding' with all the political parties about the 'acts of completion' required to fulfil the aims and objectives set in the Belfast Agreement five years earlier. Among the most important elements in a Joint Declaration due to be published at Hillsborough Castle on 10 April 2003 was an undertaking from the IRA that its campaign of violence was at an end, that all its weapons would at last be put beyond use and that it would belatedly endorse the post-Patten policing order, enabling Sinn Fein to take its seats on the Policing Board and encourage young Catholics to become police officers.

However, on the morning of the planned ceremony, the Republicans balked. Over the next month, through tortuous negotiations, they advanced their position slightly but not in the unequivocal terms of surrender demanded by Unionists or in words of sufficient clarity to convince the two governments that they were unambiguously committed to advancing their cause by exclusively peaceful means. The impasse proved to be beyond bridging and on 1 May, even though electioneering had begun, the British government indefinitely called off the long-planned elections. Their intention was to enable the terrorists and the politicians to reflect more on how tantalisingly close they had come to finally leaving violence behind them in the hope they would be sufficiently emboldened to do so in the autumn.

Postscript

By the autumn of 2003, despite the summer marching season passing off more peacefully and incident-free than at any time in the previous thirty odd years, the peace process remained firmly stalled. Hopes of running the twice-postponed elections dwindled through the summer as distrust and infighting crackled and rumbled through the entire political system like an angry thunderstorm. Diehard Republican and Loyalist paramilitaries, still wedded to violence, posed a continuing threat to the entire community with a steady stream of low-level sectarian outrages but the vigilance of the police and army, on both sides of the border, and the activities of some well-placed informers, repeatedly prevented more potentially lethal operations becoming new milestones of massacre on the long road of the troubles. The threat was not to be underestimated, however, and there was always the danger that one side or the other could fulfil its evil intent and further compromise the vulnerable peace.

The climate of instability was traditionally exacerbated by the deep divisions between the main political groupings but now there were serious internal rifts as well. The longstanding antagonistic distrust between the Ulster Unionist party and Sinn Fein, which had caused devolution to founder in October 2002, hardened as David Trimble's policies, strategy and leadership came under increasing challenge from a vociferous faction within his own party. Meanwhile, the Rev. Ian Paisley, whose apocalyptic forecasts of doom and betrayal had not been dimmed by his advancing age, continued to rail for political arrangements that would amount to a restoration of the, for him, 'golden age' of Protestant domination.

On the Catholic side, where support for the Belfast Agreement remained steadfast, the rivalry between the SDLP and Sinn Fein intensified while dissident Republicans accused both of signing up to a settlement that only prolonged partition. Mainstream Republicans wanted the elections to take place without further delay in the firm belief that they would see off their Republican rivals and convincingly eclipse the

SDLP. Then, as the only all-Ireland party, their uncompromising drive for a united Ireland, they concluded, would be unstoppable given the solid political bridgeheads established in both the northern and southern political jurisdictions. Their confidence in their cause was such that Gerry Adams, a key leadership figure, indicated that Republicans would demand the British and Irish governments create a transitional body to a united Ireland if the Good Friday Agreement was finally renounced by the Unionists, as many hoped.

Catholics had always decried what they called 'Unionist triumphalism' but as their political power and influence increased in the aftermath of the Agreement, both Sinn Fein and the SDLP demonstrated crass insensitivity to their Protestant compatriots as, under the guise of 'equality', they embarked on a series of missions that can only be described as provocative. At a time when health service provision was seriously under-funded, the Sinn Fein minister for health, social services and public safety ran up a bill for over £300,000 publishing all official documents and announcements in English and Irish. Similarly, the SDLP characterised the legislative moves to underpin north-south policing co-operation as the creation of all-Ireland policing and promoted a vision of southern officers on northern streets when all the evidence was that the last thing the overwhelming majority of Garda Siochana officers wanted was to swap their problematic enough beats for even more onerous ones across the border.

So it was that, little more than five years after the signing of the Belfast Agreement, the manoeuvrings of those in favour of it stoked up the fears and anxieties of their opponents who stifled progress and undercut the overwhelming public support with which the deal had been greeted and approved after Good Friday 1999. As ever in Northern Ireland, the fruitless preoccupation with the past was compromising efforts to shape the future and the election, whenever it would come, seemed certain only to trigger off another round of negotiation rather than overdue acts of completion and implementation.

Despite the fundamental reform that had taken place, the new police service was not exempt from this debilitating process. Sinn Fein continued to claim that Patten had not been fully implemented and initiated a campaign of distraction highlighting what it alleged was widespread 'collusion' in the past between the RUC, British Army and Loyalist killers to carry out a series of state-sponsored murders. Ulster Unionists hit back with counter-claims that the Garda had colluded with the IRA in many equally violent incidents and, angered by the extravagant £100m and rising cost of the Bloody Sunday Inquiry, called for similarly forensic public investigation of atrocities committed by the IRA.

The police accordingly came under growing pressure to redress the sense of hurt and grievance in the community and among its own former officers, who shared resentment that so many murderers and maimers remained undetected and unpunished. Nevertheless, the tide of police reform rolled steadily forward, with the new service progressively creating the new policing culture prescribed in the new beginning outlined by Patten. It was the one bright spot on an increasingly bleak landscape immediately ahead but beyond, over the horizon, there were clear signs that against the wider sweep of Irish history the much brighter future heralded by the ground-breaking and historic Good Friday accord would ultimately prevail.

The modern 'troubles', prolonged and violent even by the bloody standards of Irish history, have, nevertheless, driven profound political re-alignment. Although not yet complete, it has radically and positively transformed internal relationships within Northern Ireland, the nature of cross-border contacts and the over-arching association between Britain and Ireland to new plateaux of constructive co-operation. At the outset of events in the late 1960's, Britain still refused to concede that the Irish Republic had even a legitimate interest in the situation in Northern Ireland. Now, however, that interest has not only been underpinned by successive inter-government agreements but expanded to the point where there is virtual joint government oversight of all political and administrative matters. This process of transition is set to widen and deepen as Britain's long retreat from Northern Ireland continues.

Northern Ireland is in fact a hybrid state. Neither of the two governments really want it, despite the communities who claim allegiance to one or other, and remain involved only reluctantly because they fear the violent consequences of the 'ethnic cleansing' that would follow from withdrawal.

It is to the credit of the police in Northern Ireland that they have grasped the new realities and are striving enthusiastically to perform their duties against such an inauspicious political backdrop. They are also having to cope with the residue of civil conflict, a legacy of lucrative racketeering and organised crime and generations whose moral and legal compasses have been biased by the years of violence. In default, it is all too often the police who are left trying to set new values and standards for communities left wandering and leaderless by a political and community management all too tragically devoid of the courage, vision and drive to strike out for the bright horizon. The police and the people deserve better. Most importantly the people must prevent the new policing arrangements being hijacked by the political parties as they intend to do. Devolving police oversight powers from London to Belfast and the proposed creation of a ministry of justice would be a mistake as fatal as the decision in the early 1920s to maintain a paramilitary police force, under the tight rein of the ministry of home affairs, to defend the border and the union. Similarly, calls for 'local' control of policing must be resisted for decoded that means giving formal recognition to the ruthless paramilitary militias who wield the power of judge, jury and often executioner in some of the most deprived and disadvantaged communities in Northern Ireland by carrying out so-called 'punishment attacks' with brutal and savage alacrity.

Much progress has been made in creating a new even-handed, impartial police service, fully representative of the entire community. After the uncertainty and tumult of change, police capacity and confidence is recovering and growing and the partnerships with other agencies, who have an equally important role to play in promoting community safety and public tranquillity, are being forged. The entire community must make sure that this new beginning, purchased at such human and social cost, is not once more plundered by politicians for their own short term and devious ends. That battle is all the more important because policing arrangements in Northern Ireland for the first time stand on twin pillars of Protestant and Catholic consent, a priceless prize that must never be forfeited.

Chris Ryder
Belfast
October 2003

Bibliography

Official papers

Chief Constable's Annual Reports (Royal Ulster Constabulary and Police Service of Northern Ireland, 1969–2002)

Lord Cameron Commission, Disturbances in Northern Ireland (Cmnd. 532, 1969)

Lord Hunt Committee, Report of the Advisory Committee on Police in Northern Ireland (Cmnd. 535, 1969)

Scarman Tribunal Report, Violence and Civil Disturbances in Northern Ireland, (Cmnd. 566, 1972)

Bennett Report, Committee of Inquiry into Police Interrogation Procedures in Northern Ireland (Cmnd. 7497, 1979)

Chairman Chris Patten, Report of the Independent Commission of Policing, 'A new beginning: Policing in Northern Ireland' (1999)

Other

Richard Abbot, *Police Casualties in Ireland: 1919-1922* (Mercier Press, 2000)

Brian Barton, *Brookeborough: the Making of a Prime Minister* (Institute of Irish Studies, Belfast, 1988)

Dan Breen, *My Fight for Irish Freedom* (Talbot Press, 1924; Anvil Books, 1964)

Ken Bloomfield, *Stormont in Crisis* (Blackstaff Press, 1994)

Paddy Devlin, *Straight Left: An Autobiography* (Blackstaff Press, 1993)

Dr Garrett Fitzgerald, *All in a Life: An Autobiography* (Gill and Macmillan, 1991)

Sir John Hermon, *Holding the Line* (Gill and Macmillan, 1997)

Thomas Jones, ed. Keith Middlemas, *Whitehall Diary Vol. 2, Ireland 1918–25* (Oxford University Press, 1971)

G. B. Kenna, *Facts and Figures of the Belfast Pogrom, 1920–1922* (O'Connell Publishing, 1922); and ed. Tom Donaldson (Donaldson Archives, 1977)

Sir Robert Mark, *In the Office of Constable* (Harper Collins, 1978)

Chris Ryder and Vincent Kearney, *Drumcree: The Orange Order's Last Stand* (Methuen, 2001)

Chris Ryder, *The RUC: A Force under Fire* (Methuen, 1989)

Patrick Shea, *Voices and the Sound of Drums: Autobiography* (Blackstaff Press, 1981)

John Stalker, *Stalker* (Harper Collins, 1988)

Sir Henry Wilson, ed. Keith Jeffrey, *The Military Correspondence of Field Marshall Sir Henry Wilson 1918–1922* (Bodley Head, 1985)

Index

Note on police officers' designations
Not all ranks in the RIC/RUC (until 1969) were identical to those in the English police force.
The following abbreviations have been adopted:
CI = County Inspector (*not* Chief Inspector)
DI = District Inspector (*not* Detective Inspector)
Con. (*not* PC) = Constable
SC = Special Constable